COWBOYS

WRITER
GARY PHILLIPS

ART
BRIAN HURTT

LETTERS
CLEM ROBINS

COWBOYS

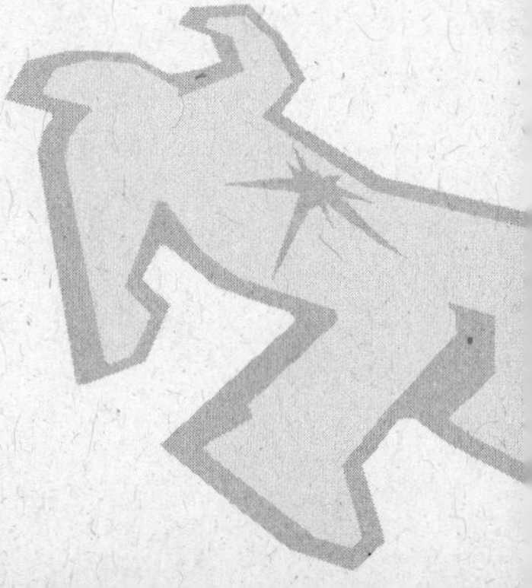

COWBOYS
VERTIGO CRIME

Published by DC Comics, 1700 Broadway, New York, NY 10019. Printed in the USA. First Printing.
DC Comics, a Warner Bros. Entertainment Company.

HC ISBN: 978-1-4012-1534-7 SC ISBN: 978-1-4012-3064-7

SUSTAINABLE FORESTRY INITIATIVE Certified Chain of Custody 80% Certified Fiber Sourcing and 40% Post-Consumer Recycled www.sfiprogram.org

NSF-SFICOC-C0001801
This label applies to the text stock.

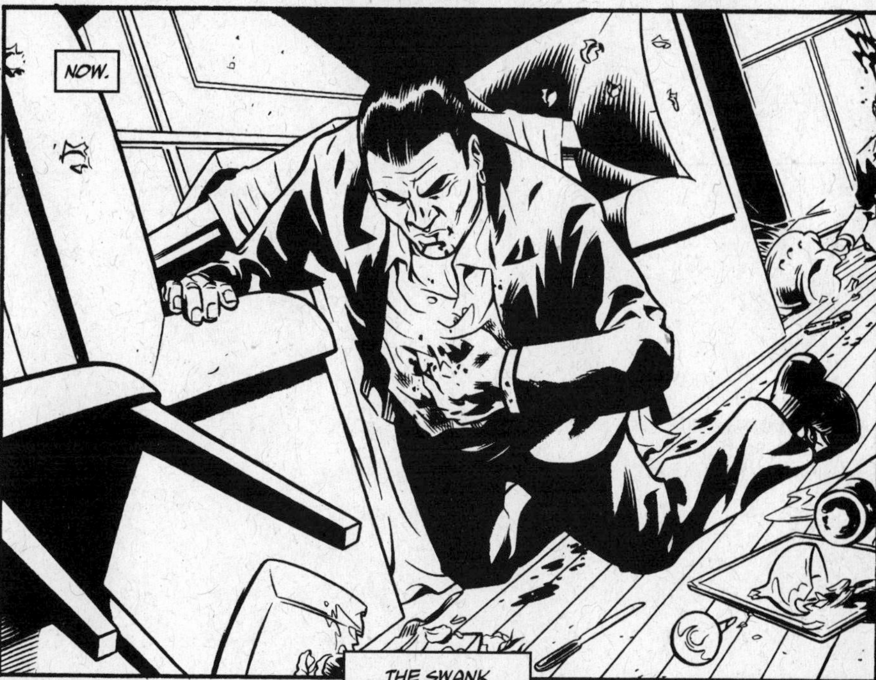
NOW.
THE SWANK THREE PENNY RESTAURANT.

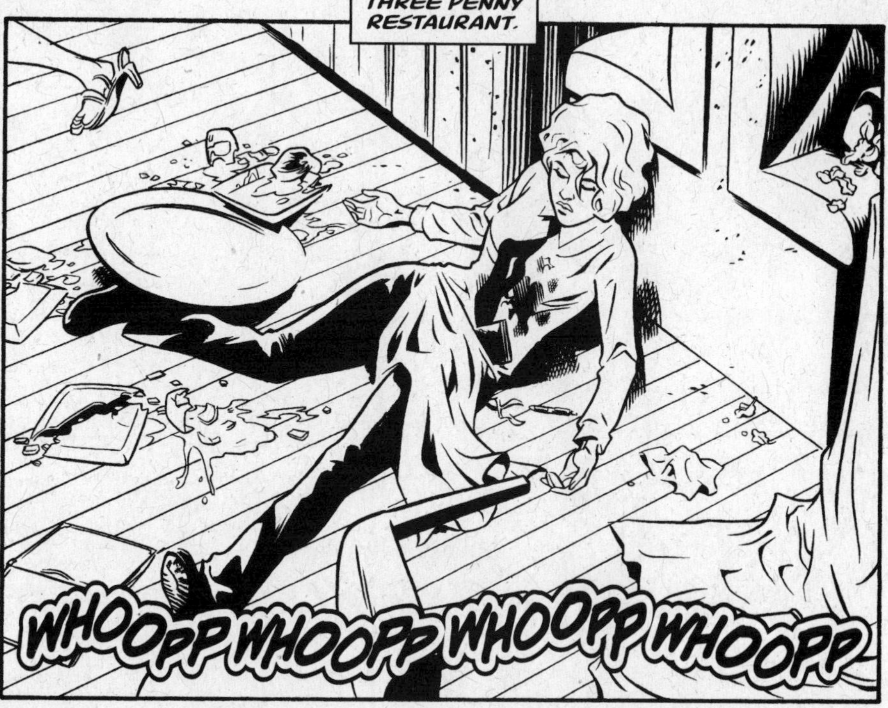
WHOOPP WHOOPP WHOOPP WHOOPP

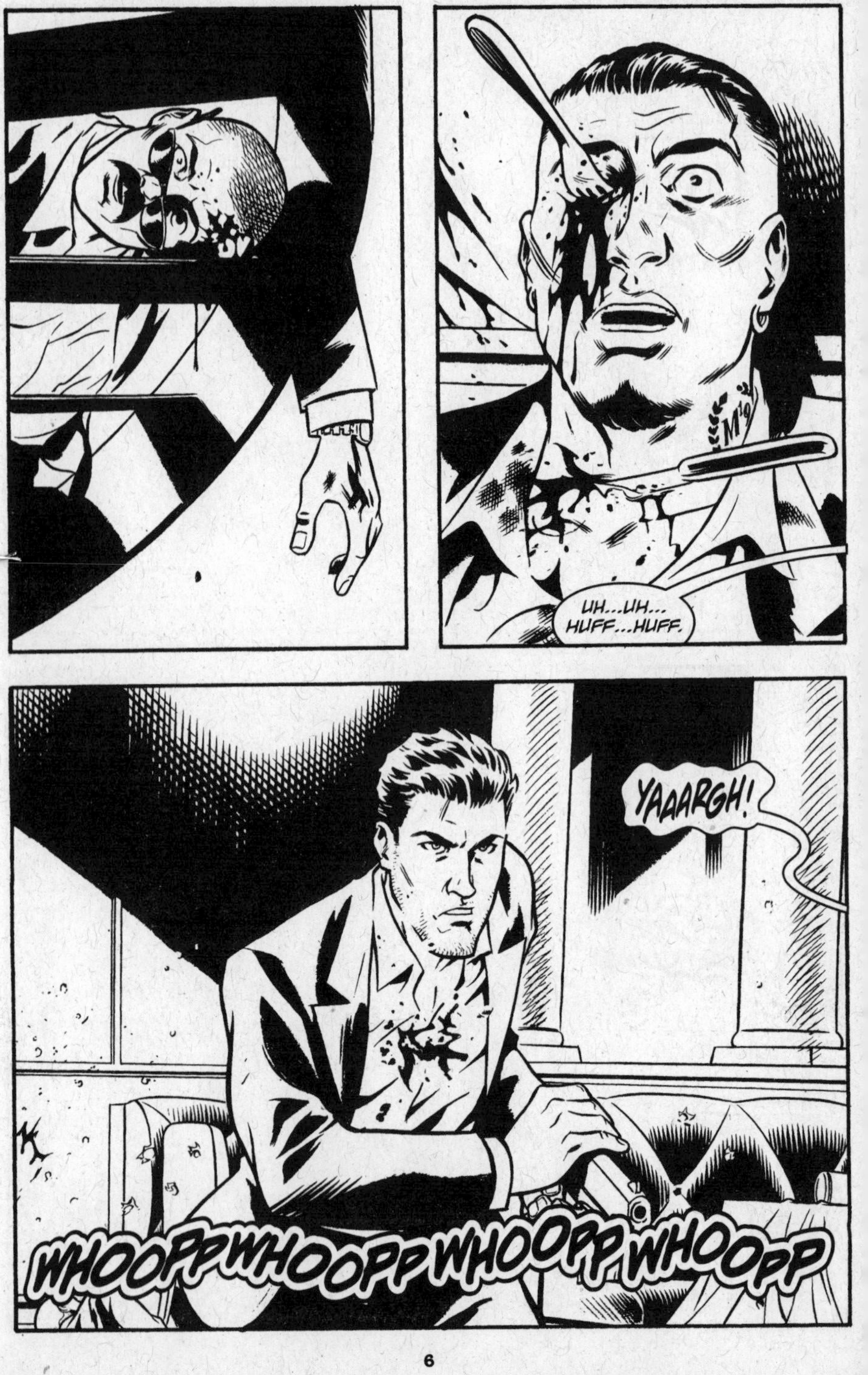
UH...UH...
HUFF...HUFF.
YAAARGH!
WHOOPP WHOOPP WHOOPP WHOOPP

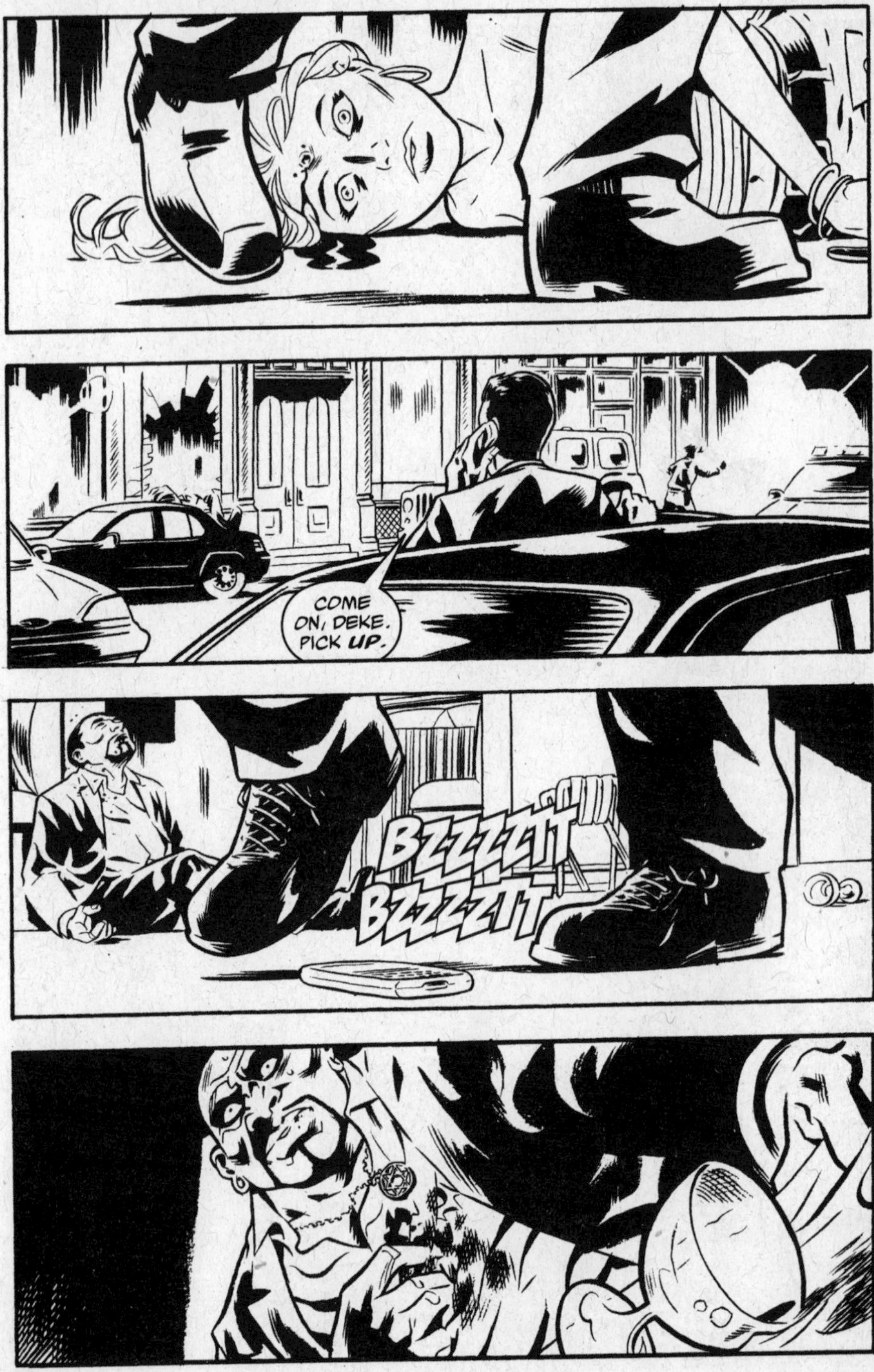
COME ON, DEKE. PICK UP.
BZZZZTT
BZZZZTT

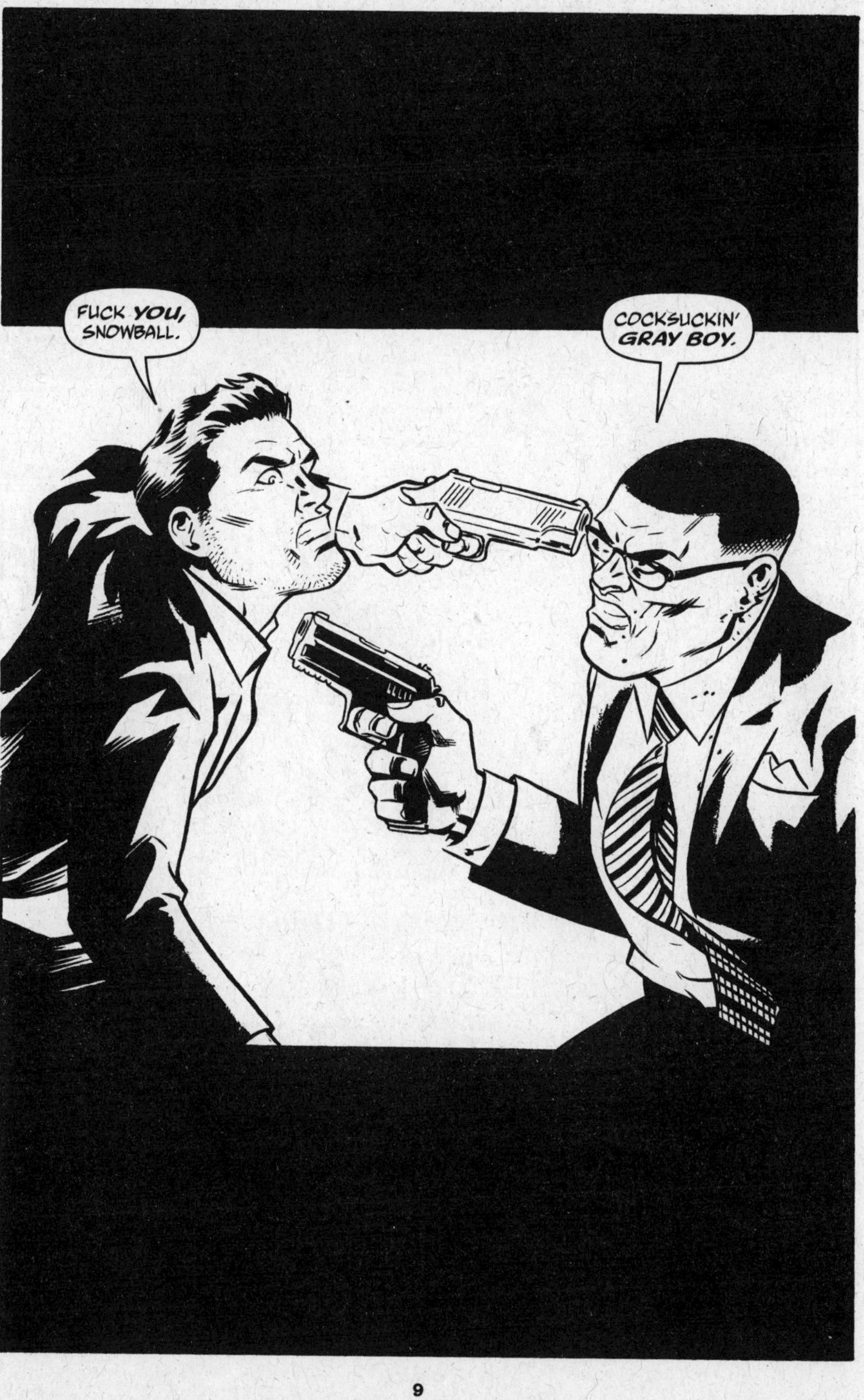
FUCK YOU, SNOWBALL.
COCKSUCKIN' GRAY BOY.

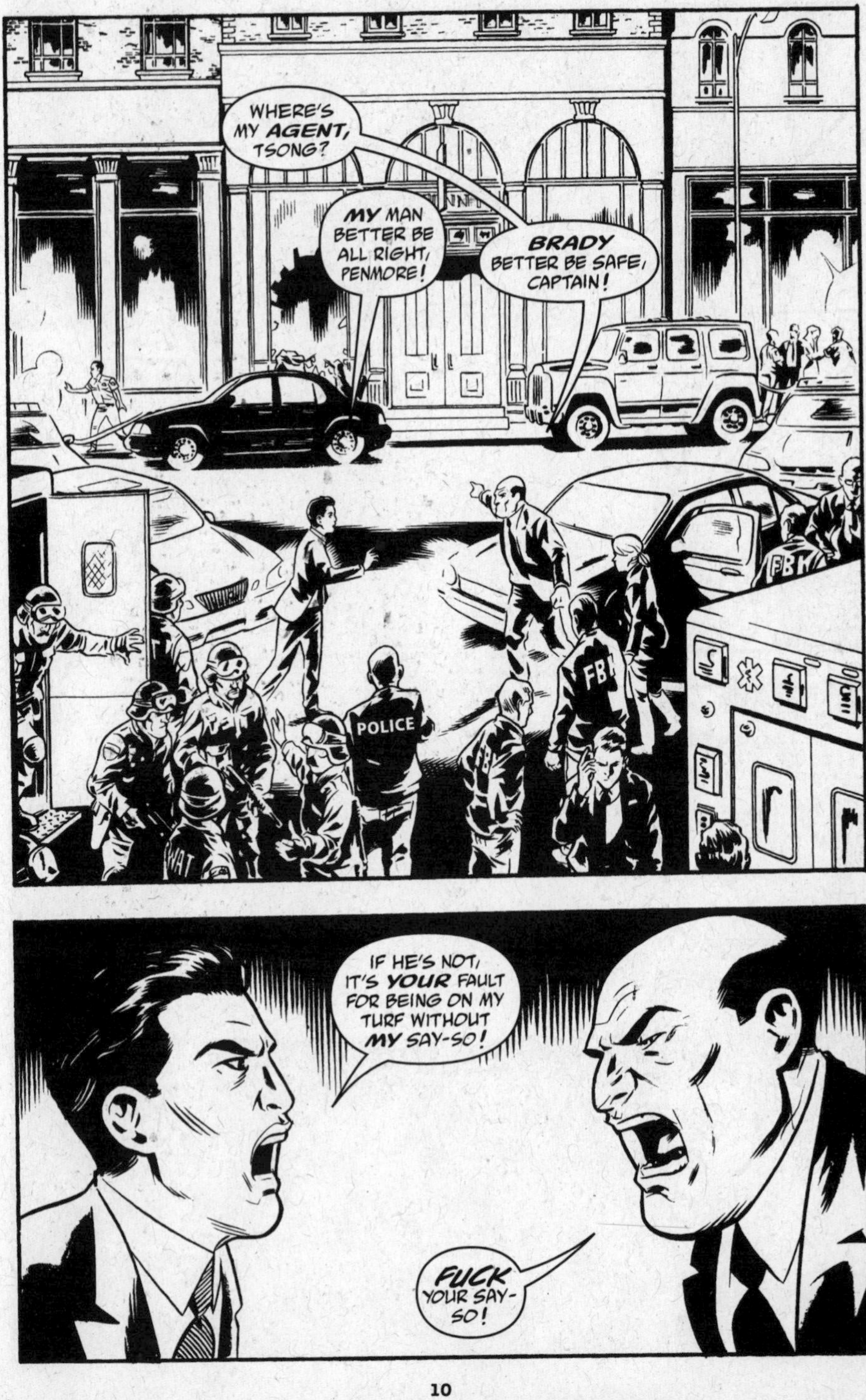
WHERE'S MY AGENT, TSONG?
MY MAN BETTER BE ALL RIGHT, PENMORE!
BRADY BETTER BE SAFE, CAPTAIN!
POLICE
FBI
FBI
IF HE'S NOT, IT'S YOUR FAULT FOR BEING ON MY TURF WITHOUT MY SAY-SO!
FUCK YOUR SAY-SO!

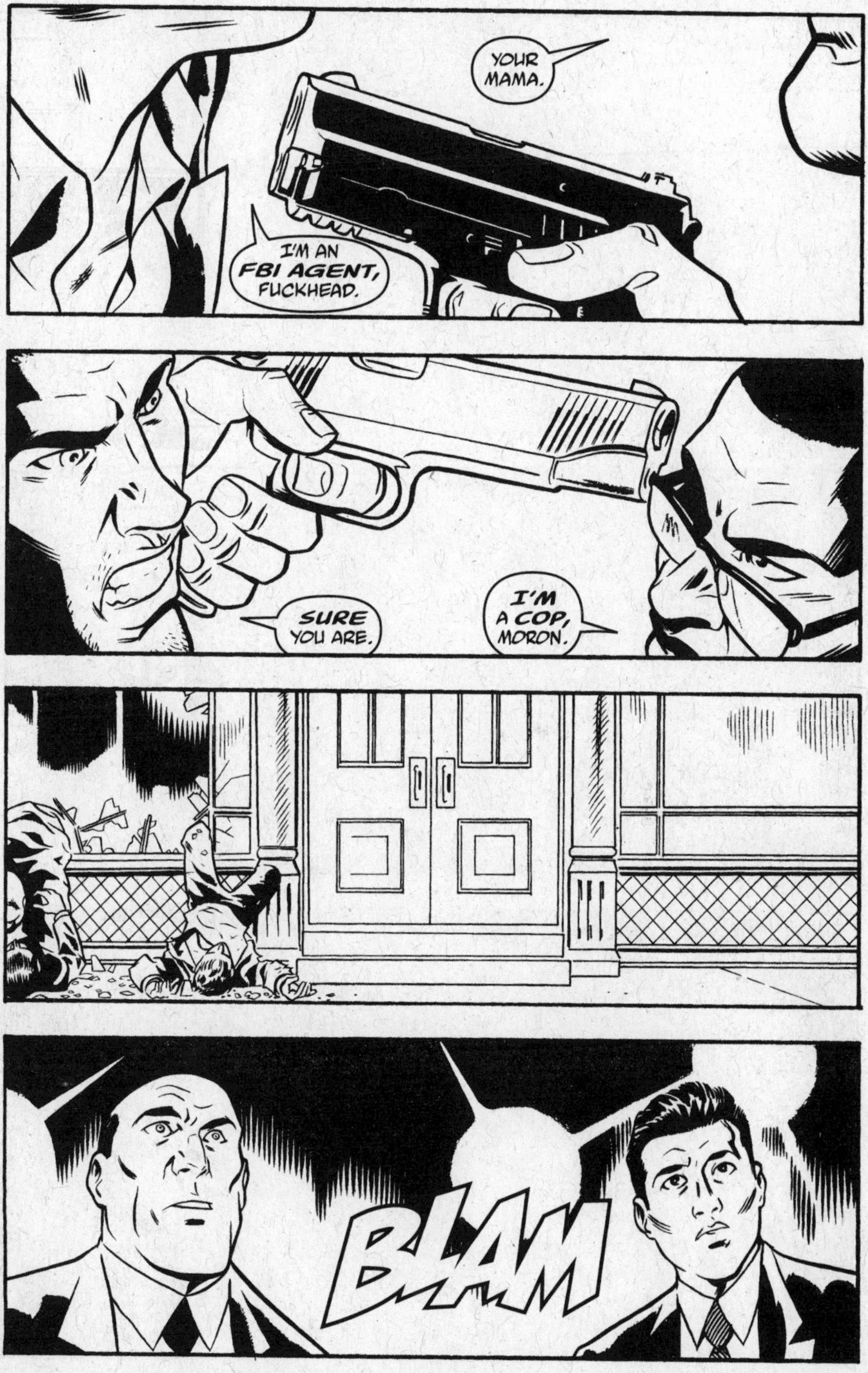
YOUR MAMA.
I'M AN FBI AGENT, FUCKHEAD.
I'M A COP, MORON.
SURE YOU ARE.
BLAM

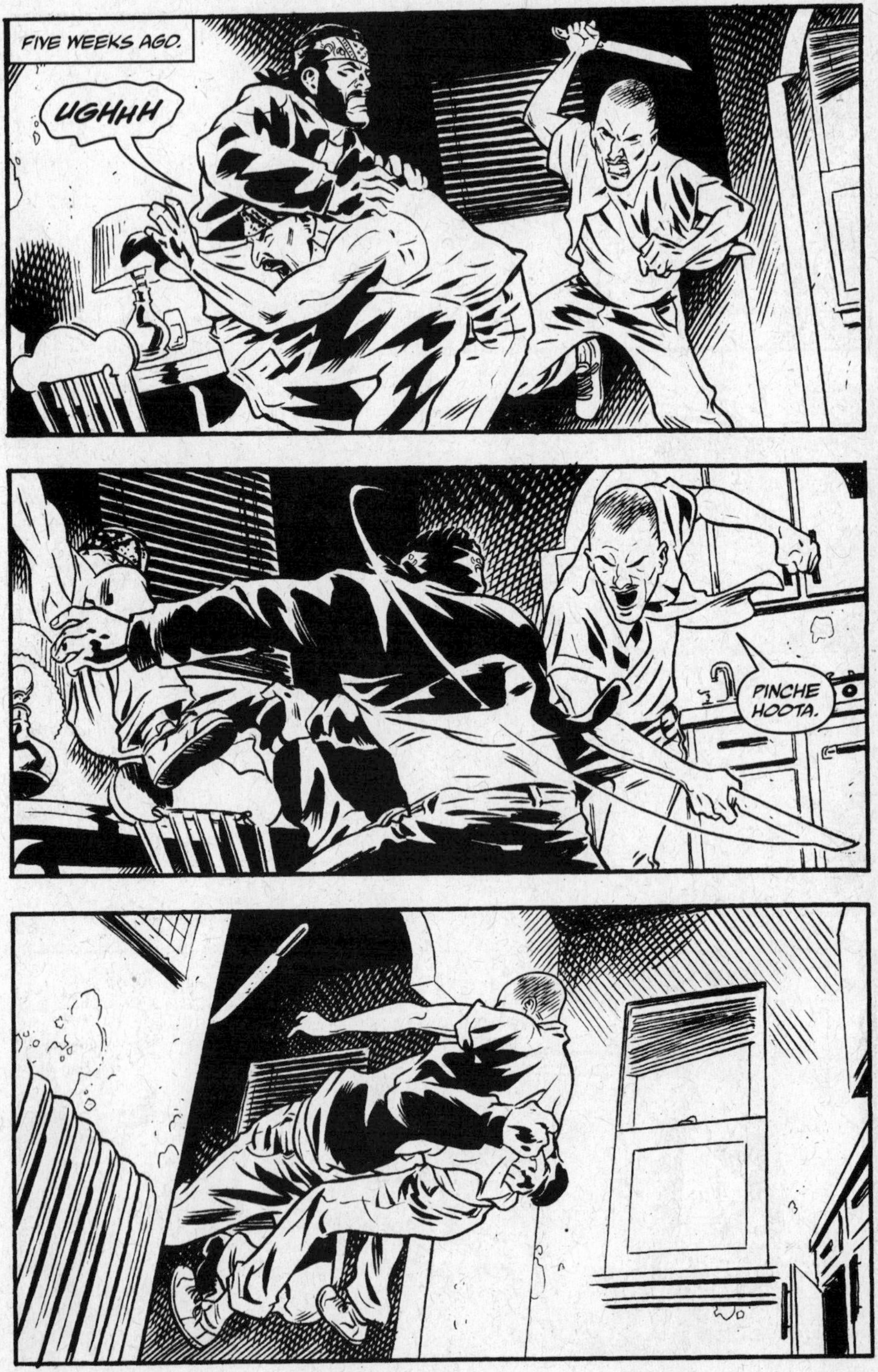
FIVE WEEKS AGO.
UGHHH
PINCHE HOOTA.

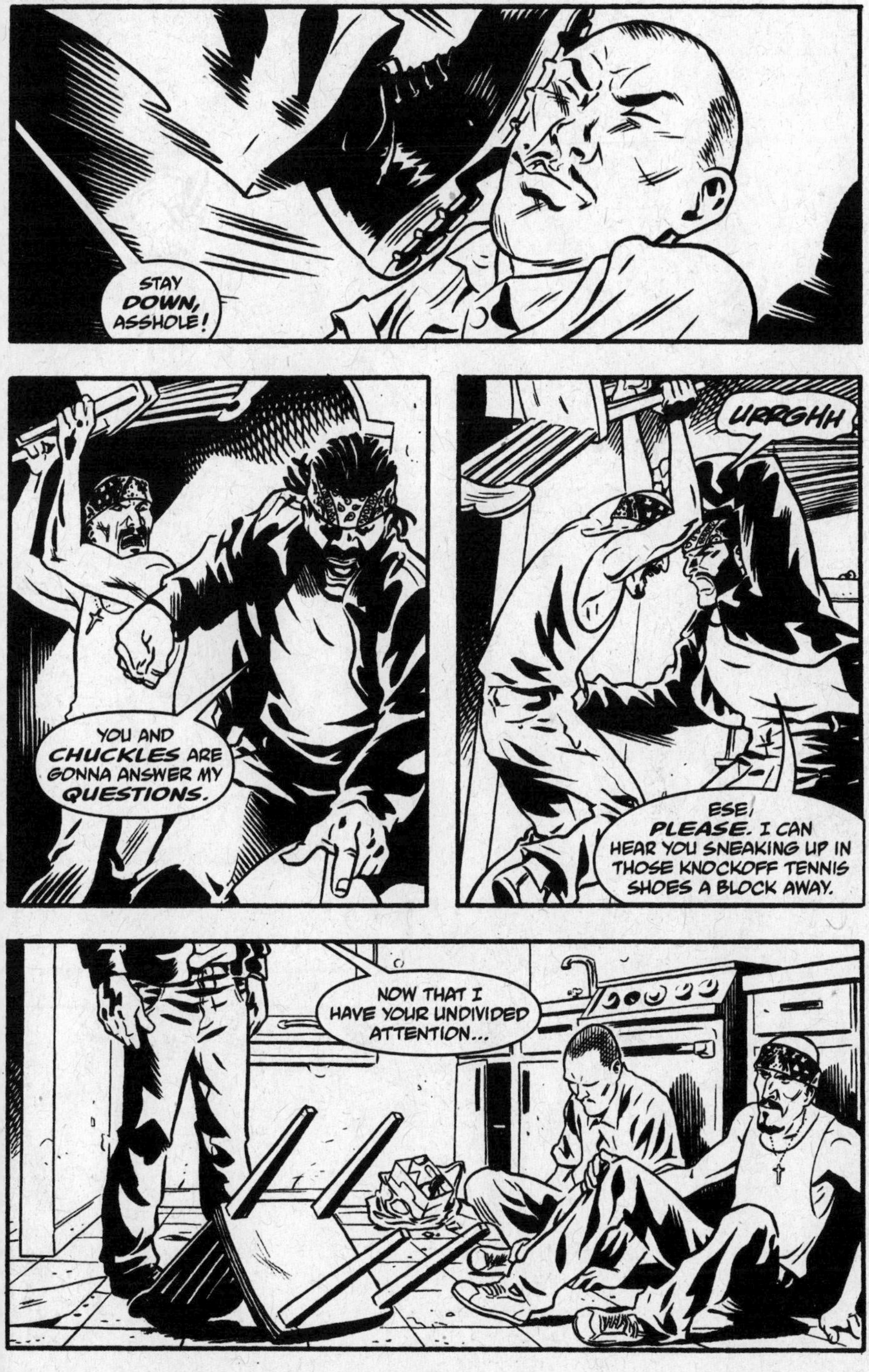
STAY DOWN, ASSHOLE!
YOU AND CHUCKLES ARE GONNA ANSWER MY QUESTIONS.
URRGHH
ESE, PLEASE. I CAN HEAR YOU SNEAKING UP IN THOSE KNOCKOFF TENNIS SHOES A BLOCK AWAY.
NOW THAT I HAVE YOUR UNDIVIDED ATTENTION...

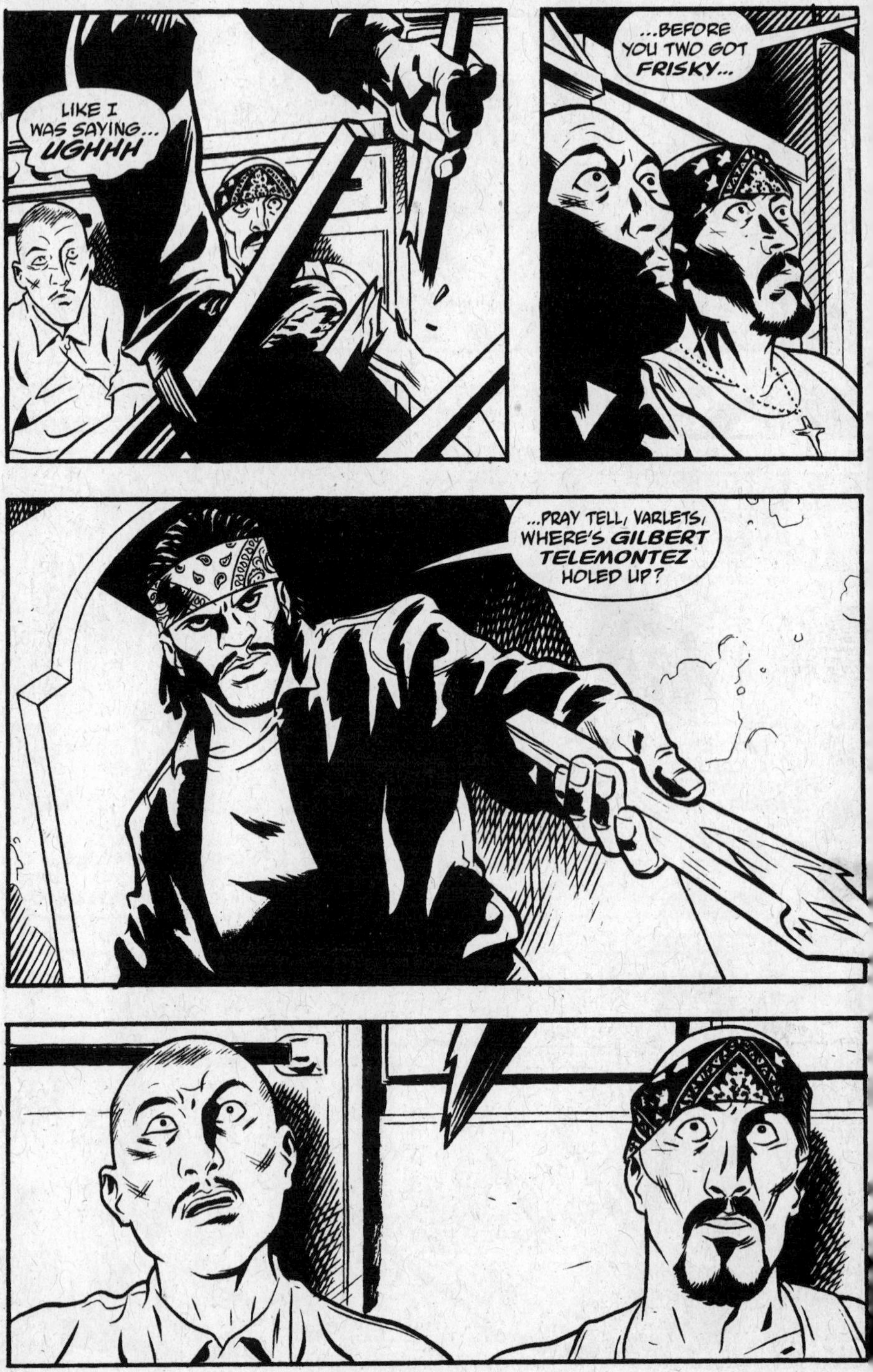
LIKE I WAS SAYING... UGHHH
...BEFORE YOU TWO GOT FRISKY...
...PRAY TELL, VARLETS, WHERE'S GILBERT TELEMONTEZ HOLED UP?

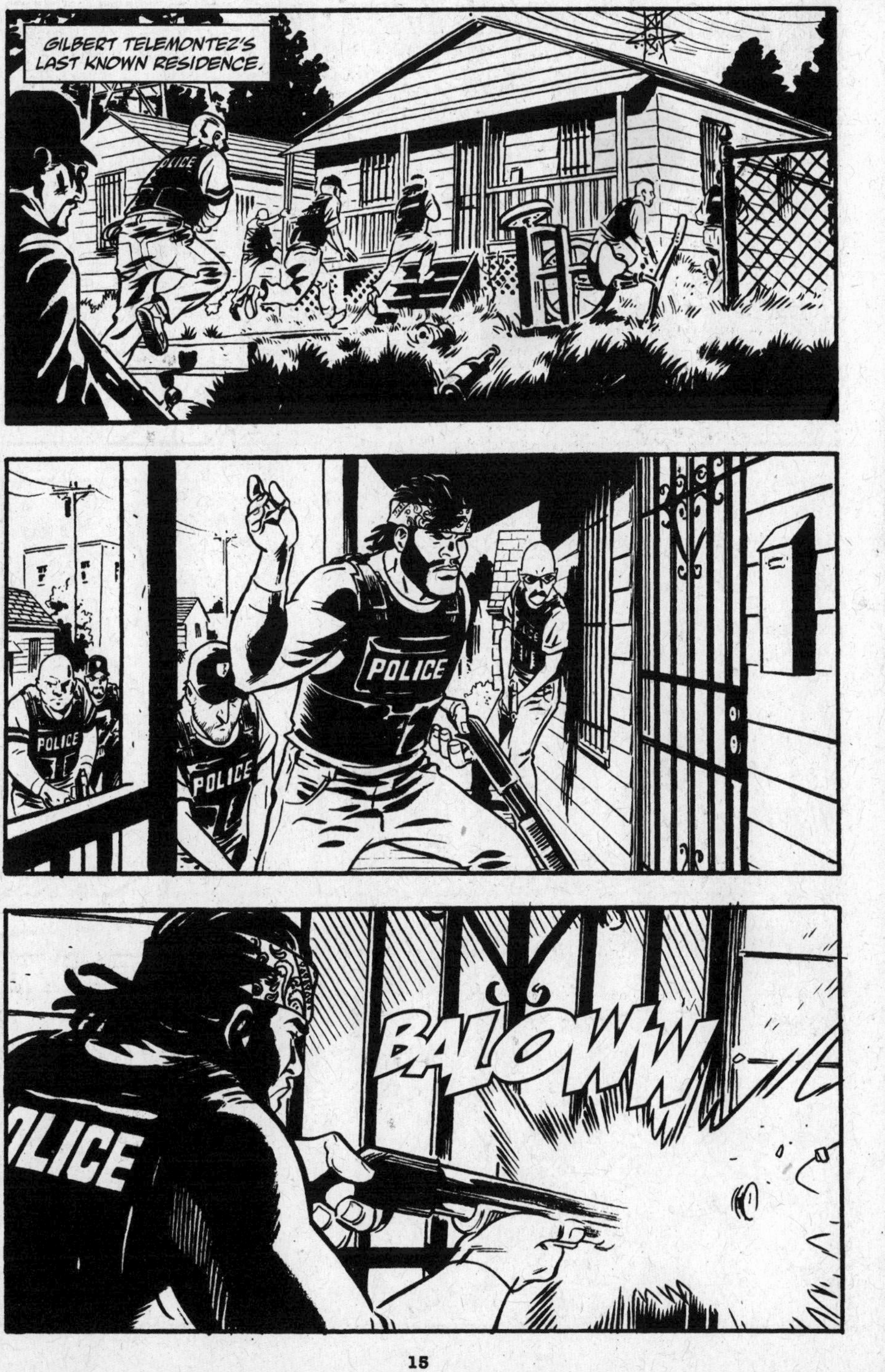
GILBERT TELEMONTEZ'S LAST KNOWN RESIDENCE.
POLICE
POLICE
POLICE
POLICE
BALOWW
OLICE

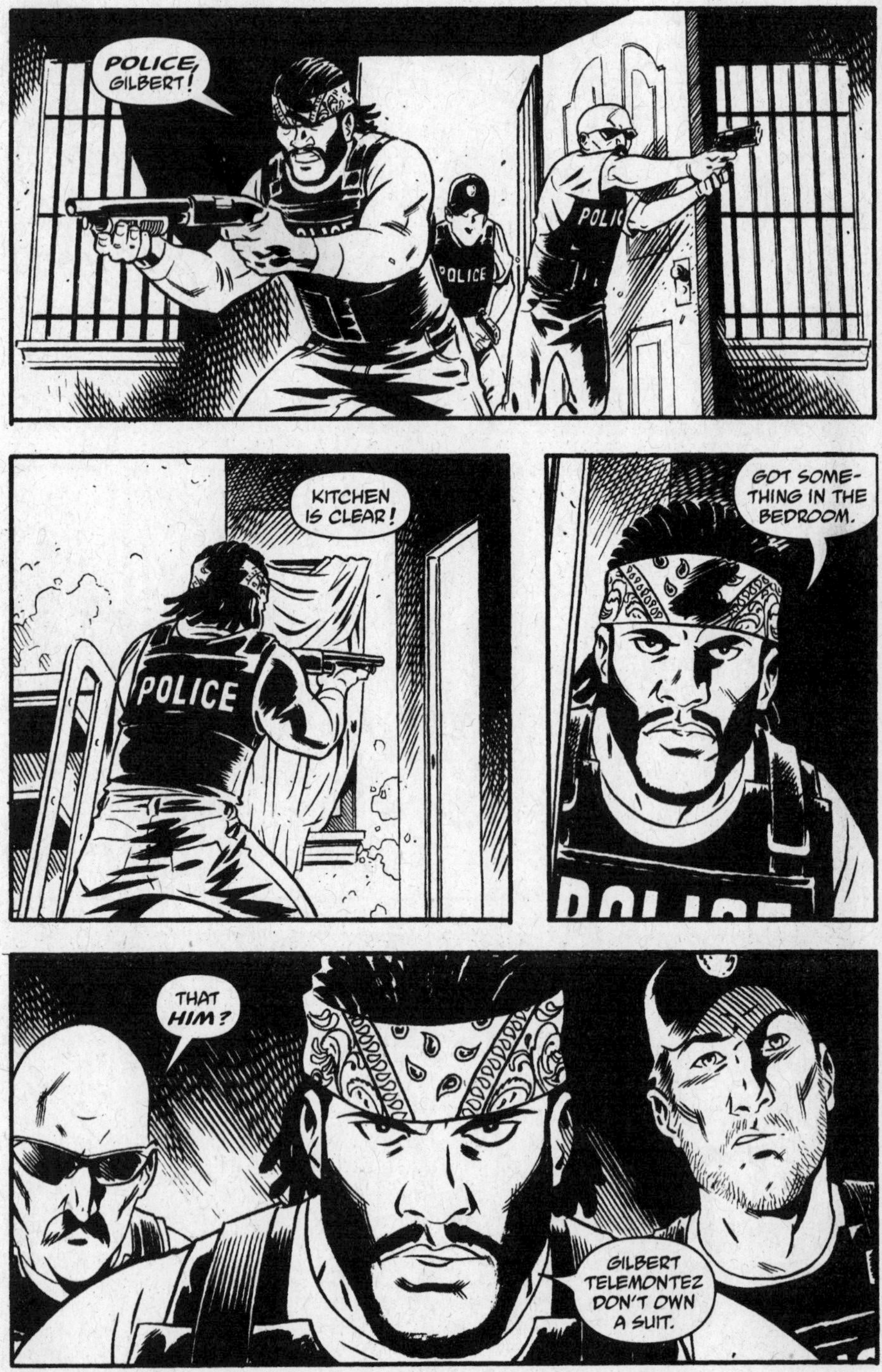
POLICE, GILBERT!
KITCHEN IS CLEAR!
POLICE
GOT SOME-THING IN THE BEDROOM.
THAT HIM?
GILBERT TELEMONTEZ DON'T OWN A SUIT.

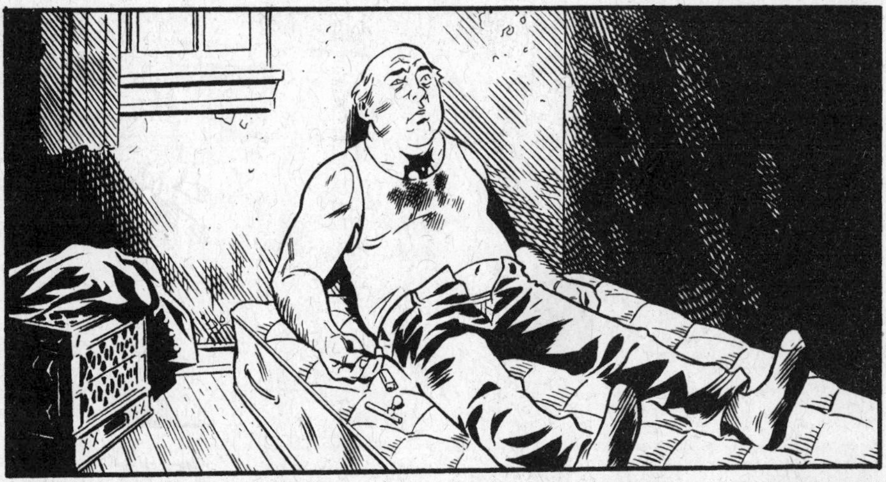
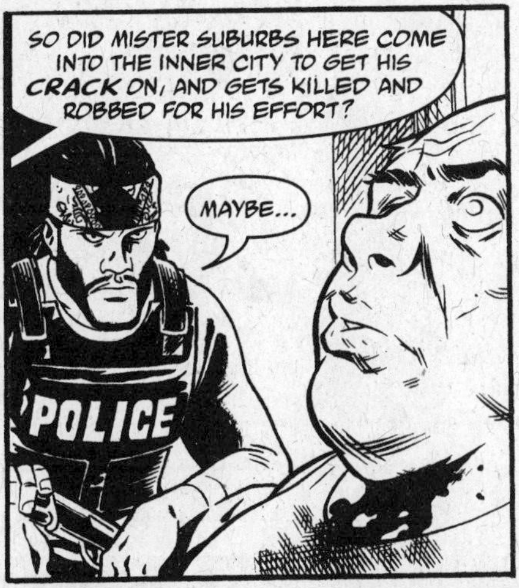
SO DID MISTER SUBURBS HERE COME INTO THE INNER CITY TO GET HIS CRACK ON, AND GETS KILLED AND ROBBED FOR HIS EFFORT?
MAYBE...
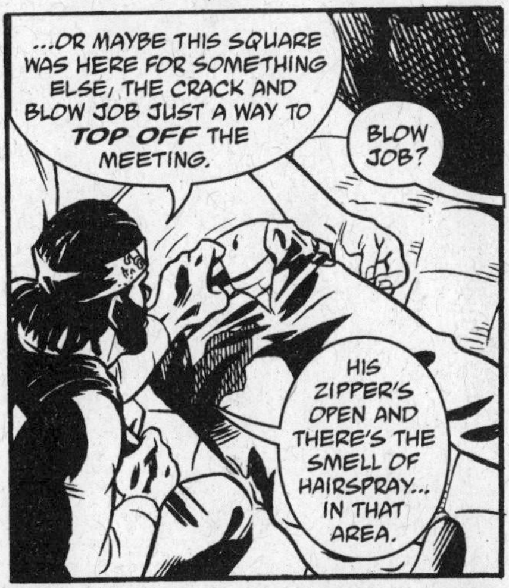
...OR MAYBE THIS SQUARE WAS HERE FOR SOMETHING ELSE, THE CRACK AND BLOW JOB JUST A WAY TO TOP OFF THE MEETING.
BLOW JOB?
HIS ZIPPER'S OPEN AND THERE'S THE SMELL OF HAIRSPRAY... IN THAT AREA.
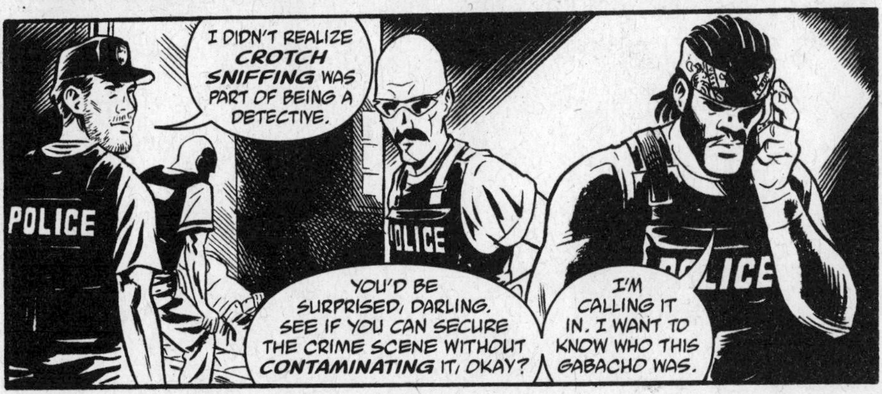
I DIDN'T REALIZE CROTCH SNIFFING WAS PART OF BEING A DETECTIVE.
POLICE
POLICE
POLICE
YOU'D BE SURPRISED, DARLING. SEE IF YOU CAN SECURE THE CRIME SCENE WITHOUT CONTAMINATING IT, OKAY?
I'M CALLING IT IN. I WANT TO KNOW WHO THIS GABACHO WAS.

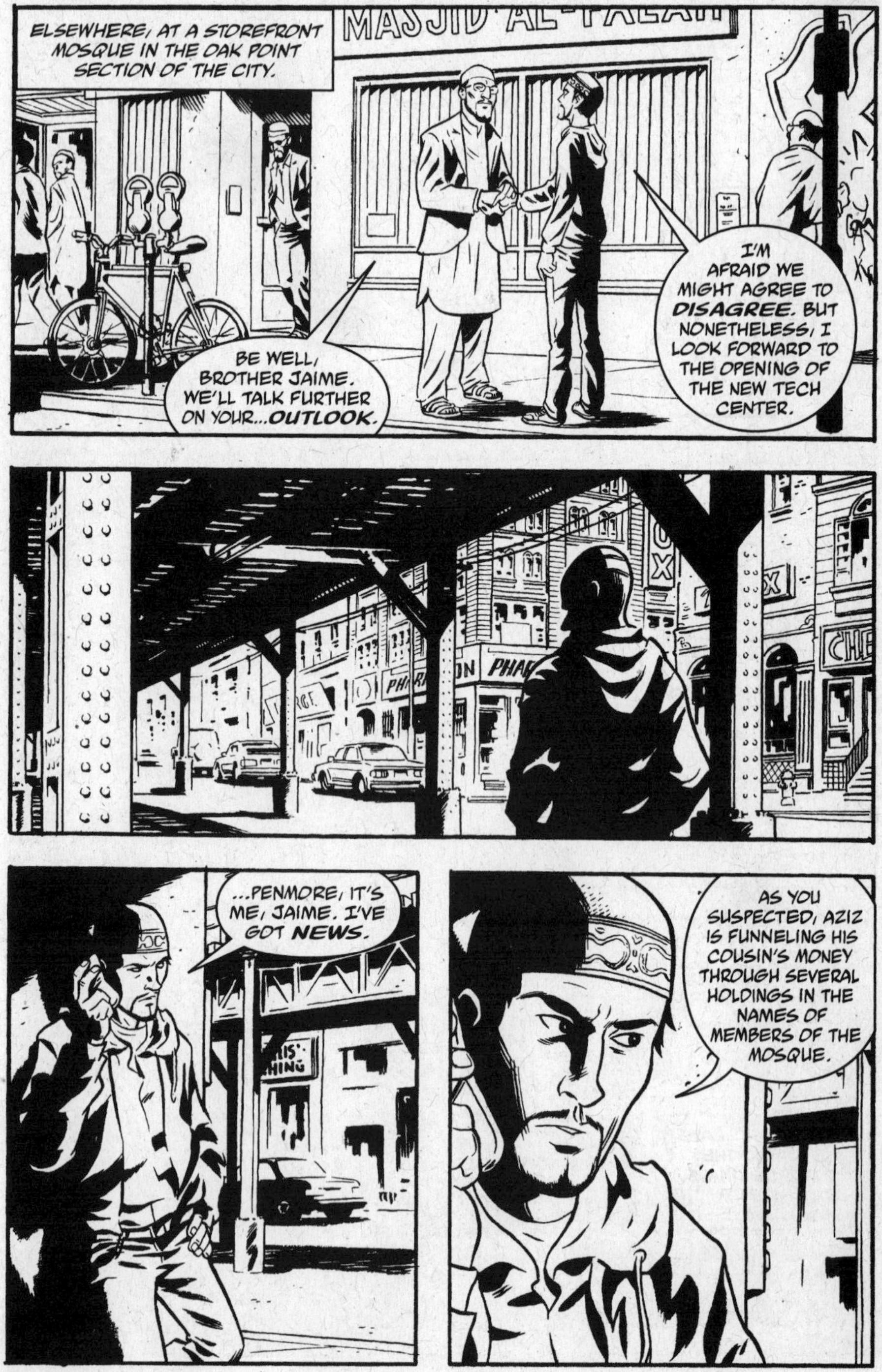
ELSEWHERE, AT A STOREFRONT MOSQUE IN THE OAK POINT SECTION OF THE CITY.
I'M AFRAID WE MIGHT AGREE TO DISAGREE. BUT NONETHELESS, I LOOK FORWARD TO THE OPENING OF THE NEW TECH CENTER.
BE WELL, BROTHER JAIME. WE'LL TALK FURTHER ON YOUR...OUTLOOK.
...PENMORE, IT'S ME, JAIME. I'VE GOT NEWS.
AS YOU SUSPECTED, AZIZ IS FUNNELING HIS COUSIN'S MONEY THROUGH SEVERAL HOLDINGS IN THE NAMES OF MEMBERS OF THE MOSQUE.

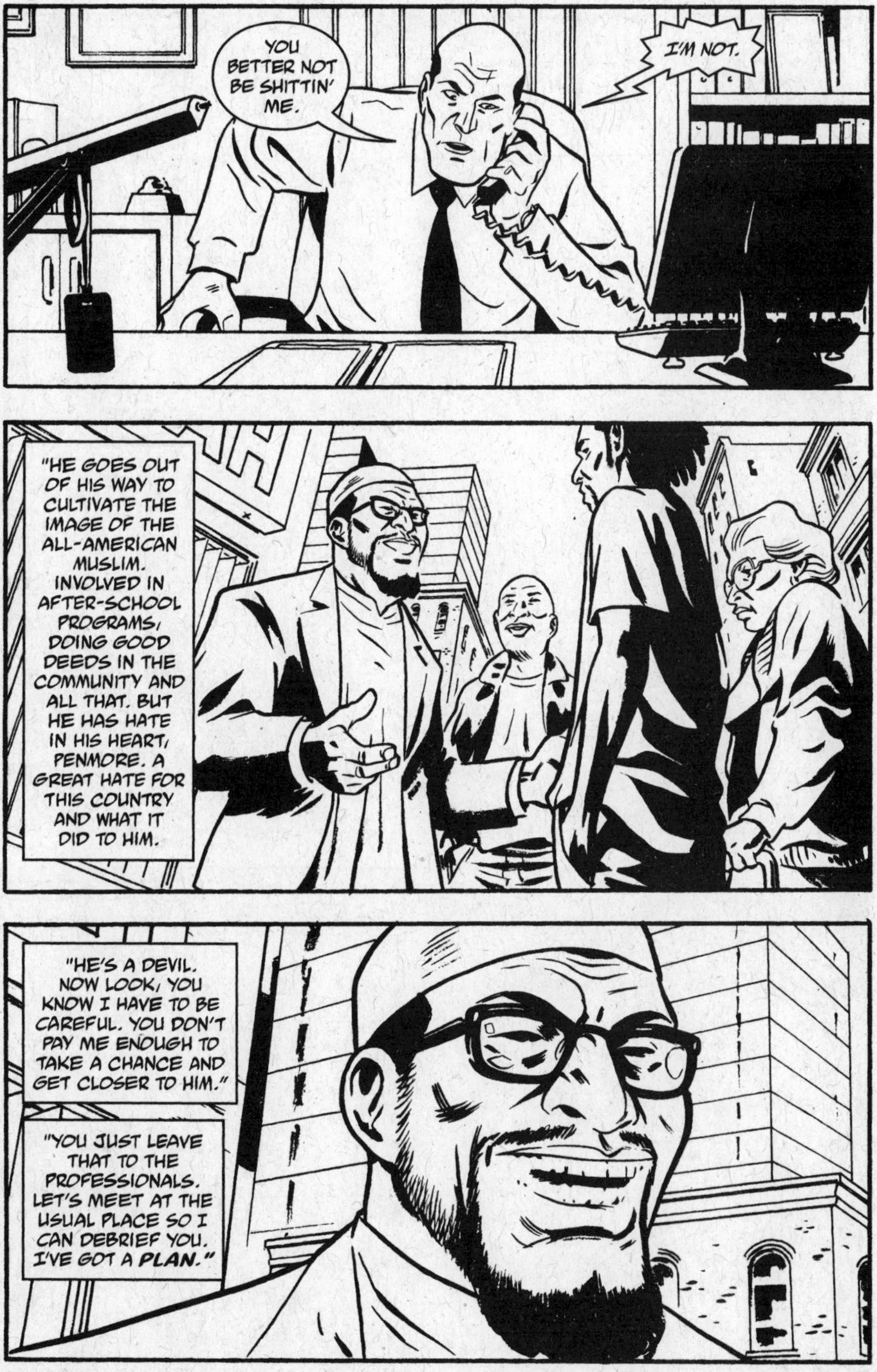
YOU BETTER NOT BE SHITTIN' ME.
I'M NOT.
"HE GOES OUT OF HIS WAY TO CULTIVATE THE IMAGE OF THE ALL-AMERICAN MUSLIM. INVOLVED IN AFTER-SCHOOL PROGRAMS, DOING GOOD DEEDS IN THE COMMUNITY AND ALL THAT. BUT HE HAS HATE IN HIS HEART, PENMORE. A GREAT HATE FOR THIS COUNTRY AND WHAT IT DID TO HIM.
"HE'S A DEVIL. NOW LOOK, YOU KNOW I HAVE TO BE CAREFUL. YOU DON'T PAY ME ENOUGH TO TAKE A CHANCE AND GET CLOSER TO HIM."
"YOU JUST LEAVE THAT TO THE PROFESSIONALS. LET'S MEET AT THE USUAL PLACE SO I CAN DEBRIEF YOU. I'VE GOT A PLAN."

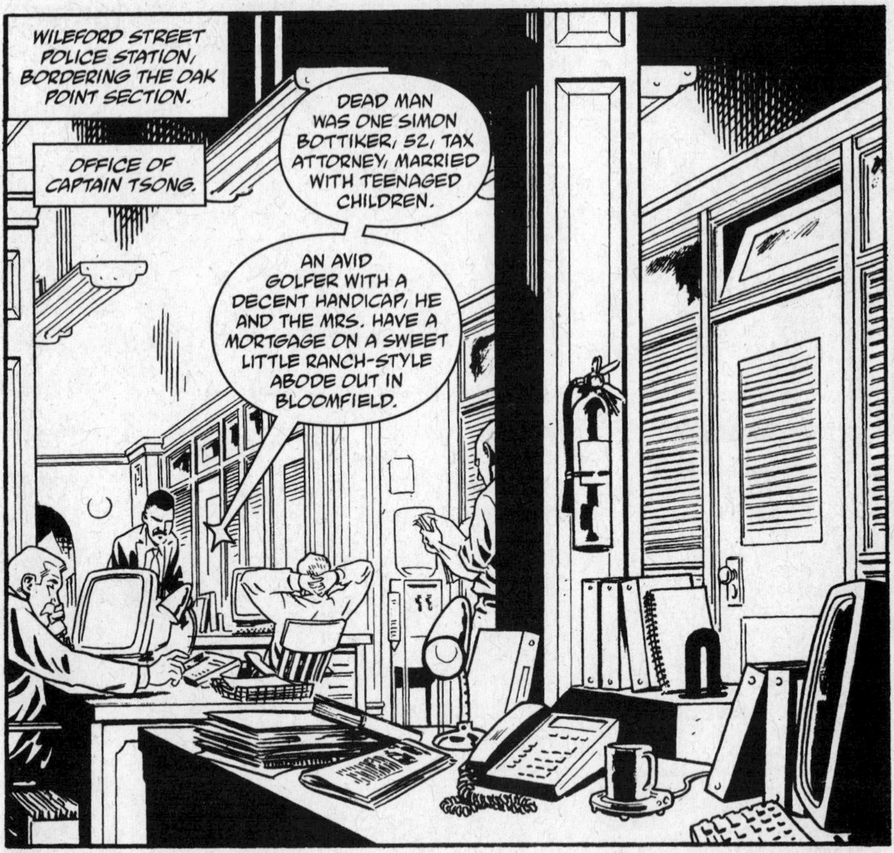
WILEFORD STREET POLICE STATION, BORDERING THE OAK POINT SECTION.
OFFICE OF CAPTAIN TSONG.
DEAD MAN WAS ONE SIMON BOTTIKER, 52, TAX ATTORNEY, MARRIED WITH TEENAGED CHILDREN.
AN AVID GOLFER WITH A DECENT HANDICAP, HE AND THE MRS. HAVE A MORTGAGE ON A SWEET LITTLE RANCH-STYLE ABODE OUT IN BLOOMFIELD.

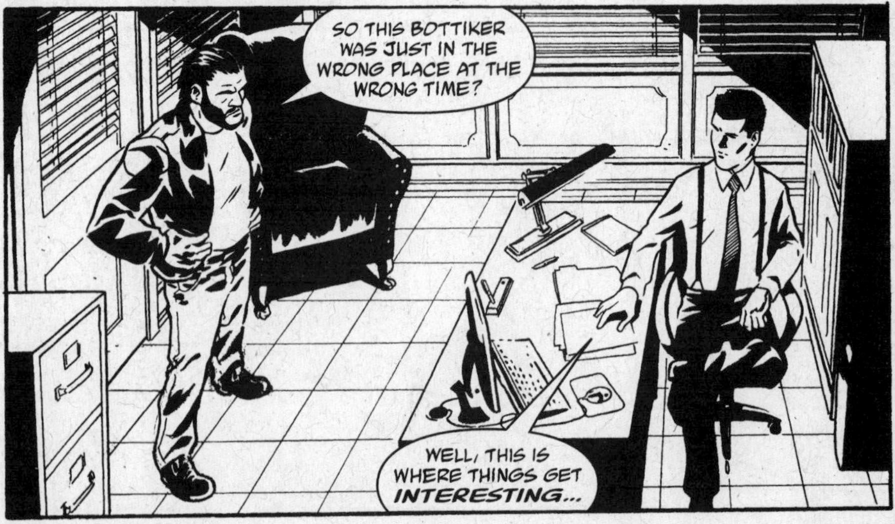
SO THIS BOTTIKER WAS JUST IN THE WRONG PLACE AT THE WRONG TIME?
WELL, THIS IS WHERE THINGS GET *INTERESTING...*

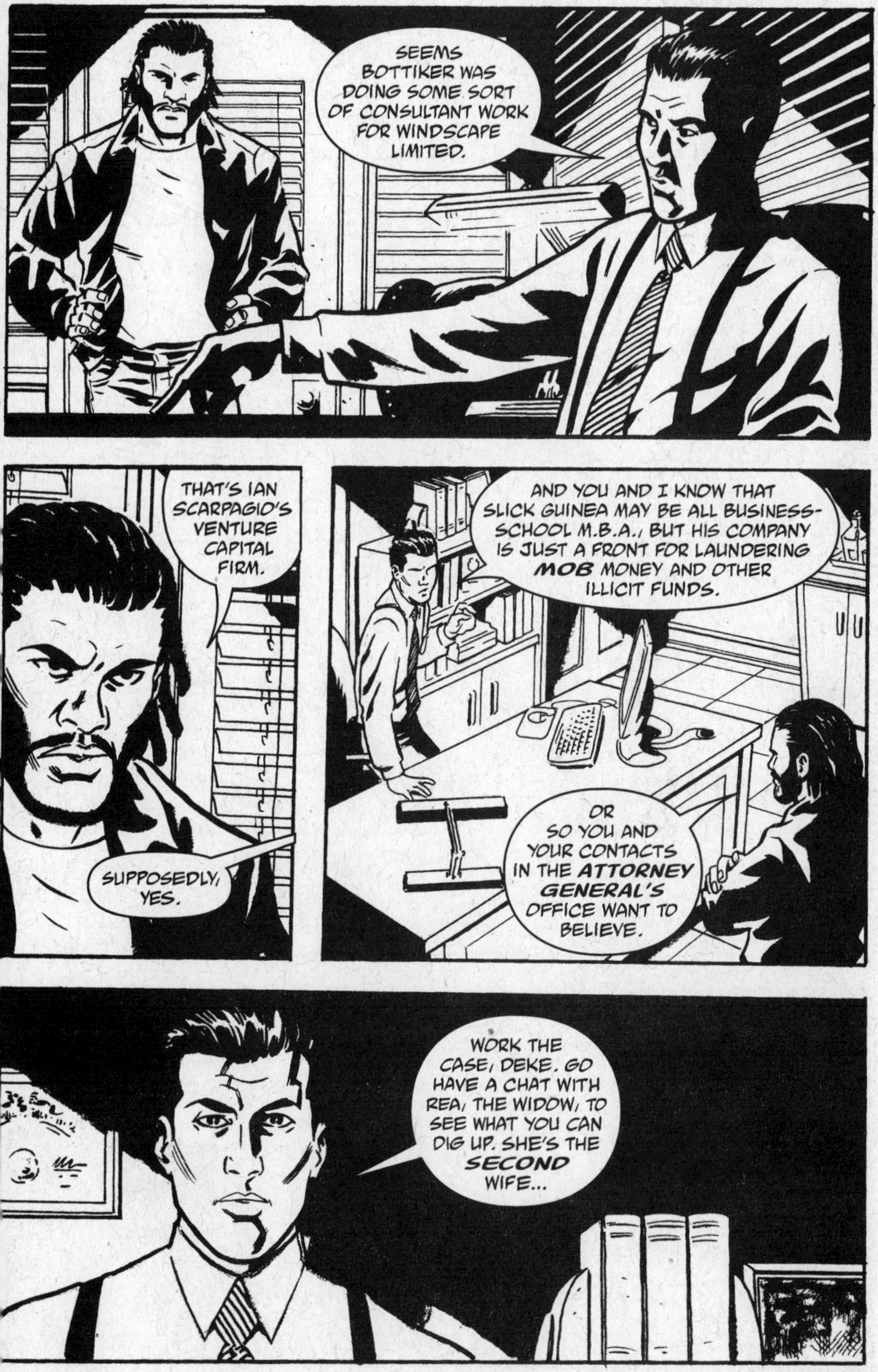
SEEMS BOTTIKER WAS DOING SOME SORT OF CONSULTANT WORK FOR WINDSCAPE LIMITED.
THAT'S IAN SCARPAGIO'S VENTURE CAPITAL FIRM.
SUPPOSEDLY, YES.
AND YOU AND I KNOW THAT SLICK GUINEA MAY BE ALL BUSINESS-SCHOOL M.B.A., BUT HIS COMPANY IS JUST A FRONT FOR LAUNDERING MOB MONEY AND OTHER ILLICIT FUNDS.
OR SO YOU AND YOUR CONTACTS IN THE ATTORNEY GENERAL'S OFFICE WANT TO BELIEVE.
WORK THE CASE, DEKE. GO HAVE A CHAT WITH REA, THE WIDOW, TO SEE WHAT YOU CAN DIG UP. SHE'S THE SECOND WIFE...

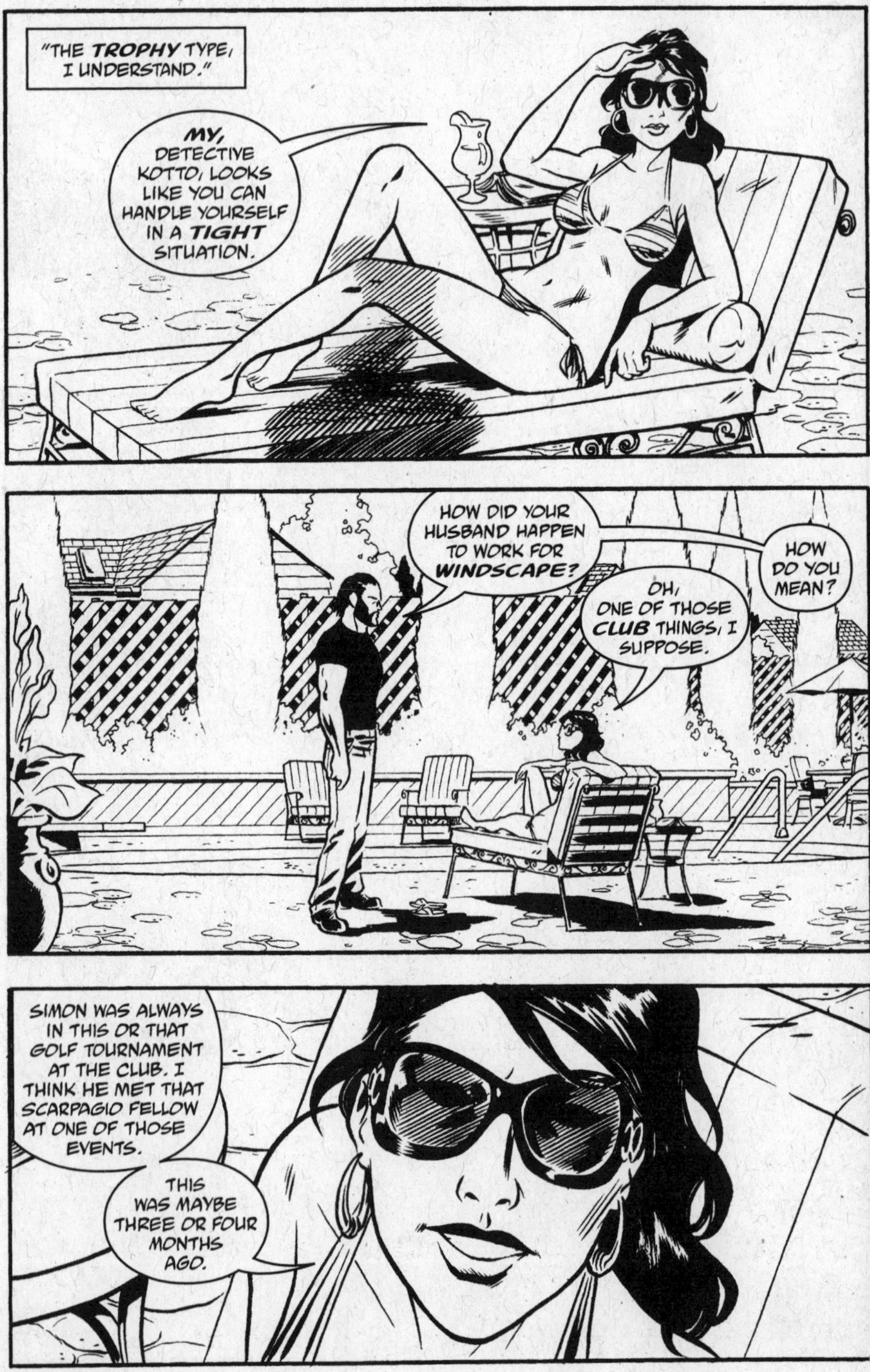
"THE TROPHY TYPE, I UNDERSTAND."
MY, DETECTIVE KOTTO, LOOKS LIKE YOU CAN HANDLE YOURSELF IN A TIGHT SITUATION.
HOW DID YOUR HUSBAND HAPPEN TO WORK FOR WINDSCAPE?
HOW DO YOU MEAN?
OH, ONE OF THOSE CLUB THINGS, I SUPPOSE.
SIMON WAS ALWAYS IN THIS OR THAT GOLF TOURNAMENT AT THE CLUB. I THINK HE MET THAT SCARPAGIO FELLOW AT ONE OF THOSE EVENTS.
THIS WAS MAYBE THREE OR FOUR MONTHS AGO.

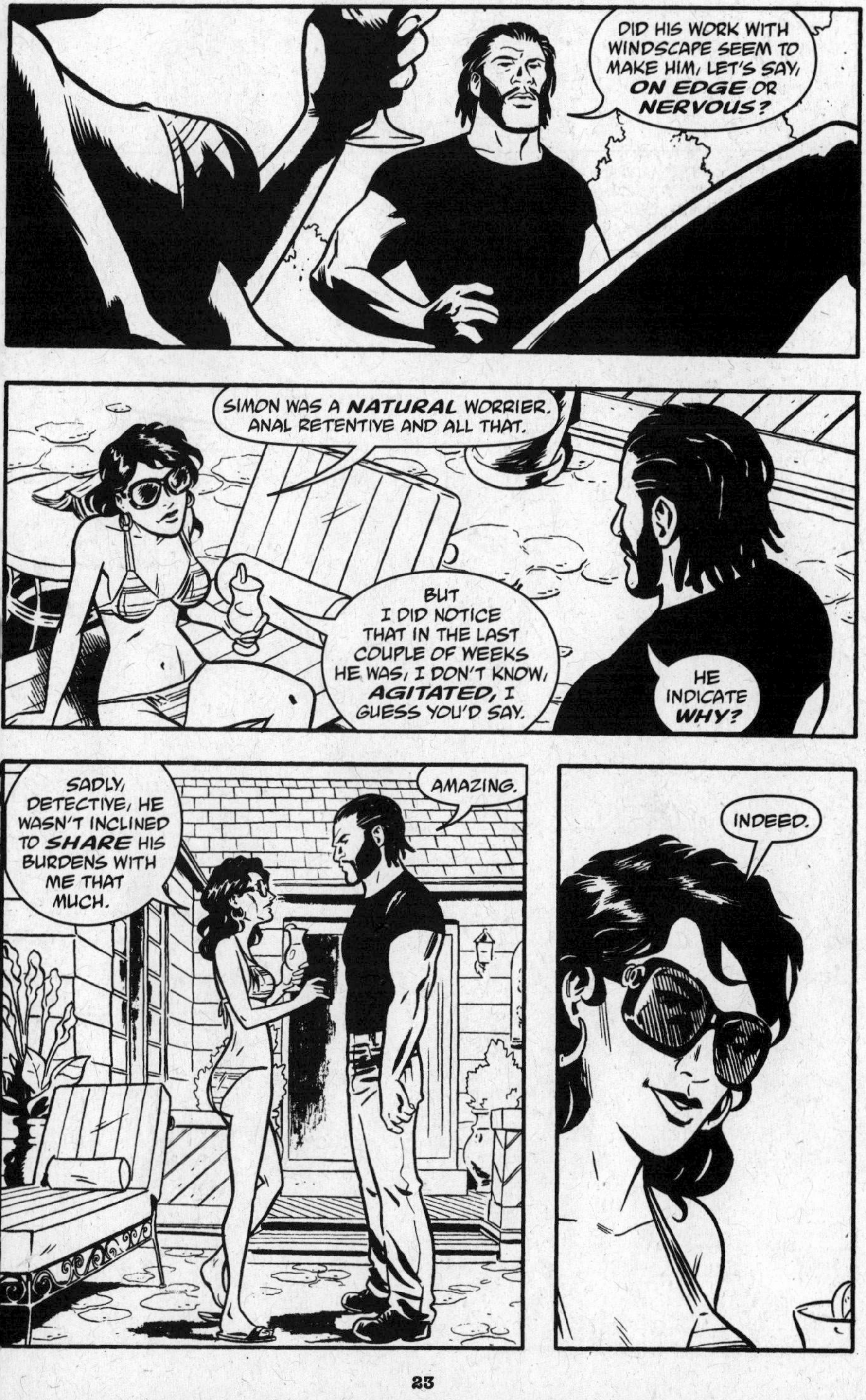
DID HIS WORK WITH WINDSCAPE SEEM TO MAKE HIM, LET'S SAY, ON EDGE OR NERVOUS?
SIMON WAS A NATURAL WORRIER. ANAL RETENTIVE AND ALL THAT.
BUT I DID NOTICE THAT IN THE LAST COUPLE OF WEEKS HE WAS, I DON'T KNOW, AGITATED, I GUESS YOU'D SAY.
HE INDICATE WHY?
SADLY, DETECTIVE, HE WASN'T INCLINED TO SHARE HIS BURDENS WITH ME THAT MUCH.
AMAZING.
INDEED.

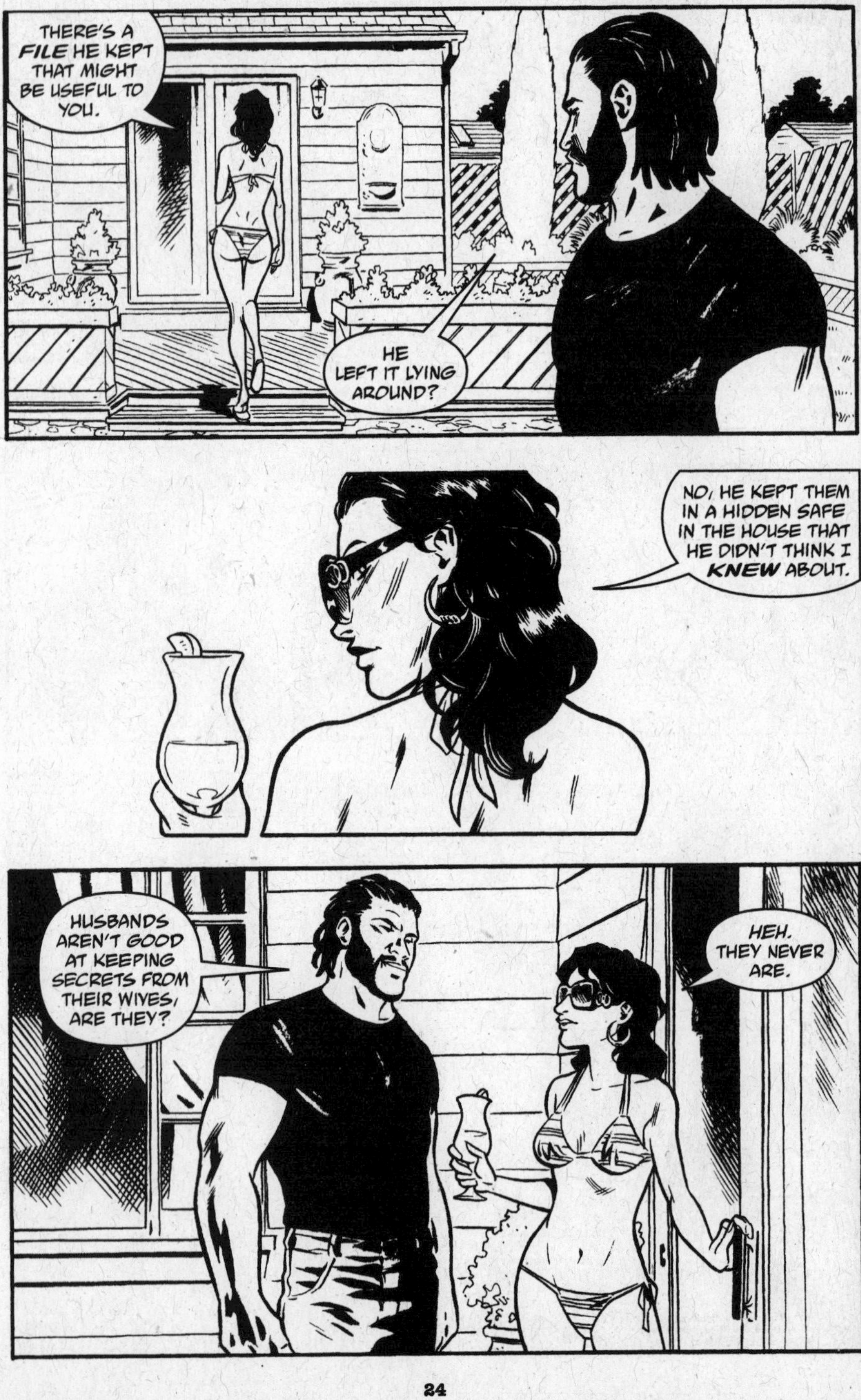
THERE'S A FILE HE KEPT THAT MIGHT BE USEFUL TO YOU.
HE LEFT IT LYING AROUND?
NO, HE KEPT THEM IN A HIDDEN SAFE IN THE HOUSE THAT HE DIDN'T THINK I KNEW ABOUT.
HUSBANDS AREN'T GOOD AT KEEPING SECRETS FROM THEIR WIVES, ARE THEY?
HEH. THEY NEVER ARE.

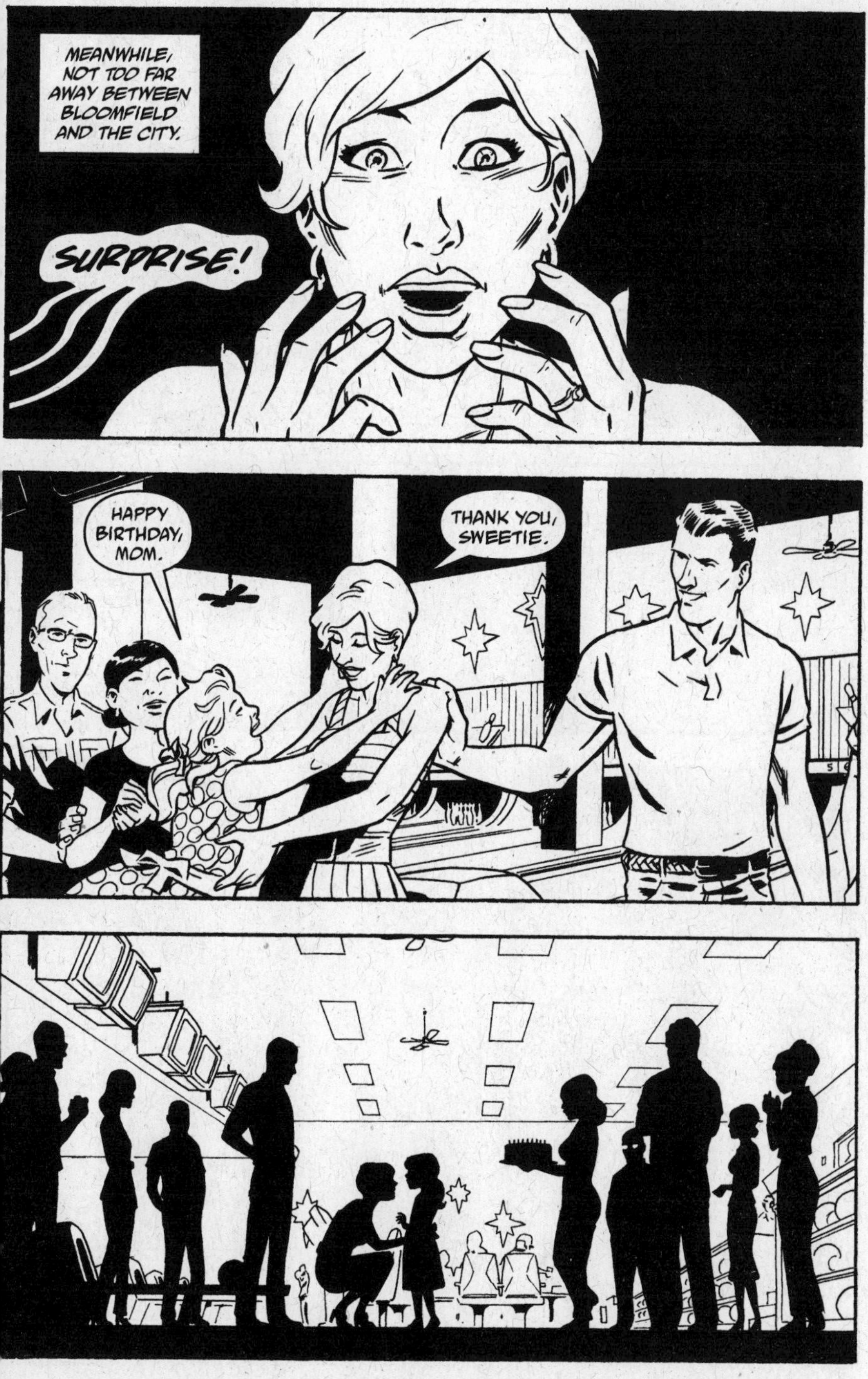
MEANWHILE, NOT TOO FAR AWAY BETWEEN BLOOMFIELD AND THE CITY.
SURPRISE!
HAPPY BIRTHDAY, MOM.
THANK YOU, SWEETIE.

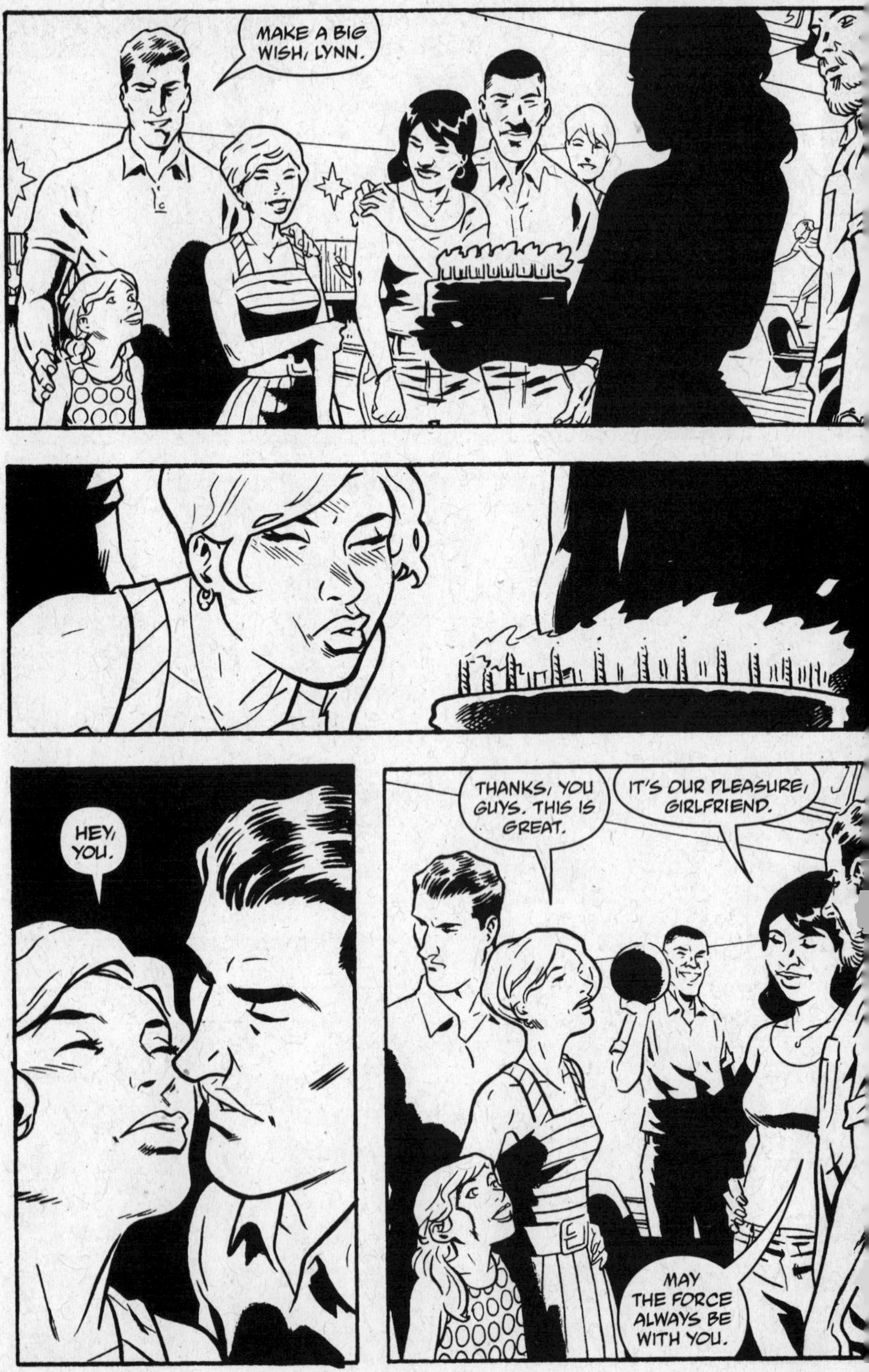
MAKE A BIG WISH, LYNN.
HEY, YOU.
THANKS, YOU GUYS. THIS IS GREAT.
IT'S OUR PLEASURE, GIRLFRIEND.
MAY THE FORCE ALWAYS BE WITH YOU.

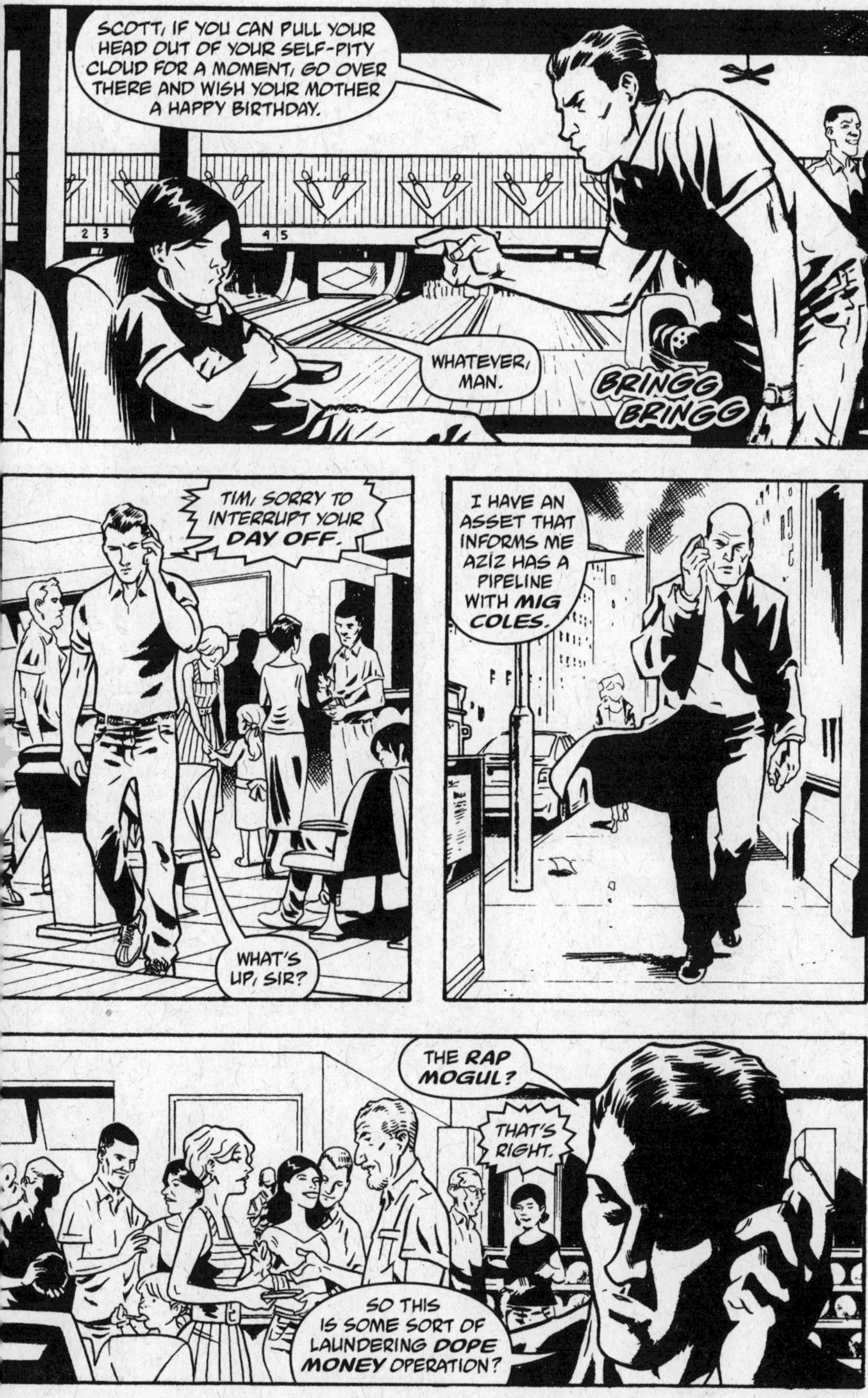
SCOTT, IF YOU CAN PULL YOUR HEAD OUT OF YOUR SELF-PITY CLOUD FOR A MOMENT, GO OVER THERE AND WISH YOUR MOTHER A HAPPY BIRTHDAY.
WHATEVER, MAN.
BRINGG BRINGG
TIM, SORRY TO INTERRUPT YOUR DAY OFF.
WHAT'S UP, SIR?
I HAVE AN ASSET THAT INFORMS ME AZIZ HAS A PIPELINE WITH MIG COLES.
THE RAP MOGUL?
THAT'S RIGHT.
SO THIS IS SOME SORT OF LAUNDERING DOPE MONEY OPERATION?

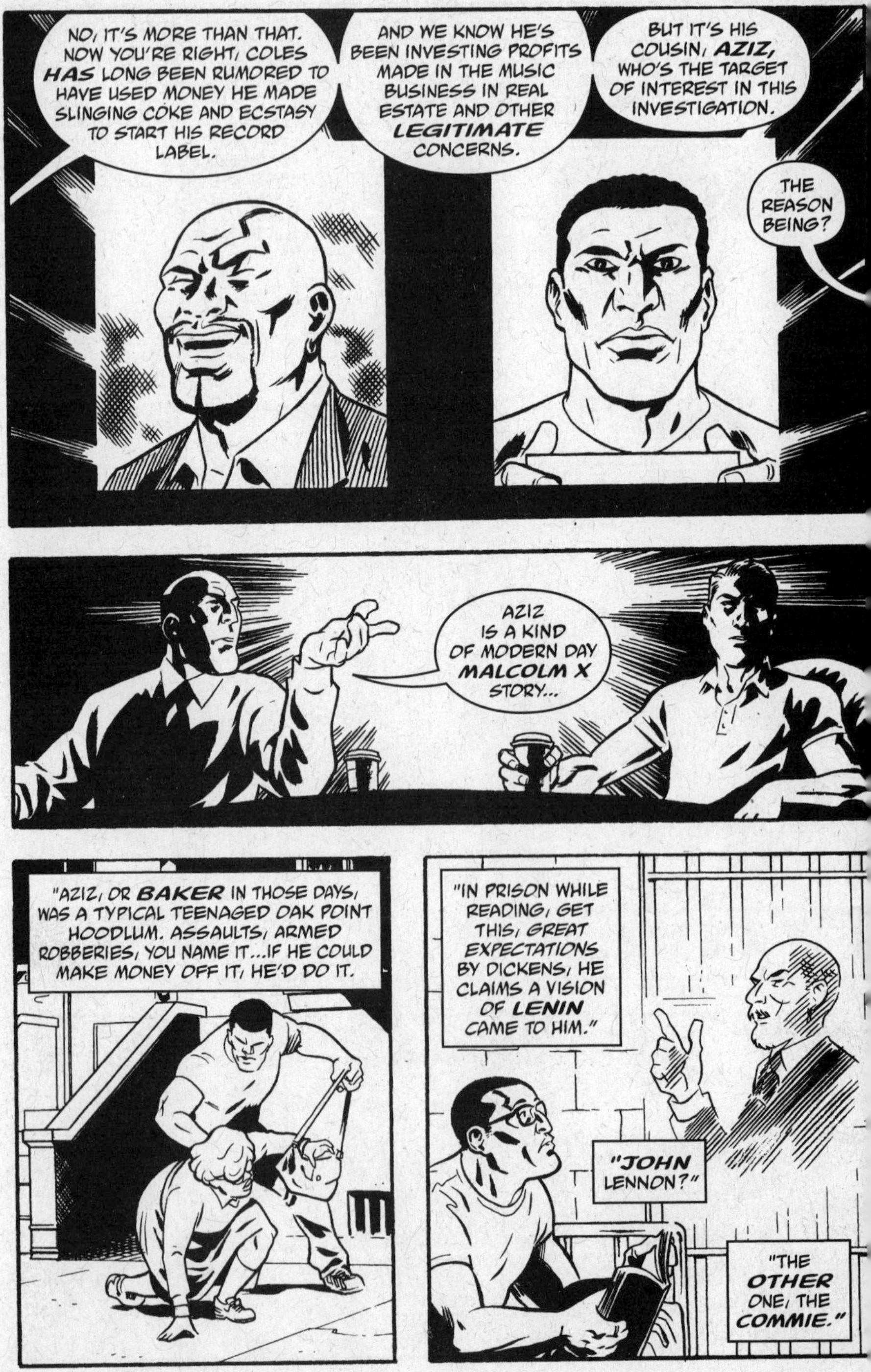
NO, IT'S MORE THAN THAT. NOW YOU'RE RIGHT, COLES HAS LONG BEEN RUMORED TO HAVE USED MONEY HE MADE SLINGING COKE AND ECSTASY TO START HIS RECORD LABEL.
AND WE KNOW HE'S BEEN INVESTING PROFITS MADE IN THE MUSIC BUSINESS IN REAL ESTATE AND OTHER LEGITIMATE CONCERNS.
BUT IT'S HIS COUSIN, AZIZ, WHO'S THE TARGET OF INTEREST IN THIS INVESTIGATION.
THE REASON BEING?
AZIZ IS A KIND OF MODERN DAY MALCOLM X STORY...
"AZIZ, OR BAKER IN THOSE DAYS, WAS A TYPICAL TEENAGED OAK POINT HOODLUM. ASSAULTS, ARMED ROBBERIES, YOU NAME IT...IF HE COULD MAKE MONEY OFF IT, HE'D DO IT.
"IN PRISON WHILE READING, GET THIS, GREAT EXPECTATIONS BY DICKENS, HE CLAIMS A VISION OF LENIN CAME TO HIM."
"JOHN LENNON?"
"THE OTHER ONE, THE COMMIE."

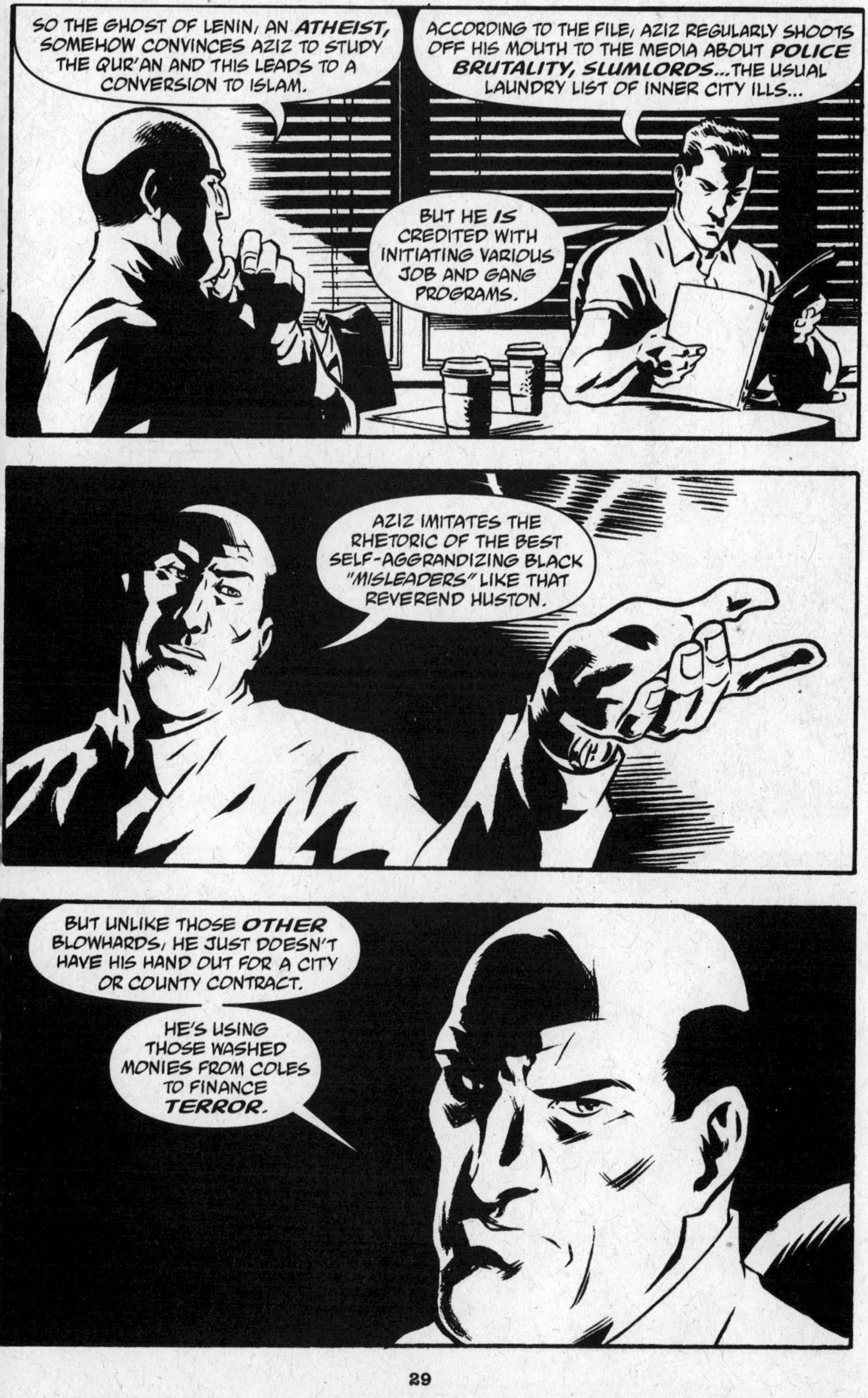
SO THE GHOST OF LENIN, AN ATHEIST, SOMEHOW CONVINCES AZIZ TO STUDY THE QUR'AN AND THIS LEADS TO A CONVERSION TO ISLAM.
ACCORDING TO THE FILE, AZIZ REGULARLY SHOOTS OFF HIS MOUTH TO THE MEDIA ABOUT POLICE BRUTALITY, SLUMLORDS...THE USUAL LAUNDRY LIST OF INNER CITY ILLS...
BUT HE IS CREDITED WITH INITIATING VARIOUS JOB AND GANG PROGRAMS.
AZIZ IMITATES THE RHETORIC OF THE BEST SELF-AGGRANDIZING BLACK "MISLEADERS" LIKE THAT REVEREND HUSTON.
BUT UNLIKE THOSE OTHER BLOWHARDS, HE JUST DOESN'T HAVE HIS HAND OUT FOR A CITY OR COUNTY CONTRACT.
HE'S USING THOSE WASHED MONIES FROM COLES TO FINANCE TERROR.

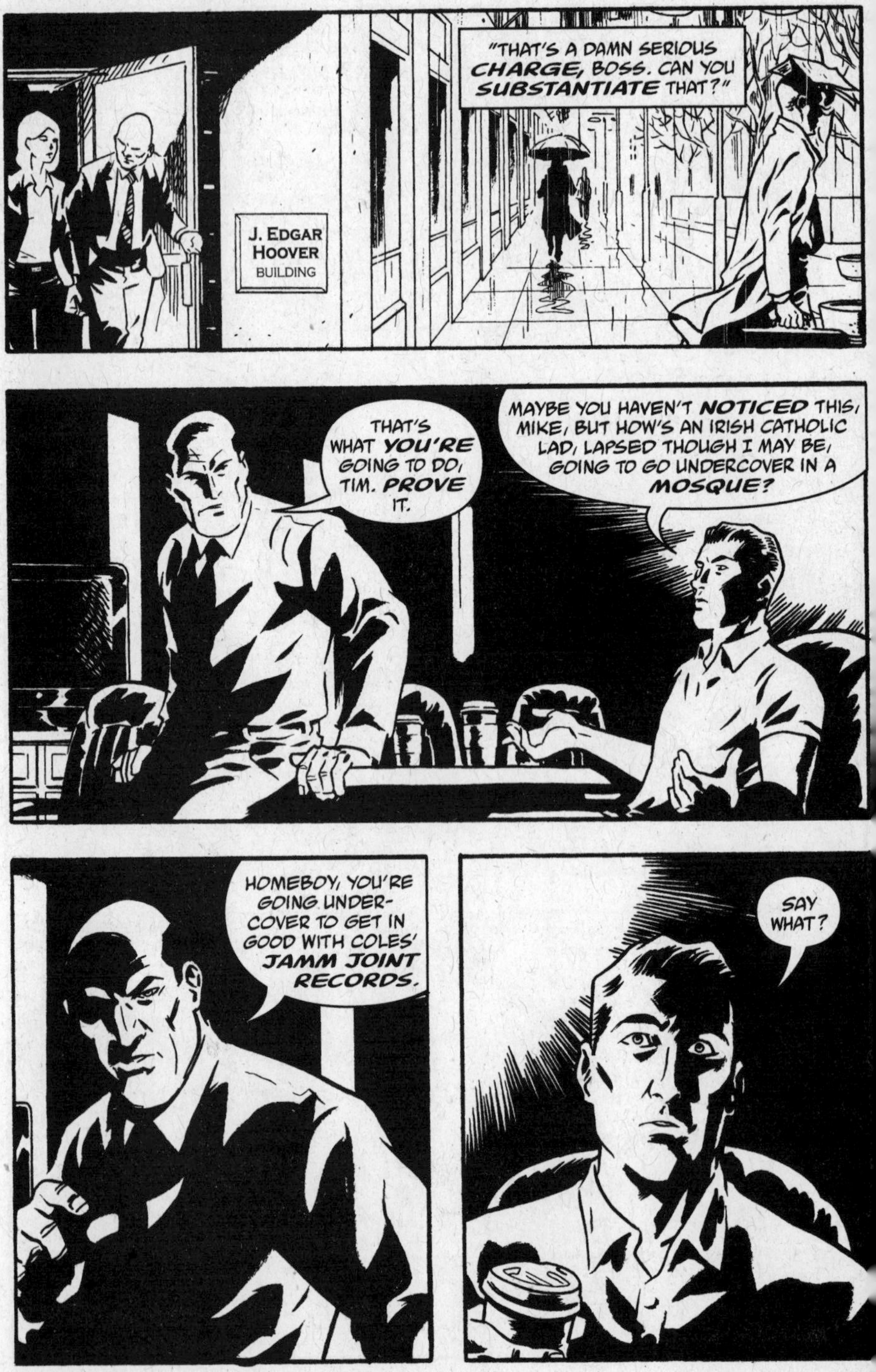
"THAT'S A DAMN SERIOUS CHARGE, BOSS. CAN YOU SUBSTANTIATE THAT?"
J. EDGAR HOOVER BUILDING
THAT'S WHAT YOU'RE GOING TO DO, TIM. PROVE IT.
MAYBE YOU HAVEN'T NOTICED THIS, MIKE, BUT HOW'S AN IRISH CATHOLIC LAD, LAPSED THOUGH I MAY BE, GOING TO GO UNDERCOVER IN A MOSQUE?
HOMEBOY, YOU'RE GOING UNDER-COVER TO GET IN GOOD WITH COLES' JAMM JOINT RECORDS.
SAY WHAT?

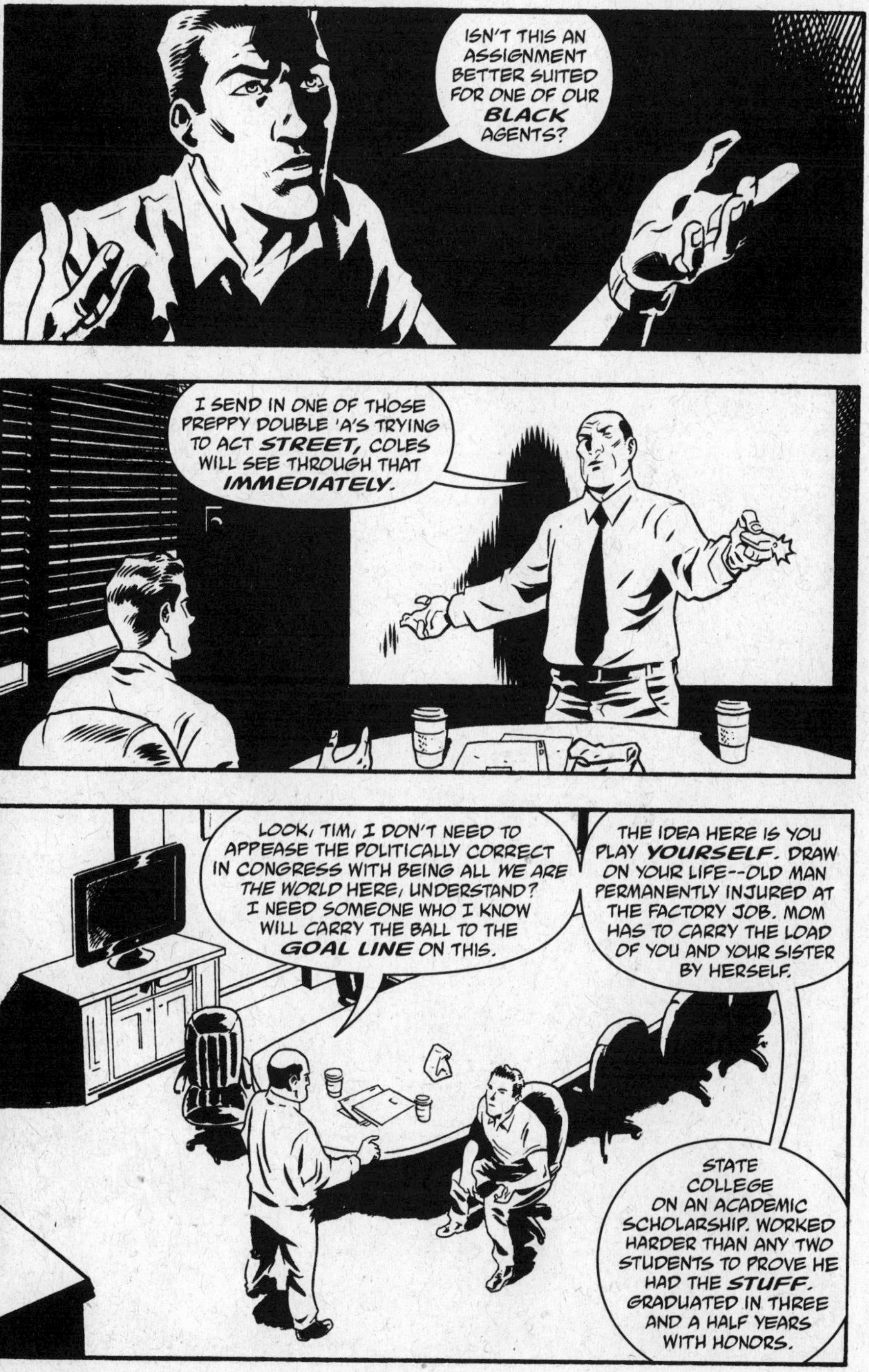
ISN'T THIS AN ASSIGNMENT BETTER SUITED FOR ONE OF OUR BLACK AGENTS?
I SEND IN ONE OF THOSE PREPPY DOUBLE 'A'S TRYING TO ACT STREET, COLES WILL SEE THROUGH THAT IMMEDIATELY.
LOOK, TIM, I DON'T NEED TO APPEASE THE POLITICALLY CORRECT IN CONGRESS WITH BEING ALL WE ARE THE WORLD HERE, UNDERSTAND? I NEED SOMEONE WHO I KNOW WILL CARRY THE BALL TO THE GOAL LINE ON THIS.
THE IDEA HERE IS YOU PLAY YOURSELF. DRAW ON YOUR LIFE--OLD MAN PERMANENTLY INJURED AT THE FACTORY JOB. MOM HAS TO CARRY THE LOAD OF YOU AND YOUR SISTER BY HERSELF.
STATE COLLEGE ON AN ACADEMIC SCHOLARSHIP. WORKED HARDER THAN ANY TWO STUDENTS TO PROVE HE HAD THE STUFF. GRADUATED IN THREE AND A HALF YEARS WITH HONORS.

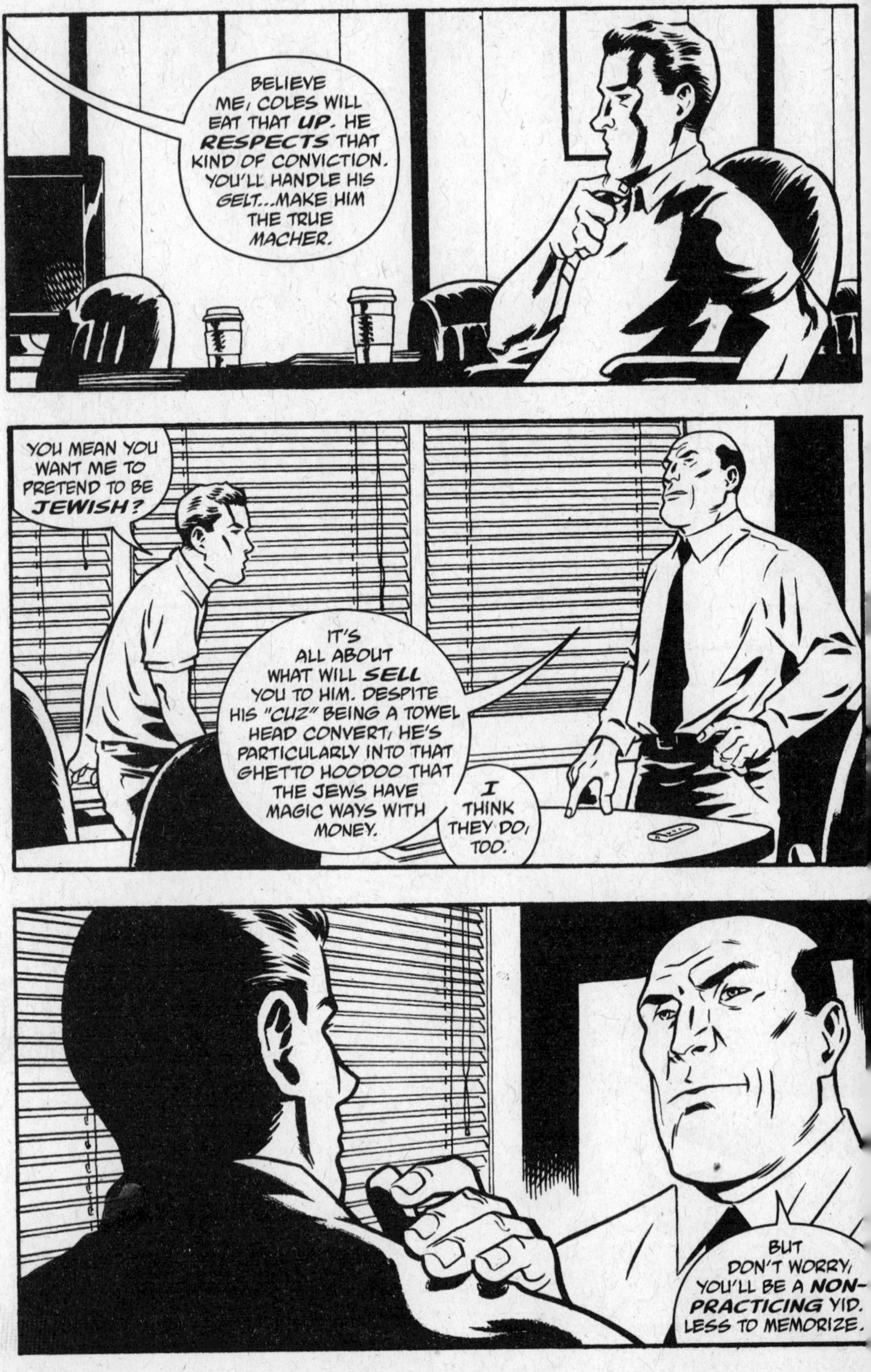
BELIEVE ME, COLES WILL EAT THAT **UP**. HE **RESPECTS** THAT KIND OF CONVICTION. YOU'LL HANDLE HIS GELT...MAKE HIM THE TRUE MACHER.
YOU MEAN YOU WANT ME TO PRETEND TO BE **JEWISH**?
IT'S ALL ABOUT WHAT WILL **SELL** YOU TO HIM. DESPITE HIS "CUZ" BEING A TOWEL HEAD CONVERT, HE'S PARTICULARLY INTO THAT GHETTO HOODOO THAT THE JEWS HAVE MAGIC WAYS WITH MONEY.
I THINK THEY DO, TOO.
BUT DON'T WORRY, YOU'LL BE A **NON-PRACTICING** YID. LESS TO MEMORIZE.

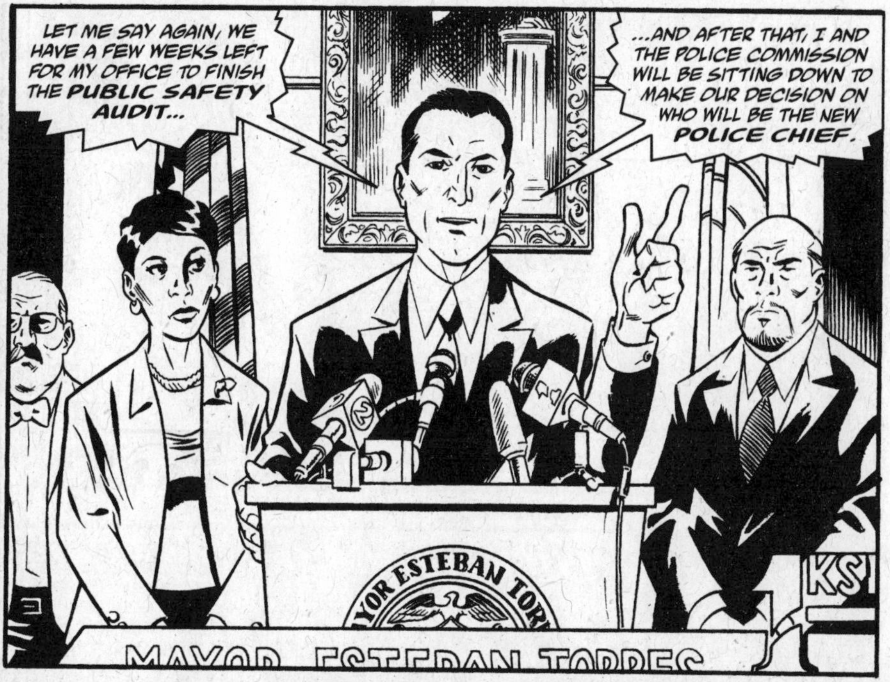
LET ME SAY AGAIN, WE HAVE A FEW WEEKS LEFT FOR MY OFFICE TO FINISH THE **PUBLIC SAFETY AUDIT...**
...AND AFTER THAT, I AND THE POLICE COMMISSION WILL BE SITTING DOWN TO MAKE OUR DECISION ON WHO WILL BE THE NEW **POLICE CHIEF.**
MAYOR ESTEBAN TORRES

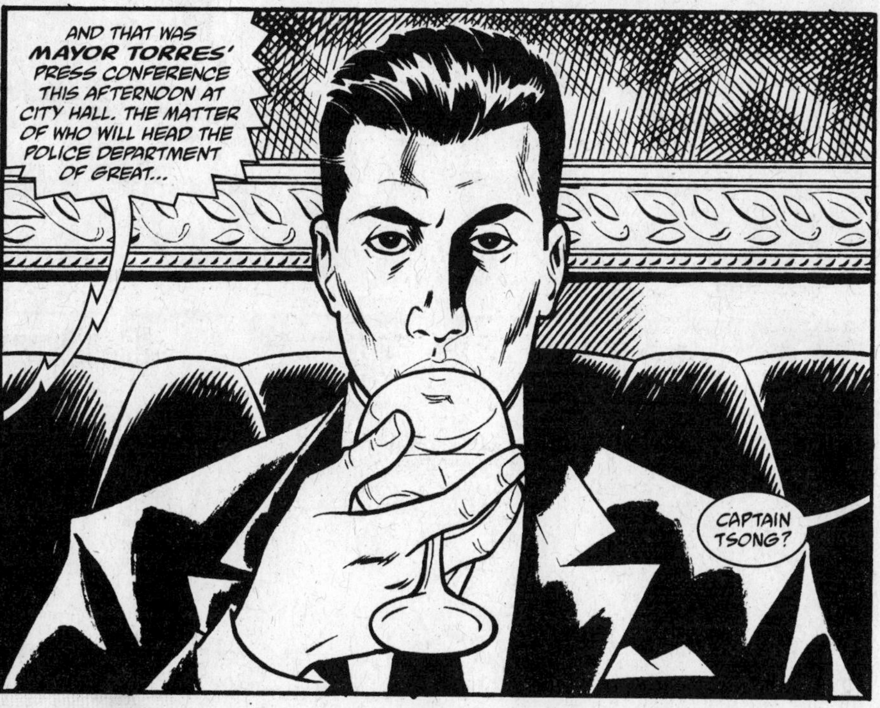
AND THAT WAS **MAYOR TORRES'** PRESS CONFERENCE THIS AFTERNOON AT CITY HALL. THE MATTER OF WHO WILL HEAD THE POLICE DEPARTMENT OF GREAT...
CAPTAIN TSONG?

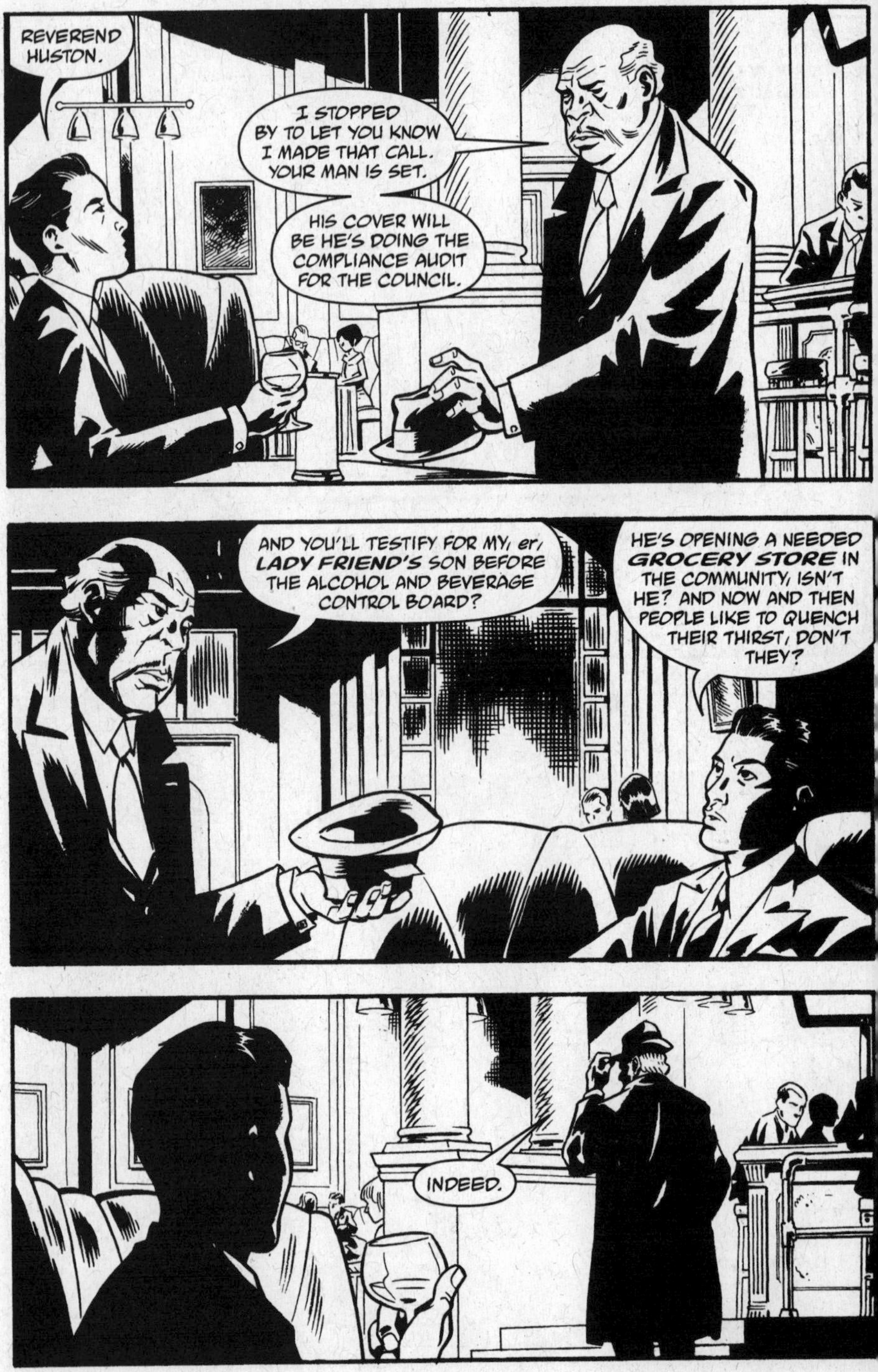
REVEREND HUSTON.
I STOPPED BY TO LET YOU KNOW I MADE THAT CALL. YOUR MAN IS SET.
HIS COVER WILL BE HE'S DOING THE COMPLIANCE AUDIT FOR THE COUNCIL.
AND YOU'LL TESTIFY FOR MY, er, LADY FRIEND'S SON BEFORE THE ALCOHOL AND BEVERAGE CONTROL BOARD?
HE'S OPENING A NEEDED GROCERY STORE IN THE COMMUNITY, ISN'T HE? AND NOW AND THEN PEOPLE LIKE TO QUENCH THEIR THIRST, DON'T THEY?
INDEED.

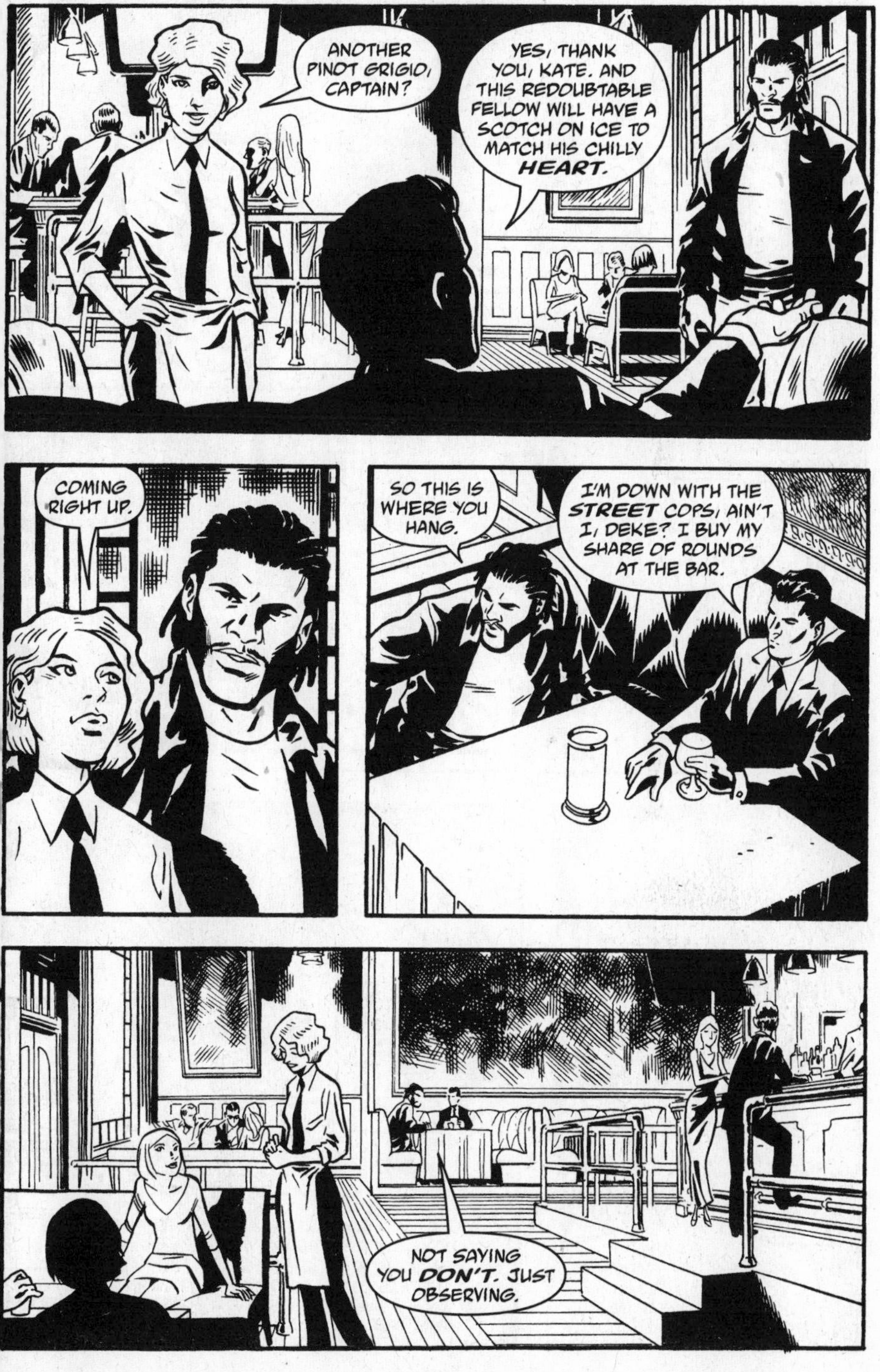
ANOTHER PINOT GRIGIO, CAPTAIN?
YES, THANK YOU, KATE. AND THIS REDOUBTABLE FELLOW WILL HAVE A SCOTCH ON ICE TO MATCH HIS CHILLY HEART.
COMING RIGHT UP.
SO THIS IS WHERE YOU HANG.
I'M DOWN WITH THE STREET COPS, AIN'T I, DEKE? I BUY MY SHARE OF ROUNDS AT THE BAR.
NOT SAYING YOU DON'T. JUST OBSERVING.

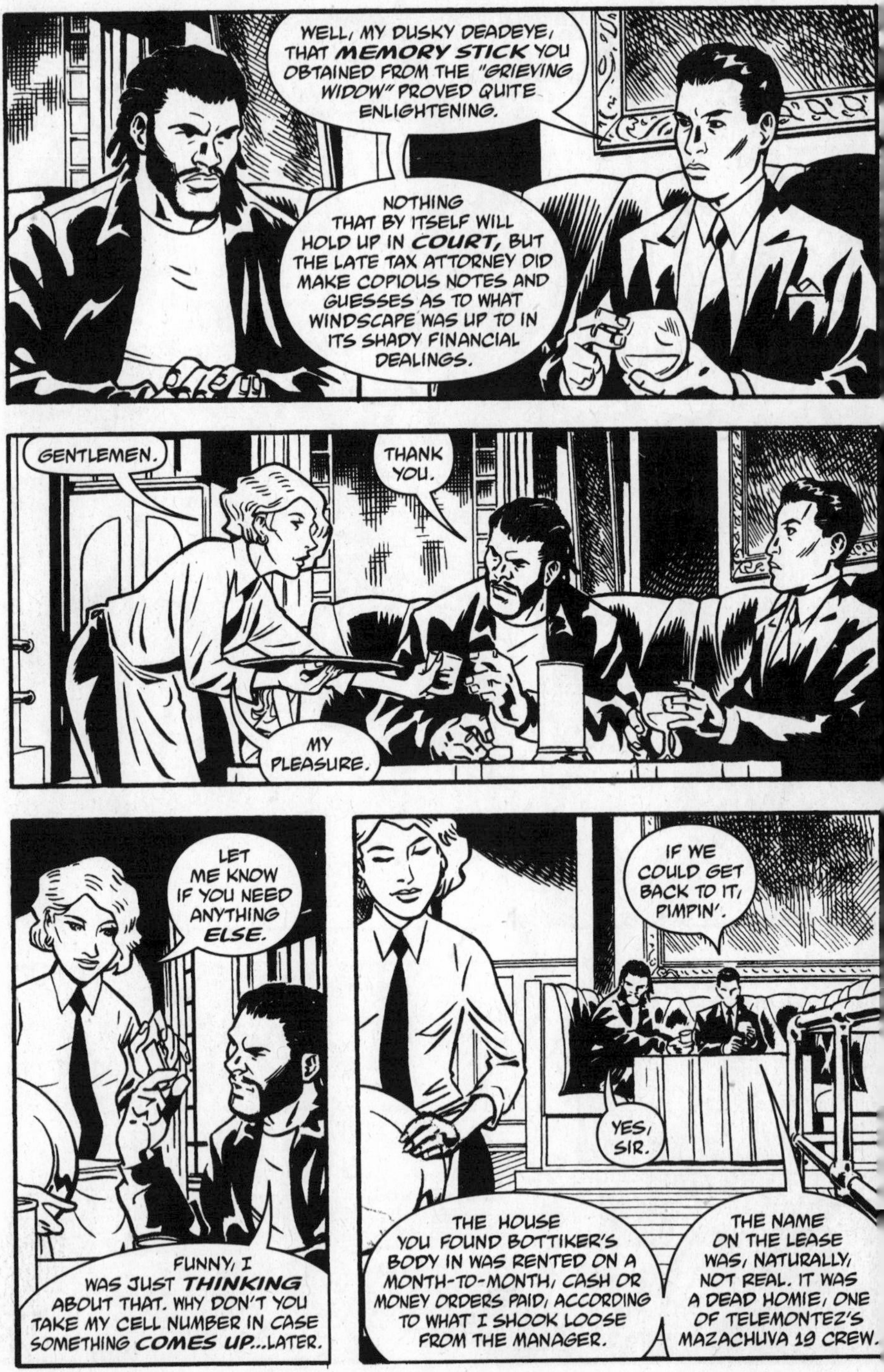
WELL, MY DUSKY DEADEYE, THAT MEMORY STICK YOU OBTAINED FROM THE "GRIEVING WIDOW" PROVED QUITE ENLIGHTENING.
NOTHING THAT BY ITSELF WILL HOLD UP IN COURT, BUT THE LATE TAX ATTORNEY DID MAKE COPIOUS NOTES AND GUESSES AS TO WHAT WINDSCAPE WAS UP TO IN ITS SHADY FINANCIAL DEALINGS.
GENTLEMEN.
THANK YOU.
MY PLEASURE.
LET ME KNOW IF YOU NEED ANYTHING ELSE.
FUNNY, I WAS JUST THINKING ABOUT THAT. WHY DON'T YOU TAKE MY CELL NUMBER IN CASE SOMETHING COMES UP...LATER.
IF WE COULD GET BACK TO IT, PIMPIN'.
YES, SIR.
THE HOUSE YOU FOUND BOTTIKER'S BODY IN WAS RENTED ON A MONTH-TO-MONTH, CASH OR MONEY ORDERS PAID, ACCORDING TO WHAT I SHOOK LOOSE FROM THE MANAGER.
THE NAME ON THE LEASE WAS, NATURALLY, NOT REAL. IT WAS A DEAD HOMIE, ONE OF TELEMONTEZ'S MAZACHUVA 19 CREW.

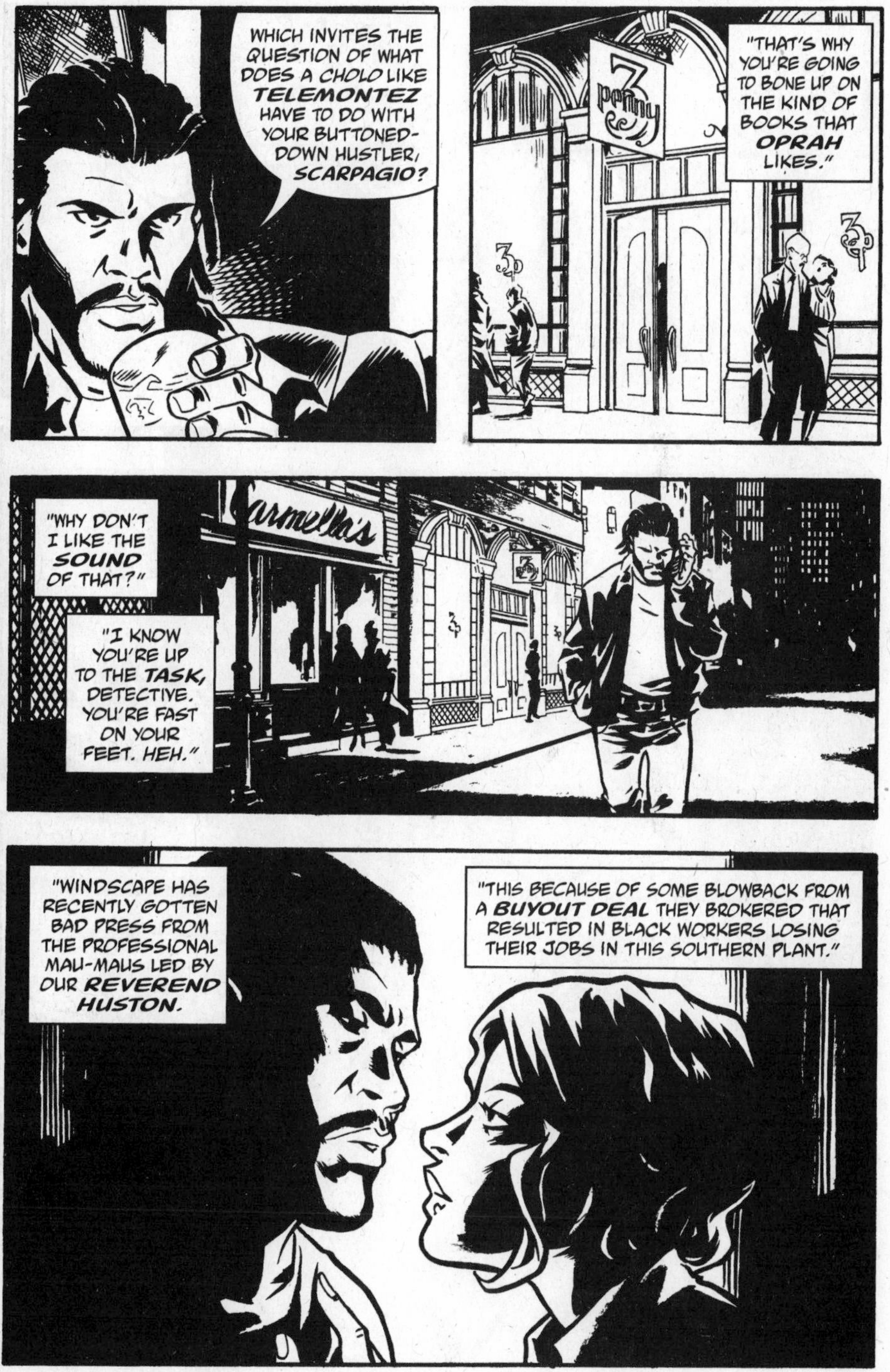
WHICH INVITES THE QUESTION OF WHAT DOES A CHOLO LIKE TELEMONTEZ HAVE TO DO WITH YOUR BUTTONED-DOWN HUSTLER, SCARPAGIO?
3 penny
"THAT'S WHY YOU'RE GOING TO BONE UP ON THE KIND OF BOOKS THAT OPRAH LIKES."
Carmella's
"WHY DON'T I LIKE THE SOUND OF THAT?"
"I KNOW YOU'RE UP TO THE TASK, DETECTIVE. YOU'RE FAST ON YOUR FEET. HEH."
"WINDSCAPE HAS RECENTLY GOTTEN BAD PRESS FROM THE PROFESSIONAL MAU-MAUS LED BY OUR REVEREND HUSTON.
"THIS BECAUSE OF SOME BLOWBACK FROM A BUYOUT DEAL THEY BROKERED THAT RESULTED IN BLACK WORKERS LOSING THEIR JOBS IN THIS SOUTHERN PLANT."

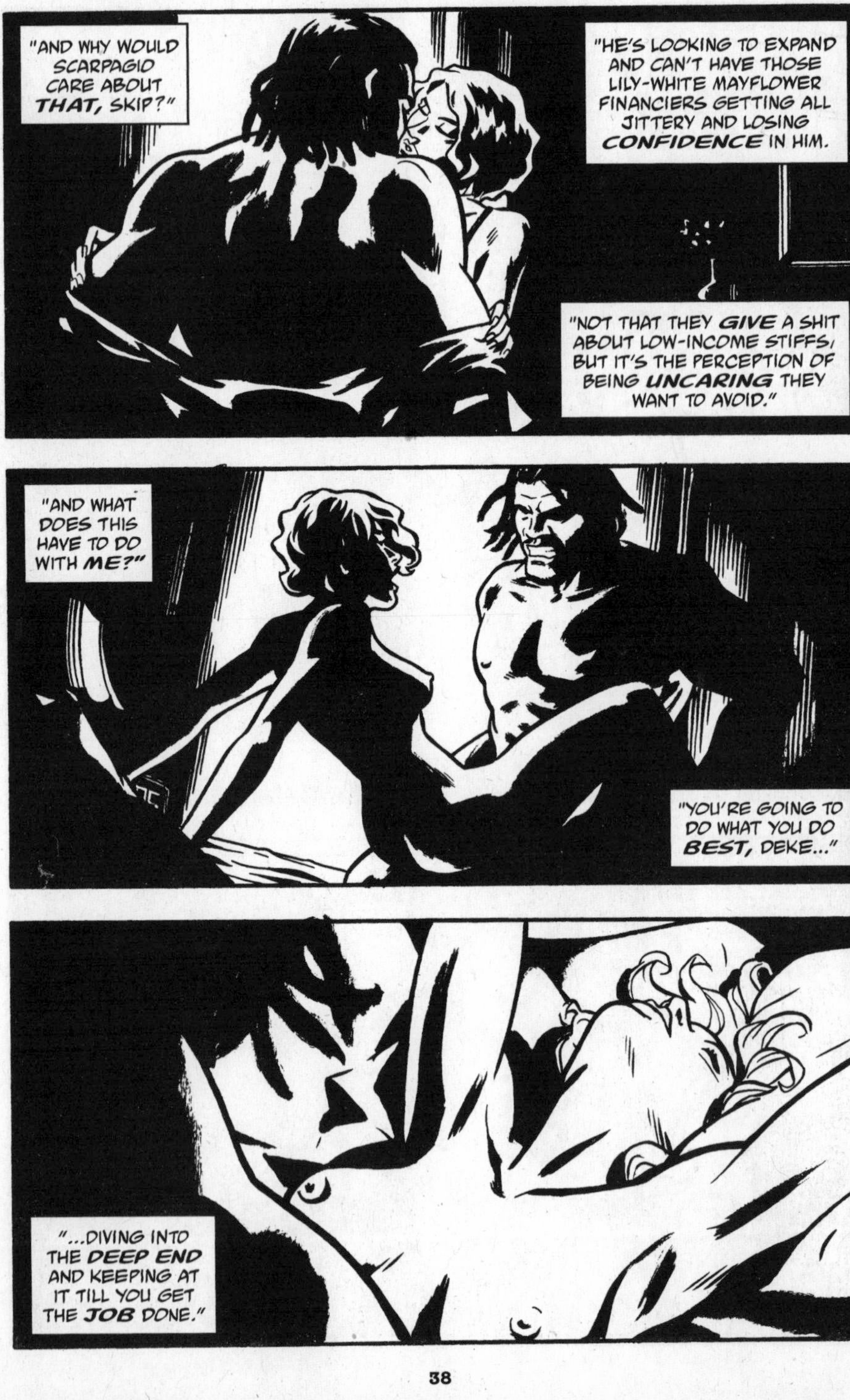
"AND WHY WOULD SCARPAGIO CARE ABOUT THAT, SKIP?"
"HE'S LOOKING TO EXPAND AND CAN'T HAVE THOSE LILY-WHITE MAYFLOWER FINANCIERS GETTING ALL JITTERY AND LOSING CONFIDENCE IN HIM.
"NOT THAT THEY GIVE A SHIT ABOUT LOW-INCOME STIFFS, BUT IT'S THE PERCEPTION OF BEING UNCARING THEY WANT TO AVOID."
"AND WHAT DOES THIS HAVE TO DO WITH ME?"
"YOU'RE GOING TO DO WHAT YOU DO BEST, DEKE..."
"...DIVING INTO THE DEEP END AND KEEPING AT IT TILL YOU GET THE JOB DONE."

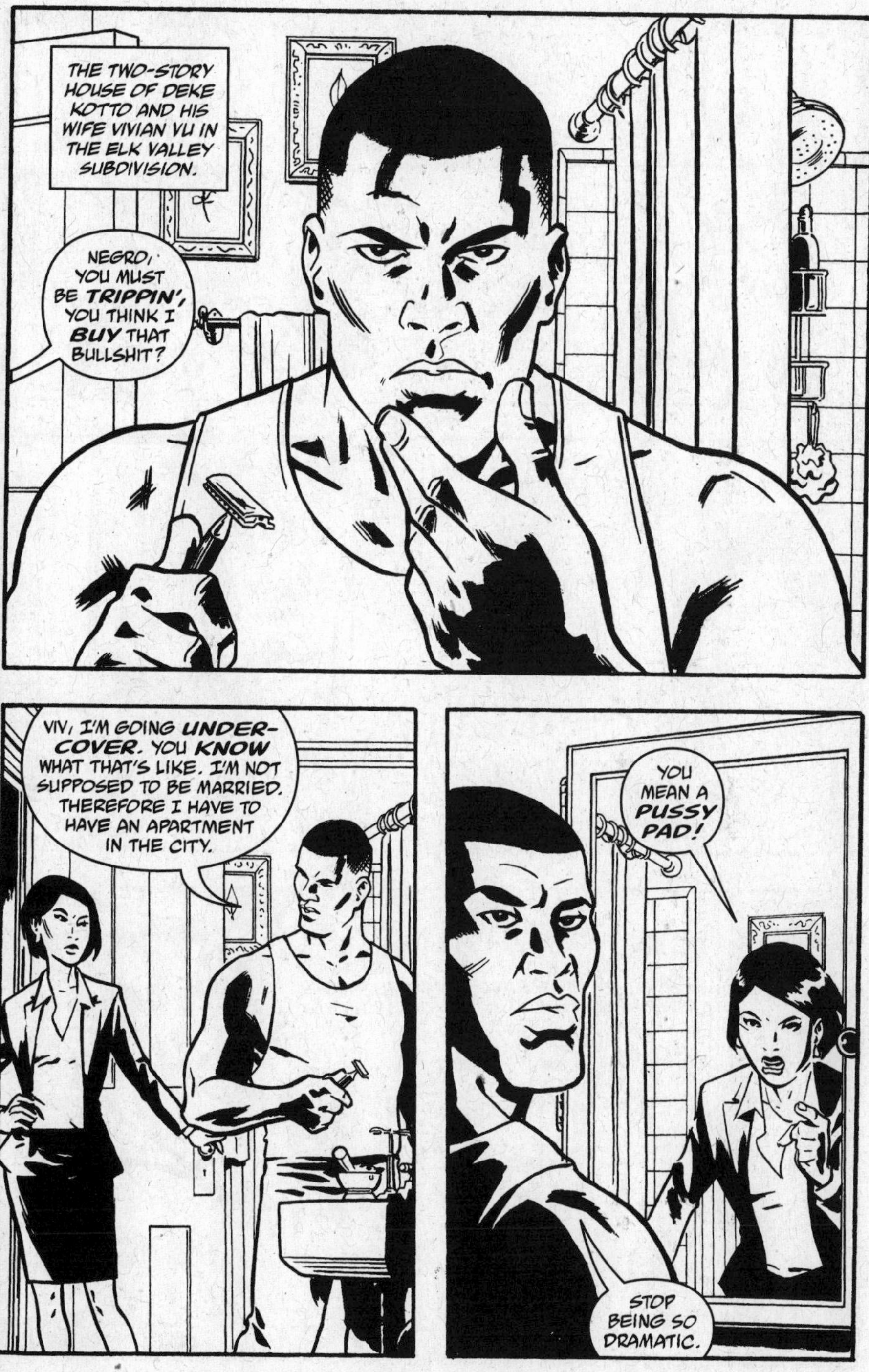
THE TWO-STORY HOUSE OF DEKE KOTTO AND HIS WIFE VIVIAN VU IN THE ELK VALLEY SUBDIVISION.
NEGRO, YOU MUST BE TRIPPIN', YOU THINK I BUY THAT BULLSHIT?
VIV, I'M GOING UNDER-COVER. YOU KNOW WHAT THAT'S LIKE. I'M NOT SUPPOSED TO BE MARRIED. THEREFORE I HAVE TO HAVE AN APARTMENT IN THE CITY.
YOU MEAN A PUSSY PAD!
STOP BEING SO DRAMATIC.

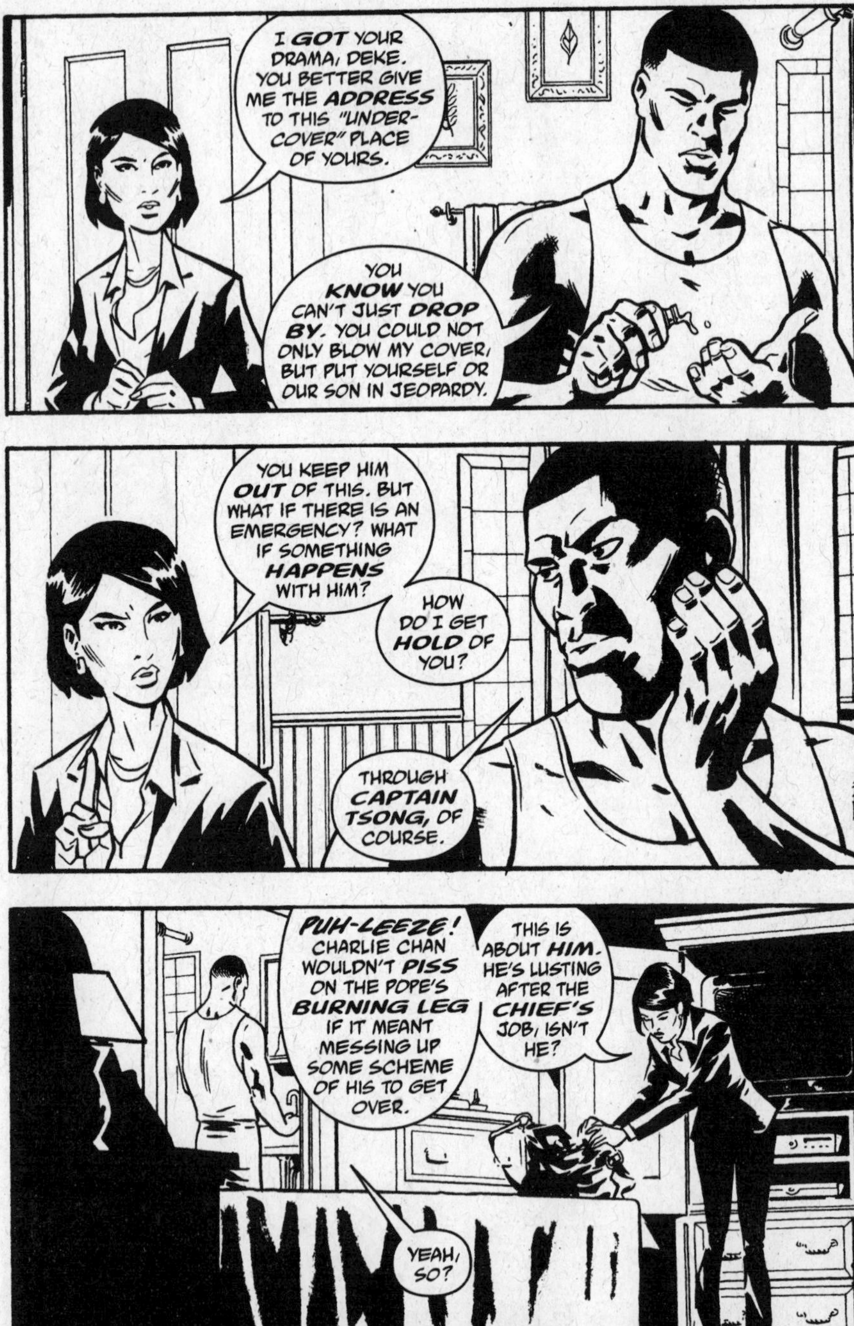
I GOT YOUR DRAMA, DEKE. YOU BETTER GIVE ME THE ADDRESS TO THIS "UNDER-COVER" PLACE OF YOURS.
YOU KNOW YOU CAN'T JUST DROP BY. YOU COULD NOT ONLY BLOW MY COVER, BUT PUT YOURSELF OR OUR SON IN JEOPARDY.
YOU KEEP HIM OUT OF THIS. BUT WHAT IF THERE IS AN EMERGENCY? WHAT IF SOMETHING HAPPENS WITH HIM?
HOW DO I GET HOLD OF YOU?
THROUGH CAPTAIN TSONG, OF COURSE.
PUH-LEEZE! CHARLIE CHAN WOULDN'T PISS ON THE POPE'S BURNING LEG IF IT MEANT MESSING UP SOME SCHEME OF HIS TO GET OVER.
THIS IS ABOUT HIM. HE'S LUSTING AFTER THE CHIEF'S JOB, ISN'T HE?
YEAH, SO?

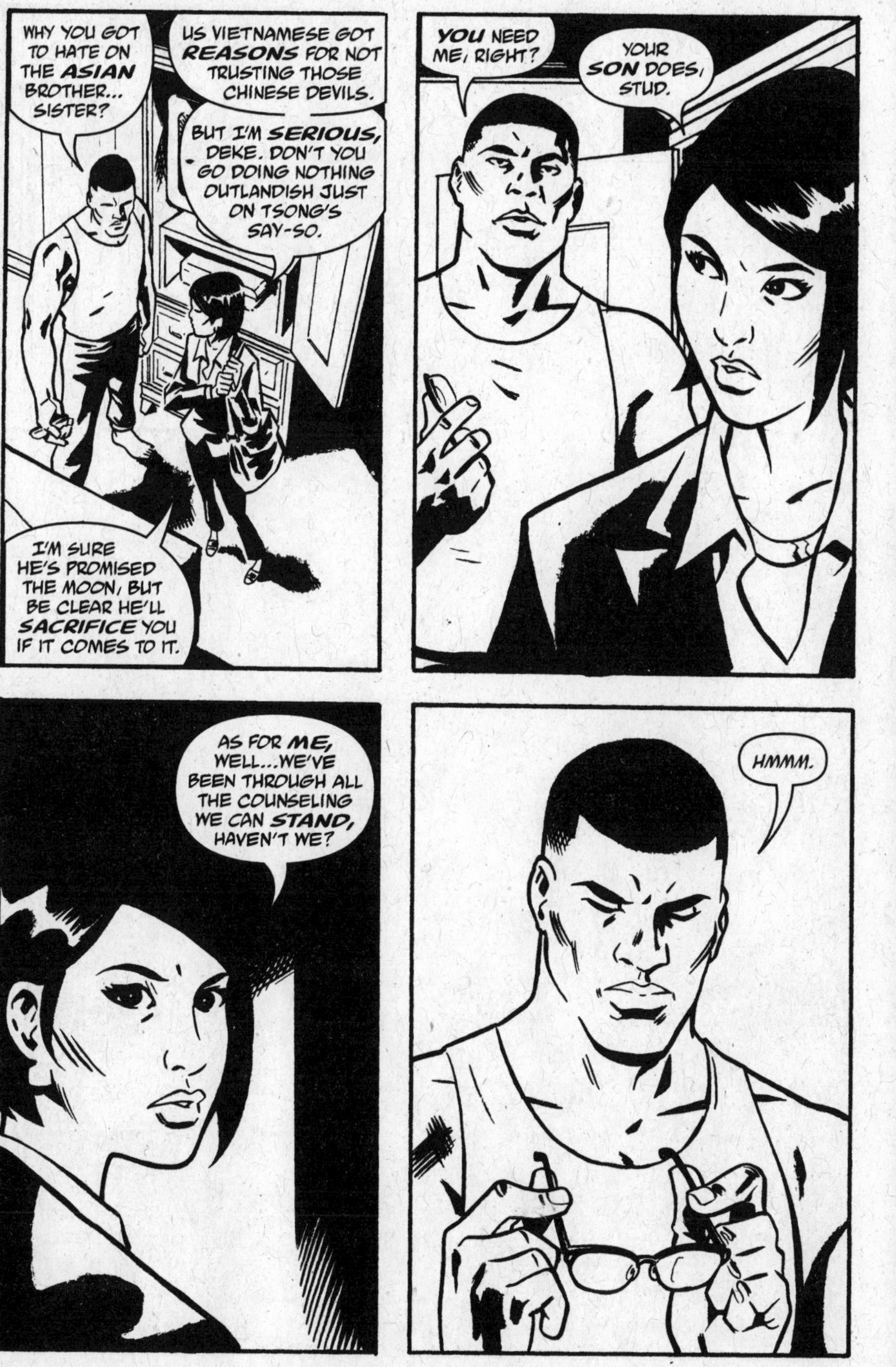
WHY YOU GOT TO HATE ON THE ASIAN BROTHER... SISTER?
US VIETNAMESE GOT REASONS FOR NOT TRUSTING THOSE CHINESE DEVILS.
BUT I'M SERIOUS, DEKE. DON'T YOU GO DOING NOTHING OUTLANDISH JUST ON TSONG'S SAY-SO.
I'M SURE HE'S PROMISED THE MOON, BUT BE CLEAR HE'LL SACRIFICE YOU IF IT COMES TO IT.
YOU NEED ME, RIGHT?
YOUR SON DOES, STUD.
AS FOR ME, WELL...WE'VE BEEN THROUGH ALL THE COUNSELING WE CAN STAND, HAVEN'T WE?
HMMM.

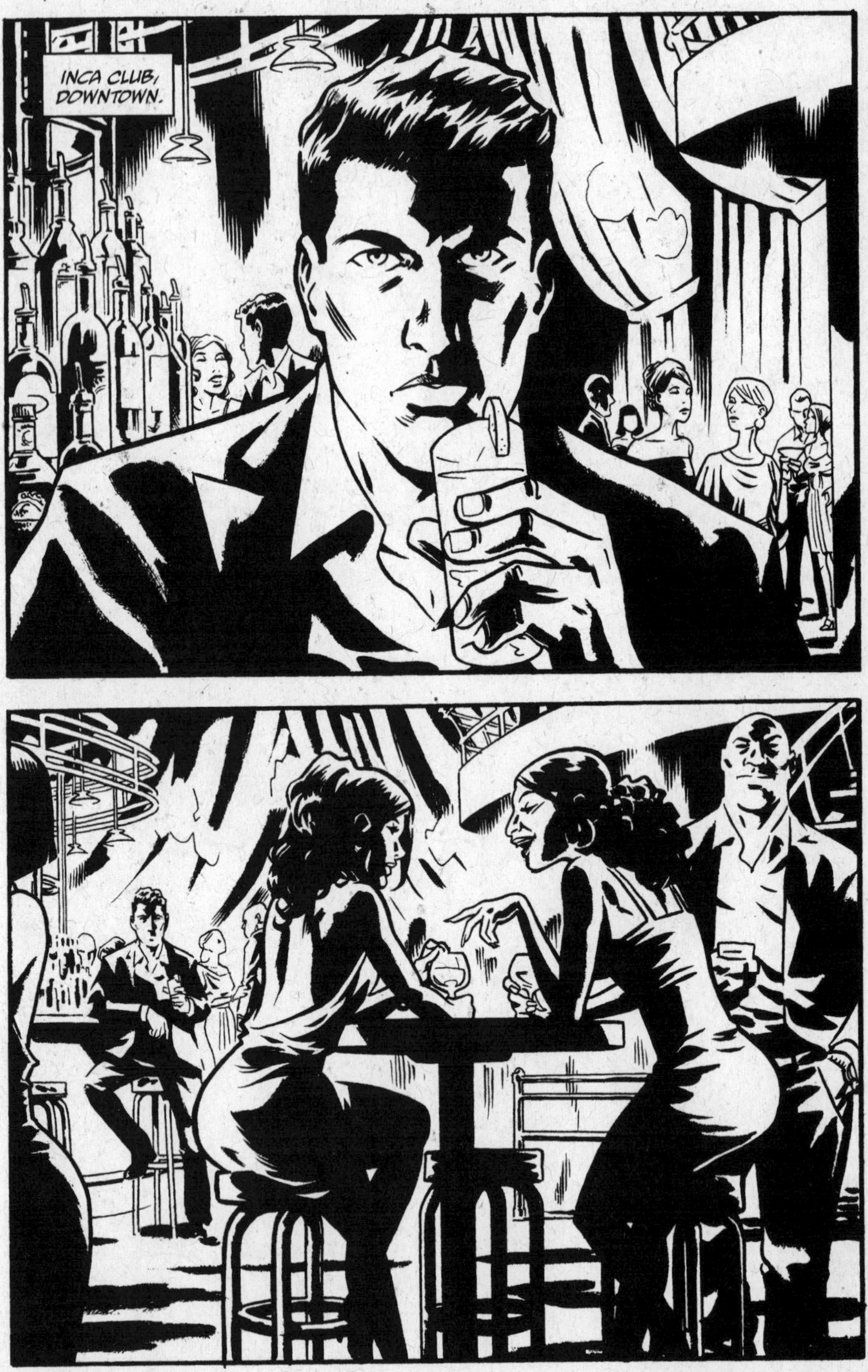
INCA CLUB, DOWNTOWN.

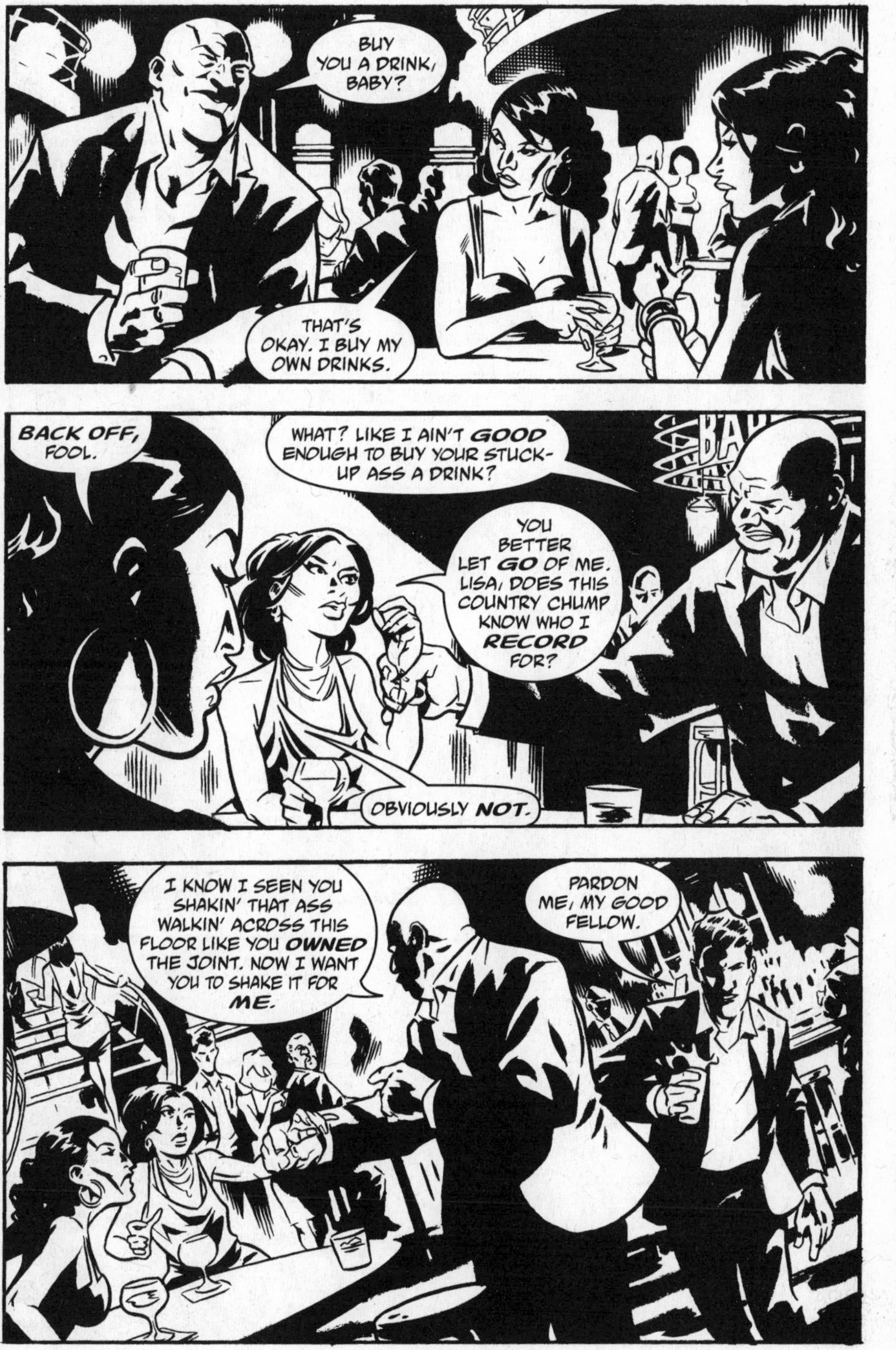
BUY YOU A DRINK, BABY?
THAT'S OKAY. I BUY MY OWN DRINKS.
BACK OFF, FOOL.
WHAT? LIKE I AIN'T **GOOD** ENOUGH TO BUY YOUR STUCK-UP ASS A DRINK?
YOU BETTER LET **GO** OF ME. LISA, DOES THIS COUNTRY CHUMP KNOW WHO I **RECORD** FOR?
OBVIOUSLY **NOT.**
I KNOW I SEEN YOU SHAKIN' THAT ASS WALKIN' ACROSS THIS FLOOR LIKE YOU **OWNED** THE JOINT. NOW I WANT YOU TO SHAKE IT FOR **ME.**
PARDON ME, MY GOOD FELLOW.

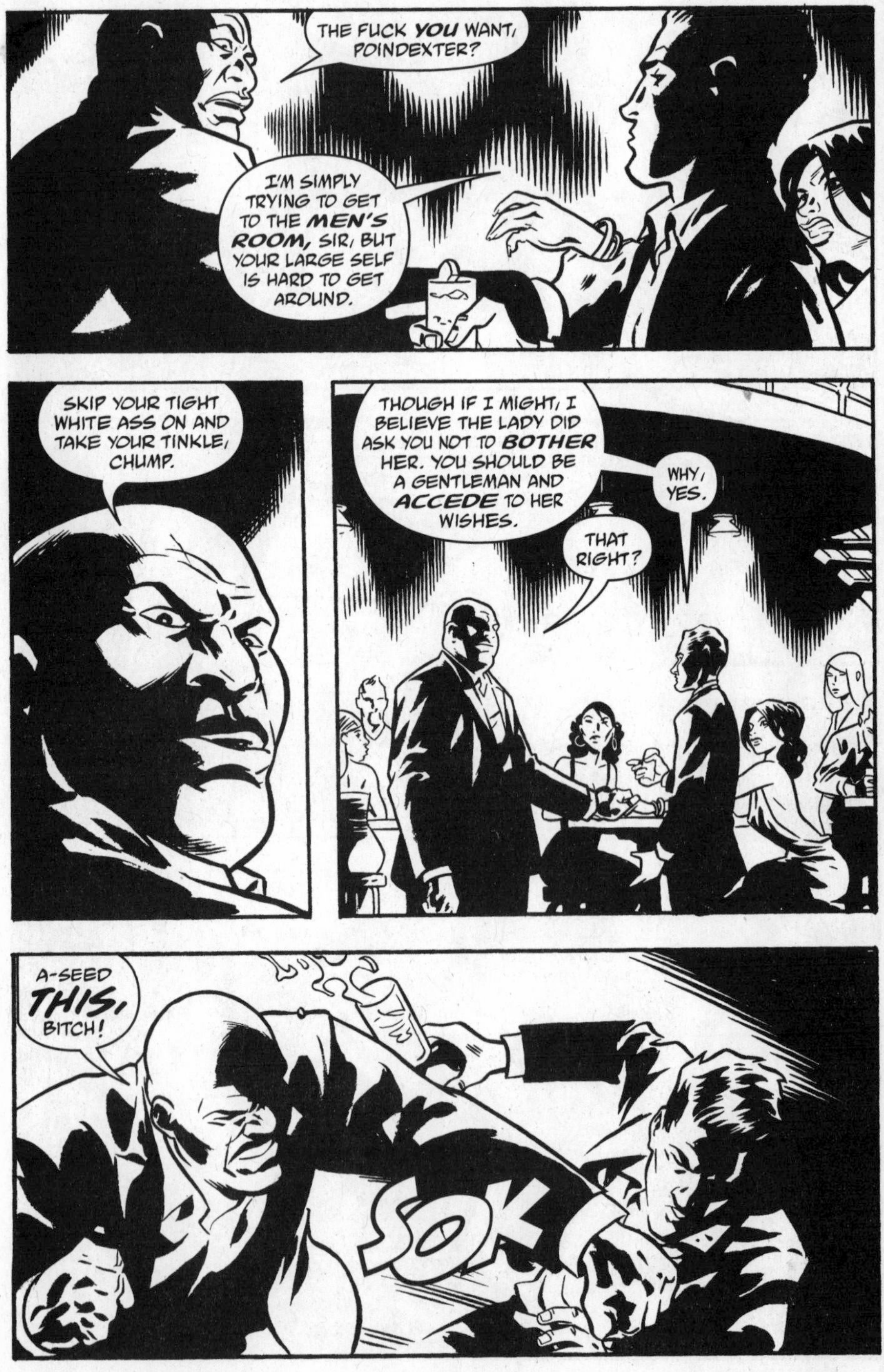
THE FUCK YOU WANT, POINDEXTER?
I'M SIMPLY TRYING TO GET TO THE MEN'S ROOM, SIR, BUT YOUR LARGE SELF IS HARD TO GET AROUND.
SKIP YOUR TIGHT WHITE ASS ON AND TAKE YOUR TINKLE, CHUMP.
THOUGH IF I MIGHT, I BELIEVE THE LADY DID ASK YOU NOT TO BOTHER HER. YOU SHOULD BE A GENTLEMAN AND ACCEDE TO HER WISHES.
THAT RIGHT?
WHY, YES.
A-SEED THIS, BITCH!
SOK

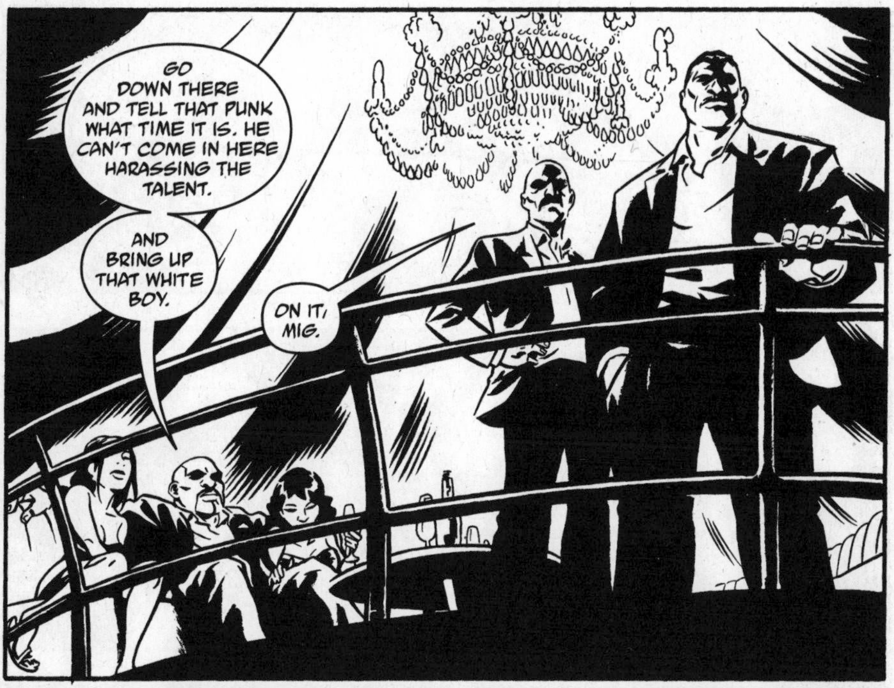
GO DOWN THERE AND TELL THAT PUNK WHAT TIME IT IS. HE CAN'T COME IN HERE HARASSING THE TALENT.
AND BRING UP THAT WHITE BOY.
ON IT, MIG.

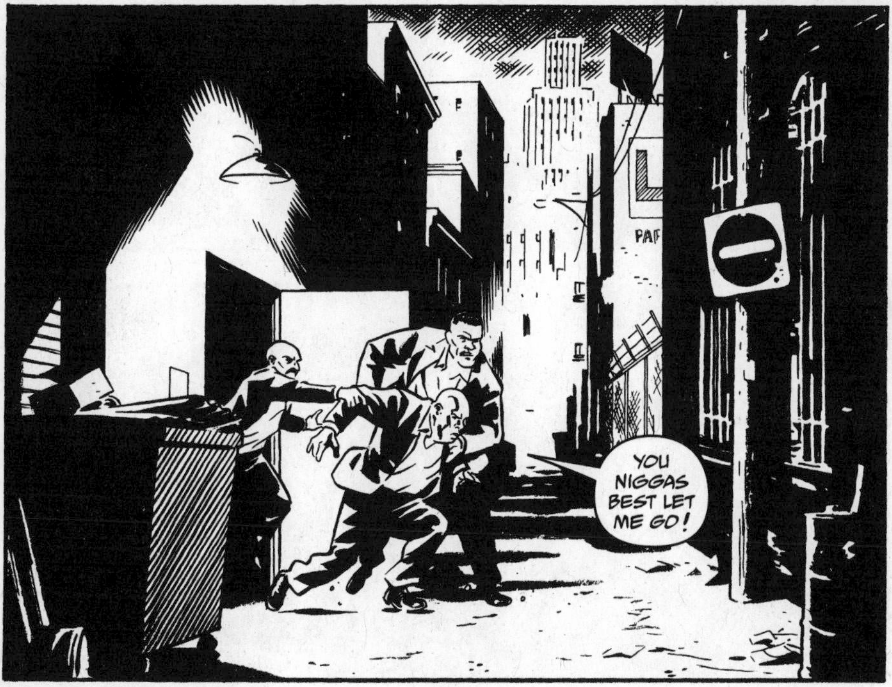
PAF
YOU NIGGAS BEST LET ME GO!

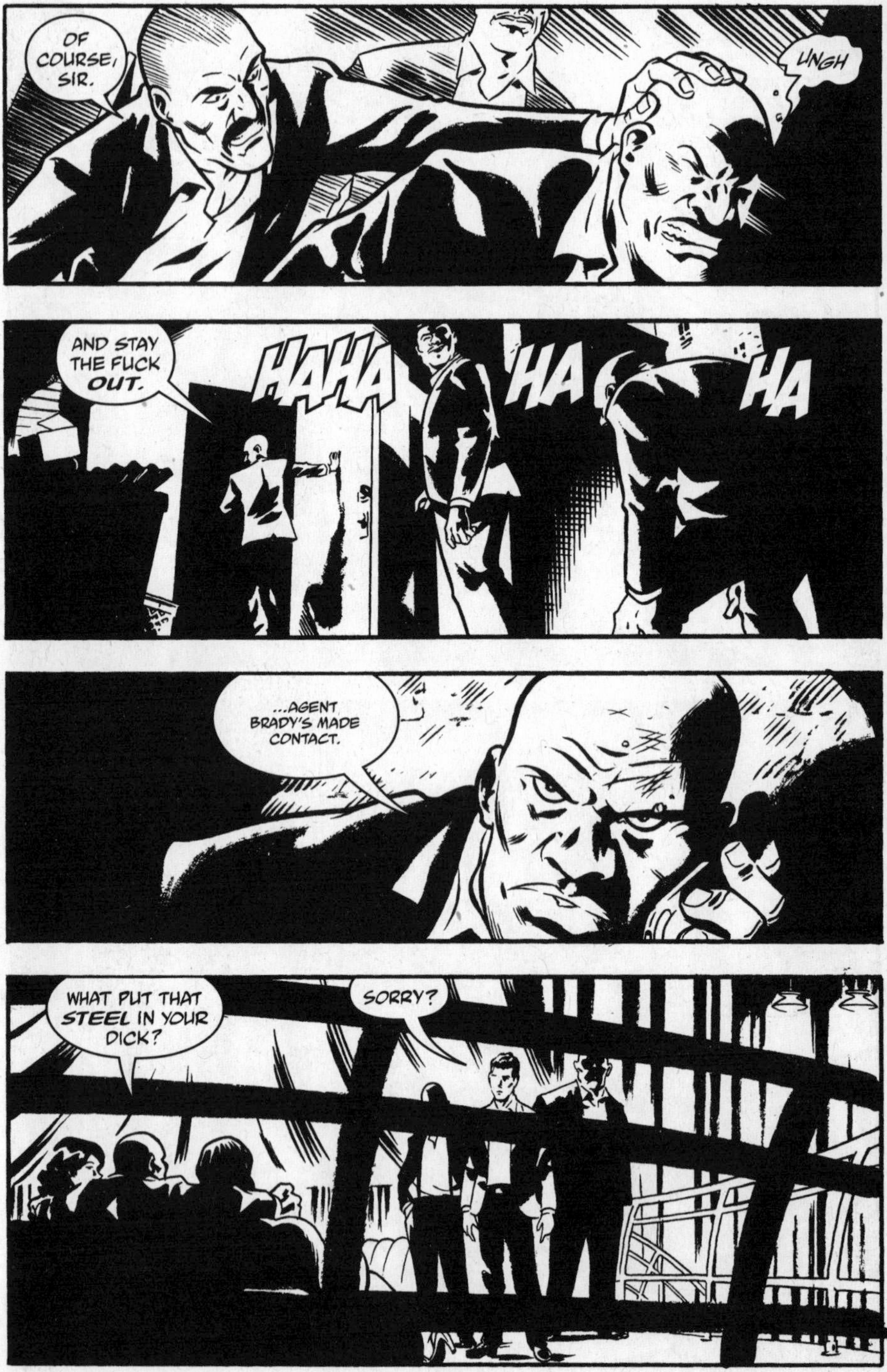
OF COURSE, SIR.
UNGH
AND STAY THE FUCK OUT.
HAHA
HA
HA
...AGENT BRADY'S MADE CONTACT.
WHAT PUT THAT STEEL IN YOUR DICK?
SORRY?

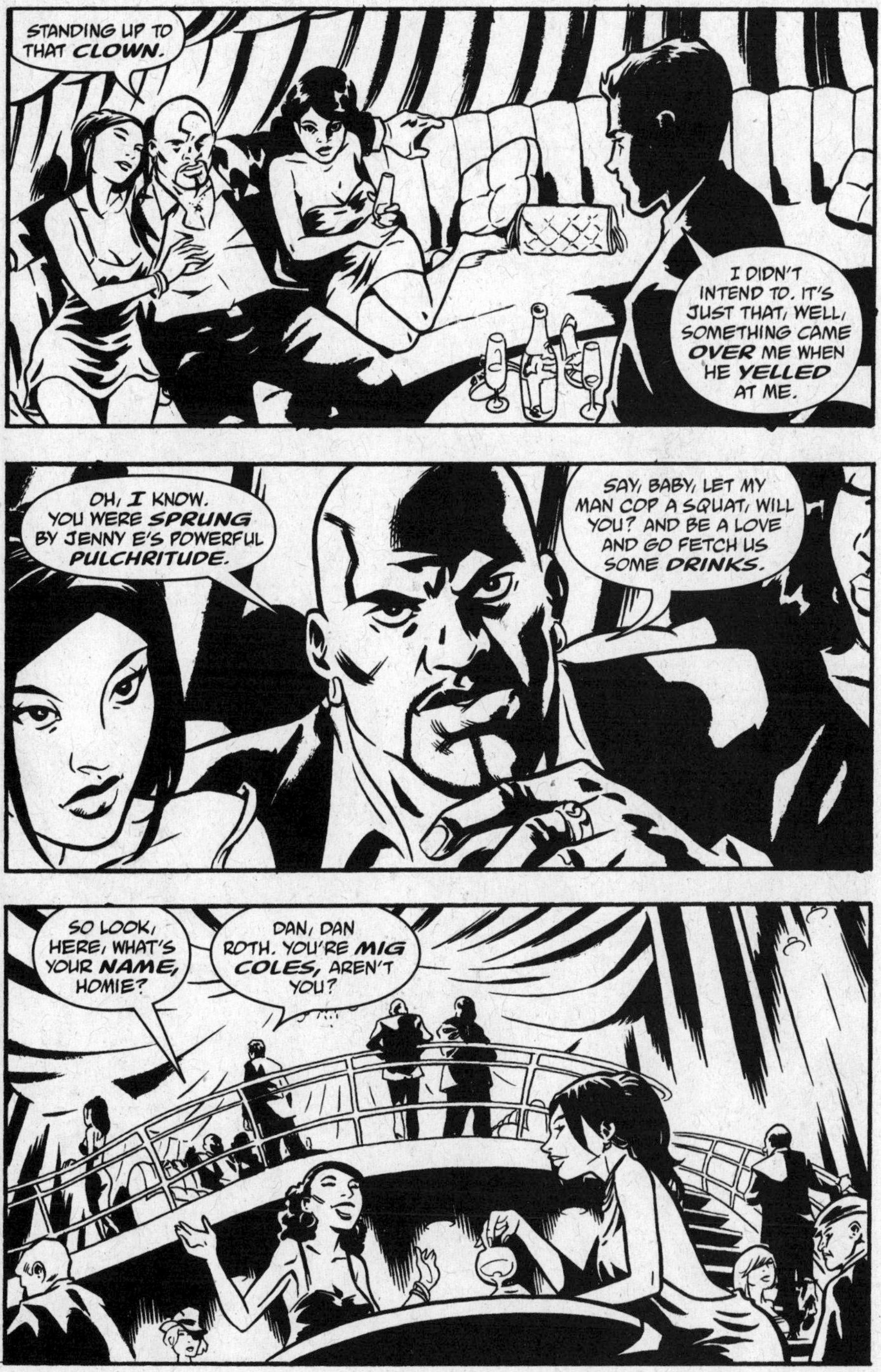
STANDING UP TO THAT CLOWN.
I DIDN'T INTEND TO. IT'S JUST THAT, WELL, SOMETHING CAME OVER ME WHEN HE YELLED AT ME.
OH, I KNOW. YOU WERE SPRUNG BY JENNY E'S POWERFUL PULCHRITUDE.
SAY, BABY, LET MY MAN COP A SQUAT, WILL YOU? AND BE A LOVE AND GO FETCH US SOME DRINKS.
SO LOOK, HERE, WHAT'S YOUR NAME, HOMIE?
DAN, DAN ROTH. YOU'RE MIG COLES, AREN'T YOU?

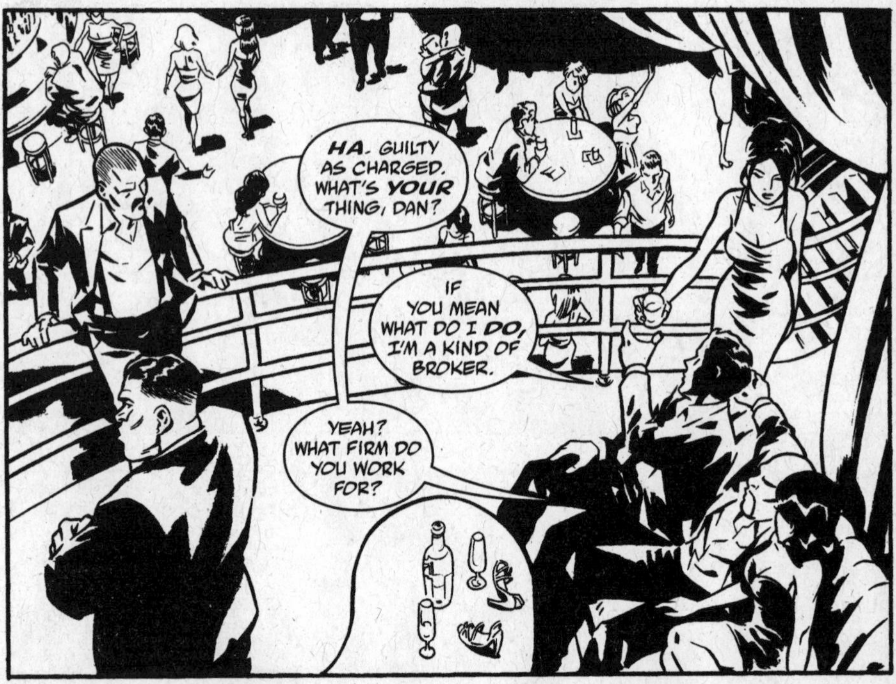
HA. GUILTY AS CHARGED. WHAT'S YOUR THING, DAN?
IF YOU MEAN WHAT DO I DO, I'M A KIND OF BROKER.
YEAH? WHAT FIRM DO YOU WORK FOR?

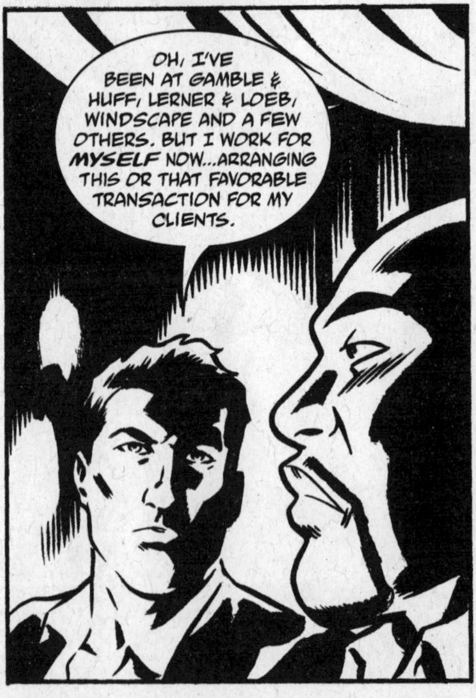
OH, I'VE BEEN AT GAMBLE & HUFF, LERNER & LOEB, WINDSCAPE AND A FEW OTHERS. BUT I WORK FOR MYSELF NOW...ARRANGING THIS OR THAT FAVORABLE TRANSACTION FOR MY CLIENTS.

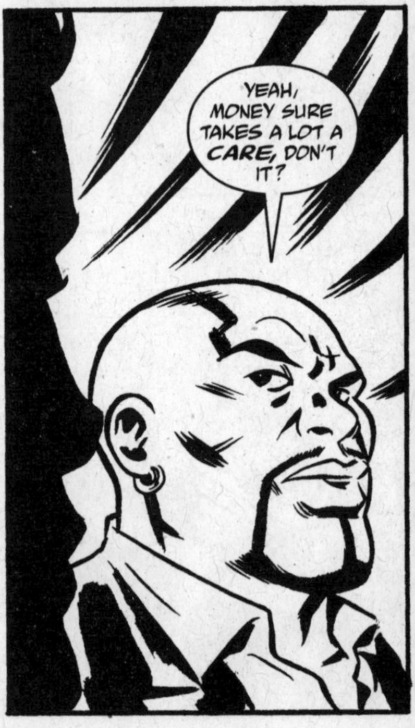
YEAH, MONEY SURE TAKES A LOT A CARE, DON'T IT?

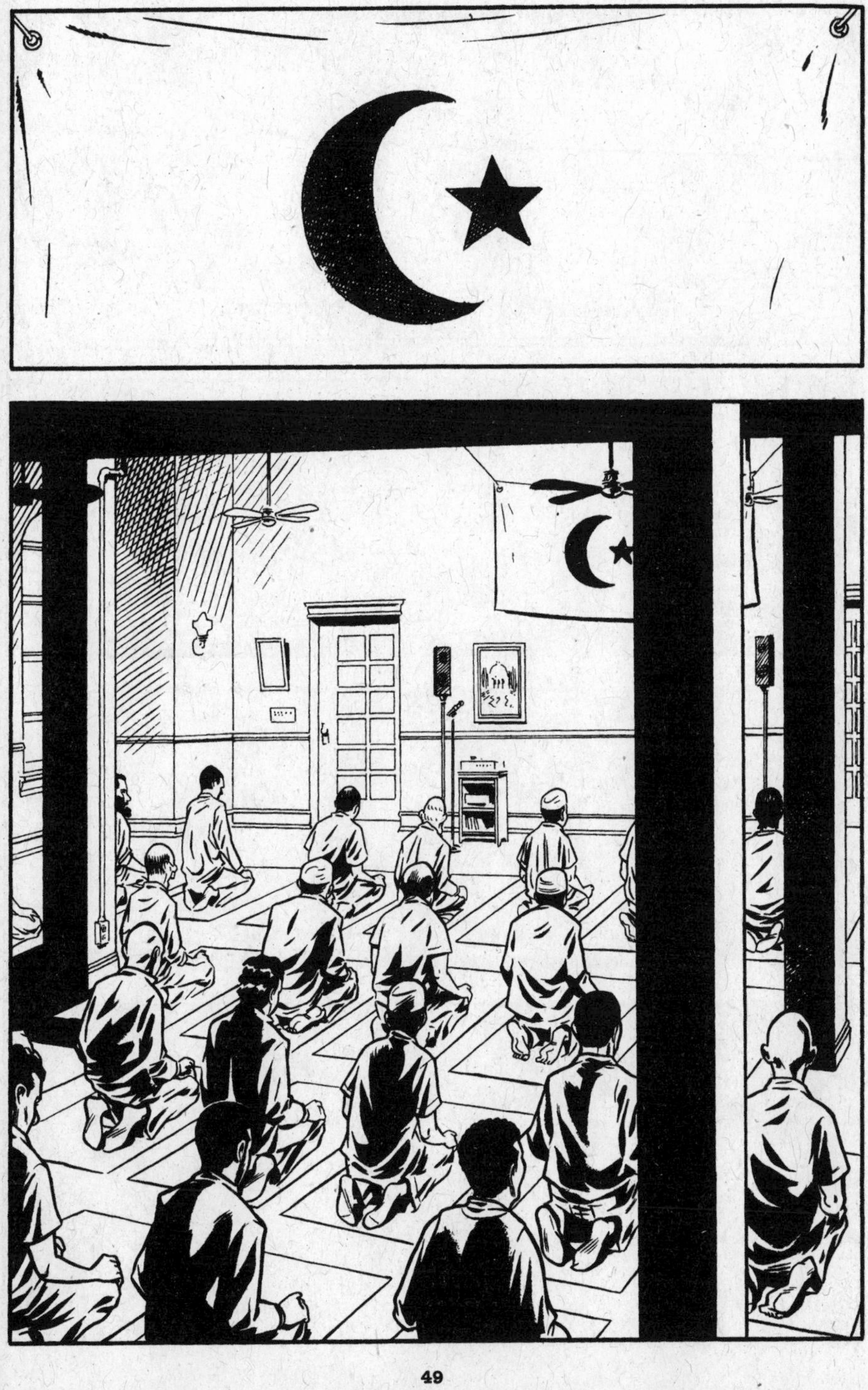

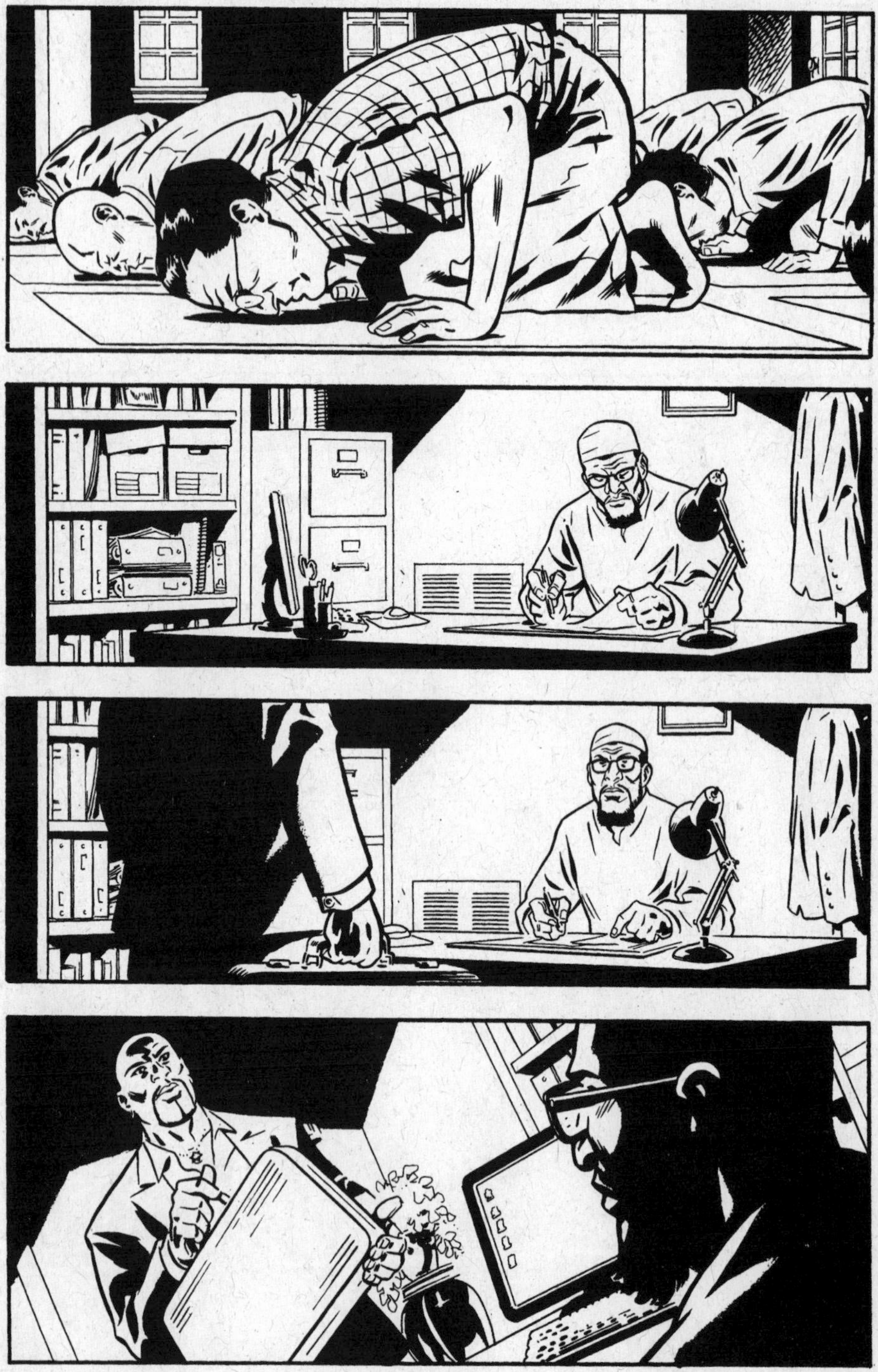

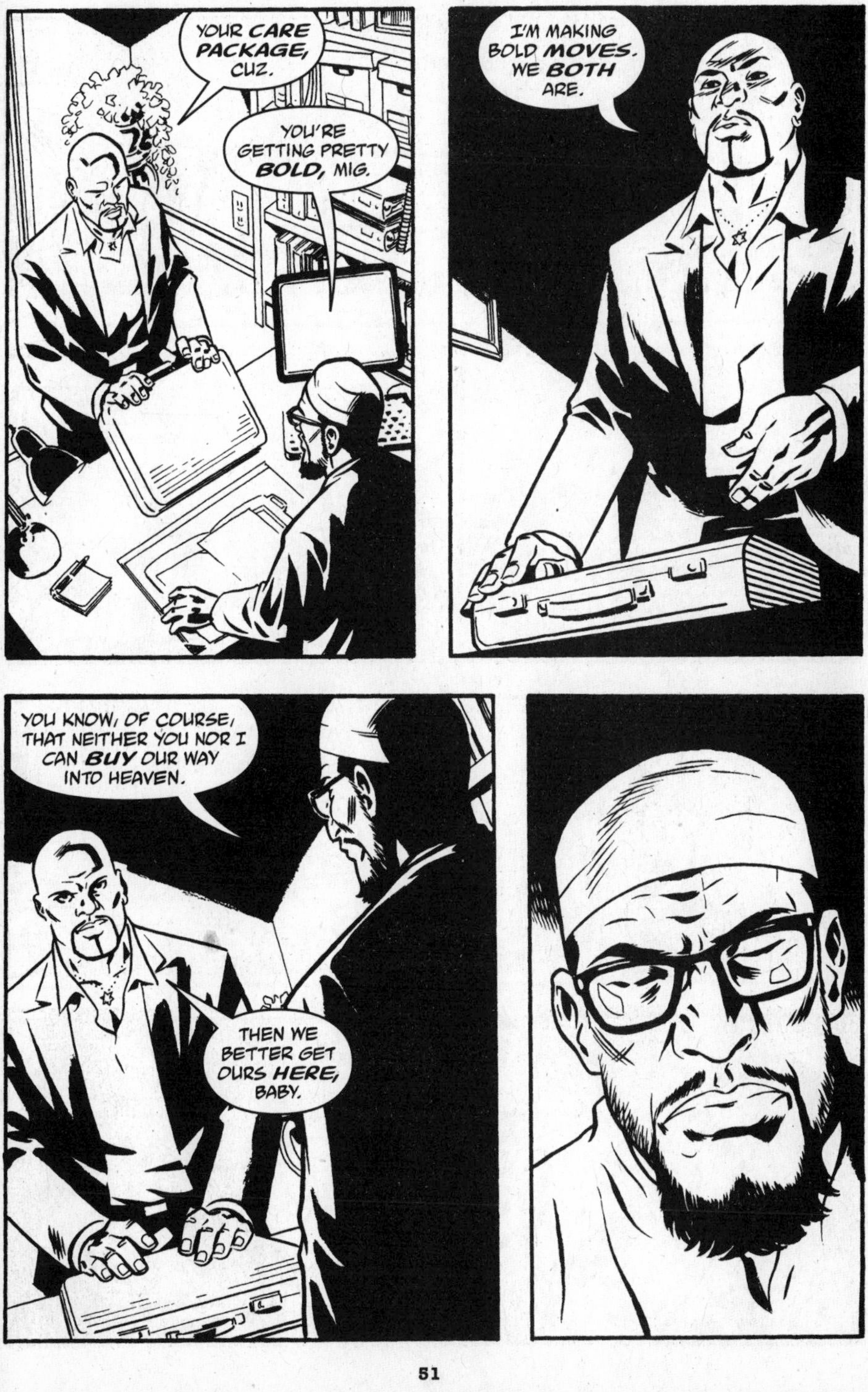
YOUR CARE PACKAGE, CUZ.
YOU'RE GETTING PRETTY BOLD, MIG.
I'M MAKING BOLD MOVES. WE BOTH ARE.
YOU KNOW, OF COURSE, THAT NEITHER YOU NOR I CAN BUY OUR WAY INTO HEAVEN.
THEN WE BETTER GET OURS HERE, BABY.

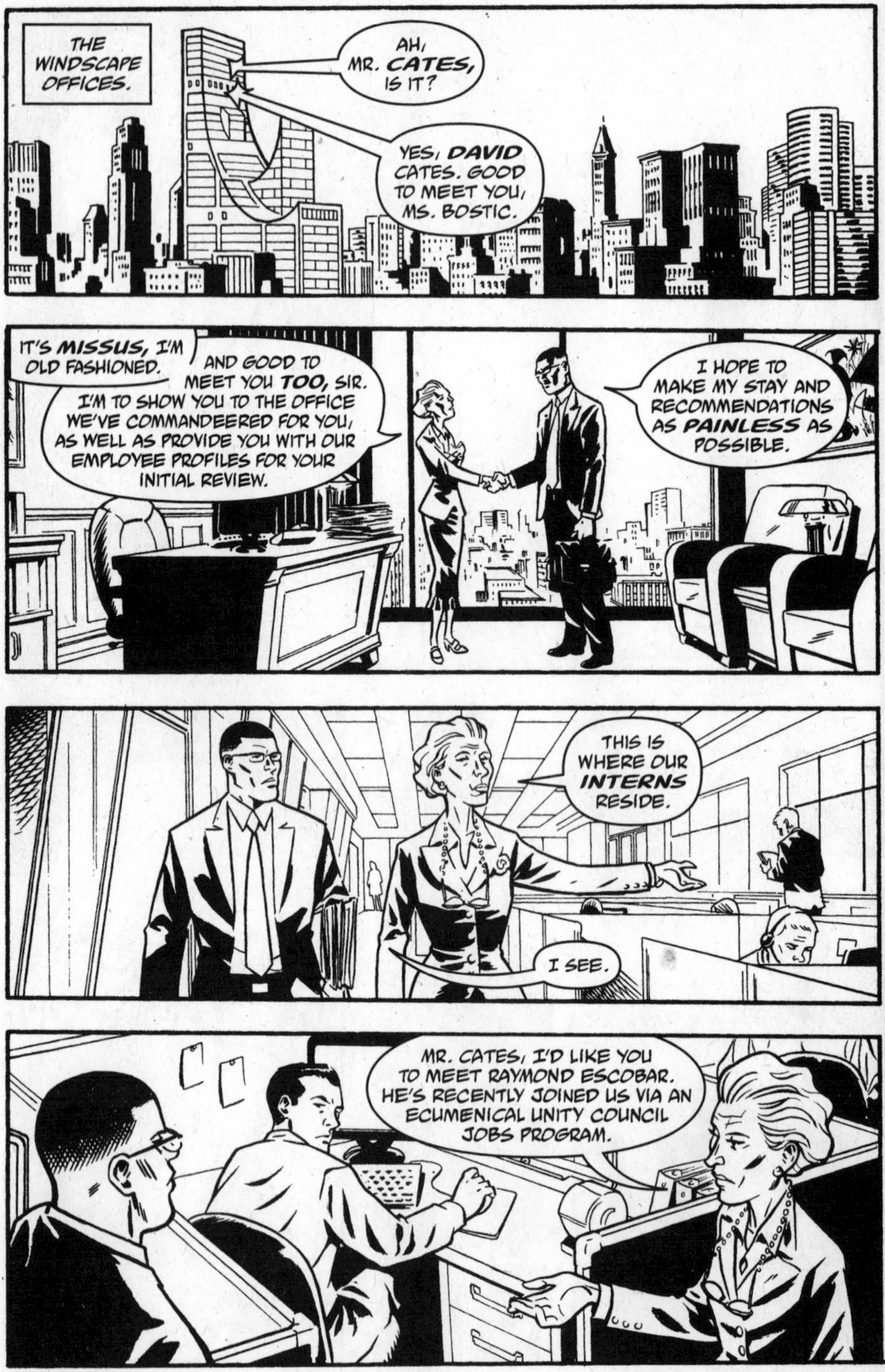
THE WINDSCAPE OFFICES.
AH, MR. CATES, IS IT?
YES, DAVID CATES. GOOD TO MEET YOU, MS. BOSTIC.
IT'S MISSUS, I'M OLD FASHIONED.
AND GOOD TO MEET YOU TOO, SIR. I'M TO SHOW YOU TO THE OFFICE WE'VE COMMANDEERED FOR YOU, AS WELL AS PROVIDE YOU WITH OUR EMPLOYEE PROFILES FOR YOUR INITIAL REVIEW.
I HOPE TO MAKE MY STAY AND RECOMMENDATIONS AS PAINLESS AS POSSIBLE.
THIS IS WHERE OUR INTERNS RESIDE.
I SEE.
MR. CATES, I'D LIKE YOU TO MEET RAYMOND ESCOBAR. HE'S RECENTLY JOINED US VIA AN ECUMENICAL UNITY COUNCIL JOBS PROGRAM.

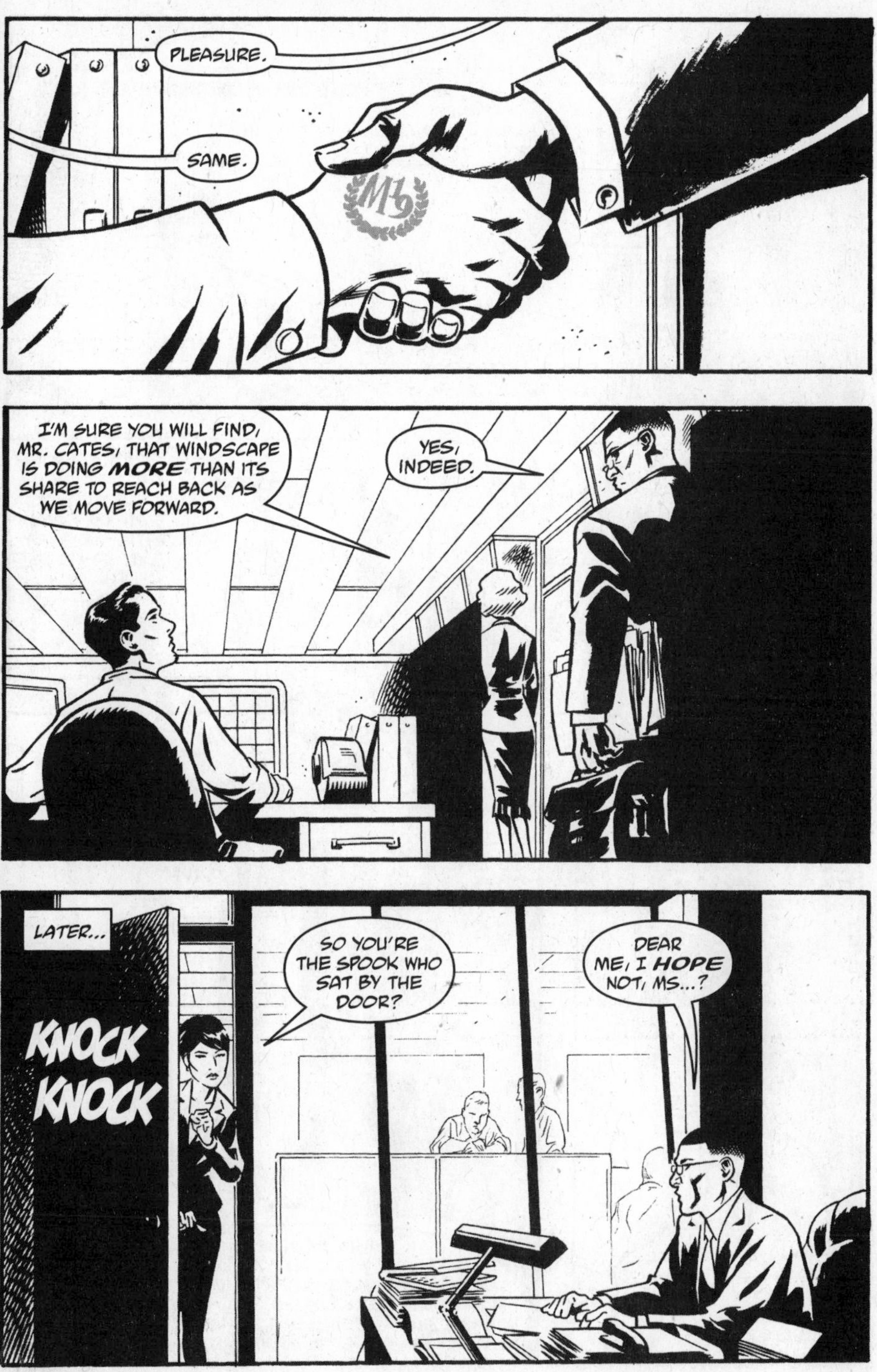
PLEASURE.
SAME.
I'M SURE YOU WILL FIND, MR. CATES, THAT WINDSCAPE IS DOING MORE THAN ITS SHARE TO REACH BACK AS WE MOVE FORWARD.
YES, INDEED.
LATER...
KNOCK KNOCK
SO YOU'RE THE SPOOK WHO SAT BY THE DOOR?
DEAR ME, I HOPE NOT, MS...?

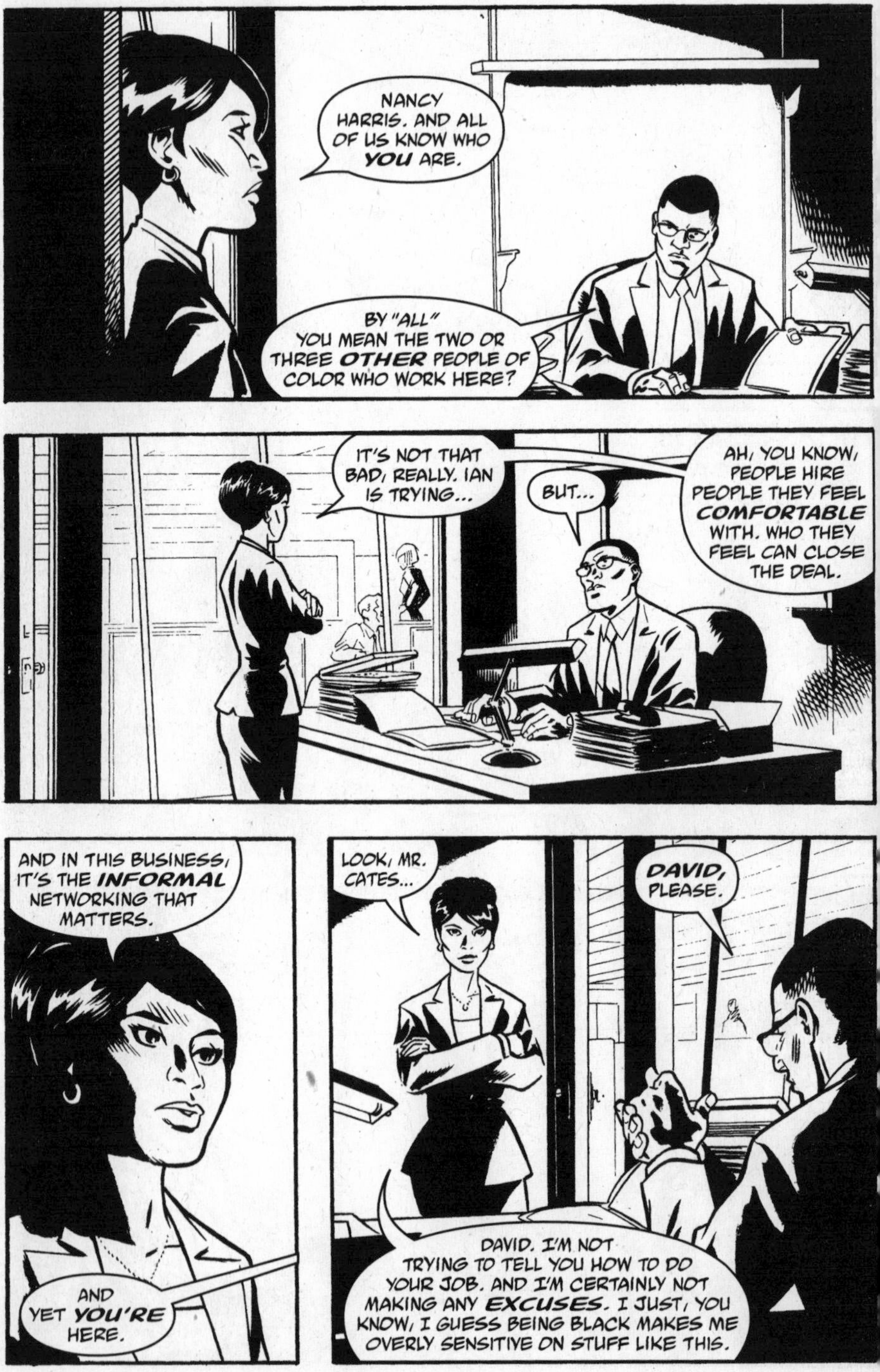
NANCY HARRIS. AND ALL OF US KNOW WHO YOU ARE.
BY "ALL" YOU MEAN THE TWO OR THREE OTHER PEOPLE OF COLOR WHO WORK HERE?
IT'S NOT THAT BAD, REALLY. IAN IS TRYING...
BUT...
AH, YOU KNOW, PEOPLE HIRE PEOPLE THEY FEEL COMFORTABLE WITH. WHO THEY FEEL CAN CLOSE THE DEAL.
AND IN THIS BUSINESS, IT'S THE INFORMAL NETWORKING THAT MATTERS.
AND YET YOU'RE HERE.
LOOK, MR. CATES...
DAVID, PLEASE.
DAVID. I'M NOT TRYING TO TELL YOU HOW TO DO YOUR JOB. AND I'M CERTAINLY NOT MAKING ANY EXCUSES. I JUST, YOU KNOW, I GUESS BEING BLACK MAKES ME OVERLY SENSITIVE ON STUFF LIKE THIS.

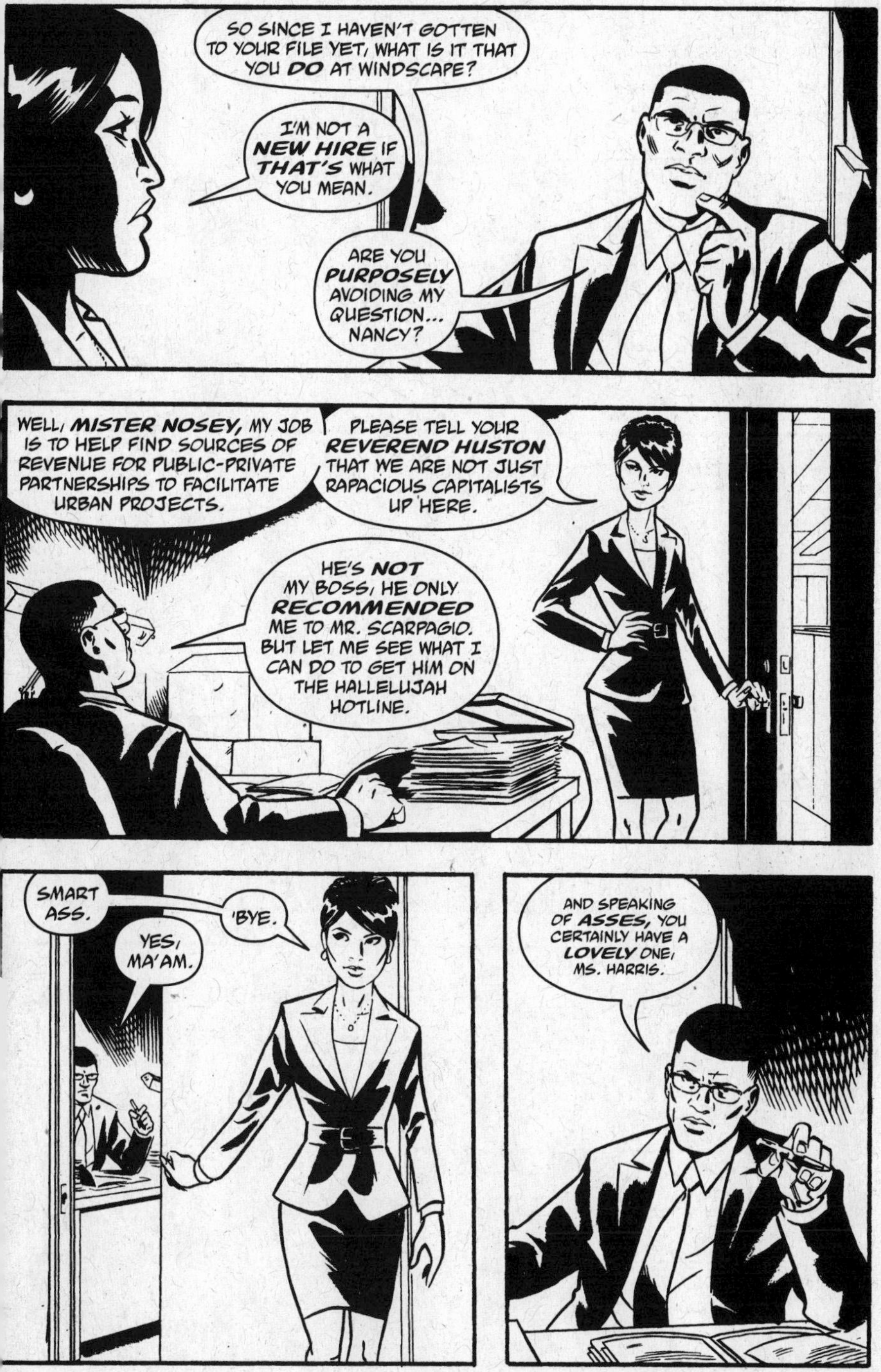
SO SINCE I HAVEN'T GOTTEN TO YOUR FILE YET, WHAT IS IT THAT YOU DO AT WINDSCAPE?
I'M NOT A NEW HIRE IF THAT'S WHAT YOU MEAN.
ARE YOU PURPOSELY AVOIDING MY QUESTION... NANCY?
WELL, MISTER NOSEY, MY JOB IS TO HELP FIND SOURCES OF REVENUE FOR PUBLIC-PRIVATE PARTNERSHIPS TO FACILITATE URBAN PROJECTS.
PLEASE TELL YOUR REVEREND HUSTON THAT WE ARE NOT JUST RAPACIOUS CAPITALISTS UP HERE.
HE'S NOT MY BOSS, HE ONLY RECOMMENDED ME TO MR. SCARPAGIO. BUT LET ME SEE WHAT I CAN DO TO GET HIM ON THE HALLELUJAH HOTLINE.
SMART ASS.
'BYE.
YES, MA'AM.
AND SPEAKING OF ASSES, YOU CERTAINLY HAVE A LOVELY ONE, MS. HARRIS.

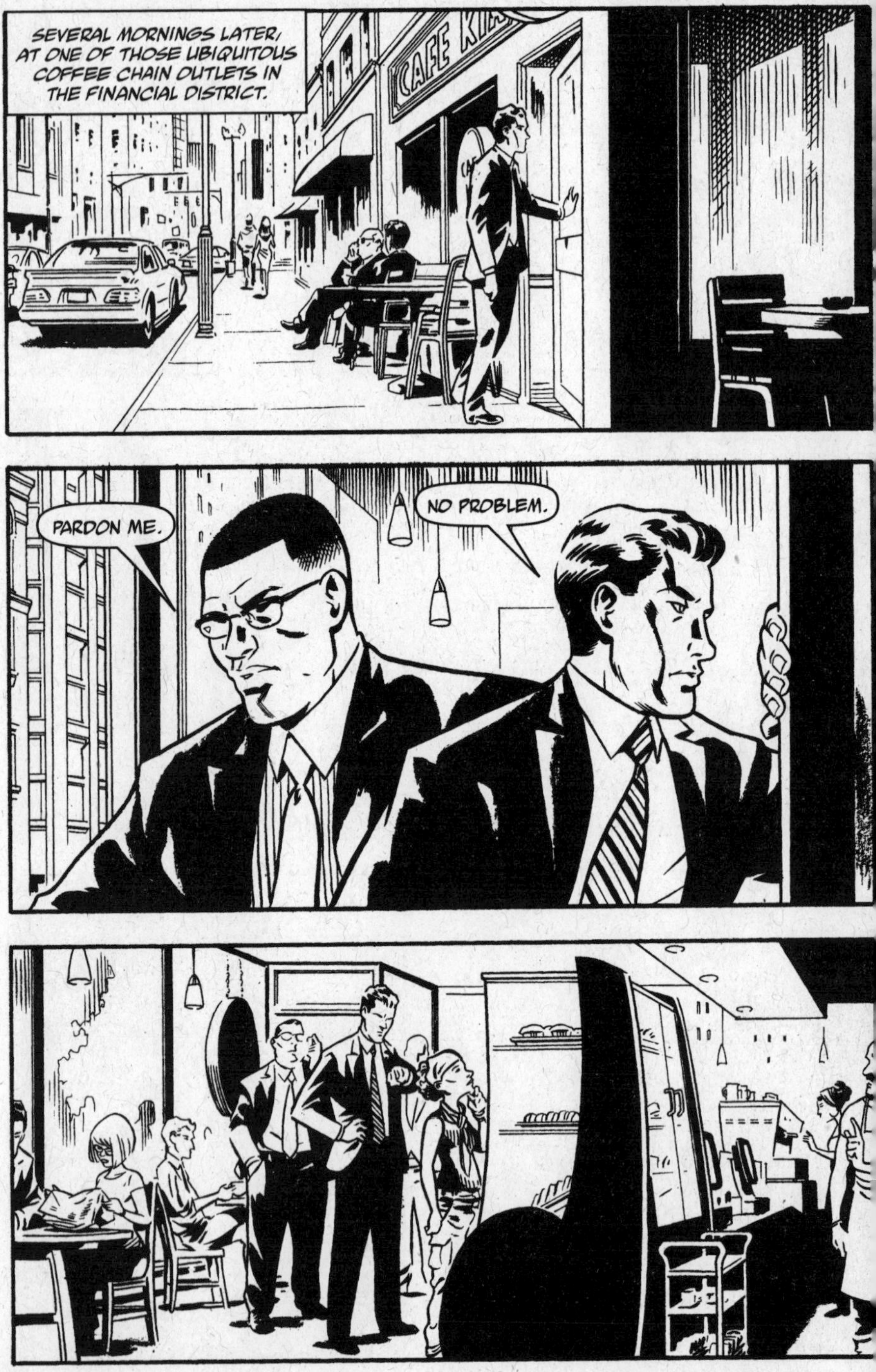
SEVERAL MORNINGS LATER, AT ONE OF THOSE UBIQUITOUS COFFEE CHAIN OUTLETS IN THE FINANCIAL DISTRICT.
CAFE KI
PARDON ME.
NO PROBLEM.

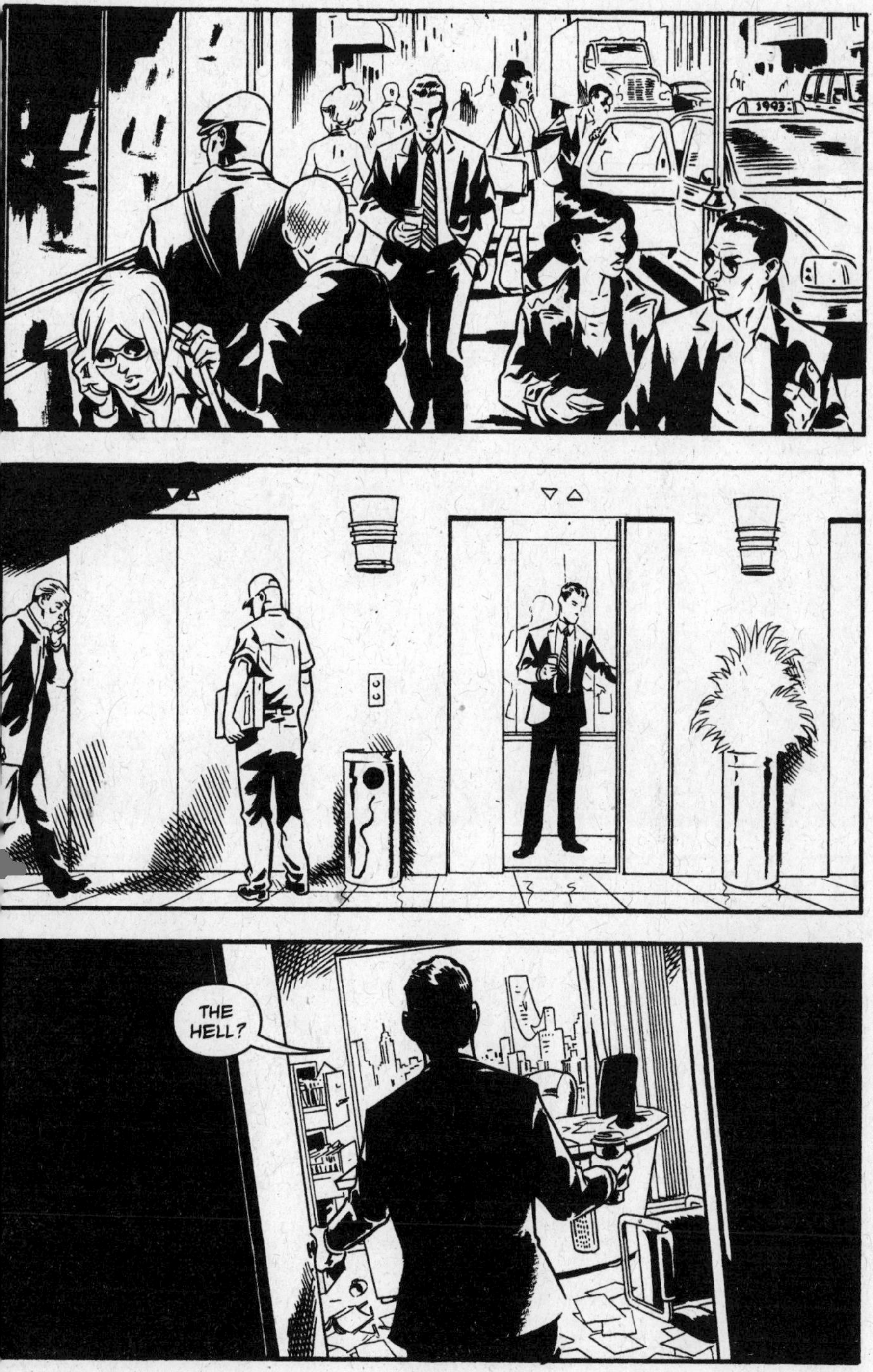
THE HELL?

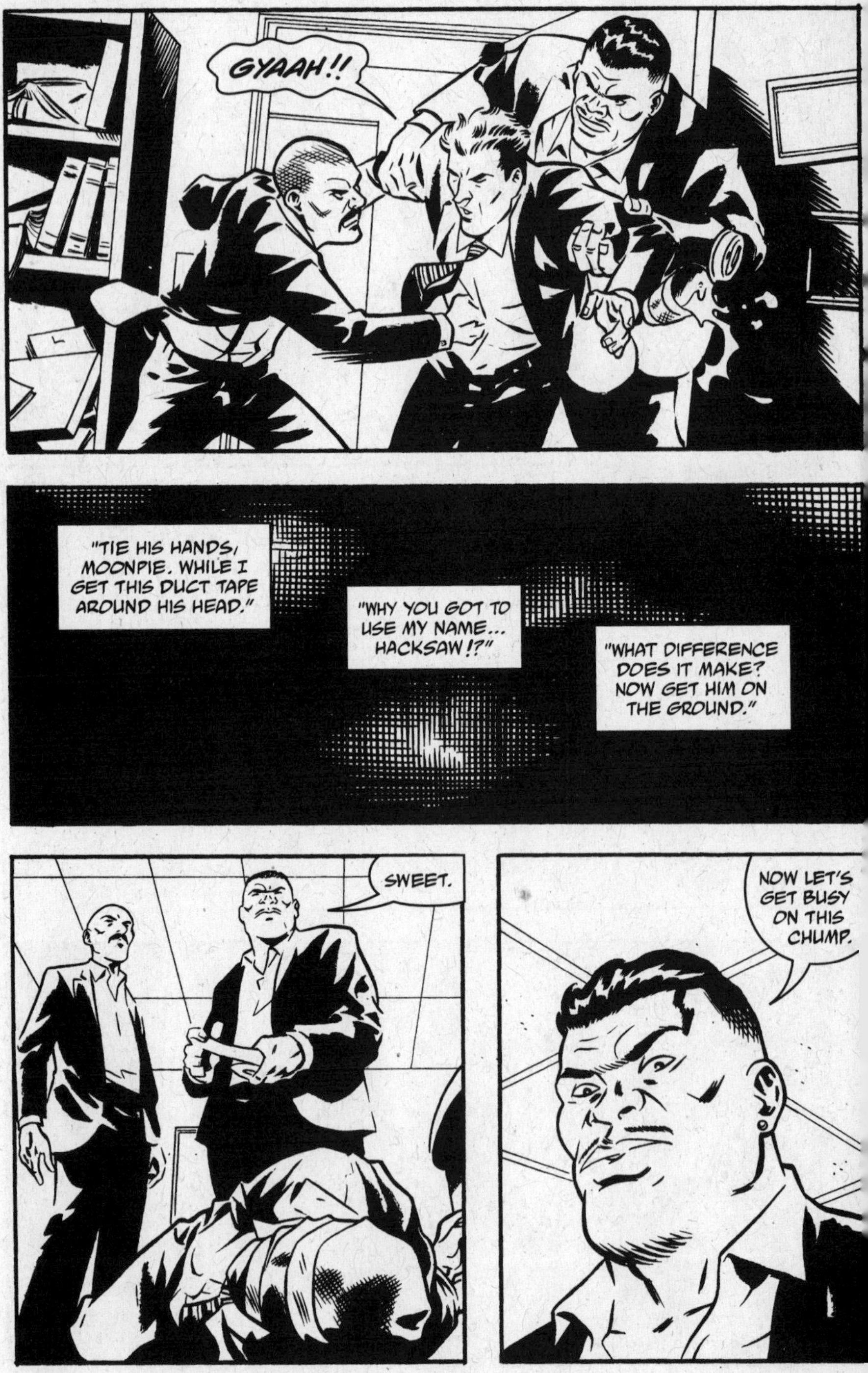
GYAAH!!
"TIE HIS HANDS, MOONPIE. WHILE I GET THIS DUCT TAPE AROUND HIS HEAD."
"WHY YOU GOT TO USE MY NAME... HACKSAW!?"
"WHAT DIFFERENCE DOES IT MAKE? NOW GET HIM ON THE GROUND."
SWEET.
NOW LET'S GET BUSY ON THIS CHUMP.

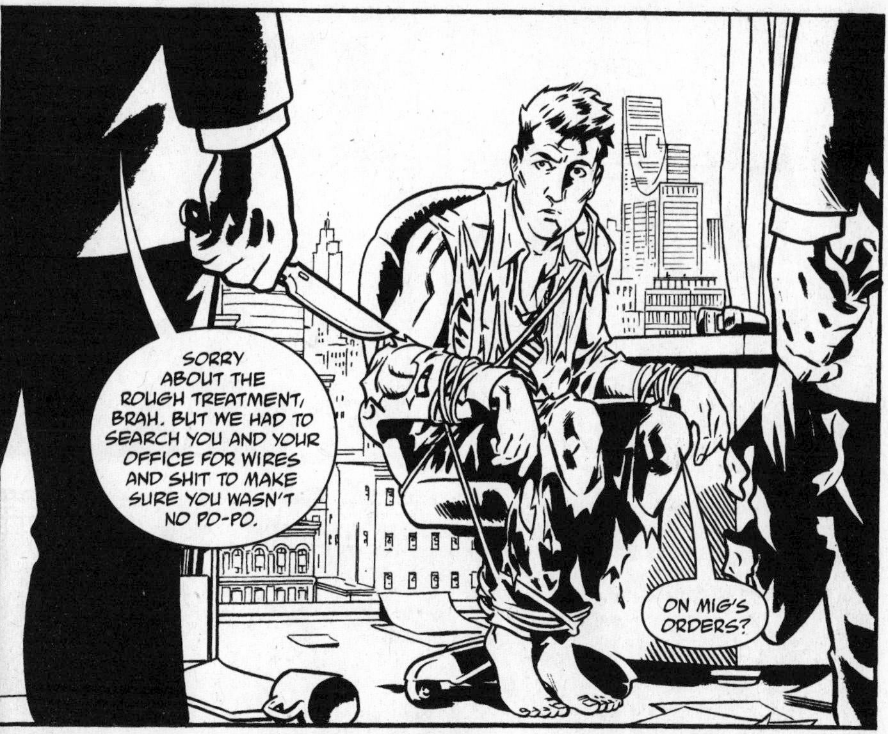
SORRY ABOUT THE ROUGH TREATMENT, BRAH. BUT WE HAD TO SEARCH YOU AND YOUR OFFICE FOR WIRES AND SHIT TO MAKE SURE YOU WASN'T NO PO-PO.
ON MIG'S ORDERS?

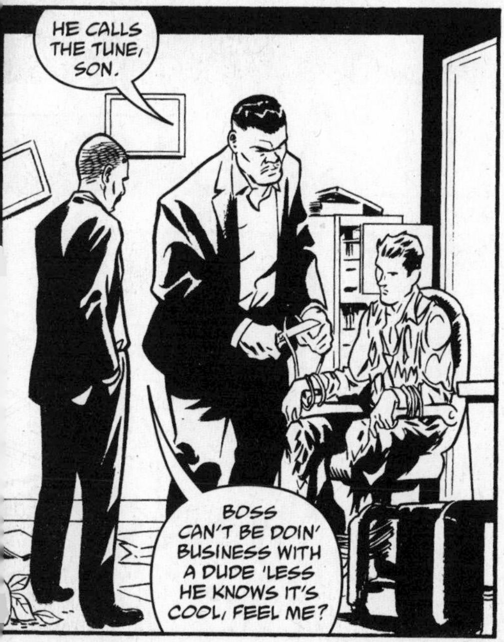
HE CALLS THE TUNE, SON.
BOSS CAN'T BE DOIN' BUSINESS WITH A DUDE 'LESS HE KNOWS IT'S COOL, FEEL ME?

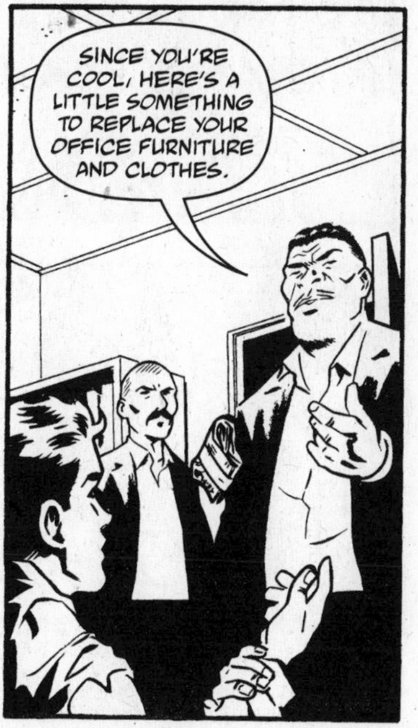
SINCE YOU'RE COOL, HERE'S A LITTLE SOMETHING TO REPLACE YOUR OFFICE FURNITURE AND CLOTHES.

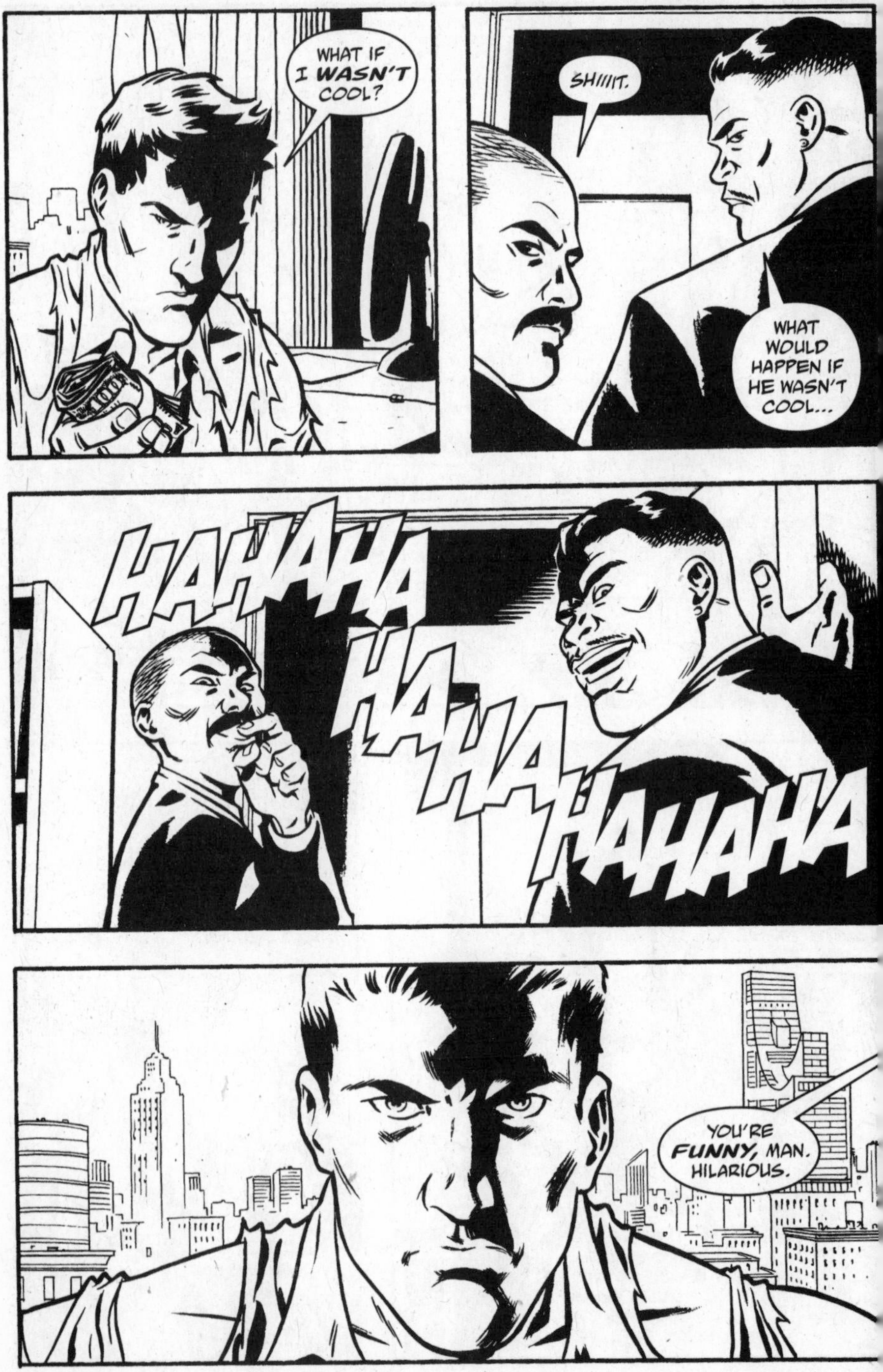

WHAT IF I WASN'T COOL?
SH////IT.
WHAT WOULD HAPPEN IF HE WASN'T COOL...
HAHAHA HA HAHA HAHAHA
YOU'RE FUNNY, MAN. HILARIOUS.

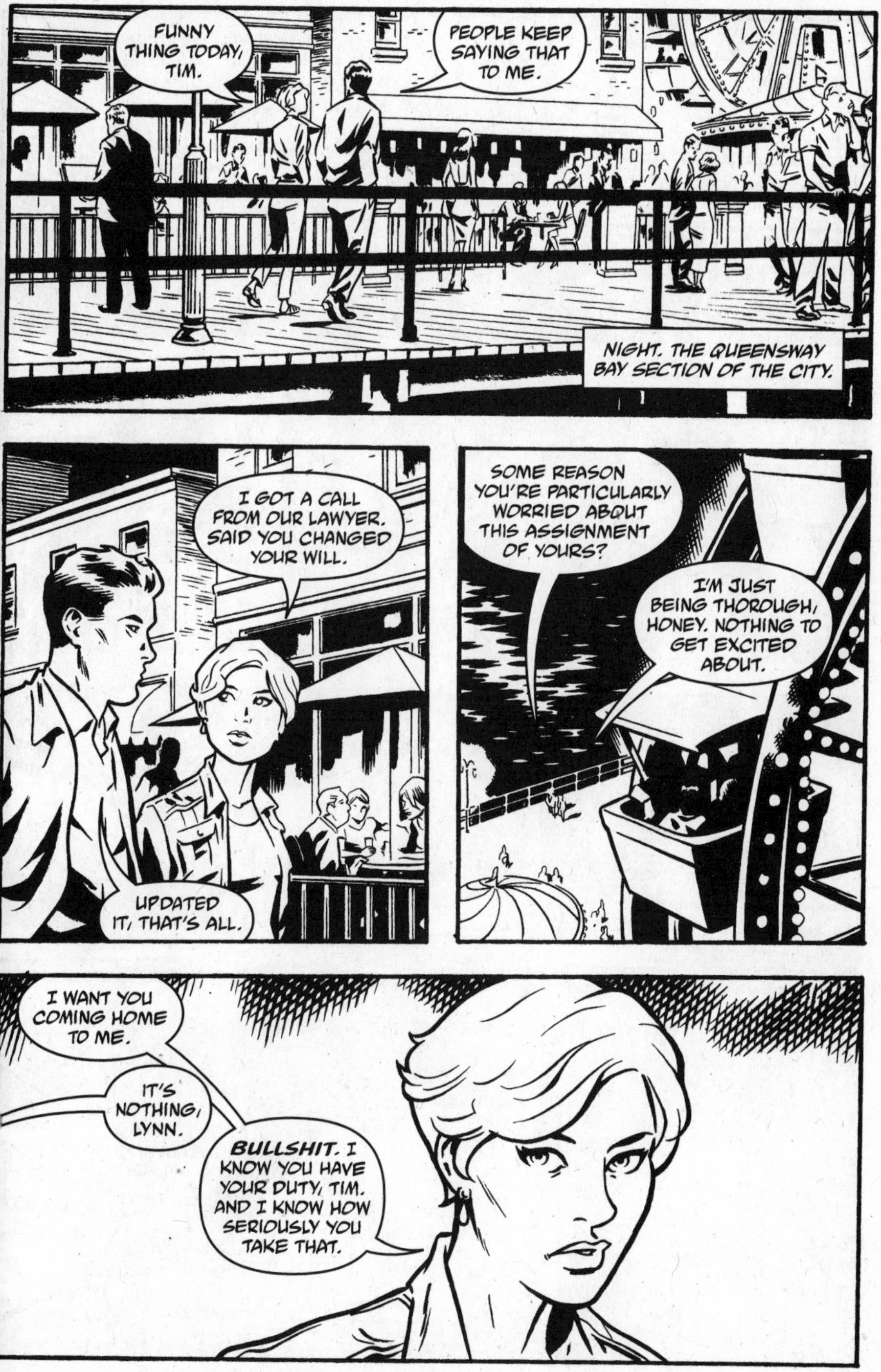

FUNNY THING TODAY, TIM.
PEOPLE KEEP SAYING THAT TO ME.
NIGHT. THE QUEENSWAY BAY SECTION OF THE CITY.
I GOT A CALL FROM OUR LAWYER. SAID YOU CHANGED YOUR WILL.
UPDATED IT, THAT'S ALL.
SOME REASON YOU'RE PARTICULARLY WORRIED ABOUT THIS ASSIGNMENT OF YOURS?
I'M JUST BEING THOROUGH, HONEY. NOTHING TO GET EXCITED ABOUT.
I WANT YOU COMING HOME TO ME.
IT'S NOTHING, LYNN.
BULLSHIT. I KNOW YOU HAVE YOUR DUTY, TIM. AND I KNOW HOW SERIOUSLY YOU TAKE THAT.

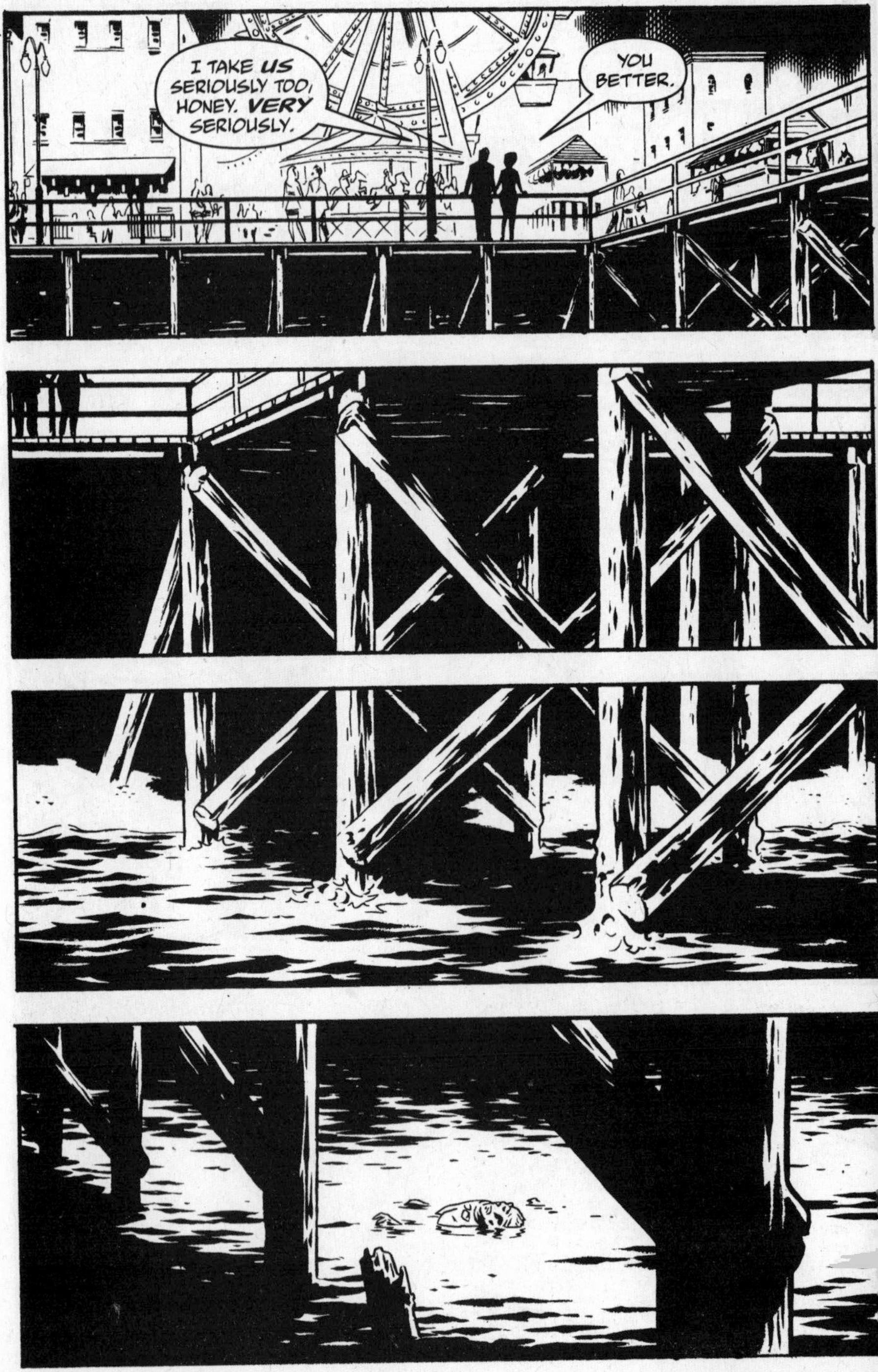
I TAKE US SERIOUSLY TOO, HONEY. VERY SERIOUSLY.
YOU BETTER.

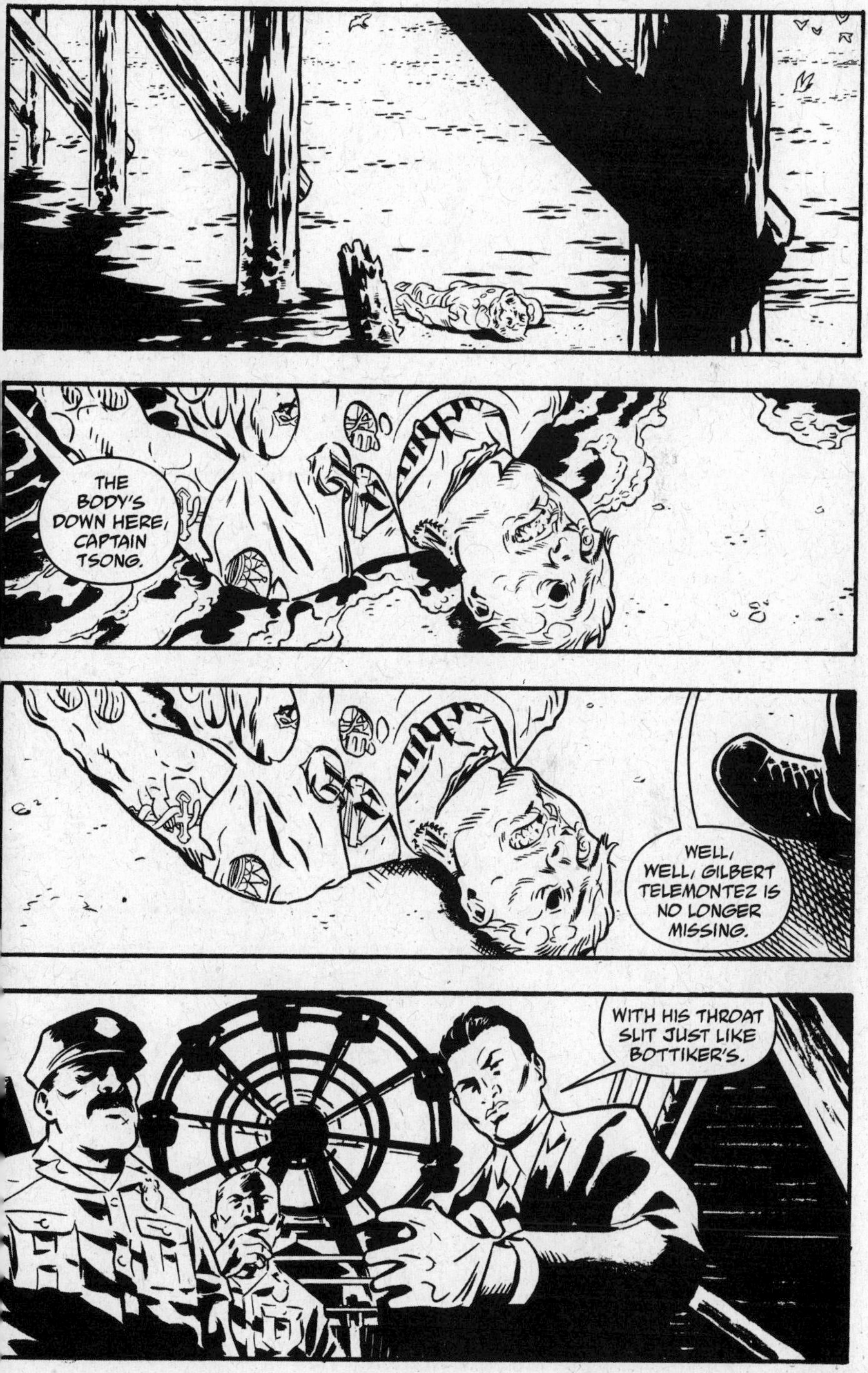
THE BODY'S DOWN HERE, CAPTAIN TSONG.
WELL, WELL, GILBERT TELEMONTEZ IS NO LONGER MISSING.
WITH HIS THROAT SLIT JUST LIKE BOTTIKER'S.

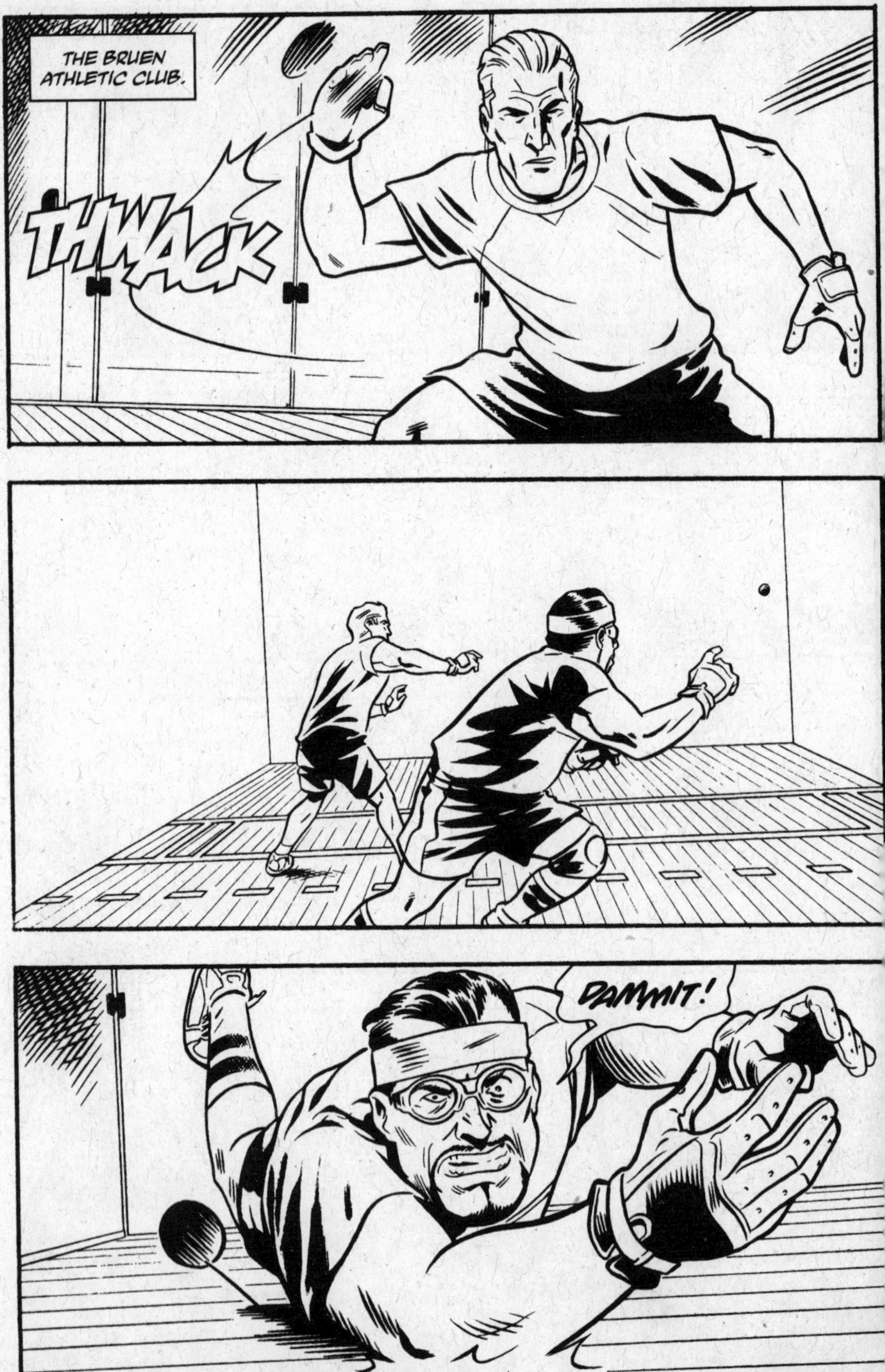
THE BRUEN ATHLETIC CLUB.
THWACK
DAMMIT!

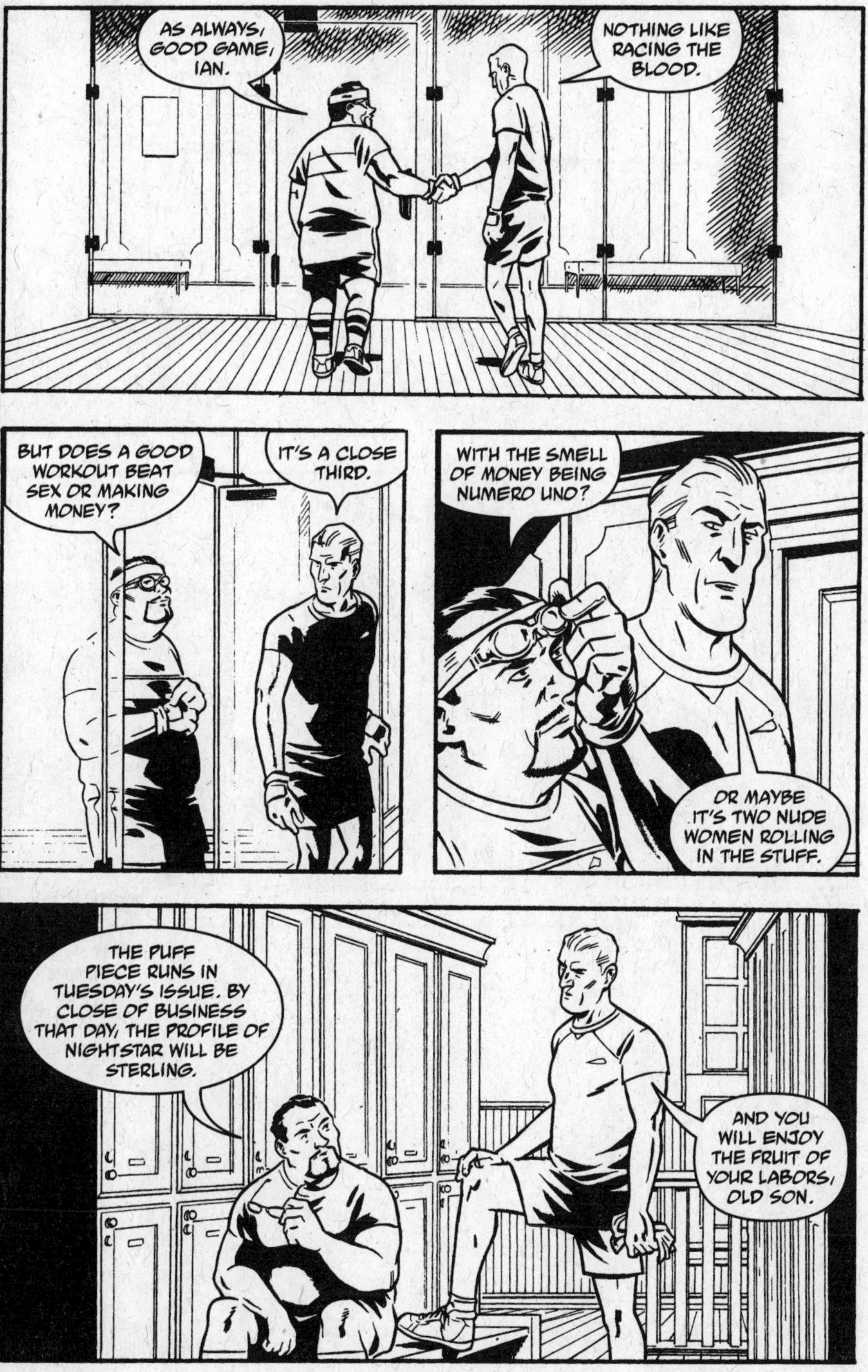
AS ALWAYS, GOOD GAME, IAN.
NOTHING LIKE RACING THE BLOOD.
BUT DOES A GOOD WORKOUT BEAT SEX OR MAKING MONEY?
IT'S A CLOSE THIRD.
WITH THE SMELL OF MONEY BEING NUMERO UNO?
OR MAYBE IT'S TWO NUDE WOMEN ROLLING IN THE STUFF.
THE PUFF PIECE RUNS IN TUESDAY'S ISSUE. BY CLOSE OF BUSINESS THAT DAY, THE PROFILE OF NIGHTSTAR WILL BE STERLING.
AND YOU WILL ENJOY THE FRUIT OF YOUR LABORS, OLD SON.

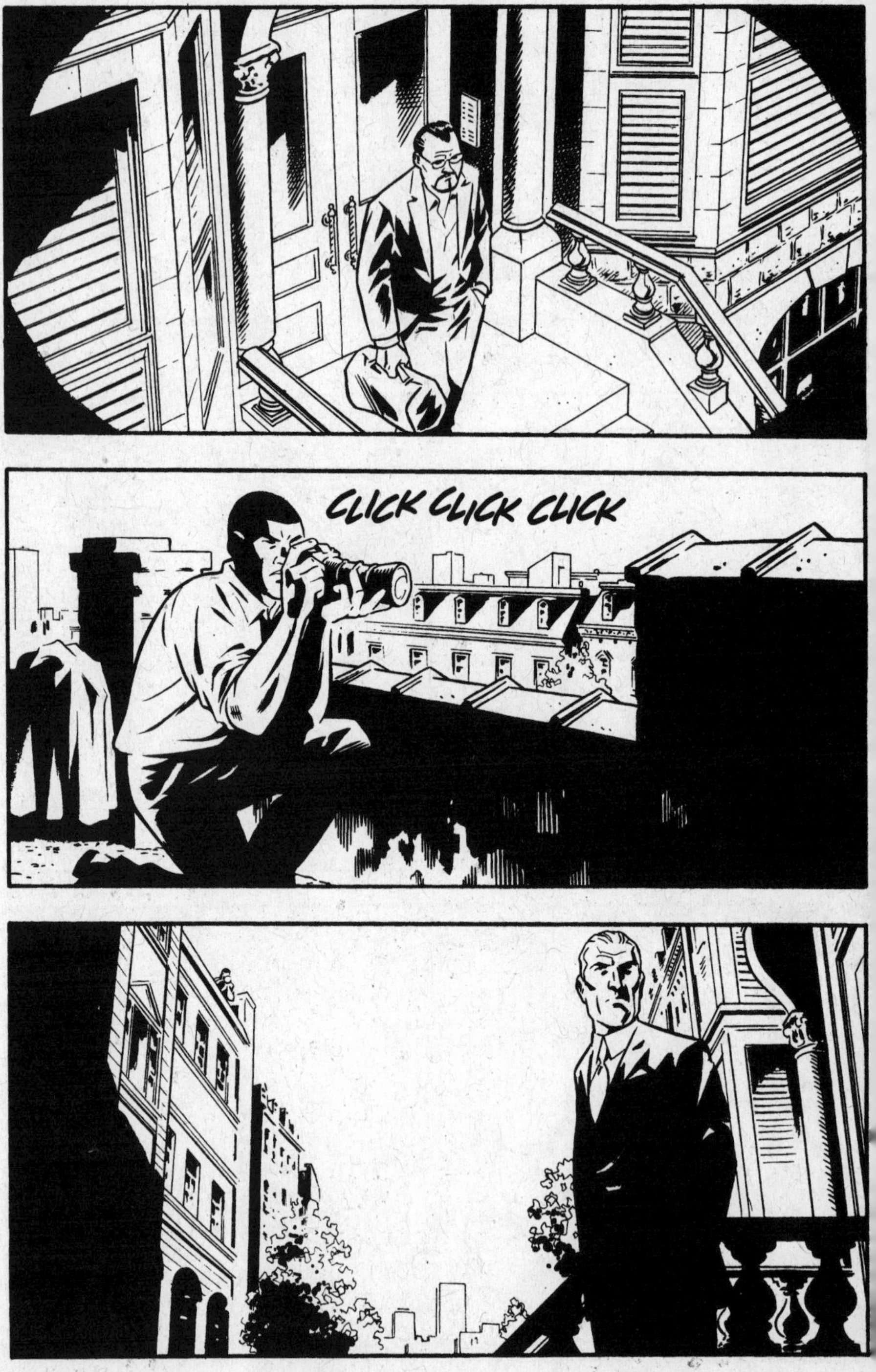
CLICK CLICK CLICK

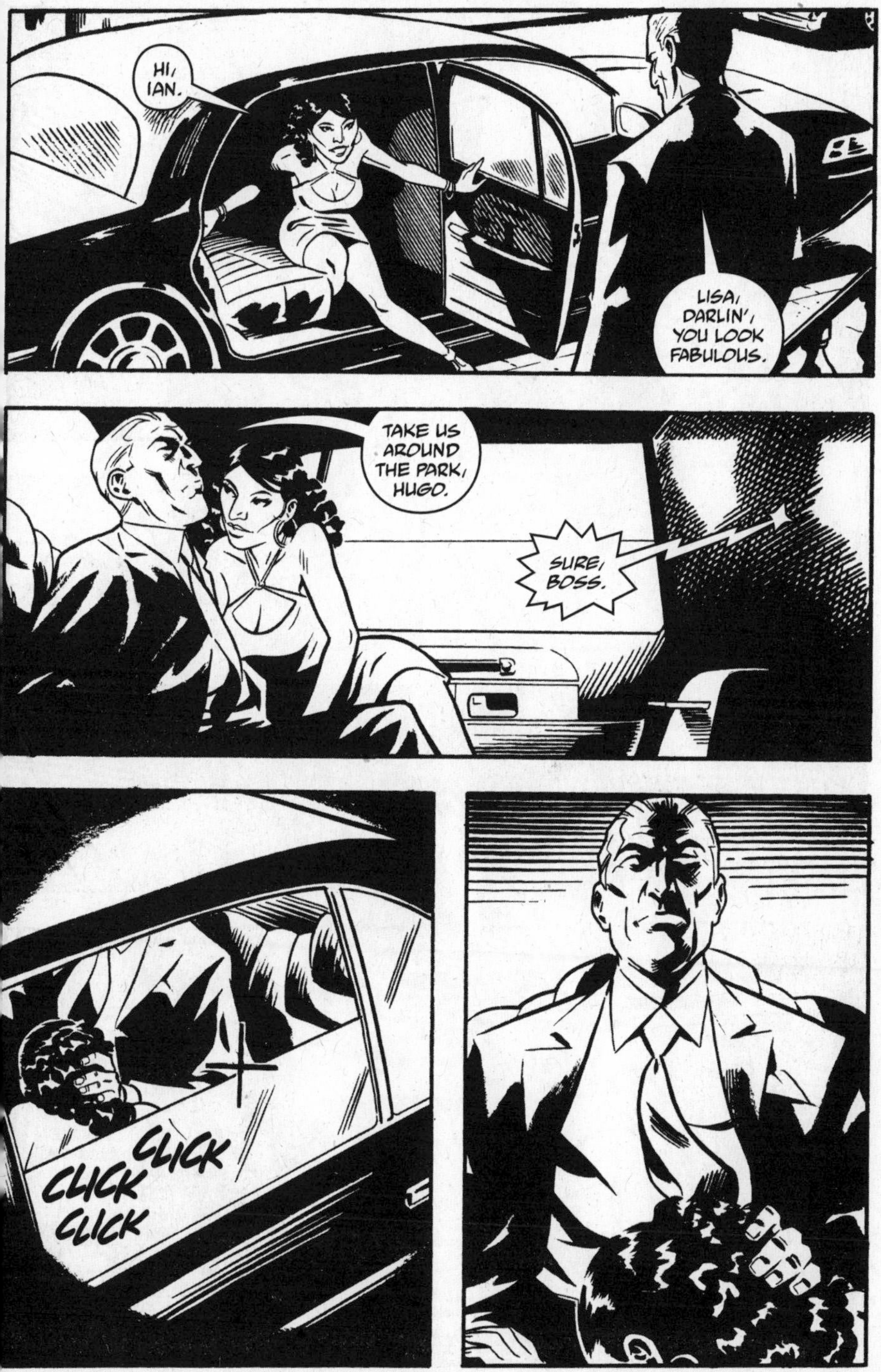
HI, IAN.
LISA, DARLIN', YOU LOOK FABULOUS.
TAKE US AROUND THE PARK, HUGO.
SURE, BOSS.
CLICK
CLICK
CLICK

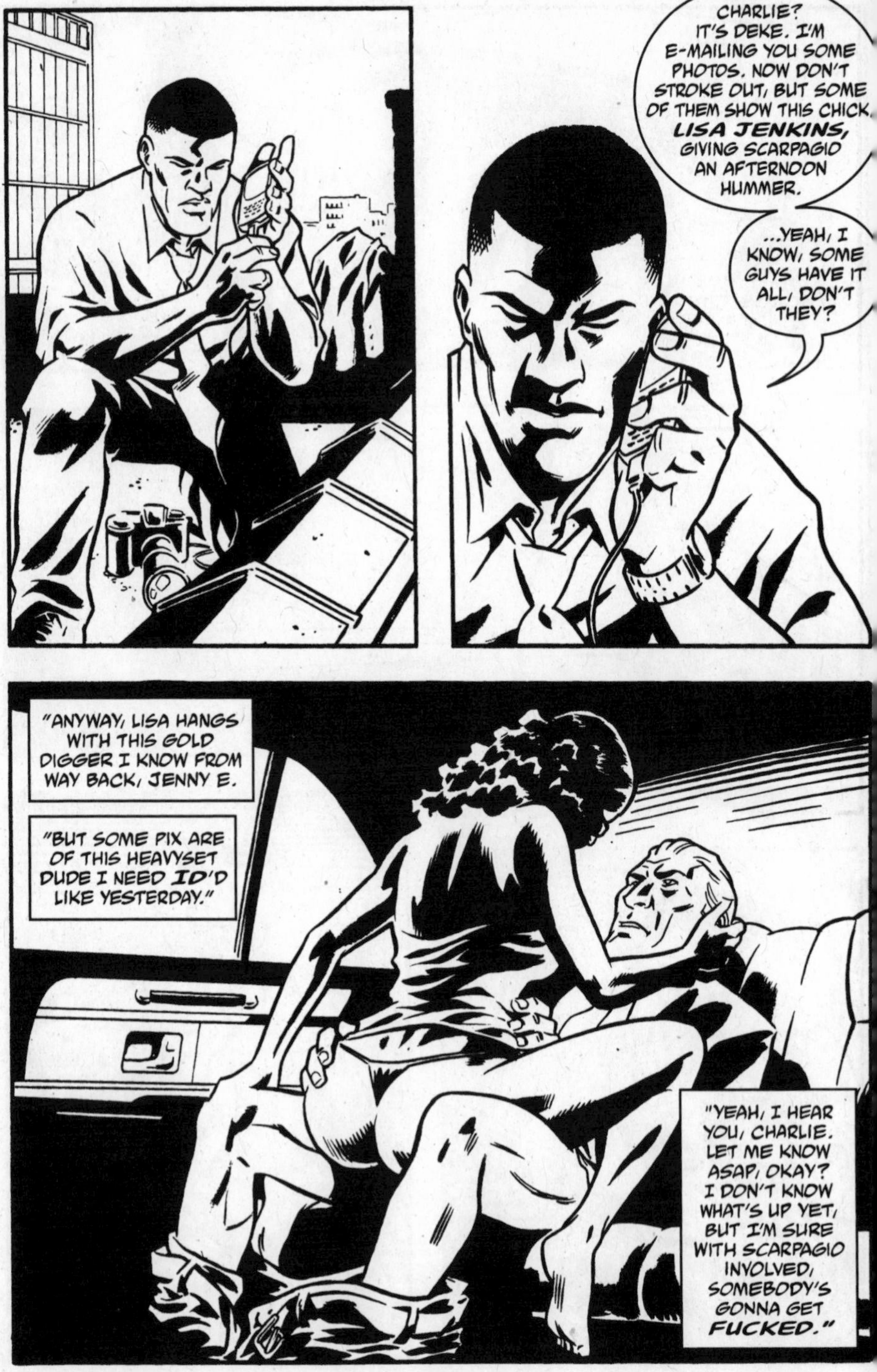
CHARLIE? IT'S DEKE. I'M E-MAILING YOU SOME PHOTOS. NOW DON'T STROKE OUT, BUT SOME OF THEM SHOW THIS CHICK, *LISA JENKINS,* GIVING SCARPAGIO AN AFTERNOON HUMMER.
...YEAH, I KNOW, SOME GUYS HAVE IT ALL, DON'T THEY?
"ANYWAY, LISA HANGS WITH THIS GOLD DIGGER I KNOW FROM WAY BACK, JENNY E.
"BUT SOME PIX ARE OF THIS HEAVYSET DUDE I NEED *ID*'D LIKE YESTERDAY."
"YEAH, I HEAR YOU, CHARLIE. LET ME KNOW ASAP, OKAY? I DON'T KNOW WHAT'S UP YET, BUT I'M SURE WITH SCARPAGIO INVOLVED, SOMEBODY'S GONNA GET *FUCKED.*"

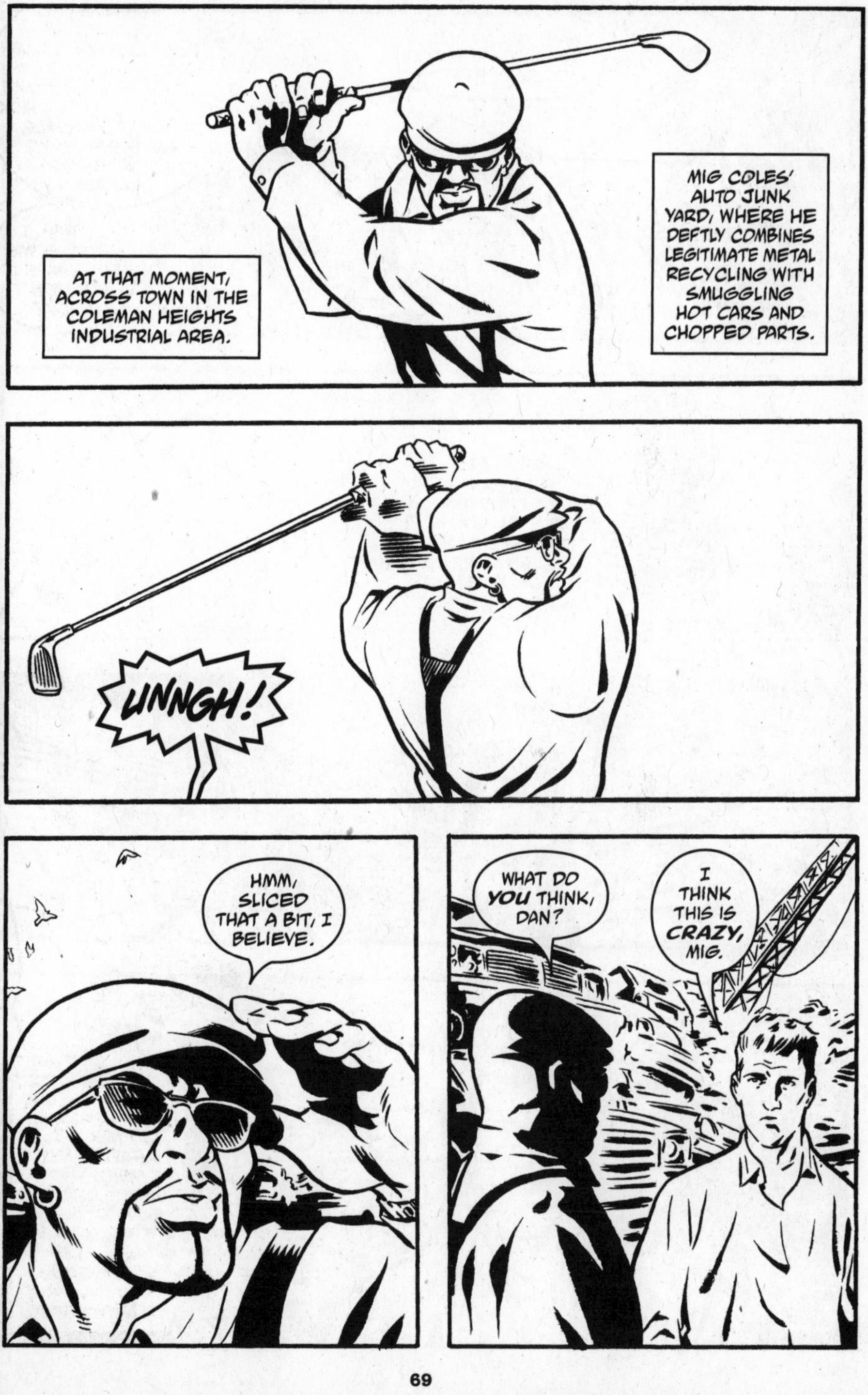
AT THAT MOMENT, ACROSS TOWN IN THE COLEMAN HEIGHTS INDUSTRIAL AREA.
MIG COLES' AUTO JUNK YARD, WHERE HE DEFTLY COMBINES LEGITIMATE METAL RECYCLING WITH SMUGGLING HOT CARS AND CHOPPED PARTS.
UNNGH!
HMM, SLICED THAT A BIT, I BELIEVE.
WHAT DO YOU THINK, DAN?
I THINK THIS IS CRAZY, MIG.

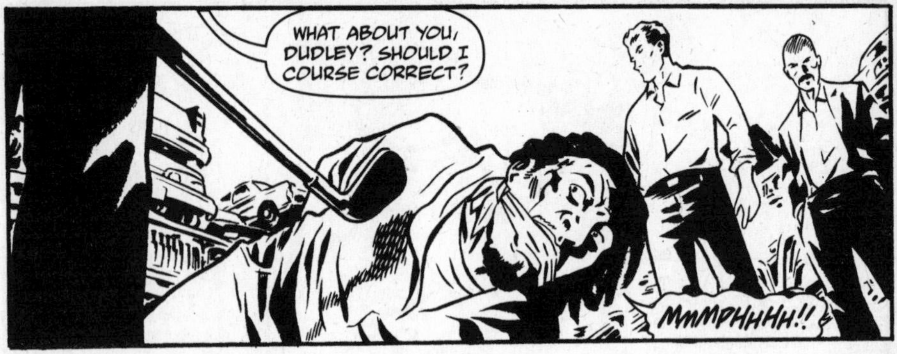
WHAT ABOUT YOU, DUDLEY? SHOULD I COURSE CORRECT?
MMMPHHHH!!

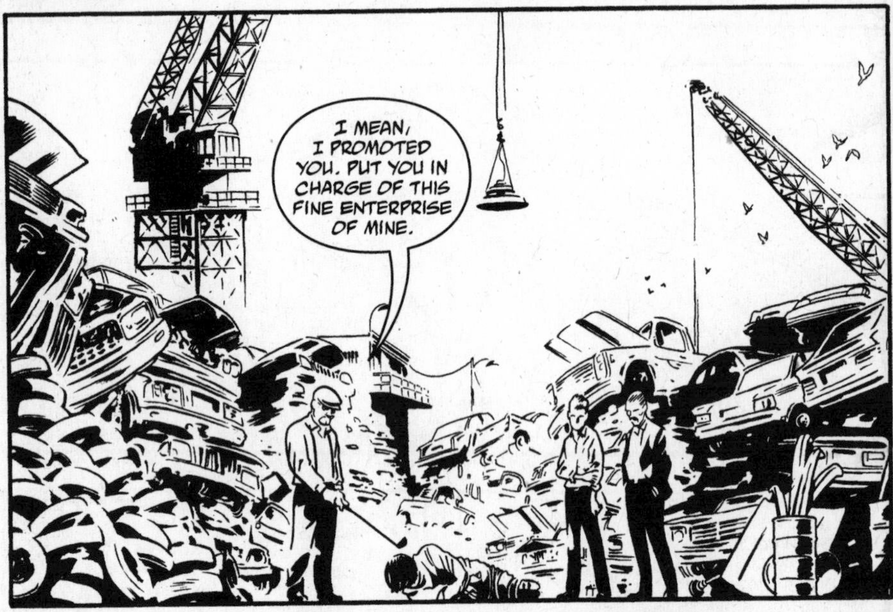
I MEAN, I PROMOTED YOU. PUT YOU IN CHARGE OF THIS FINE ENTERPRISE OF MINE.

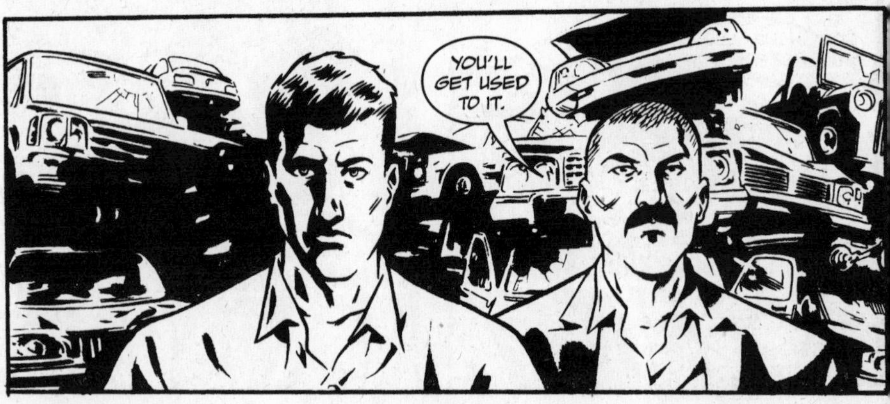
YOU'LL GET USED TO IT.

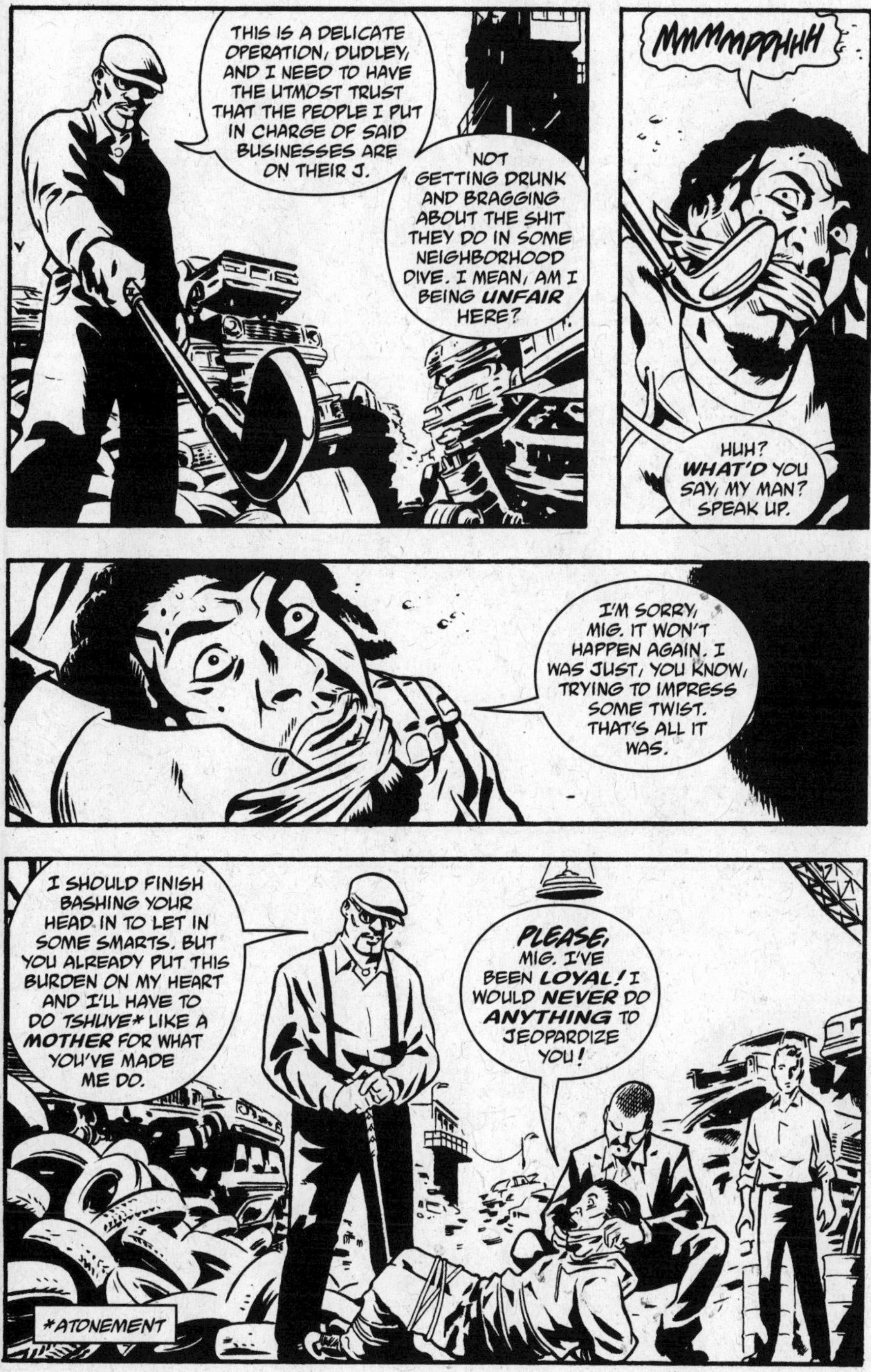
THIS IS A DELICATE OPERATION, DUDLEY, AND I NEED TO HAVE THE UTMOST TRUST THAT THE PEOPLE I PUT IN CHARGE OF SAID BUSINESSES ARE ON THEIR J.
NOT GETTING DRUNK AND BRAGGING ABOUT THE SHIT THEY DO IN SOME NEIGHBORHOOD DIVE. I MEAN, AM I BEING UNFAIR HERE?
MMMMPPHHH
HUH? WHAT'D YOU SAY, MY MAN? SPEAK UP.
I'M SORRY, MIG. IT WON'T HAPPEN AGAIN. I WAS JUST, YOU KNOW, TRYING TO IMPRESS SOME TWIST. THAT'S ALL IT WAS.
I SHOULD FINISH BASHING YOUR HEAD IN TO LET IN SOME SMARTS. BUT YOU ALREADY PUT THIS BURDEN ON MY HEART AND I'LL HAVE TO DO TSHUVE* LIKE A MOTHER FOR WHAT YOU'VE MADE ME DO.
PLEASE, MIG. I'VE BEEN LOYAL! I WOULD NEVER DO ANYTHING TO JEOPARDIZE YOU!
*ATONEMENT

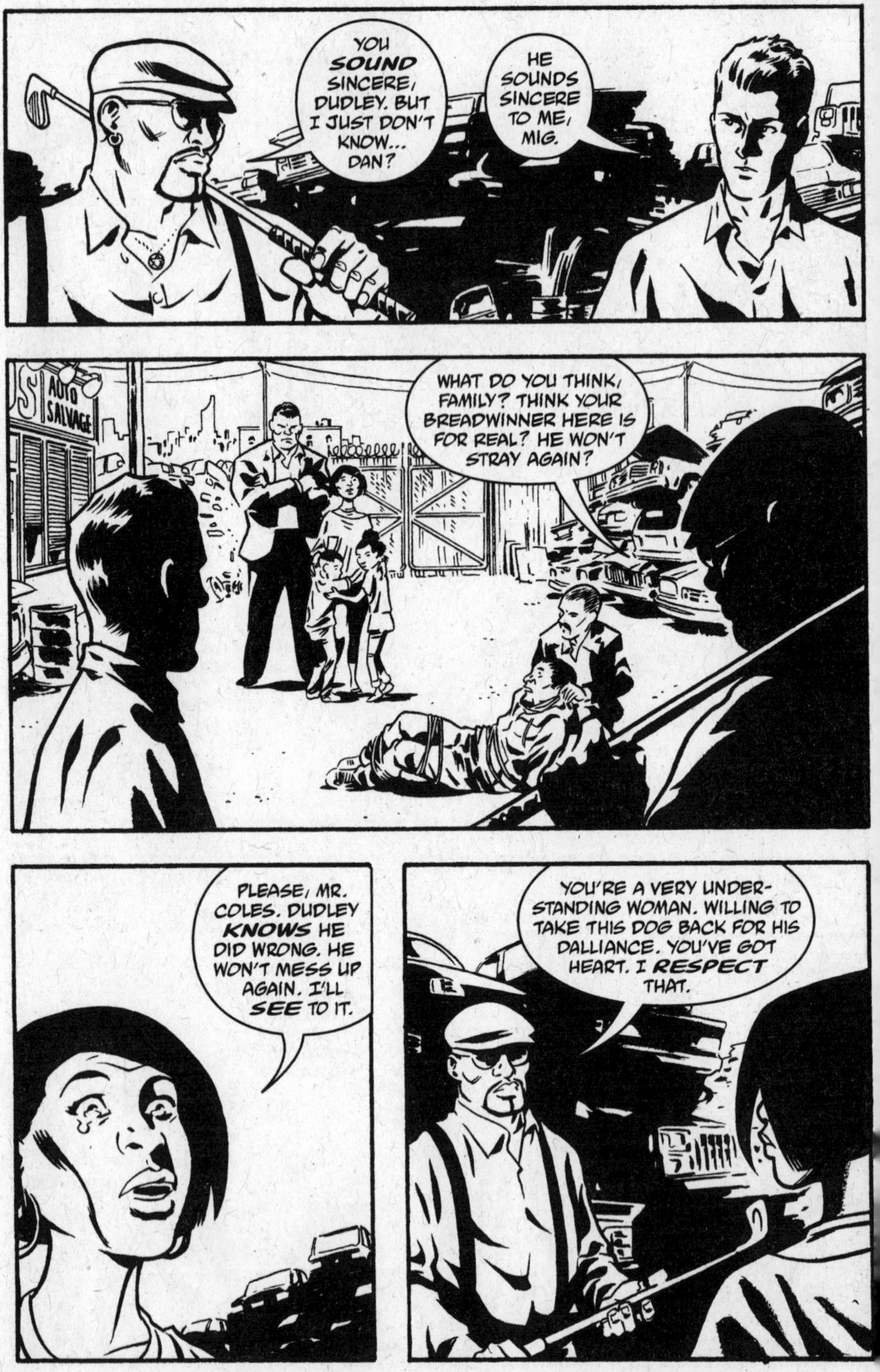
YOU *SOUND* SINCERE, DUDLEY. BUT I JUST DON'T KNOW... DAN?
HE SOUNDS SINCERE TO ME, MIG.
AUTO SALVAGE
WHAT DO YOU THINK, FAMILY? THINK YOUR BREADWINNER HERE IS FOR REAL? HE WON'T STRAY AGAIN?
PLEASE, MR. COLES. DUDLEY *KNOWS* HE DID WRONG. HE WON'T MESS UP AGAIN. I'LL *SEE* TO IT.
YOU'RE A VERY UNDER-STANDING WOMAN. WILLING TO TAKE THIS DOG BACK FOR HIS DALLIANCE. YOU'VE GOT HEART. I *RESPECT* THAT.

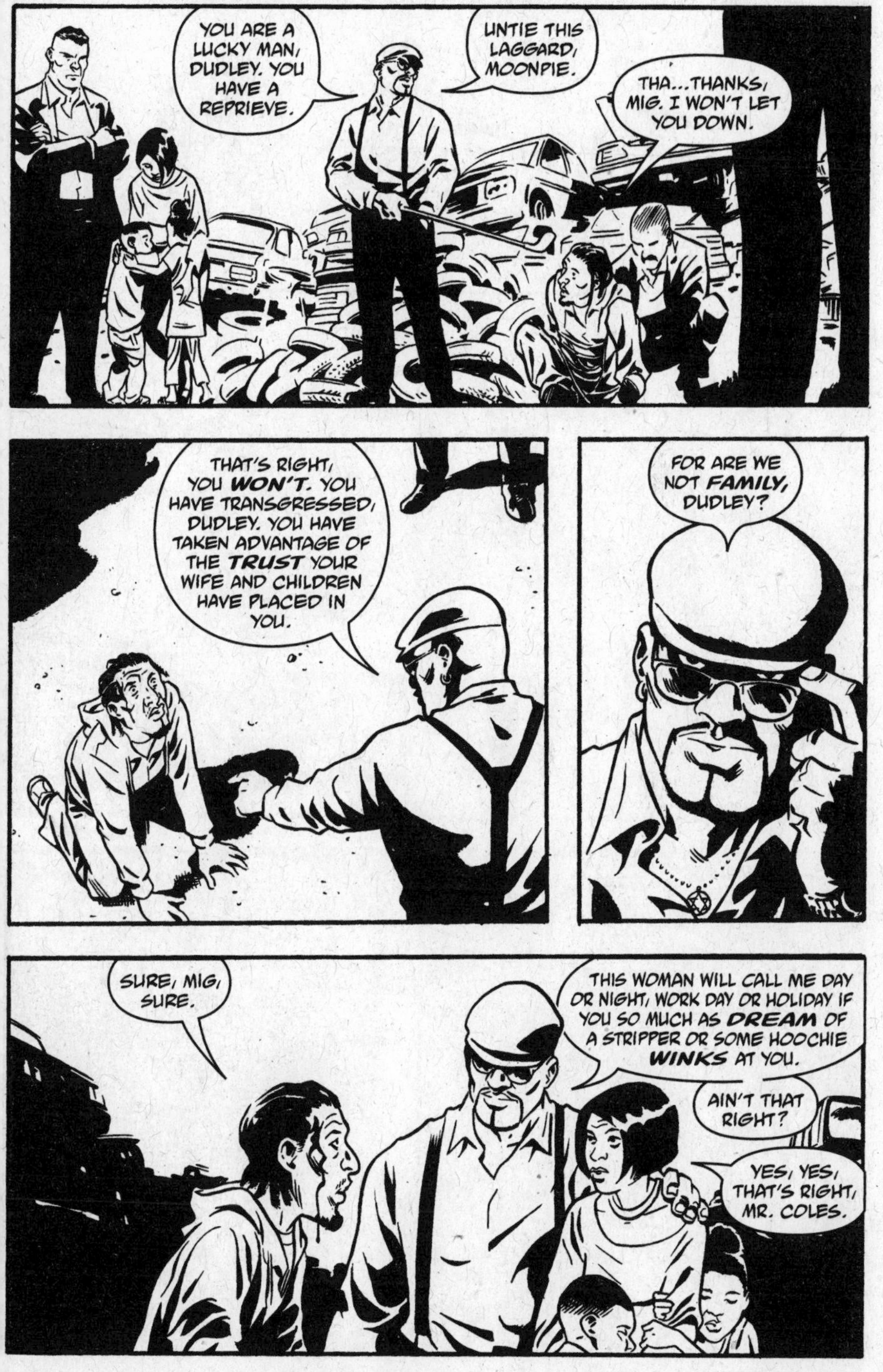
YOU ARE A LUCKY MAN, DUDLEY. YOU HAVE A REPRIEVE.
UNTIE THIS LAGGARD, MOONPIE.
THA...THANKS, MIG. I WON'T LET YOU DOWN.
THAT'S RIGHT, YOU WON'T. YOU HAVE TRANSGRESSED, DUDLEY. YOU HAVE TAKEN ADVANTAGE OF THE TRUST YOUR WIFE AND CHILDREN HAVE PLACED IN YOU.
FOR ARE WE NOT FAMILY, DUDLEY?
SURE, MIG, SURE.
THIS WOMAN WILL CALL ME DAY OR NIGHT, WORK DAY OR HOLIDAY IF YOU SO MUCH AS DREAM OF A STRIPPER OR SOME HOOCHIE WINKS AT YOU.
AIN'T THAT RIGHT?
YES, YES, THAT'S RIGHT, MR. COLES.

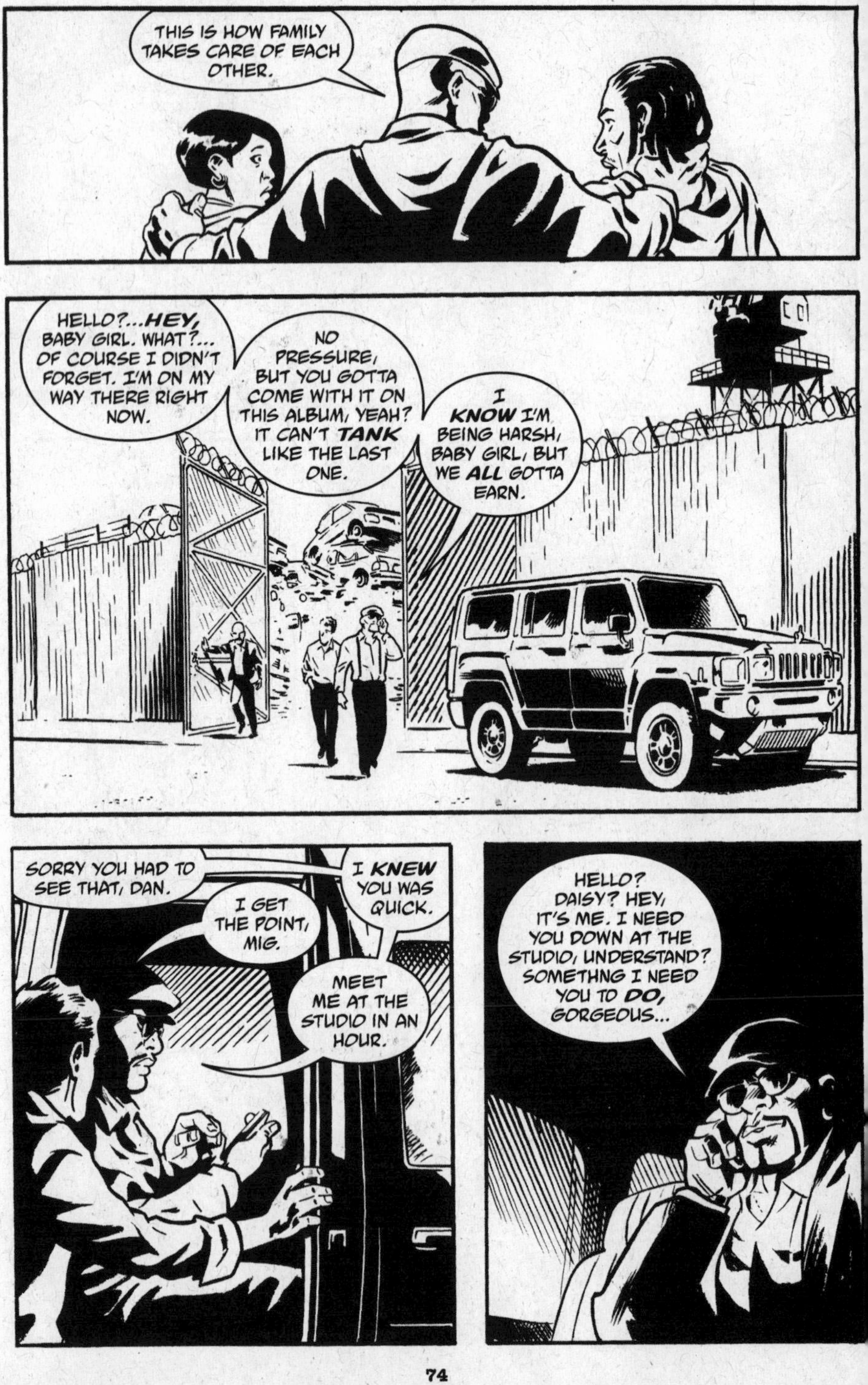
THIS IS HOW FAMILY TAKES CARE OF EACH OTHER.
HELLO?...HEY, BABY GIRL. WHAT?... OF COURSE I DIDN'T FORGET. I'M ON MY WAY THERE RIGHT NOW.
NO PRESSURE, BUT YOU GOTTA COME WITH IT ON THIS ALBUM, YEAH? IT CAN'T TANK LIKE THE LAST ONE.
I KNOW I'M BEING HARSH, BABY GIRL, BUT WE ALL GOTTA EARN.
SORRY YOU HAD TO SEE THAT, DAN.
I GET THE POINT, MIG.
I KNEW YOU WAS QUICK.
MEET ME AT THE STUDIO IN AN HOUR.
HELLO? DAISY? HEY, IT'S ME. I NEED YOU DOWN AT THE STUDIO, UNDERSTAND? SOMETHNG I NEED YOU TO DO, GORGEOUS...

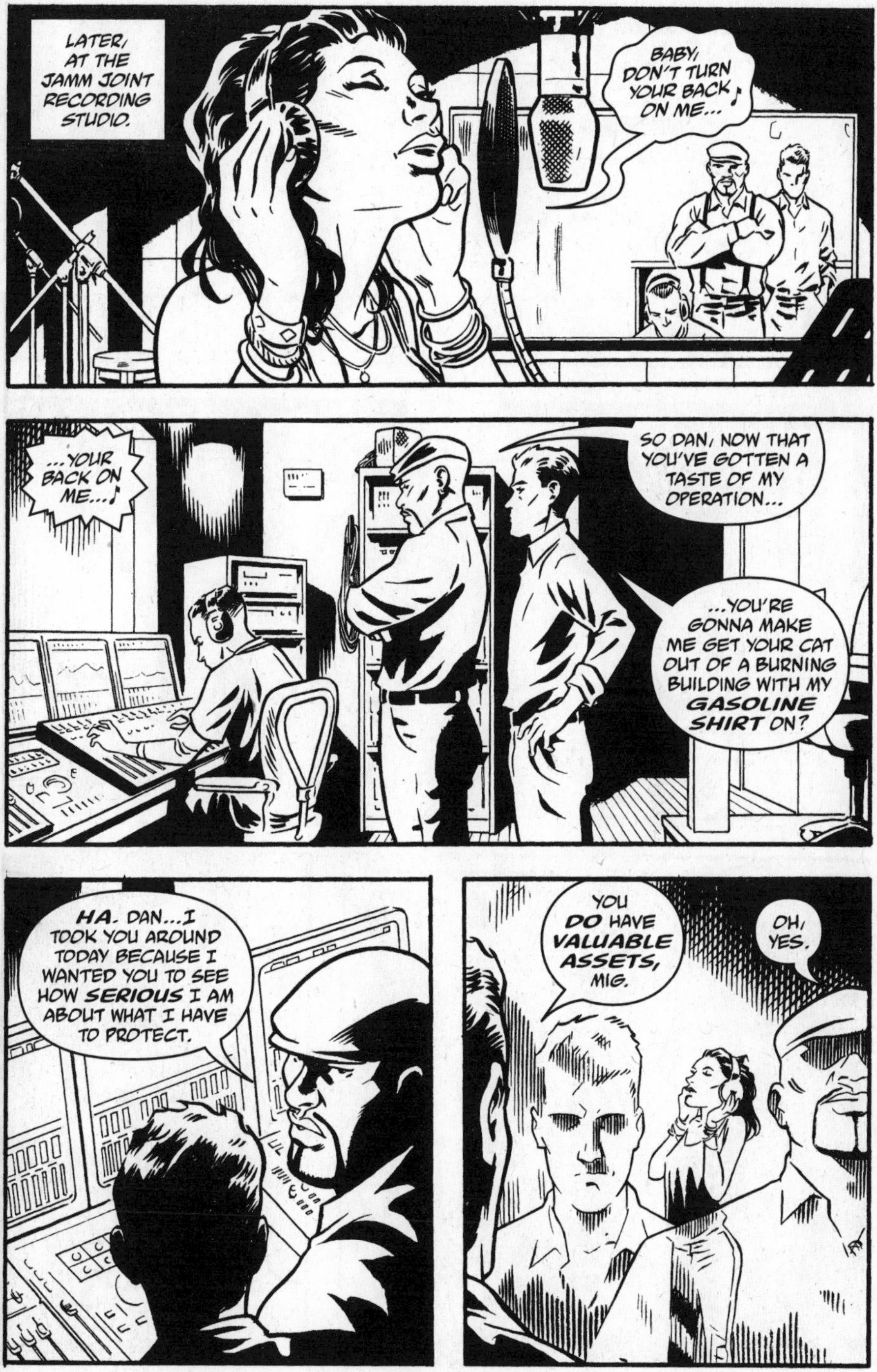
LATER, AT THE JAMM JOINT RECORDING STUDIO.
BABY, DON'T TURN YOUR BACK ON ME...♪
...YOUR BACK ON ME...♪
SO DAN, NOW THAT YOU'VE GOTTEN A TASTE OF MY OPERATION...
...YOU'RE GONNA MAKE ME GET YOUR CAT OUT OF A BURNING BUILDING WITH MY GASOLINE SHIRT ON?
HA. DAN...I TOOK YOU AROUND TODAY BECAUSE I WANTED YOU TO SEE HOW SERIOUS I AM ABOUT WHAT I HAVE TO PROTECT.
YOU DO HAVE VALUABLE ASSETS, MIG.
OH, YES.

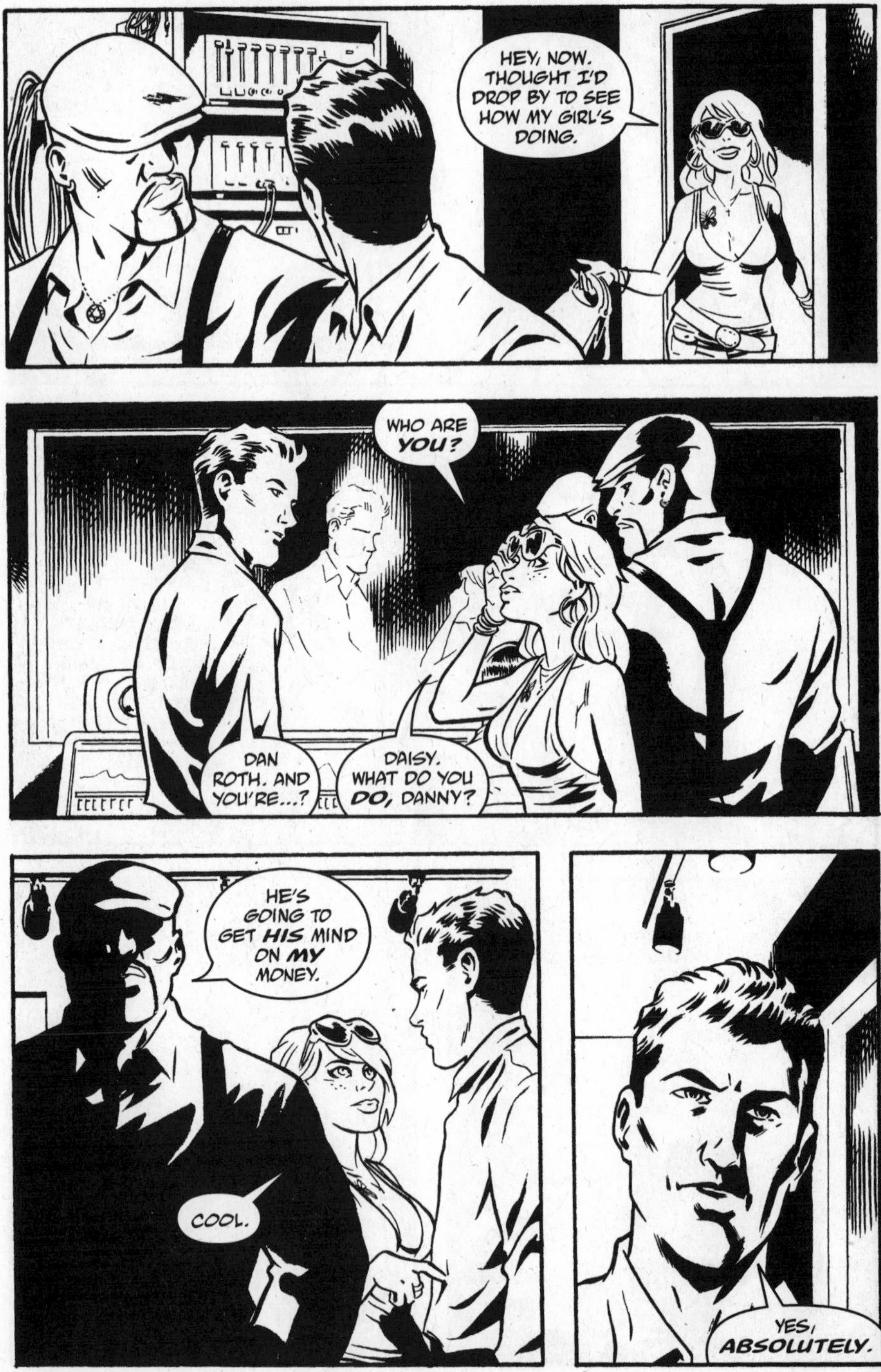
HEY, NOW. THOUGHT I'D DROP BY TO SEE HOW MY GIRL'S DOING.
WHO ARE *YOU?*
DAN ROTH. AND YOU'RE...?
DAISY. WHAT DO YOU *DO,* DANNY?
HE'S GOING TO GET *HIS* MIND ON *MY* MONEY.
COOL.
YES, *ABSOLUTELY.*

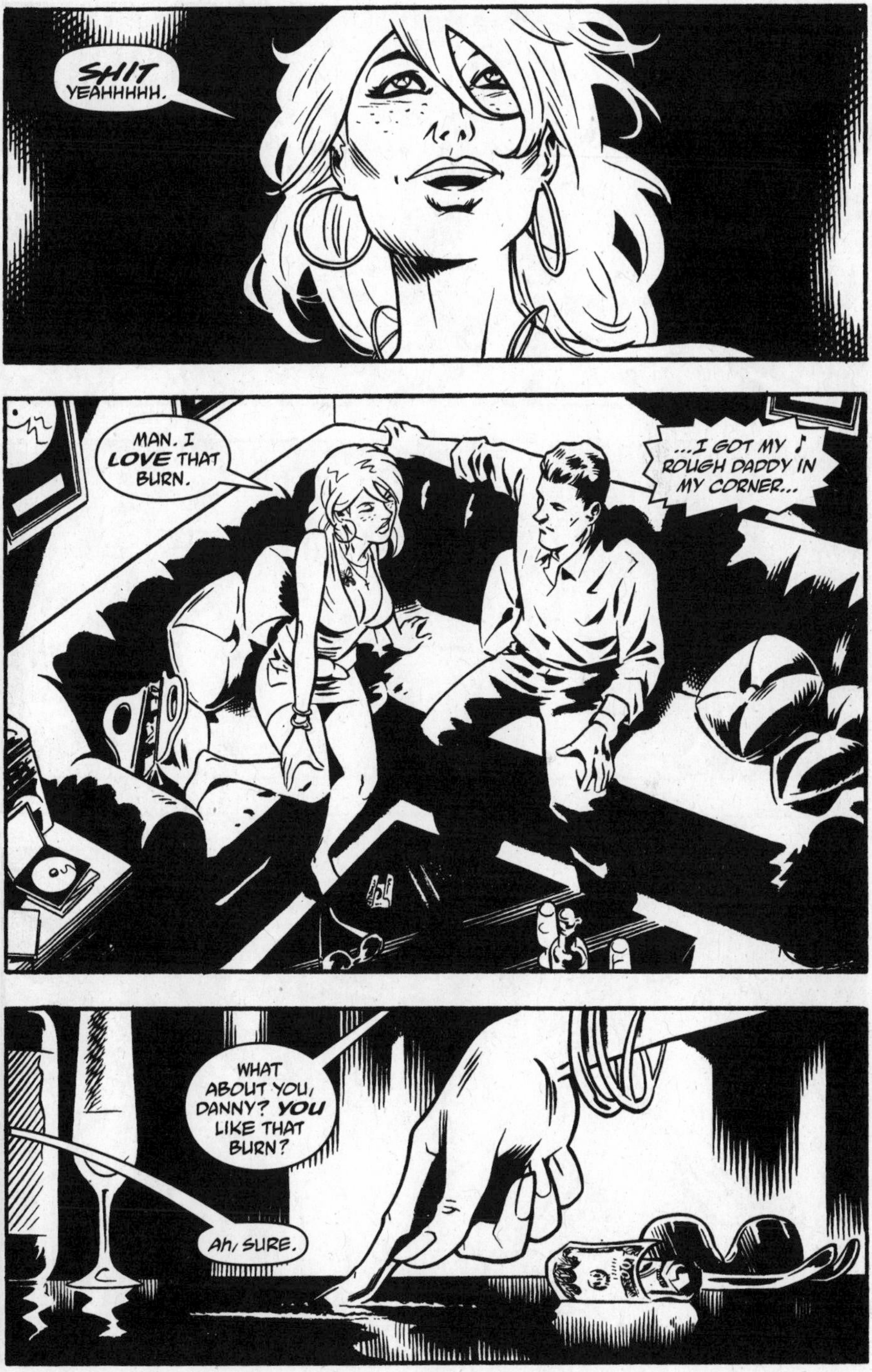
SHIT YEAHHHHH.
MAN. I LOVE THAT BURN.
...I GOT MY ♪ ROUGH DADDY IN MY CORNER...
WHAT ABOUT YOU, DANNY? YOU LIKE THAT BURN?
Ah, SURE.

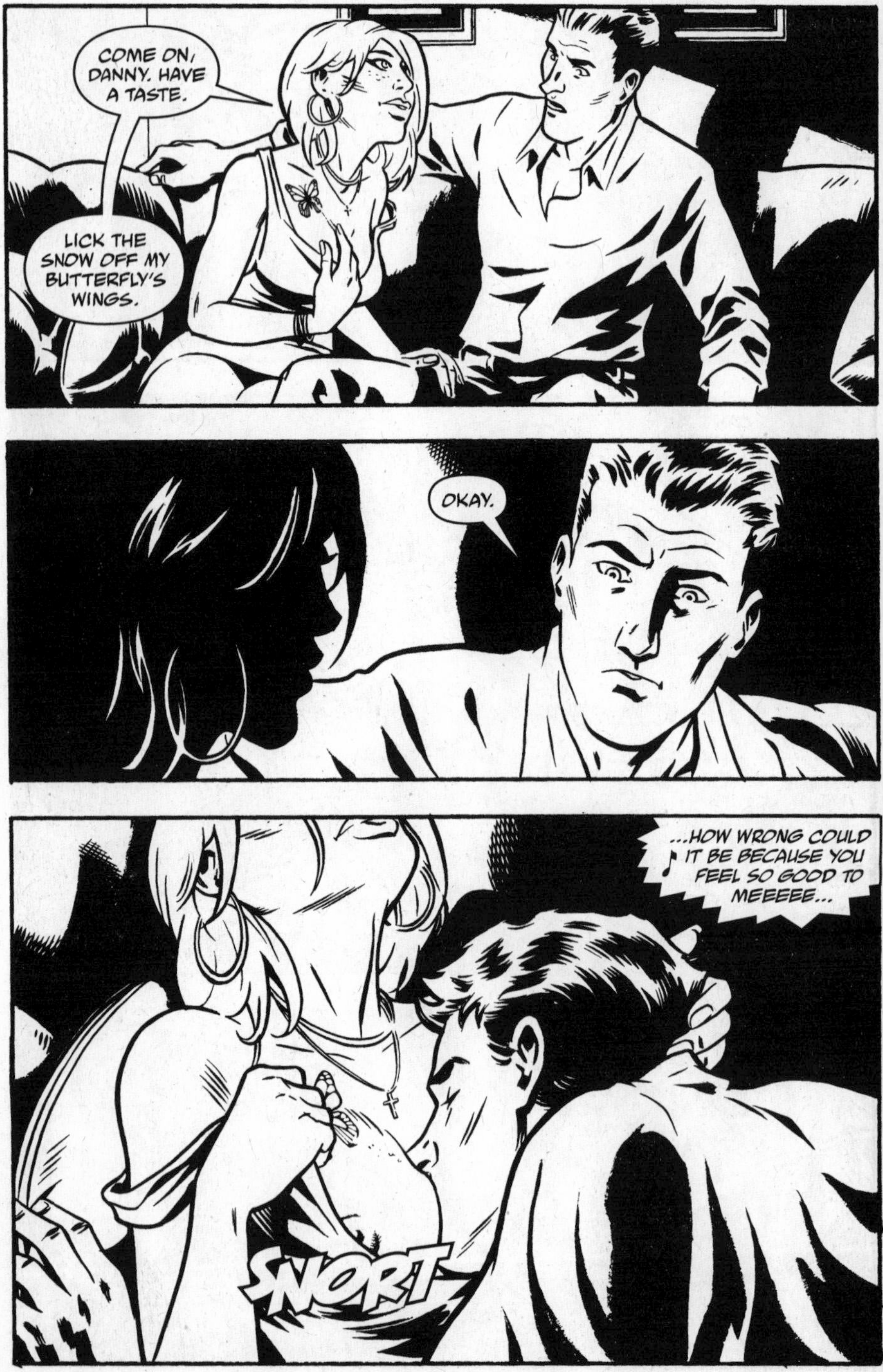

COME ON, DANNY. HAVE A TASTE.
LICK THE SNOW OFF MY BUTTERFLY'S WINGS.
OKAY.
...HOW WRONG COULD IT BE BECAUSE YOU FEEL SO GOOD TO MEEEEE...
SNORT

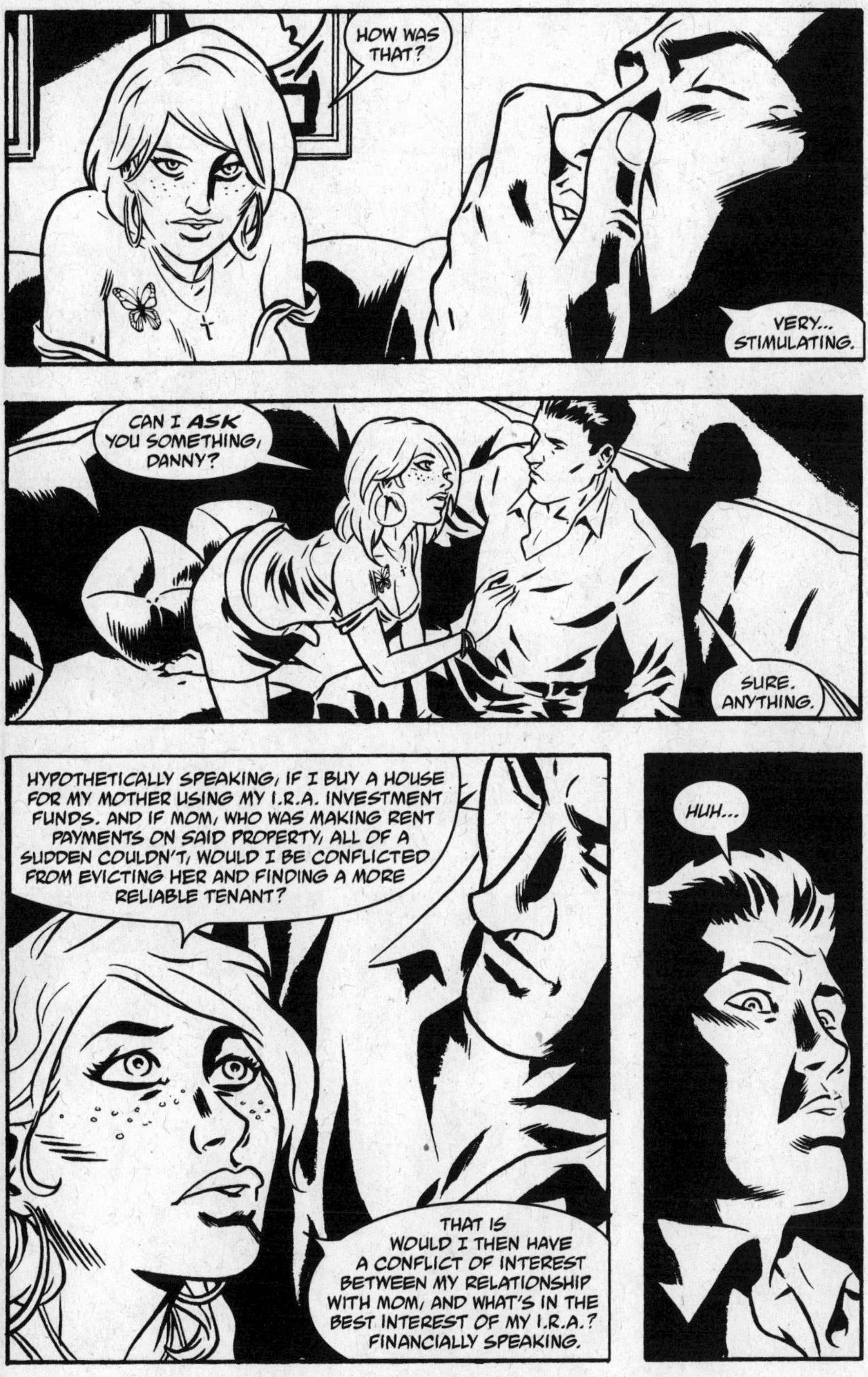
HOW WAS THAT?
VERY... STIMULATING.
CAN I ASK YOU SOMETHING, DANNY?
SURE. ANYTHING.
HYPOTHETICALLY SPEAKING, IF I BUY A HOUSE FOR MY MOTHER USING MY I.R.A. INVESTMENT FUNDS. AND IF MOM, WHO WAS MAKING RENT PAYMENTS ON SAID PROPERTY, ALL OF A SUDDEN COULDN'T, WOULD I BE CONFLICTED FROM EVICTING HER AND FINDING A MORE RELIABLE TENANT?
THAT IS WOULD I THEN HAVE A CONFLICT OF INTEREST BETWEEN MY RELATIONSHIP WITH MOM, AND WHAT'S IN THE BEST INTEREST OF MY I.R.A.? FINANCIALLY SPEAKING.
HUH...

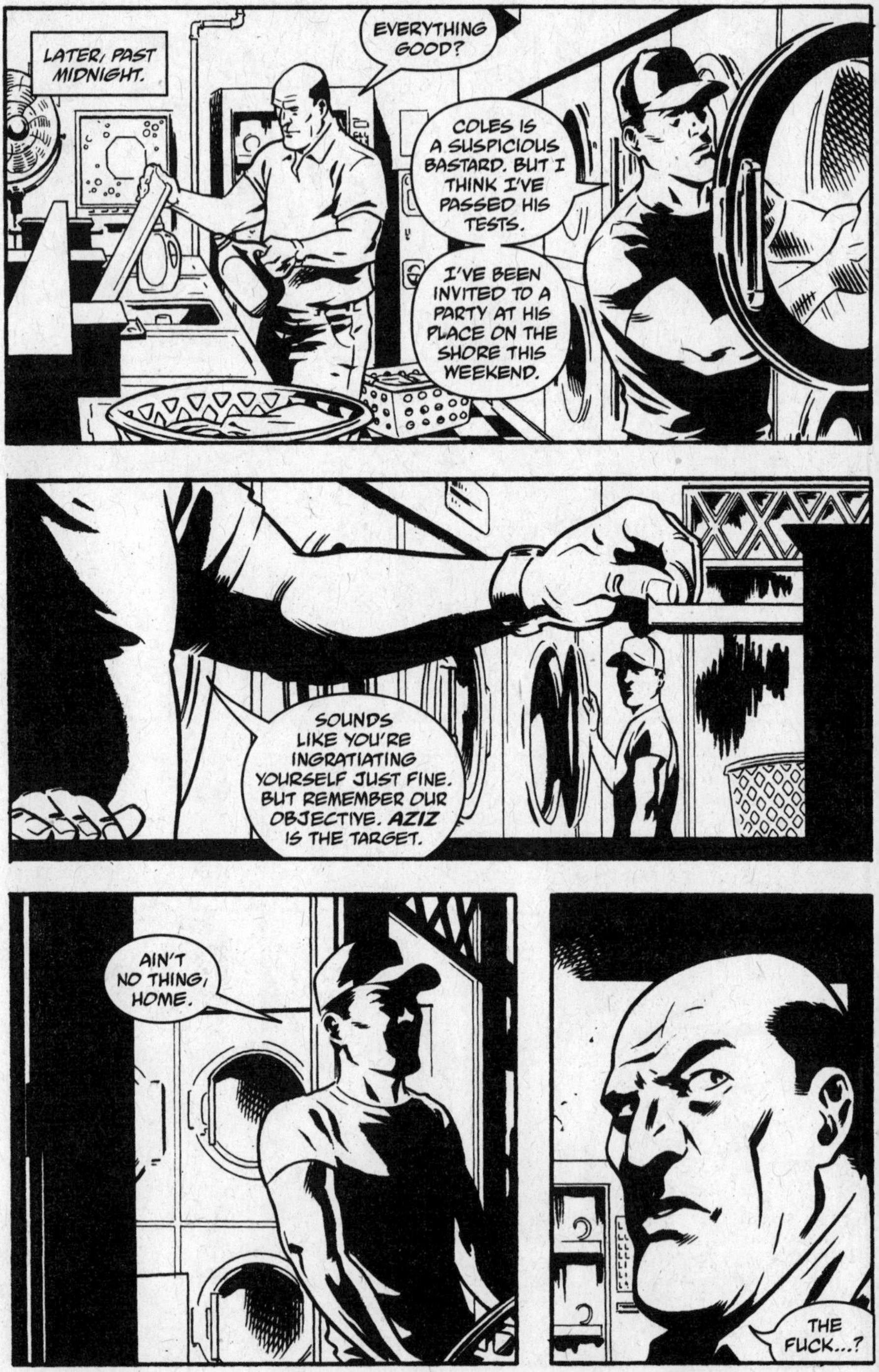
LATER, PAST MIDNIGHT.
EVERYTHING GOOD?
COLES IS A SUSPICIOUS BASTARD. BUT I THINK I'VE PASSED HIS TESTS.
I'VE BEEN INVITED TO A PARTY AT HIS PLACE ON THE SHORE THIS WEEKEND.
SOUNDS LIKE YOU'RE INGRATIATING YOURSELF JUST FINE. BUT REMEMBER OUR OBJECTIVE. AZIZ IS THE TARGET.
AIN'T NO THING, HOME.
THE FUCK...?

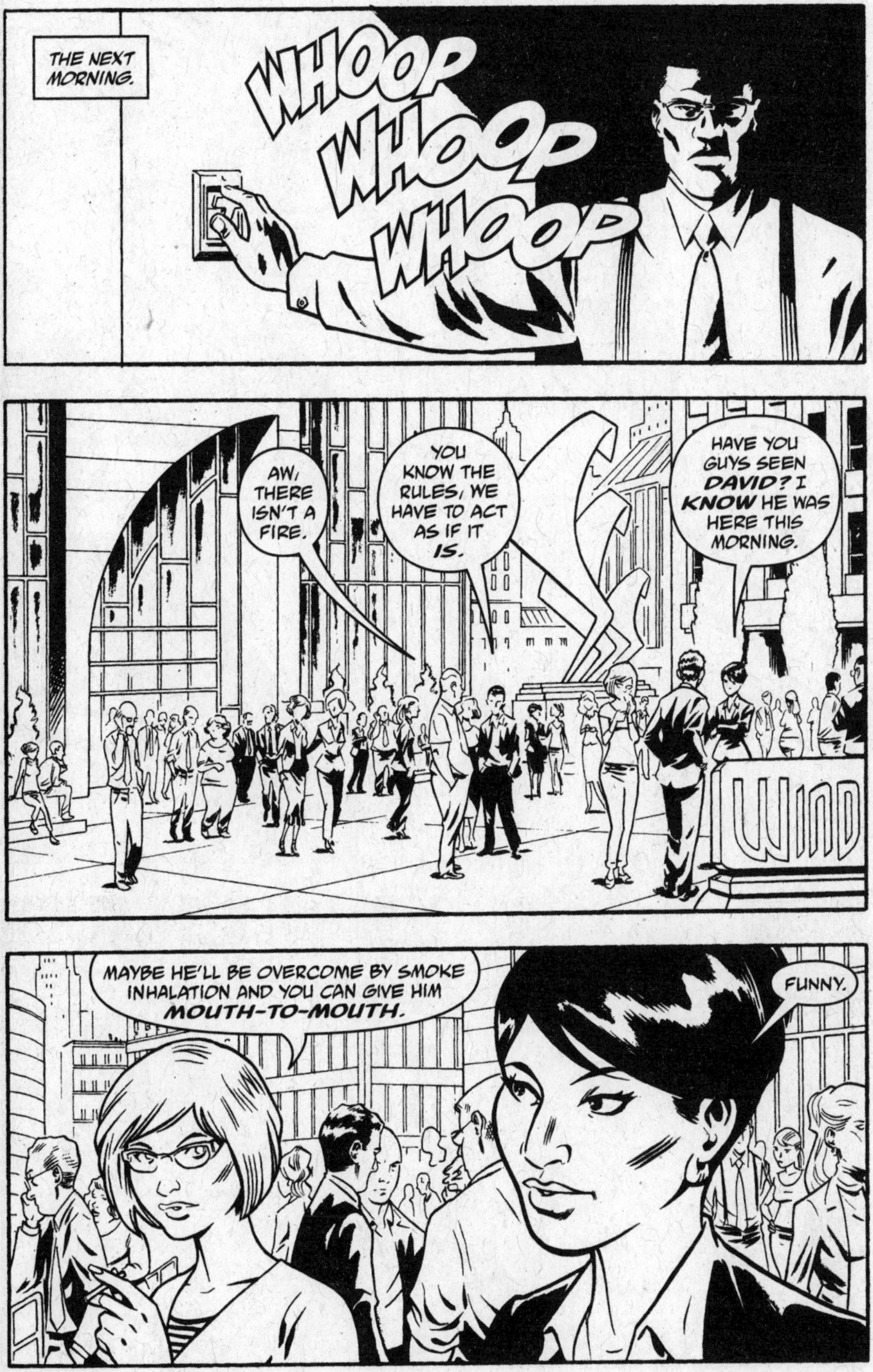
THE NEXT MORNING.
WHOOP WHOOP WHOOP
AW, THERE ISN'T A FIRE.
YOU KNOW THE RULES, WE HAVE TO ACT AS IF IT IS.
HAVE YOU GUYS SEEN DAVID? I KNOW HE WAS HERE THIS MORNING.
WIND
MAYBE HE'LL BE OVERCOME BY SMOKE INHALATION AND YOU CAN GIVE HIM MOUTH-TO-MOUTH.
FUNNY.

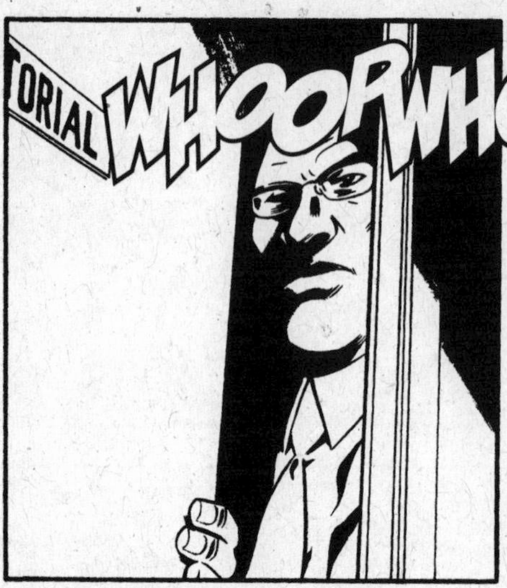
TORIAL
WHOOPWHOOPWHOOP
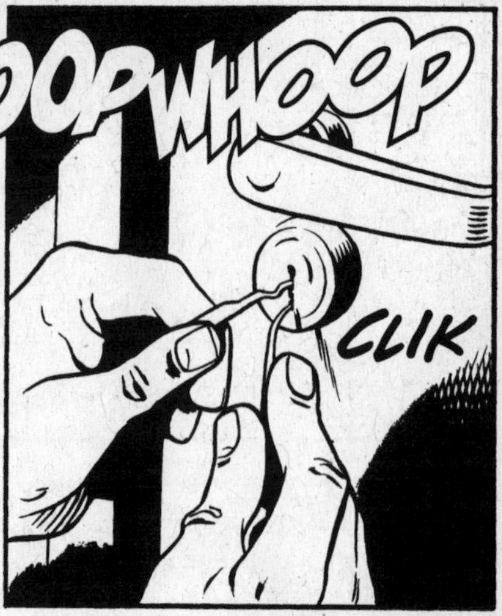
CLIK
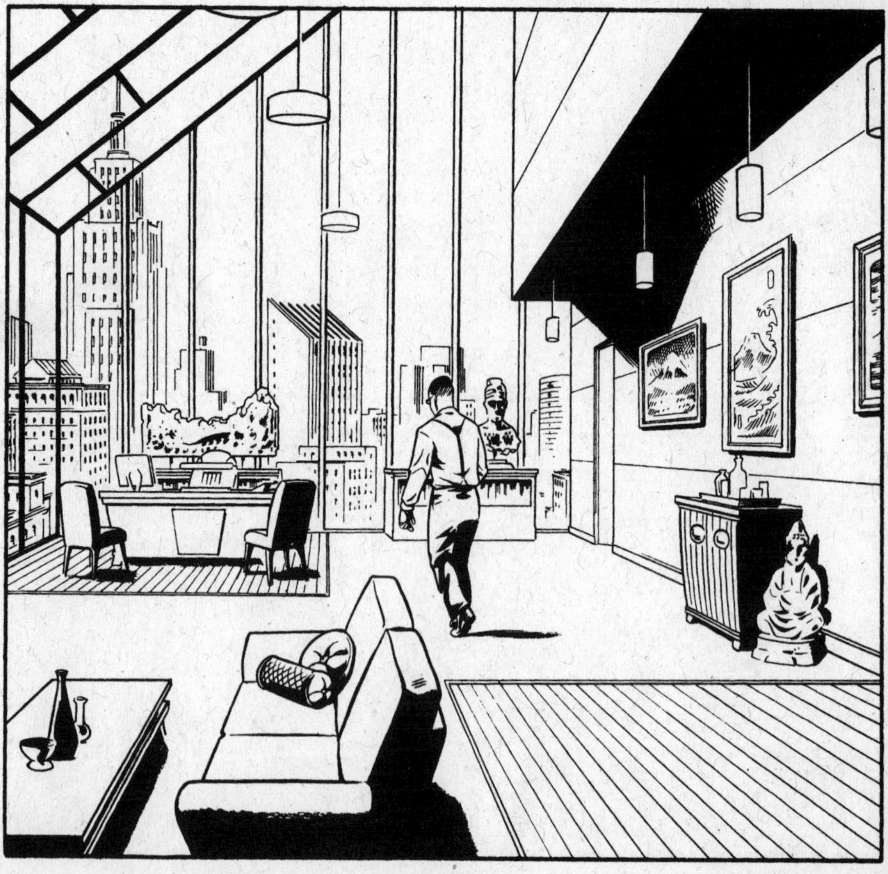

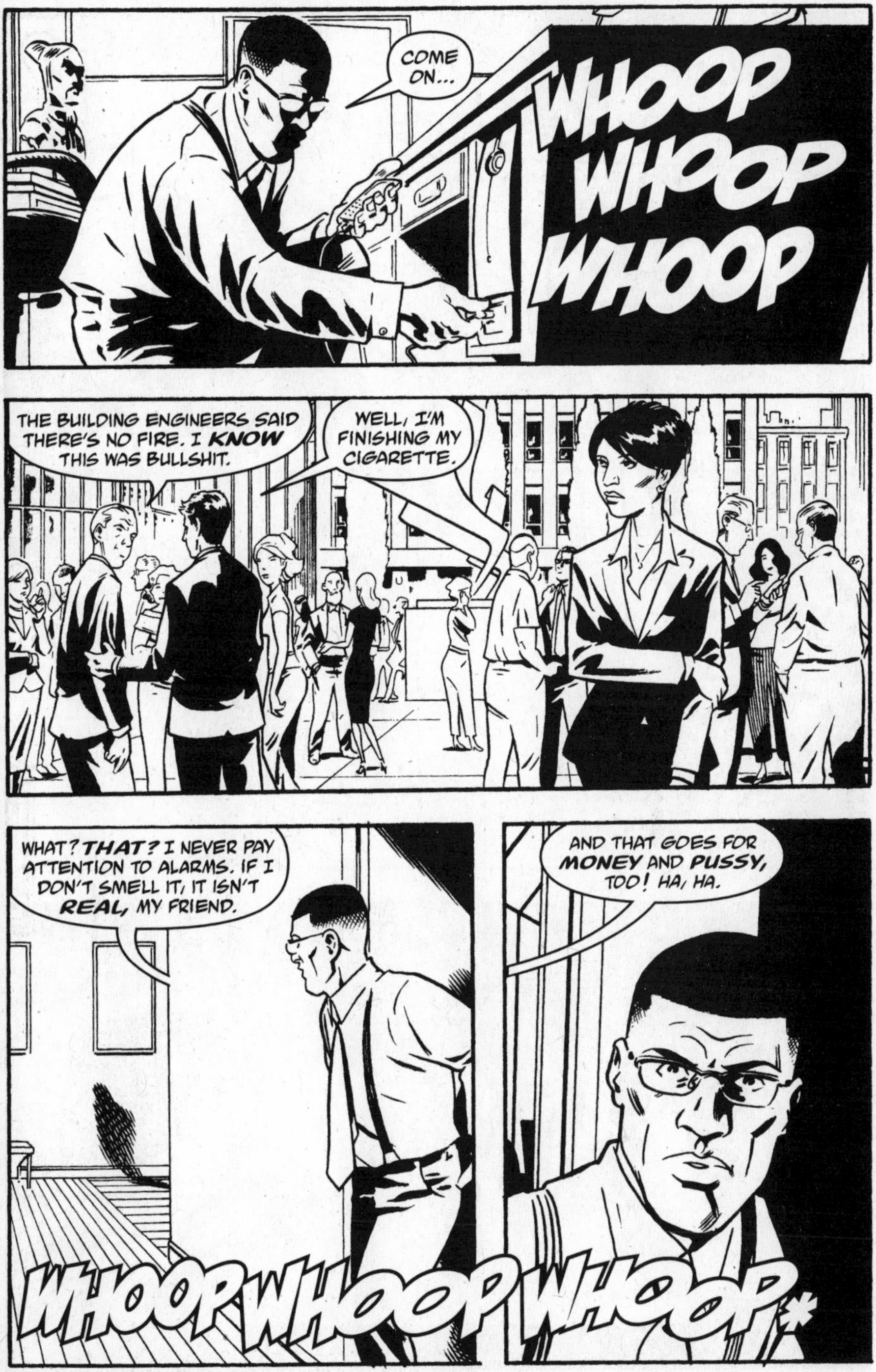
COME ON...
WHOOP WHOOP WHOOP
THE BUILDING ENGINEERS SAID THERE'S NO FIRE. I KNOW THIS WAS BULLSHIT.
WELL, I'M FINISHING MY CIGARETTE.
WHAT? THAT? I NEVER PAY ATTENTION TO ALARMS. IF I DON'T SMELL IT, IT ISN'T REAL, MY FRIEND.
AND THAT GOES FOR MONEY AND PUSSY, TOO! HA, HA.
WHOOP WHOOP WHOOP*

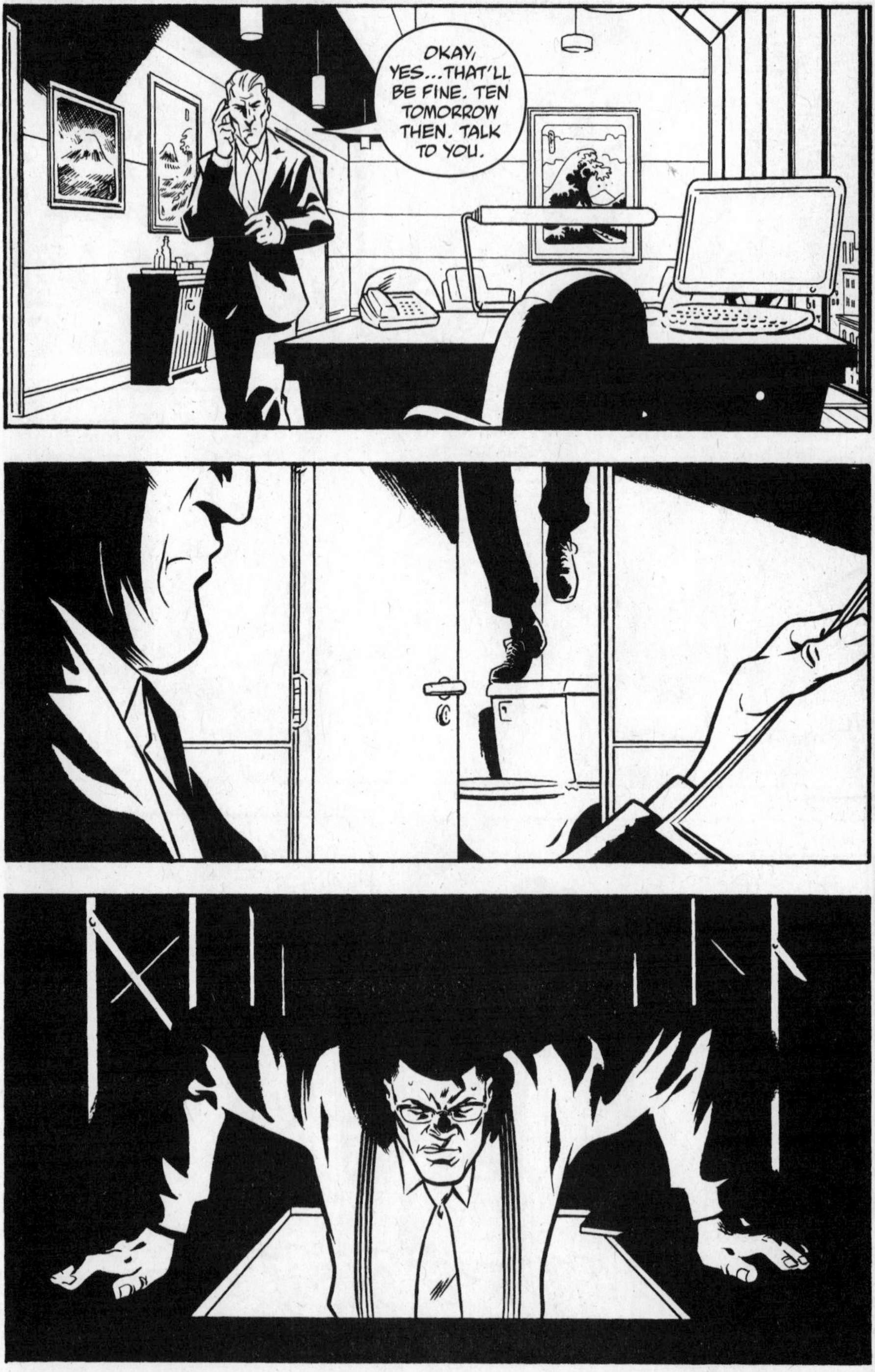
OKAY, YES...THAT'LL BE FINE. TEN TOMORROW THEN. TALK TO YOU.

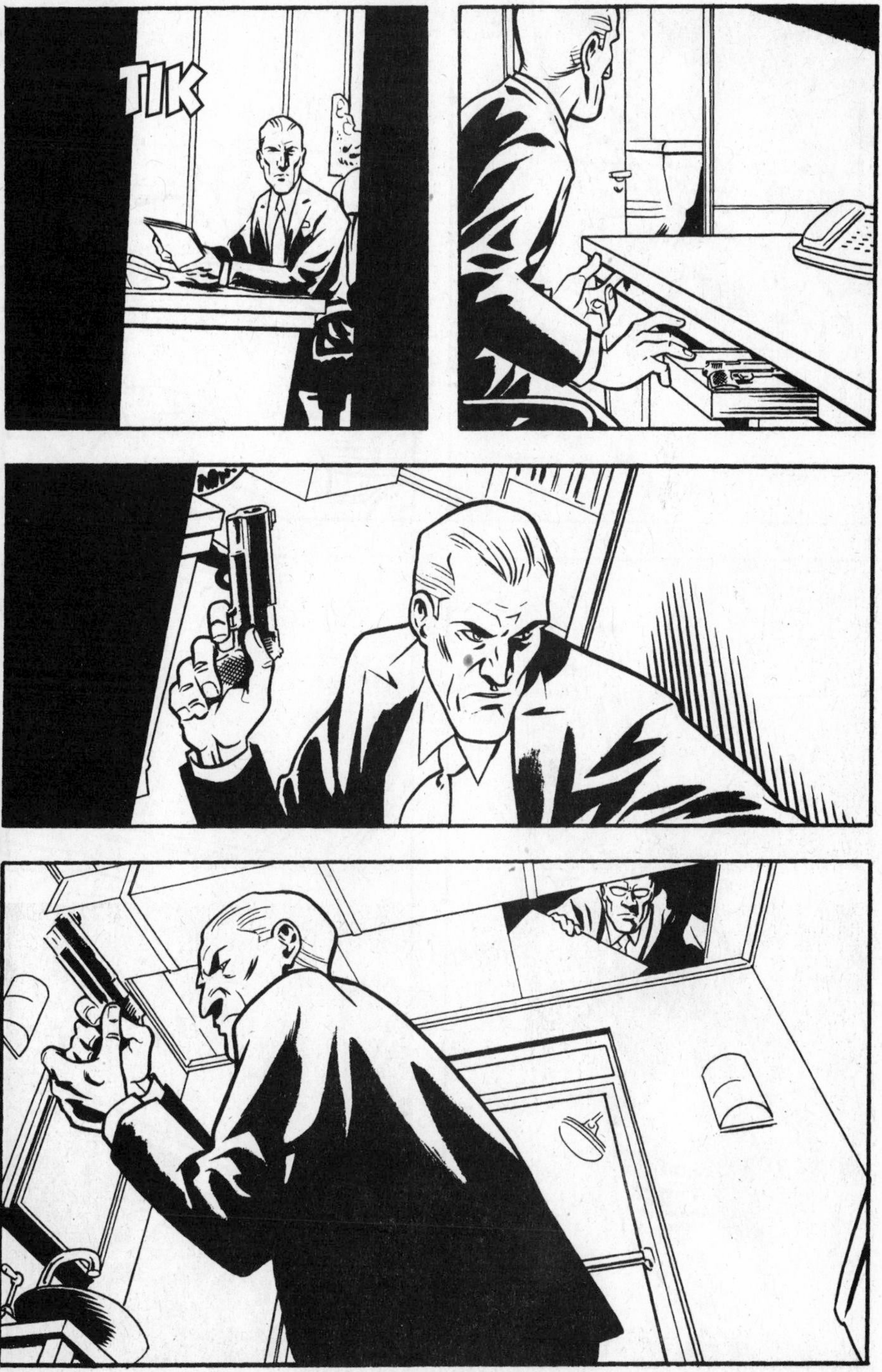
TIK

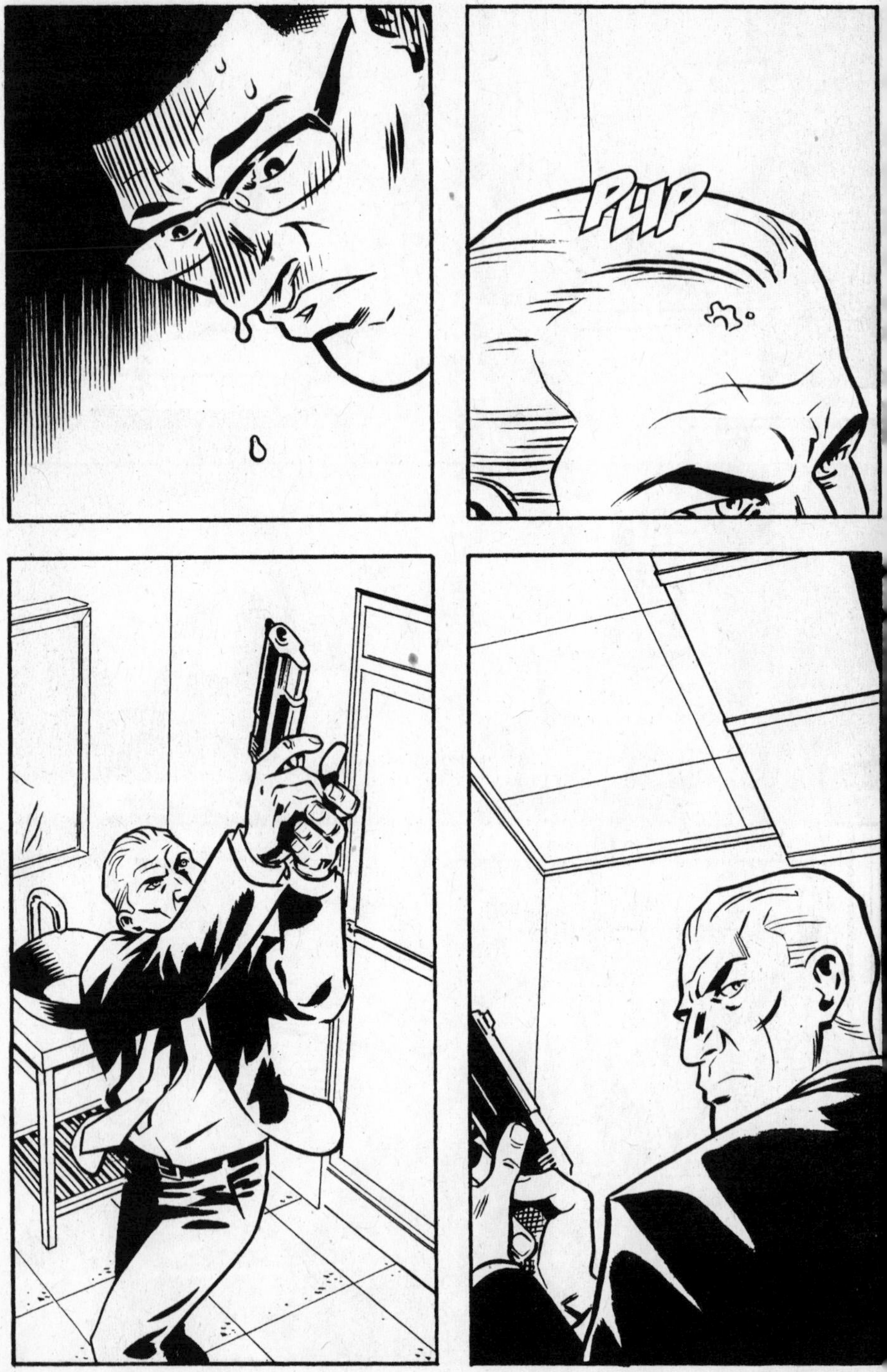
PLIP

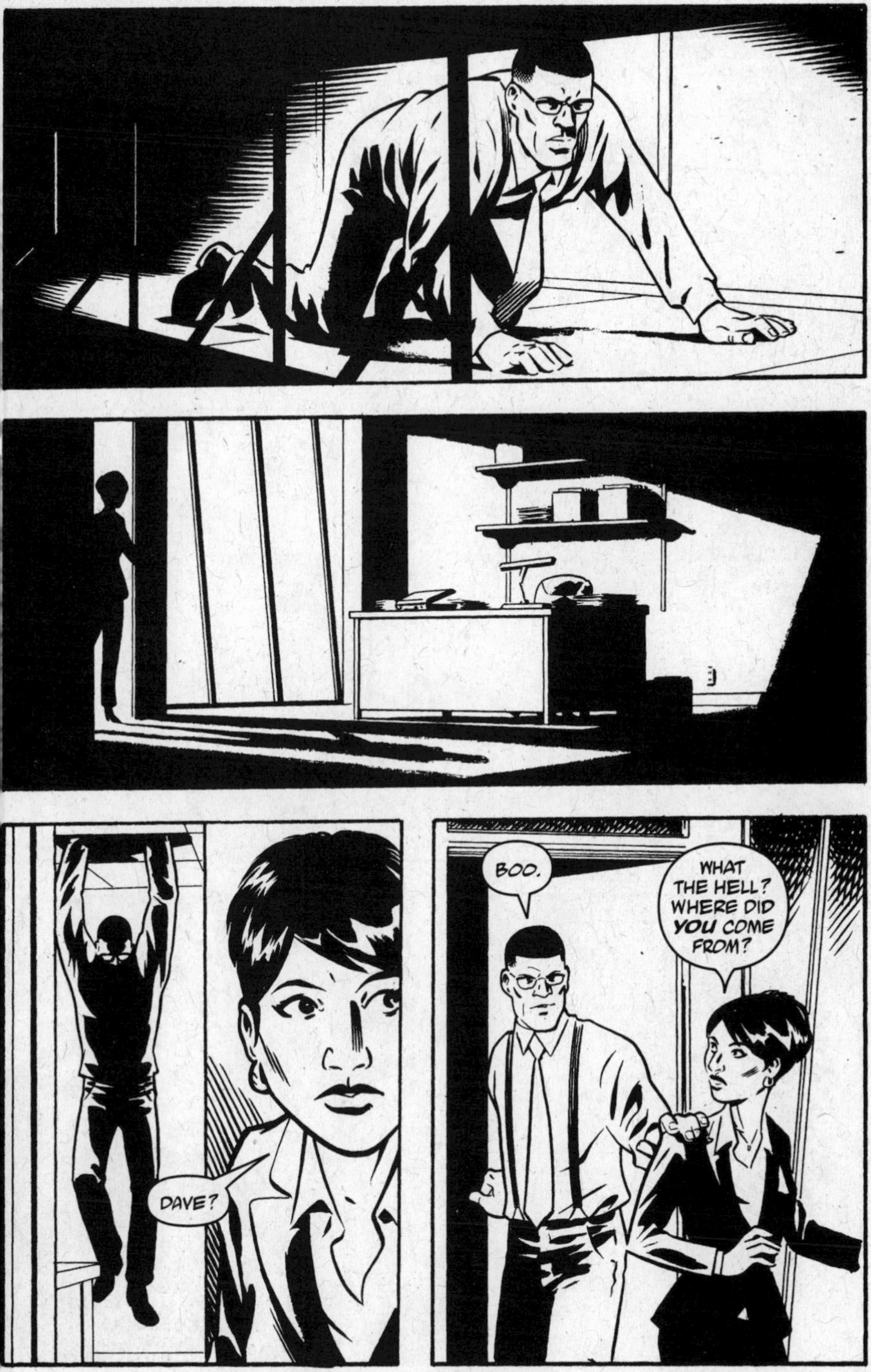
DAVE?
BOO.
WHAT THE HELL? WHERE DID YOU COME FROM?

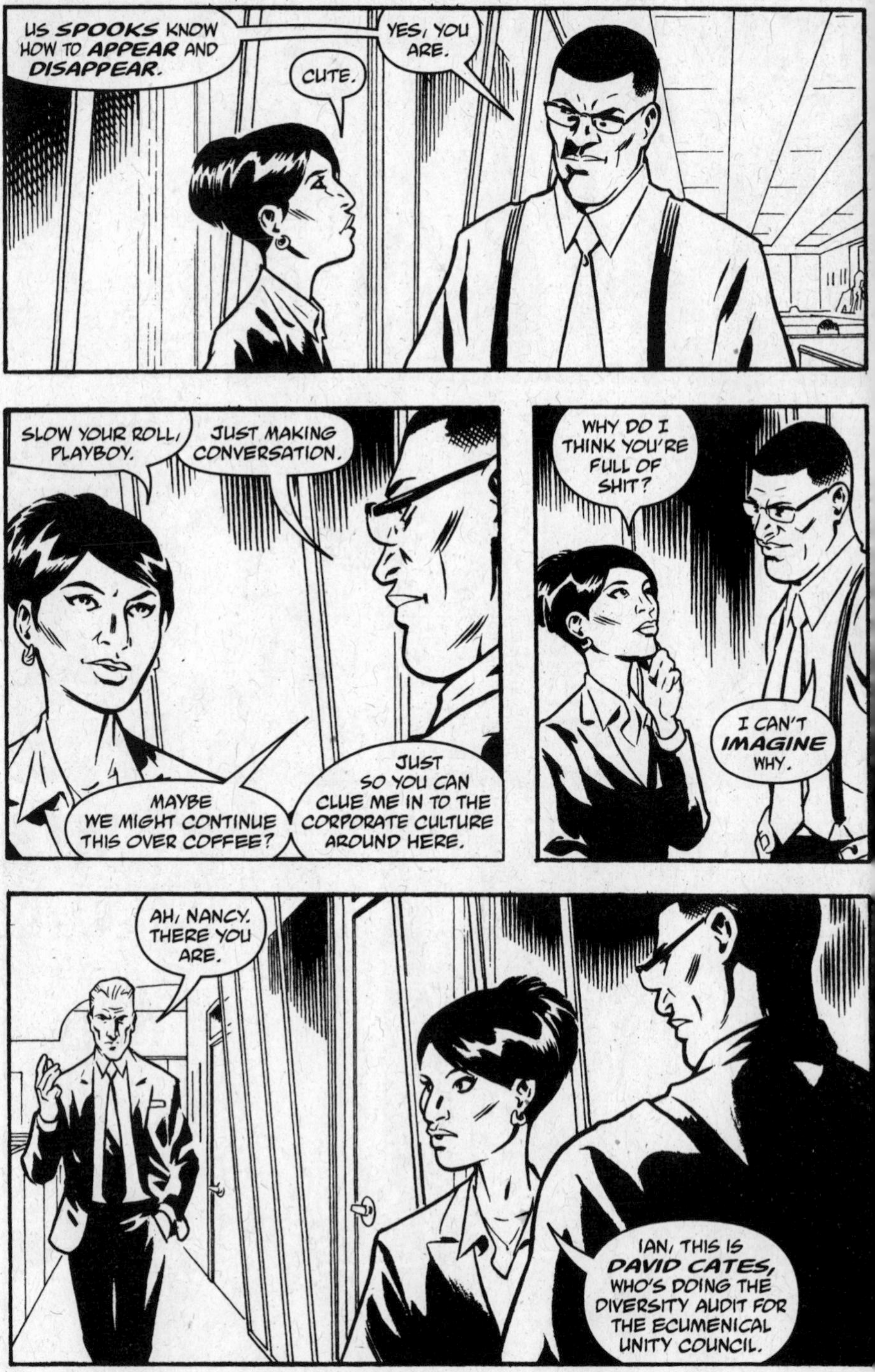
US SPOOKS KNOW HOW TO APPEAR AND DISAPPEAR.
YES, YOU ARE.
CUTE.
SLOW YOUR ROLL, PLAYBOY.
JUST MAKING CONVERSATION.
MAYBE WE MIGHT CONTINUE THIS OVER COFFEE?
JUST SO YOU CAN CLUE ME IN TO THE CORPORATE CULTURE AROUND HERE.
WHY DO I THINK YOU'RE FULL OF SHIT?
I CAN'T IMAGINE WHY.
AH, NANCY. THERE YOU ARE.
IAN, THIS IS DAVID CATES, WHO'S DOING THE DIVERSITY AUDIT FOR THE ECUMENICAL UNITY COUNCIL.

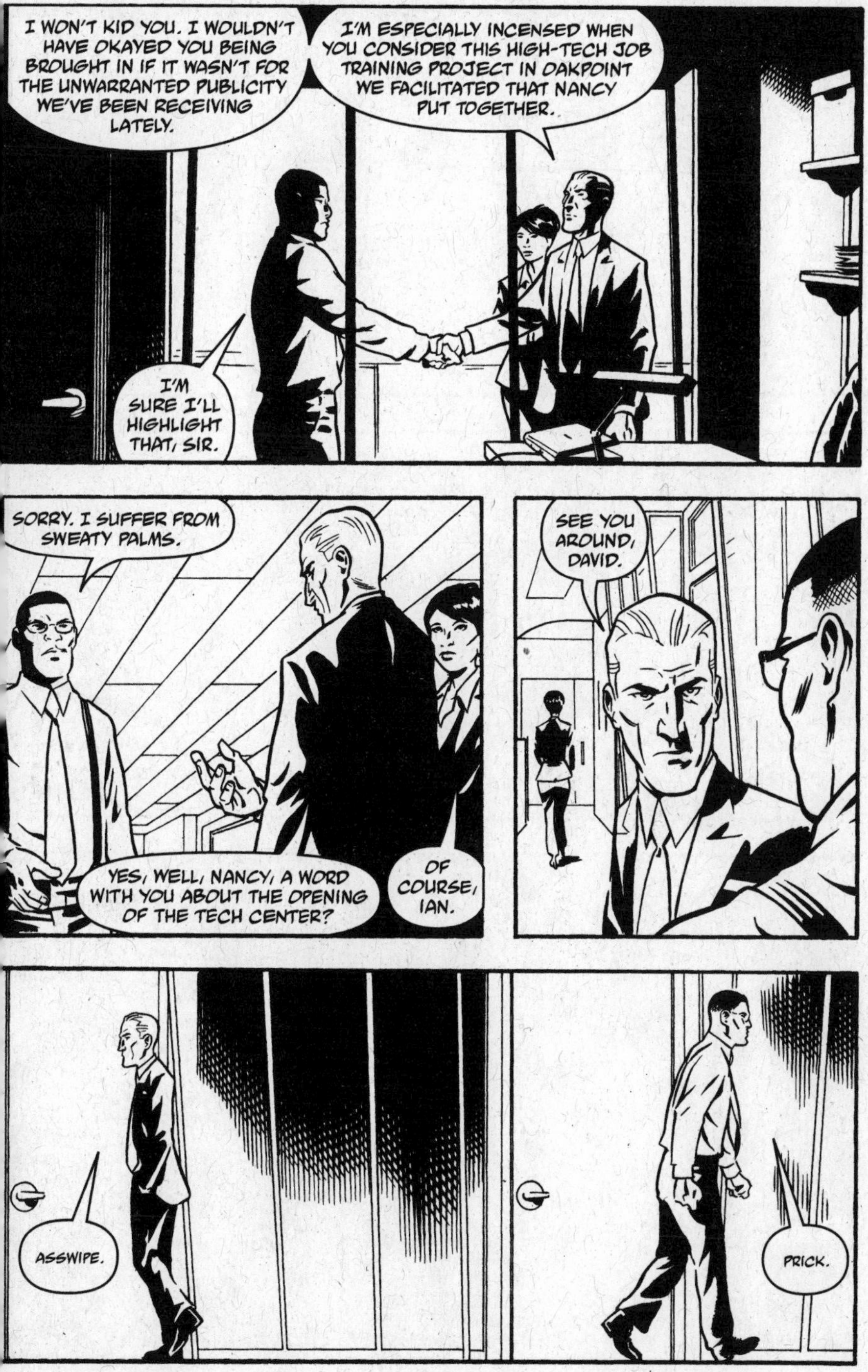

I WON'T KID YOU. I WOULDN'T HAVE OKAYED YOU BEING BROUGHT IN IF IT WASN'T FOR THE UNWARRANTED PUBLICITY WE'VE BEEN RECEIVING LATELY.
I'M ESPECIALLY INCENSED WHEN YOU CONSIDER THIS HIGH-TECH JOB TRAINING PROJECT IN OAKPOINT WE FACILITATED THAT NANCY PUT TOGETHER.
I'M SURE I'LL HIGHLIGHT THAT, SIR.
SORRY. I SUFFER FROM SWEATY PALMS.
YES, WELL, NANCY, A WORD WITH YOU ABOUT THE OPENING OF THE TECH CENTER?
OF COURSE, IAN.
SEE YOU AROUND, DAVID.
ASSWIPE.
PRICK.

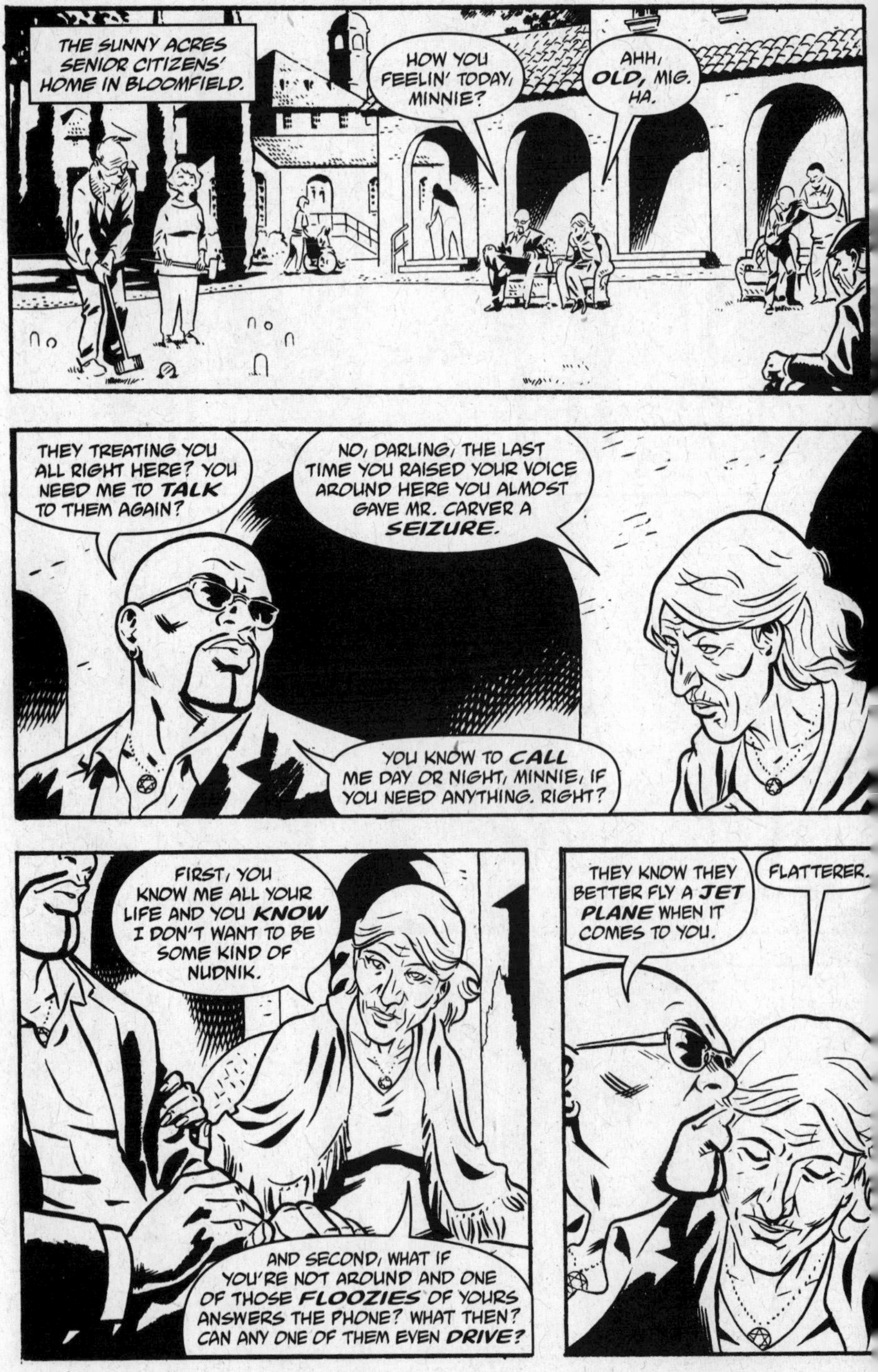
THE SUNNY ACRES SENIOR CITIZENS' HOME IN BLOOMFIELD.
HOW YOU FEELIN' TODAY, MINNIE?
AHH, OLD, MIG. HA.
THEY TREATING YOU ALL RIGHT HERE? YOU NEED ME TO TALK TO THEM AGAIN?
NO, DARLING, THE LAST TIME YOU RAISED YOUR VOICE AROUND HERE YOU ALMOST GAVE MR. CARVER A SEIZURE.
YOU KNOW TO CALL ME DAY OR NIGHT, MINNIE, IF YOU NEED ANYTHING. RIGHT?
FIRST, YOU KNOW ME ALL YOUR LIFE AND YOU KNOW I DON'T WANT TO BE SOME KIND OF NUDNIK.
AND SECOND, WHAT IF YOU'RE NOT AROUND AND ONE OF THOSE FLOOZIES OF YOURS ANSWERS THE PHONE? WHAT THEN? CAN ANY ONE OF THEM EVEN DRIVE?
THEY KNOW THEY BETTER FLY A JET PLANE WHEN IT COMES TO YOU.
FLATTERER.

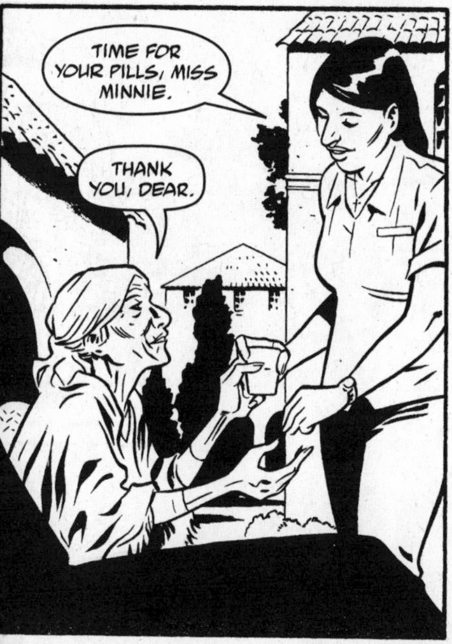
TIME FOR YOUR PILLS, MISS MINNIE.
THANK YOU, DEAR.

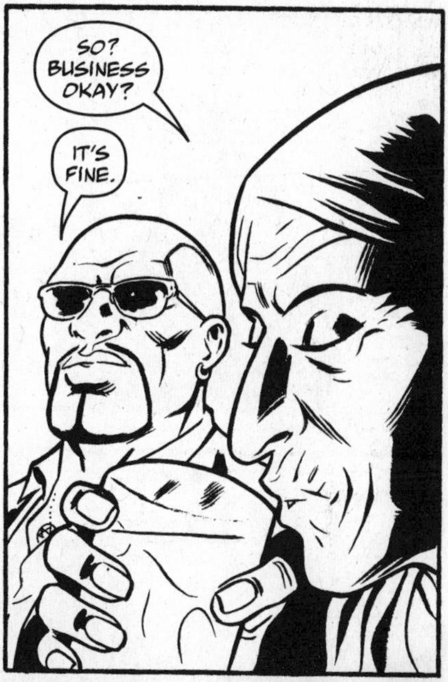
SO? BUSINESS OKAY?
IT'S FINE.

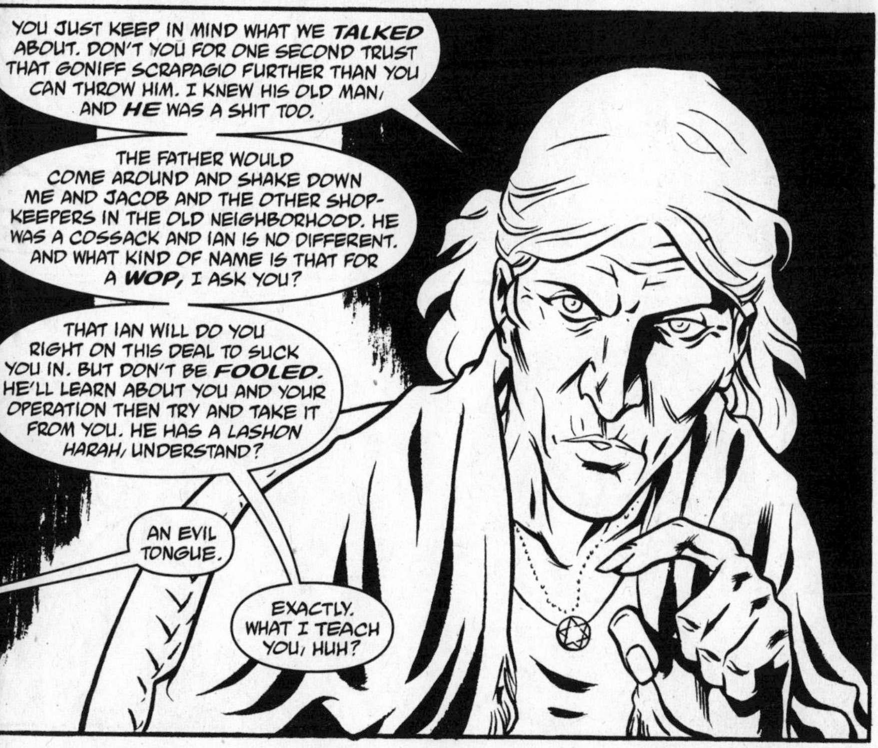
YOU JUST KEEP IN MIND WHAT WE TALKED ABOUT. DON'T YOU FOR ONE SECOND TRUST THAT GONIFF SCRAPAGIO FURTHER THAN YOU CAN THROW HIM. I KNEW HIS OLD MAN, AND HE WAS A SHIT TOO.
THE FATHER WOULD COME AROUND AND SHAKE DOWN ME AND JACOB AND THE OTHER SHOP-KEEPERS IN THE OLD NEIGHBORHOOD. HE WAS A COSSACK AND IAN IS NO DIFFERENT. AND WHAT KIND OF NAME IS THAT FOR A WOP, I ASK YOU?
THAT IAN WILL DO YOU RIGHT ON THIS DEAL TO SUCK YOU IN. BUT DON'T BE FOOLED. HE'LL LEARN ABOUT YOU AND YOUR OPERATION THEN TRY AND TAKE IT FROM YOU. HE HAS A LASHON HARAH, UNDERSTAND?
AN EVIL TONGUE.
EXACTLY. WHAT I TEACH YOU, HUH?

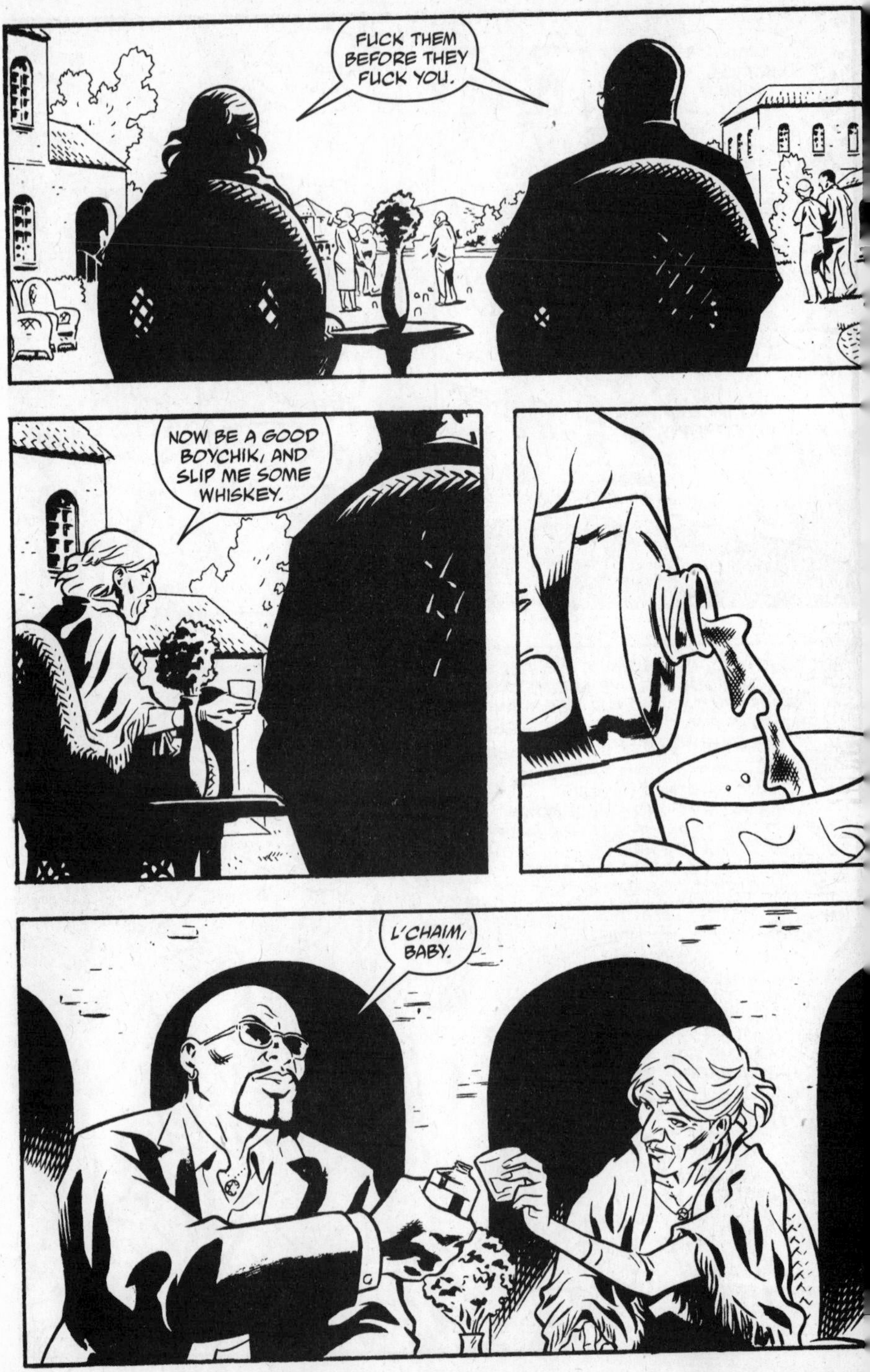
FUCK THEM BEFORE THEY FUCK YOU.
NOW BE A GOOD BOYCHIK, AND SLIP ME SOME WHISKEY.
L'CHAIM, BABY.

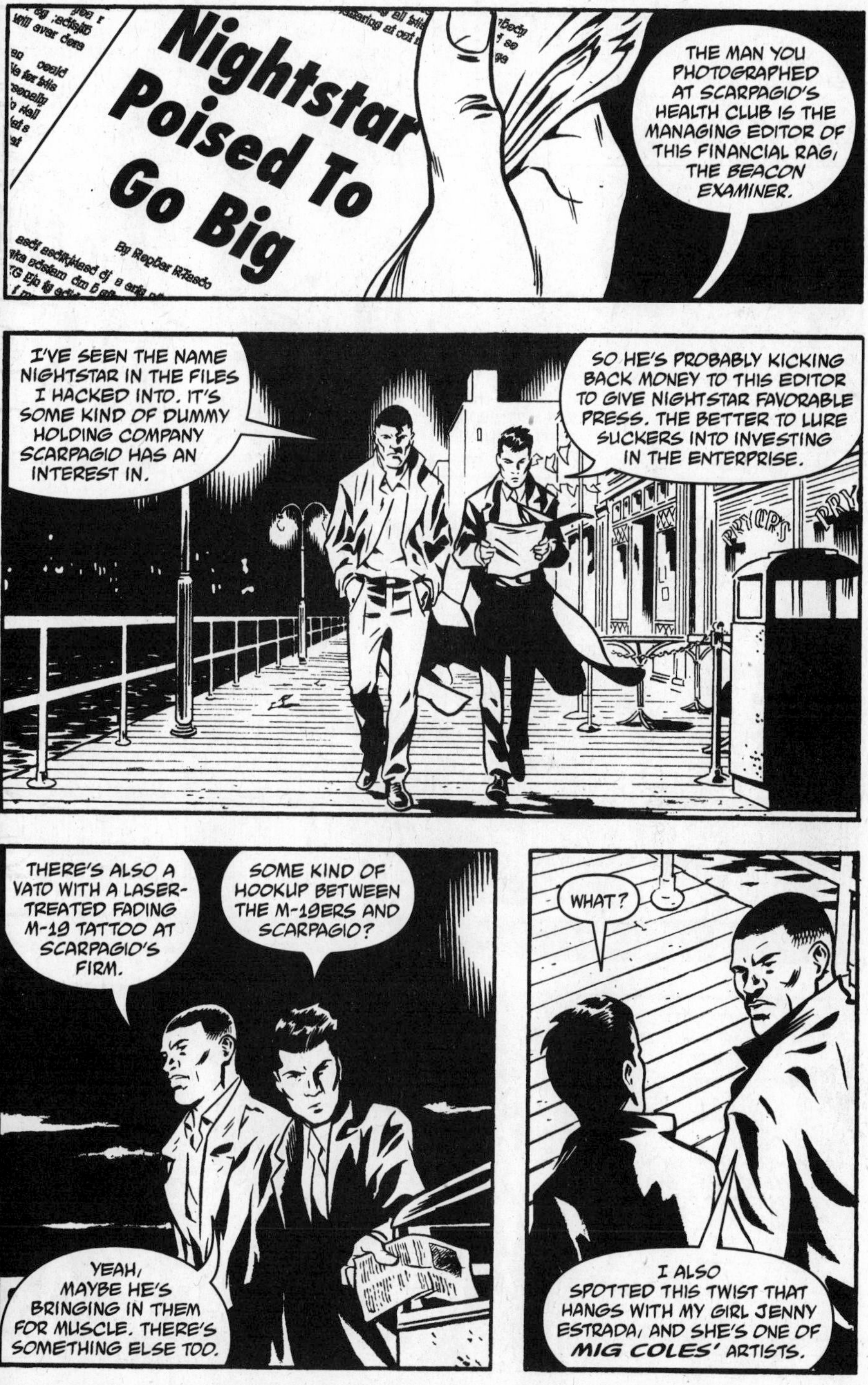
Nightstar Poised To Go Big
THE MAN YOU PHOTOGRAPHED AT SCARPAGIO'S HEALTH CLUB IS THE MANAGING EDITOR OF THIS FINANCIAL RAG, THE *BEACON EXAMINER.*
I'VE SEEN THE NAME NIGHTSTAR IN THE FILES I HACKED INTO. IT'S SOME KIND OF DUMMY HOLDING COMPANY SCARPAGIO HAS AN INTEREST IN.
SO HE'S PROBABLY KICKING BACK MONEY TO THIS EDITOR TO GIVE NIGHTSTAR FAVORABLE PRESS. THE BETTER TO LURE SUCKERS INTO INVESTING IN THE ENTERPRISE.
THERE'S ALSO A VATO WITH A LASER-TREATED FADING M-19 TATTOO AT SCARPAGIO'S FIRM.
SOME KIND OF HOOKUP BETWEEN THE M-19ERS AND SCARPAGIO?
YEAH, MAYBE HE'S BRINGING IN THEM FOR MUSCLE. THERE'S SOMETHING ELSE TOO.
WHAT?
I ALSO SPOTTED THIS TWIST THAT HANGS WITH MY GIRL JENNY ESTRADA, AND SHE'S ONE OF ***MIG COLES'*** ARTISTS.

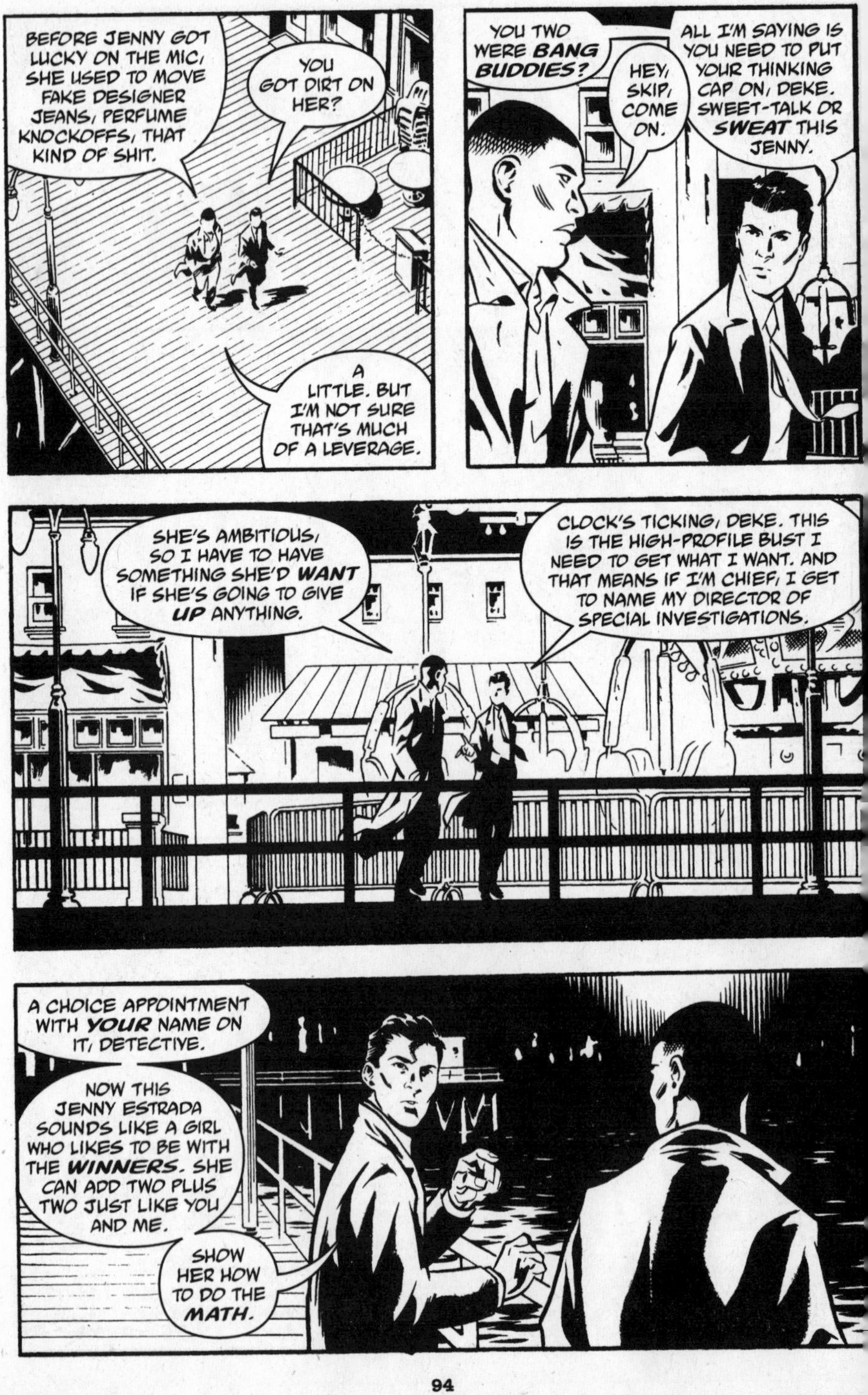
BEFORE JENNY GOT LUCKY ON THE MIC, SHE USED TO MOVE FAKE DESIGNER JEANS, PERFUME KNOCKOFFS, THAT KIND OF SHIT.
YOU GOT DIRT ON HER?
A LITTLE. BUT I'M NOT SURE THAT'S MUCH OF A LEVERAGE.
YOU TWO WERE BANG BUDDIES?
HEY, SKIP, COME ON.
ALL I'M SAYING IS YOU NEED TO PUT YOUR THINKING CAP ON, DEKE. SWEET-TALK OR SWEAT THIS JENNY.
SHE'S AMBITIOUS, SO I HAVE TO HAVE SOMETHING SHE'D WANT IF SHE'S GOING TO GIVE UP ANYTHING.
CLOCK'S TICKING, DEKE. THIS IS THE HIGH-PROFILE BUST I NEED TO GET WHAT I WANT. AND THAT MEANS IF I'M CHIEF, I GET TO NAME MY DIRECTOR OF SPECIAL INVESTIGATIONS.
A CHOICE APPOINTMENT WITH YOUR NAME ON IT, DETECTIVE.
NOW THIS JENNY ESTRADA SOUNDS LIKE A GIRL WHO LIKES TO BE WITH THE WINNERS. SHE CAN ADD TWO PLUS TWO JUST LIKE YOU AND ME.
SHOW HER HOW TO DO THE MATH.

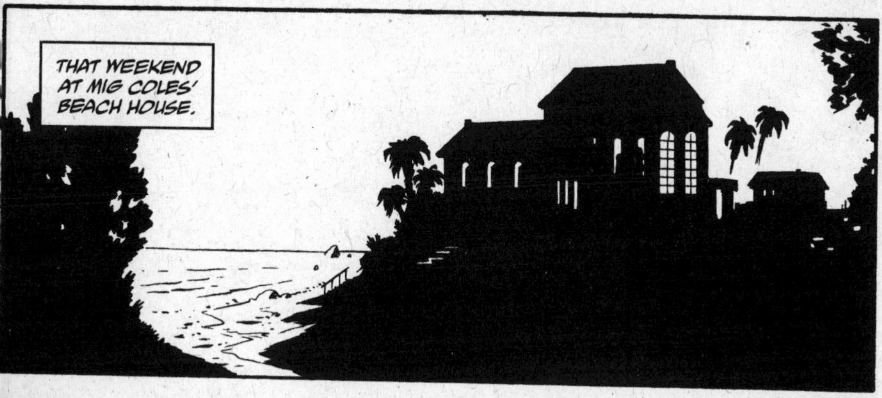
THAT WEEKEND AT MIG COLES' BEACH HOUSE.

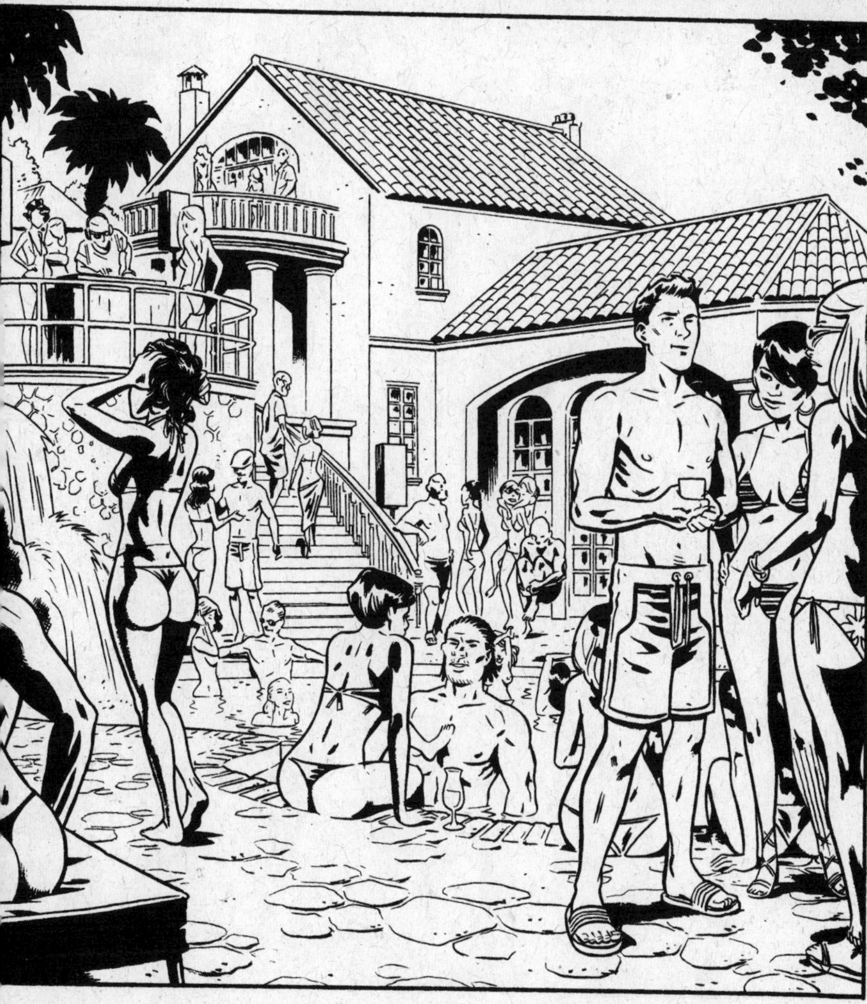

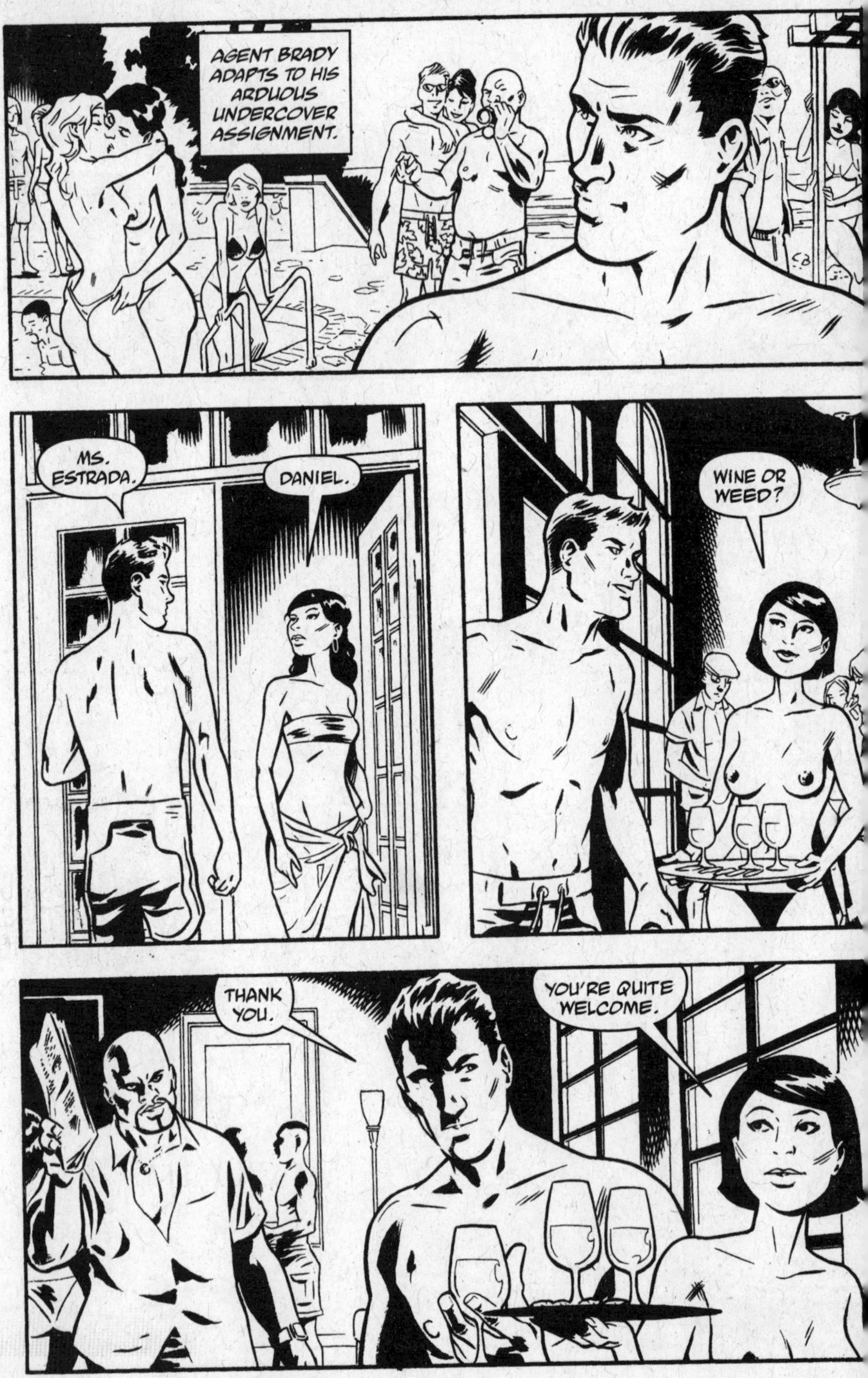
AGENT BRADY ADAPTS TO HIS ARDUOUS UNDERCOVER ASSIGNMENT.
MS. ESTRADA.
DANIEL.
WINE OR WEED?
THANK YOU.
YOU'RE QUITE WELCOME.

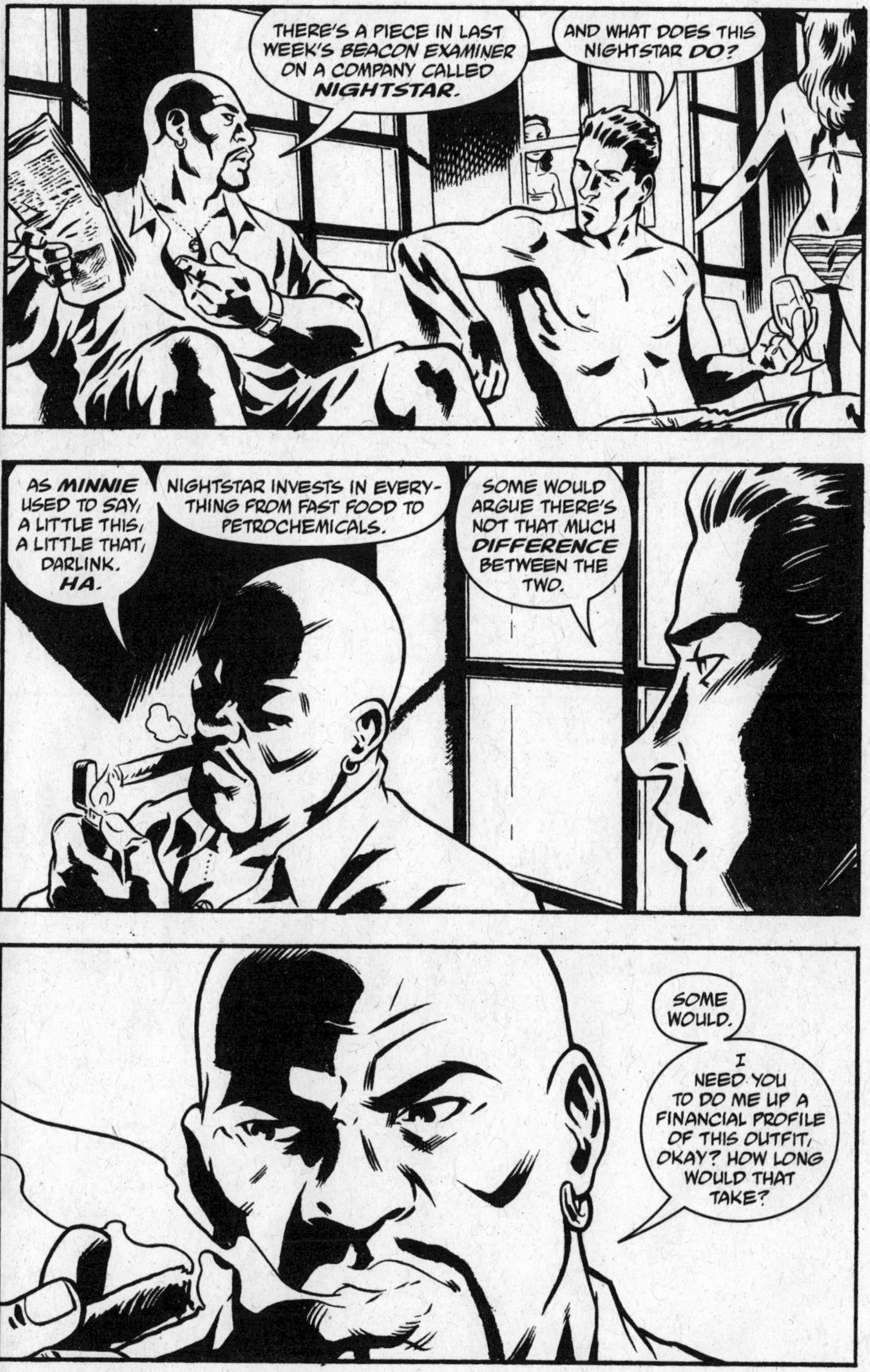
THERE'S A PIECE IN LAST WEEK'S BEACON EXAMINER ON A COMPANY CALLED NIGHTSTAR.
AND WHAT DOES THIS NIGHTSTAR DO?
AS MINNIE USED TO SAY, A LITTLE THIS, A LITTLE THAT, DARLINK. HA.
NIGHTSTAR INVESTS IN EVERYTHING FROM FAST FOOD TO PETROCHEMICALS.
SOME WOULD ARGUE THERE'S NOT THAT MUCH DIFFERENCE BETWEEN THE TWO.
SOME WOULD.
I NEED YOU TO DO ME UP A FINANCIAL PROFILE OF THIS OUTFIT, OKAY? HOW LONG WOULD THAT TAKE?

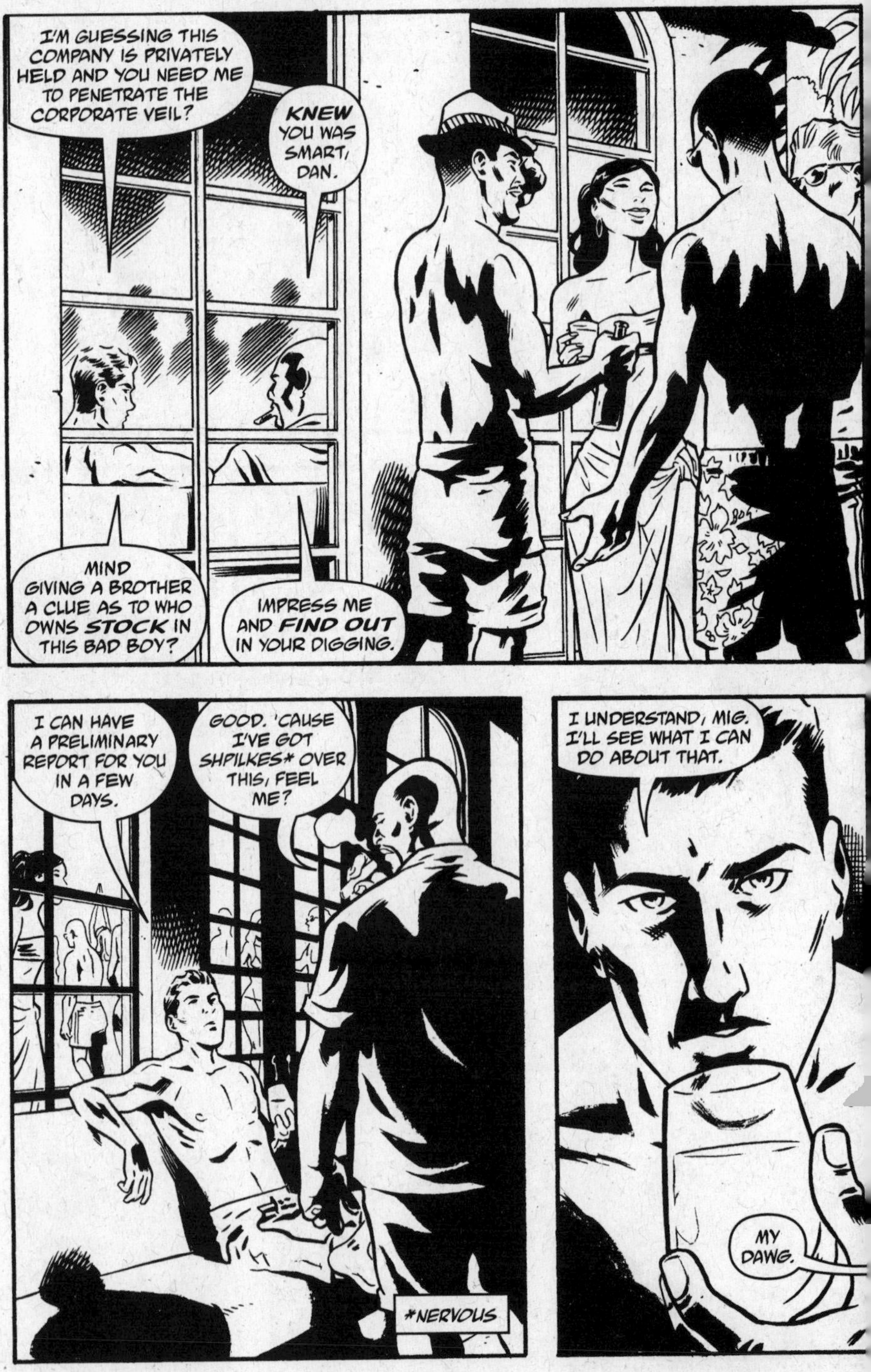
I'M GUESSING THIS COMPANY IS PRIVATELY HELD AND YOU NEED ME TO PENETRATE THE CORPORATE VEIL?
KNEW YOU WAS SMART, DAN.
MIND GIVING A BROTHER A CLUE AS TO WHO OWNS STOCK IN THIS BAD BOY?
IMPRESS ME AND FIND OUT IN YOUR DIGGING.
I CAN HAVE A PRELIMINARY REPORT FOR YOU IN A FEW DAYS.
GOOD. 'CAUSE I'VE GOT SHPILKES* OVER THIS, FEEL ME?
*NERVOUS
I UNDERSTAND, MIG. I'LL SEE WHAT I CAN DO ABOUT THAT.
MY DAWG.

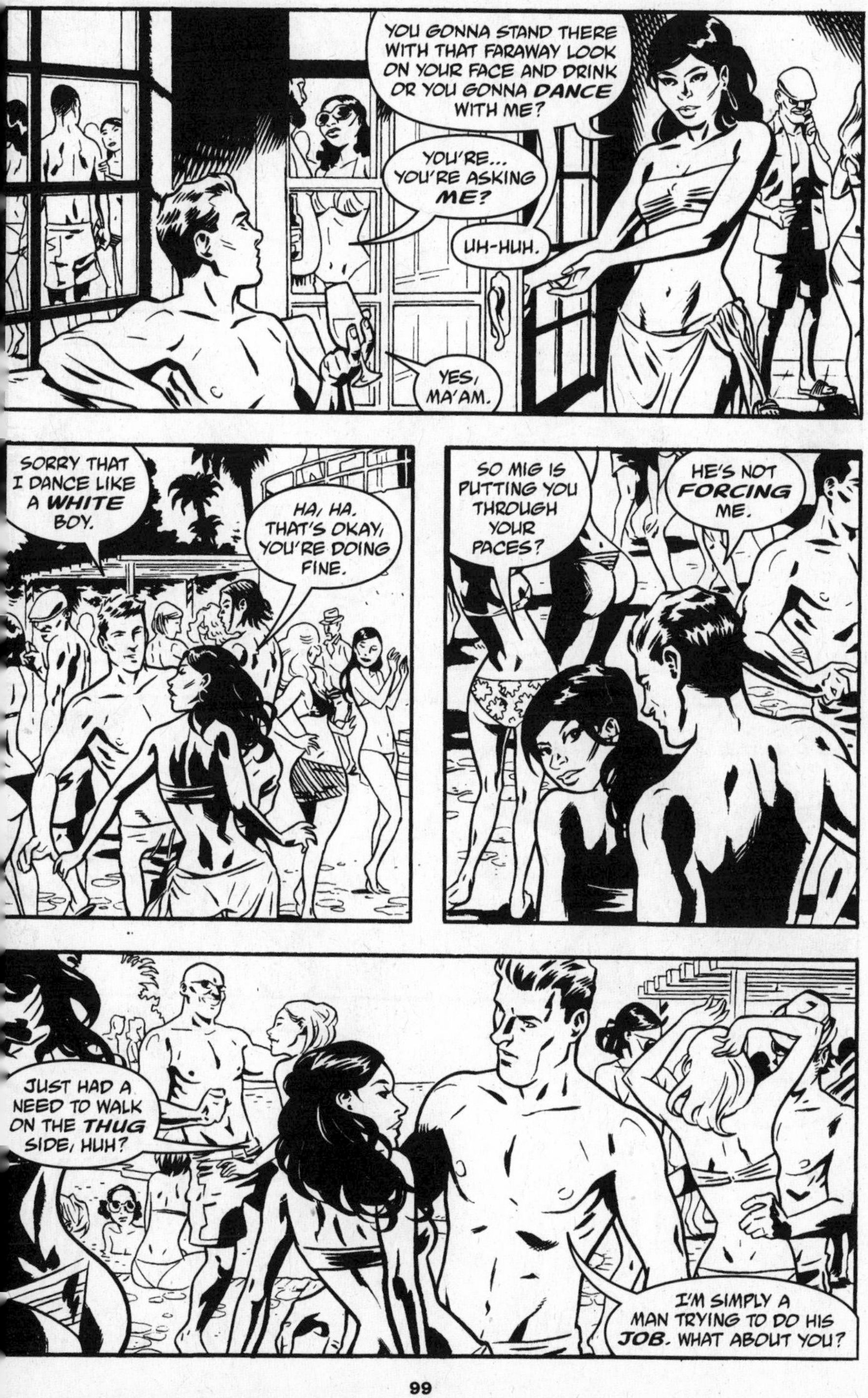
YOU GONNA STAND THERE WITH THAT FARAWAY LOOK ON YOUR FACE AND DRINK OR YOU GONNA DANCE WITH ME?
YOU'RE... YOU'RE ASKING ME?
UH-HUH.
YES, MA'AM.
SORRY THAT I DANCE LIKE A WHITE BOY.
HA, HA. THAT'S OKAY, YOU'RE DOING FINE.
SO MIG IS PUTTING YOU THROUGH YOUR PACES?
HE'S NOT FORCING ME.
JUST HAD A NEED TO WALK ON THE THUG SIDE, HUH?
I'M SIMPLY A MAN TRYING TO DO HIS JOB. WHAT ABOUT YOU?

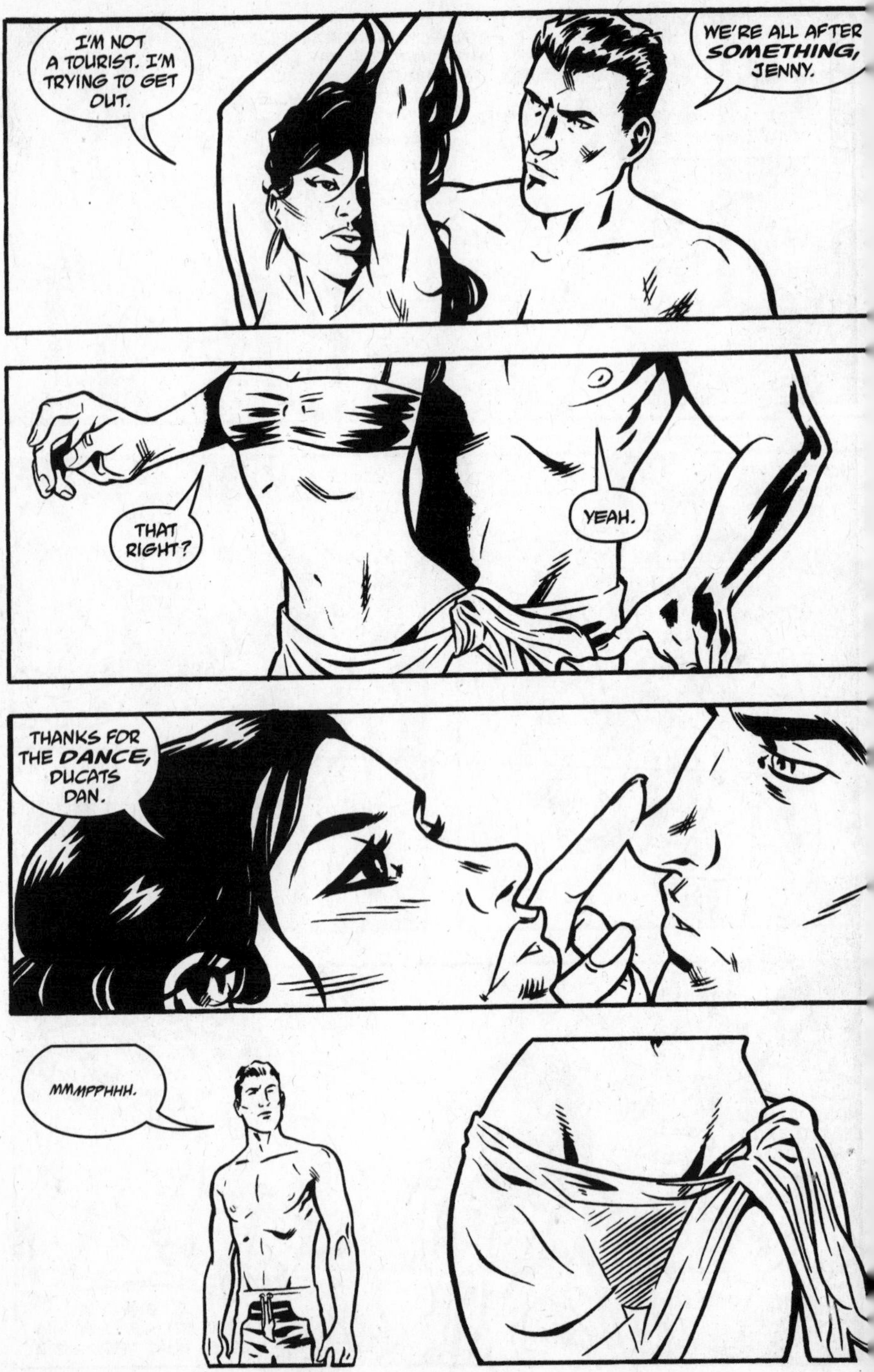
I'M NOT A TOURIST. I'M TRYING TO GET OUT.
WE'RE ALL AFTER *SOMETHING,* JENNY.
THAT RIGHT?
YEAH.
THANKS FOR THE *DANCE,* DUCATS DAN.
MMMPPHHH.

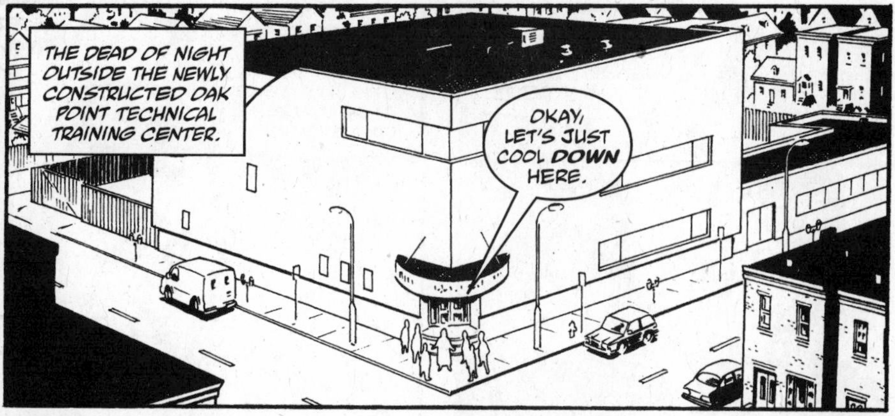
THE DEAD OF NIGHT OUTSIDE THE NEWLY CONSTRUCTED OAK POINT TECHNICAL TRAINING CENTER.
OKAY, LET'S JUST COOL DOWN HERE.

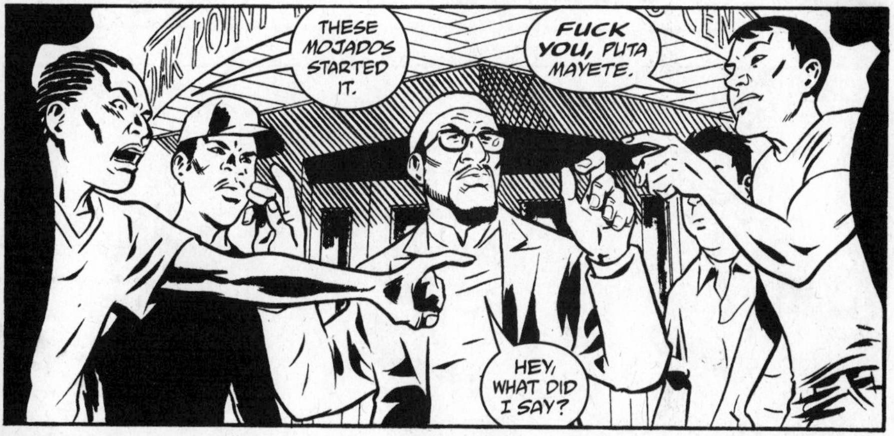
THESE MOJADOS STARTED IT.
FUCK YOU, PUTA MAYETE.
HEY, WHAT DID I SAY?

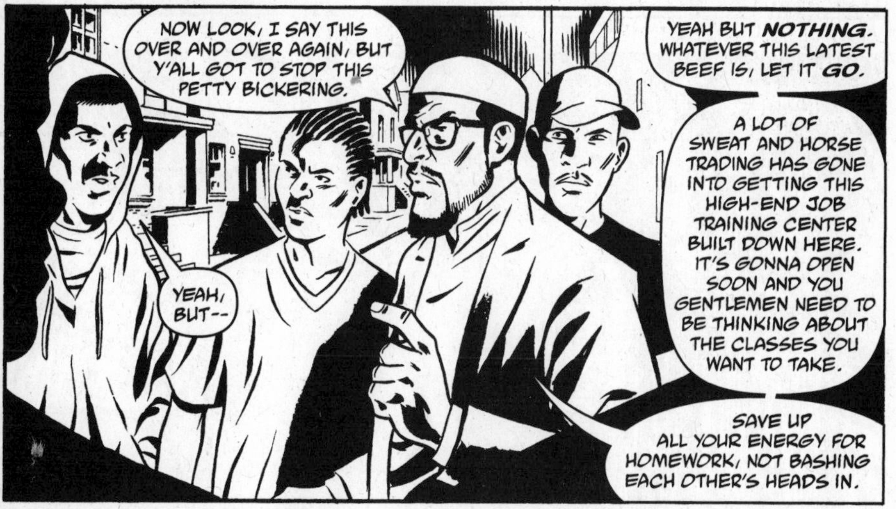
NOW LOOK, I SAY THIS OVER AND OVER AGAIN, BUT Y'ALL GOT TO STOP THIS PETTY BICKERING.
YEAH, BUT--
YEAH BUT NOTHING. WHATEVER THIS LATEST BEEF IS, LET IT GO.
A LOT OF SWEAT AND HORSE TRADING HAS GONE INTO GETTING THIS HIGH-END JOB TRAINING CENTER BUILT DOWN HERE. IT'S GONNA OPEN SOON AND YOU GENTLEMEN NEED TO BE THINKING ABOUT THE CLASSES YOU WANT TO TAKE.
SAVE UP ALL YOUR ENERGY FOR HOMEWORK, NOT BASHING EACH OTHER'S HEADS IN.

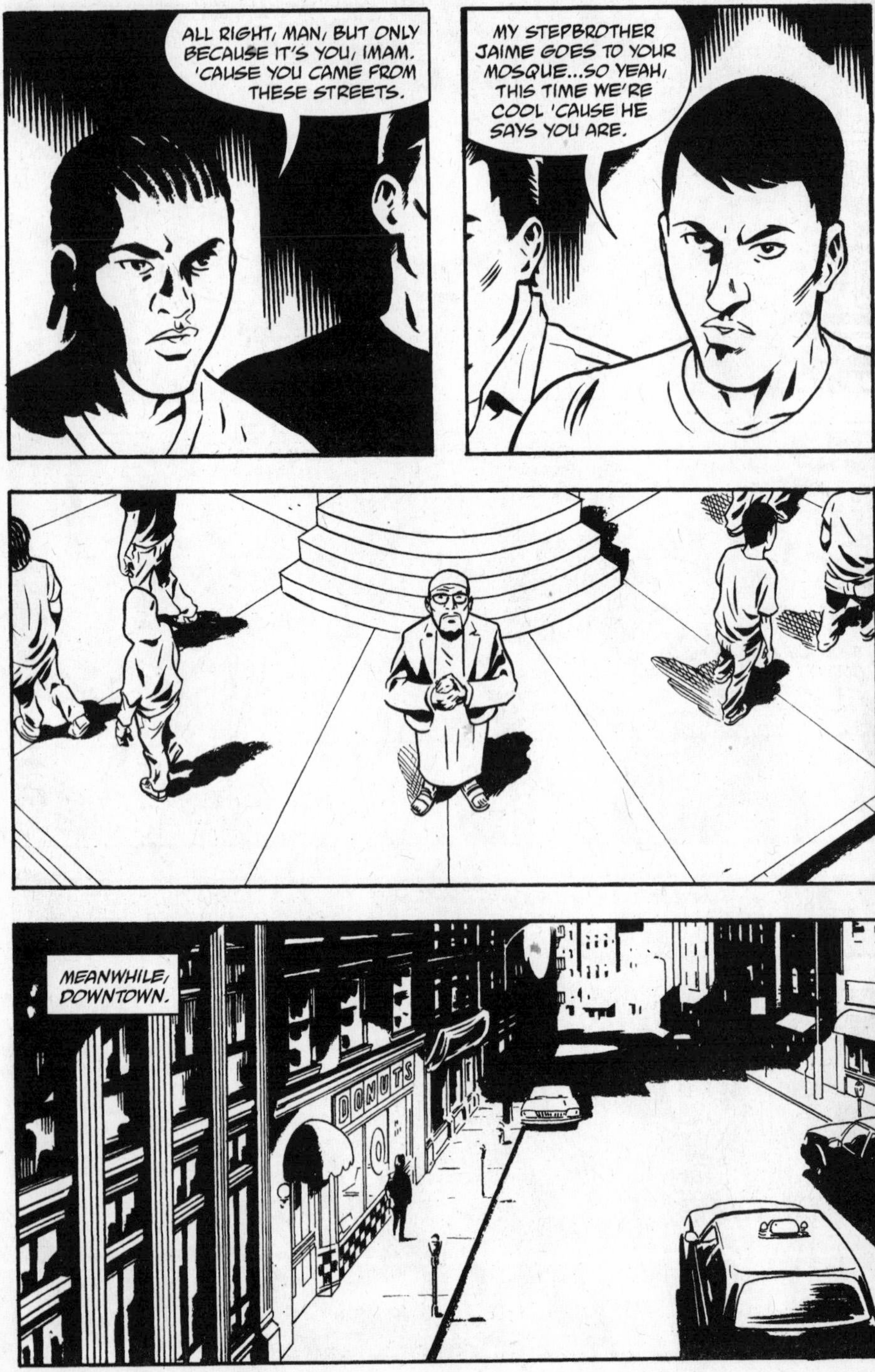
ALL RIGHT, MAN, BUT ONLY BECAUSE IT'S YOU, IMAM. 'CAUSE YOU CAME FROM THESE STREETS.
MY STEPBROTHER JAIME GOES TO YOUR MOSQUE...SO YEAH, THIS TIME WE'RE COOL 'CAUSE HE SAYS YOU ARE.
MEANWHILE, DOWNTOWN.
DONUTS

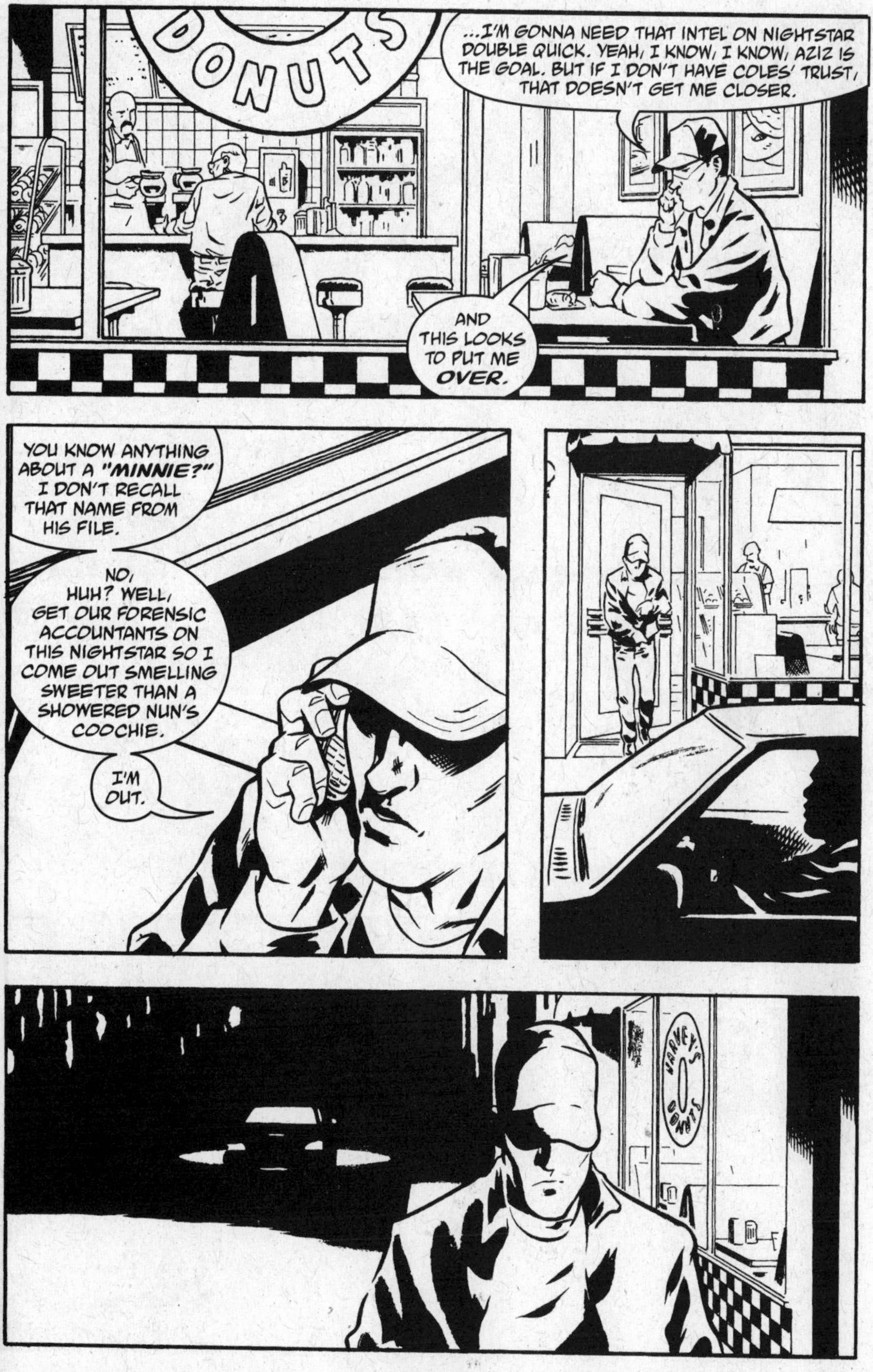
DONUTS
...I'M GONNA NEED THAT INTEL ON NIGHTSTAR DOUBLE QUICK. YEAH, I KNOW, I KNOW, AZIZ IS THE GOAL. BUT IF I DON'T HAVE COLES' TRUST, THAT DOESN'T GET ME CLOSER.
AND THIS LOOKS TO PUT ME *OVER.*
YOU KNOW ANYTHING ABOUT A *"MINNIE?"* I DON'T RECALL THAT NAME FROM HIS FILE.
NO, HUH? WELL, GET OUR FORENSIC ACCOUNTANTS ON THIS NIGHTSTAR SO I COME OUT SMELLING SWEETER THAN A SHOWERED NUN'S COOCHIE.
I'M OUT.
HARVEY'S DONUTS

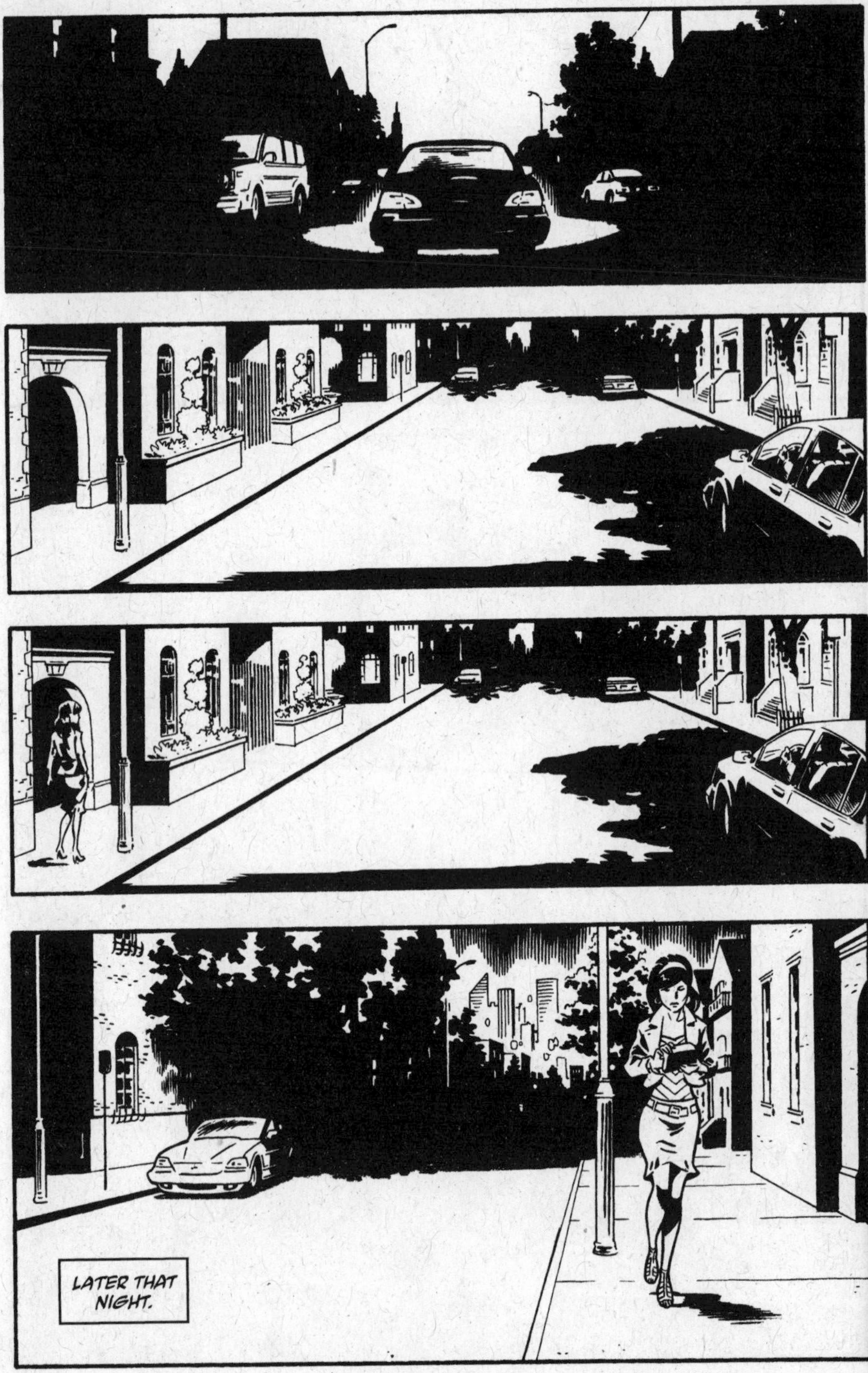
LATER THAT NIGHT.

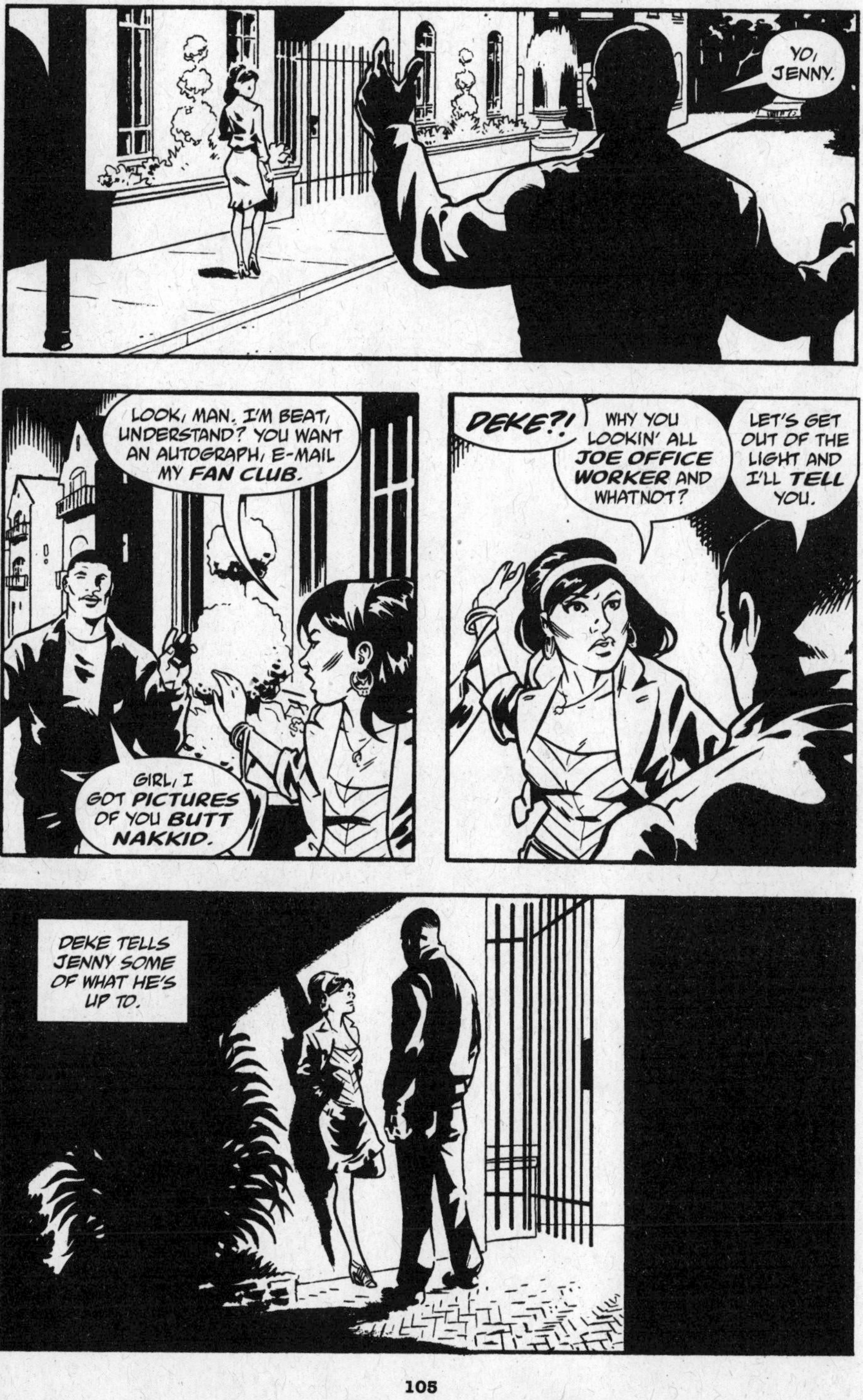
YO, JENNY.
LOOK, MAN. I'M BEAT, UNDERSTAND? YOU WANT AN AUTOGRAPH, E-MAIL MY FAN CLUB.
GIRL, I GOT PICTURES OF YOU BUTT NAKKID.
DEKE?!
WHY YOU LOOKIN' ALL JOE OFFICE WORKER AND WHATNOT?
LET'S GET OUT OF THE LIGHT AND I'LL TELL YOU.
DEKE TELLS JENNY SOME OF WHAT HE'S UP TO.

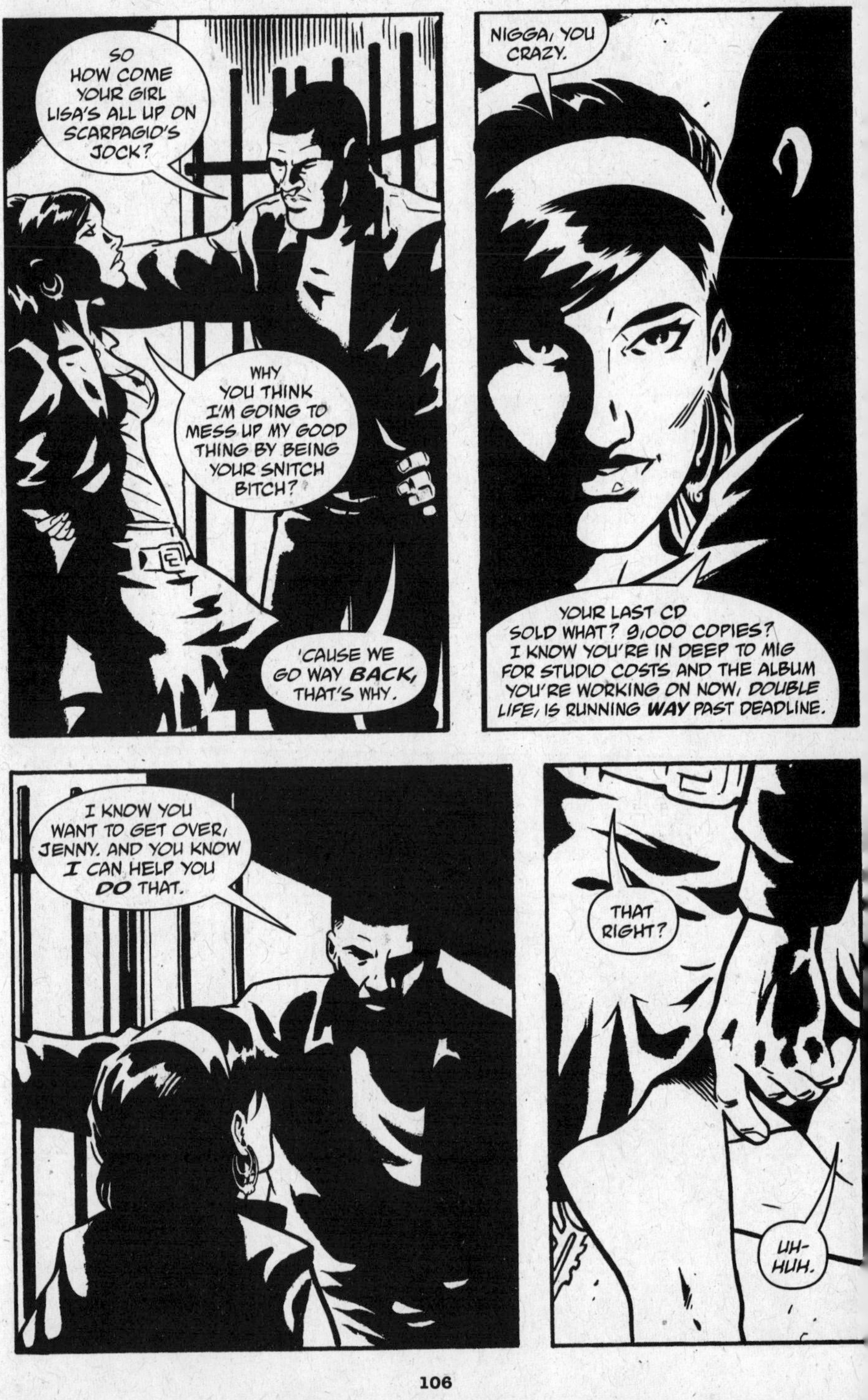
SO HOW COME YOUR GIRL LISA'S ALL UP ON SCARPAGIO'S JOCK?
WHY YOU THINK I'M GOING TO MESS UP MY GOOD THING BY BEING YOUR SNITCH BITCH?
'CAUSE WE GO WAY **BACK**, THAT'S WHY.
NIGGA, YOU CRAZY.
YOUR LAST CD SOLD WHAT? 9,000 COPIES? I KNOW YOU'RE IN DEEP TO MIG FOR STUDIO COSTS AND THE ALBUM YOU'RE WORKING ON NOW, *DOUBLE LIFE*, IS RUNNING **WAY** PAST DEADLINE.
I KNOW YOU WANT TO GET OVER, JENNY. AND YOU KNOW *I* CAN HELP YOU **DO** THAT.
THAT RIGHT?
UH-HUH.

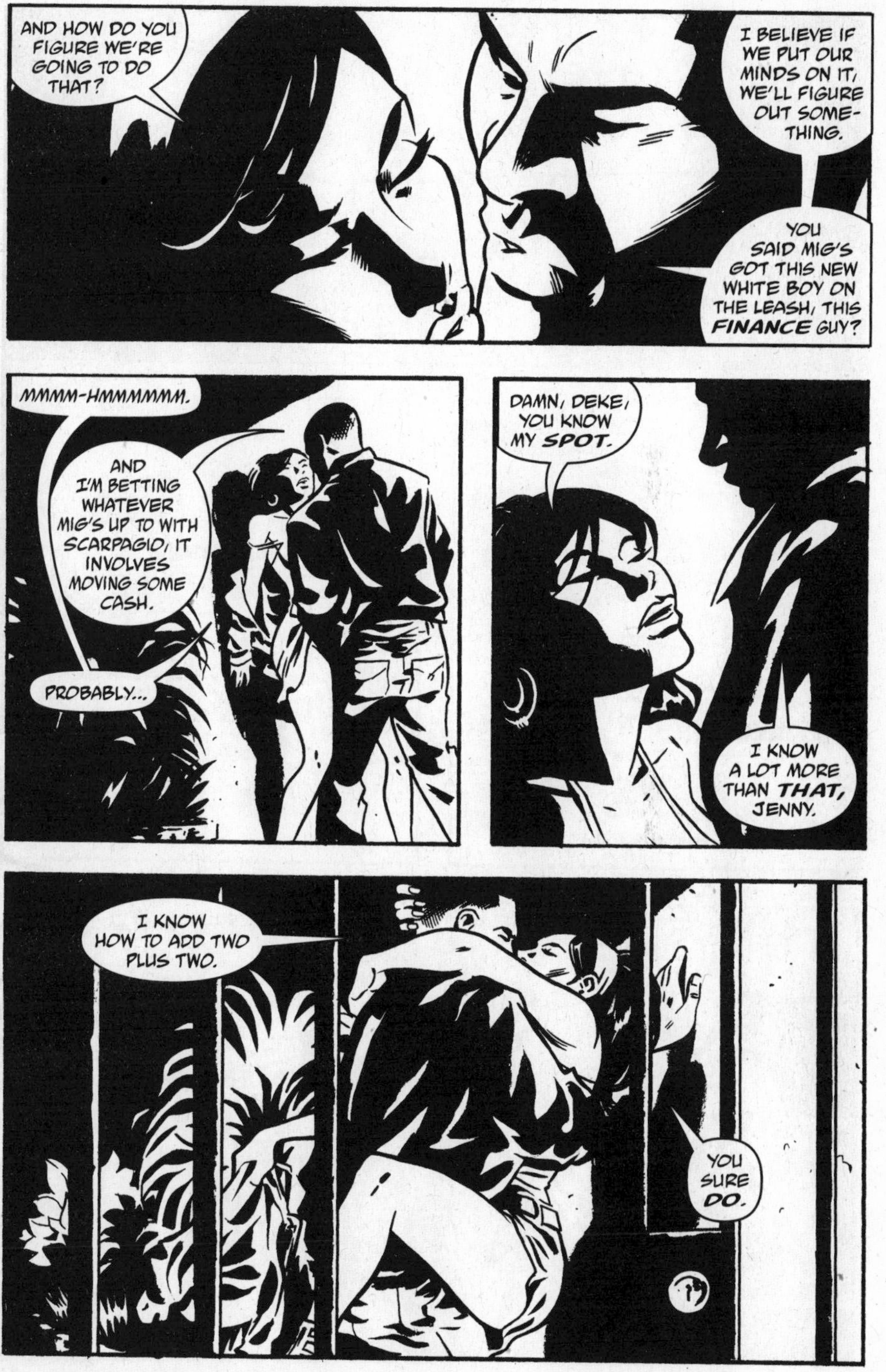
AND HOW DO YOU FIGURE WE'RE GOING TO DO THAT?
I BELIEVE IF WE PUT OUR MINDS ON IT, WE'LL FIGURE OUT SOME-THING.
YOU SAID MIG'S GOT THIS NEW WHITE BOY ON THE LEASH, THIS ***FINANCE*** GUY?
MMMM-HMMMMMM.
AND I'M BETTING WHATEVER MIG'S UP TO WITH SCARPAGIO, IT INVOLVES MOVING SOME CASH.
PROBABLY...
DAMN, DEKE, YOU KNOW MY ***SPOT***.
I KNOW A LOT MORE THAN ***THAT,*** JENNY.
I KNOW HOW TO ADD TWO PLUS TWO.
YOU SURE ***DO***.

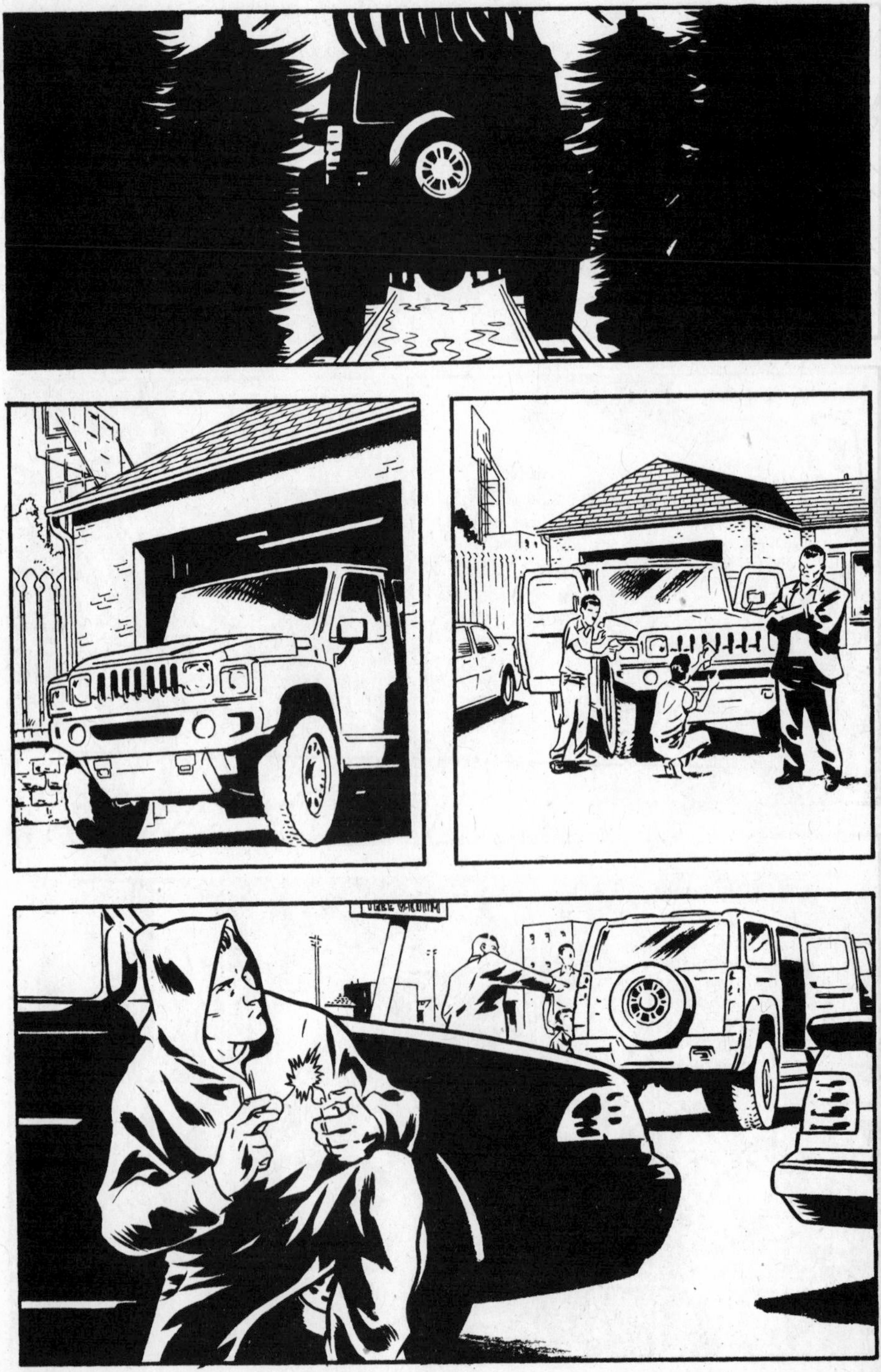

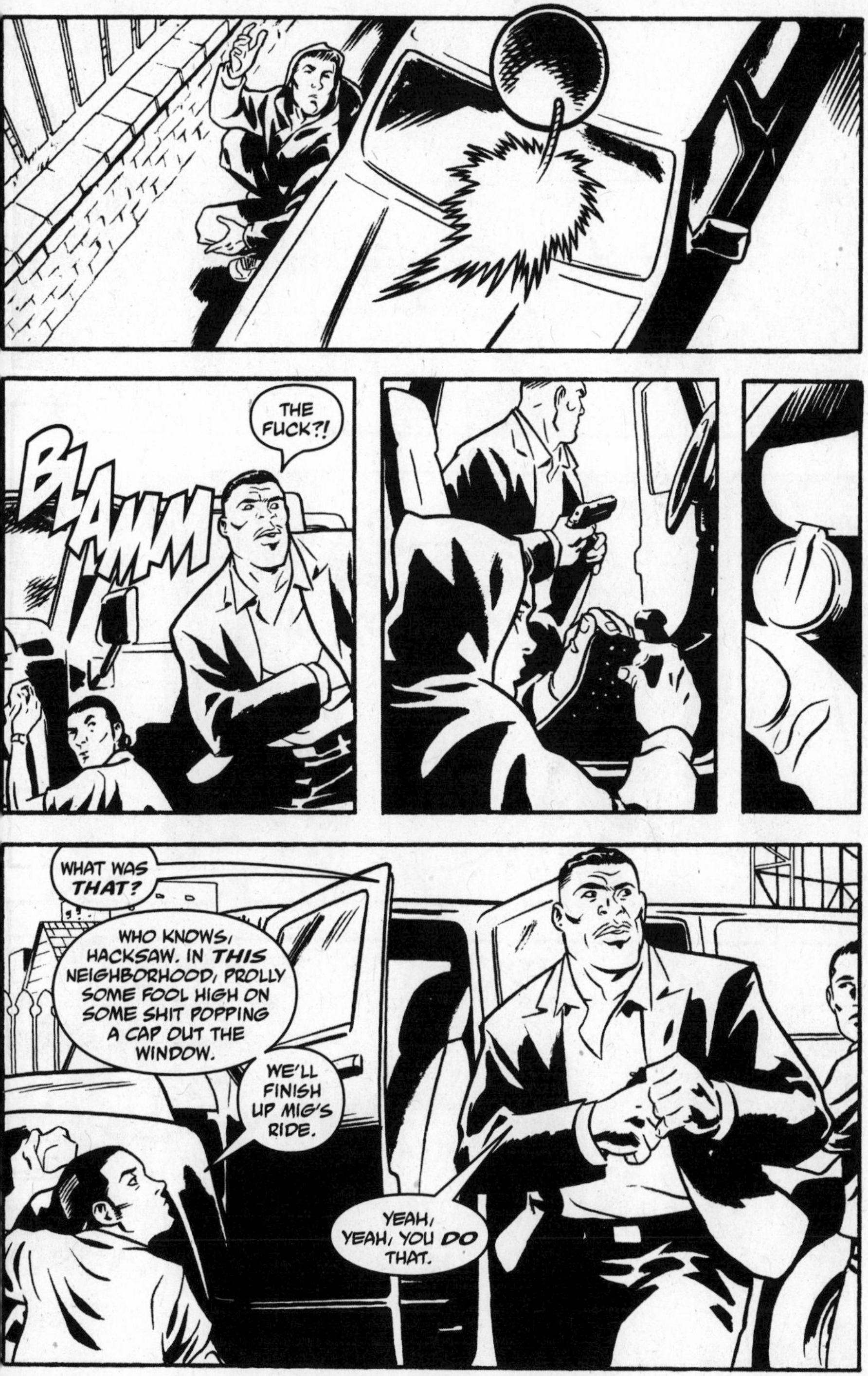

BLAMM
THE FUCK?!
WHAT WAS THAT?
WHO KNOWS, HACKSAW. IN THIS NEIGHBORHOOD, PROLLY SOME FOOL HIGH ON SOME SHIT POPPING A CAP OUT THE WINDOW.
WE'LL FINISH UP MIG'S RIDE.
YEAH, YEAH, YOU DO THAT.

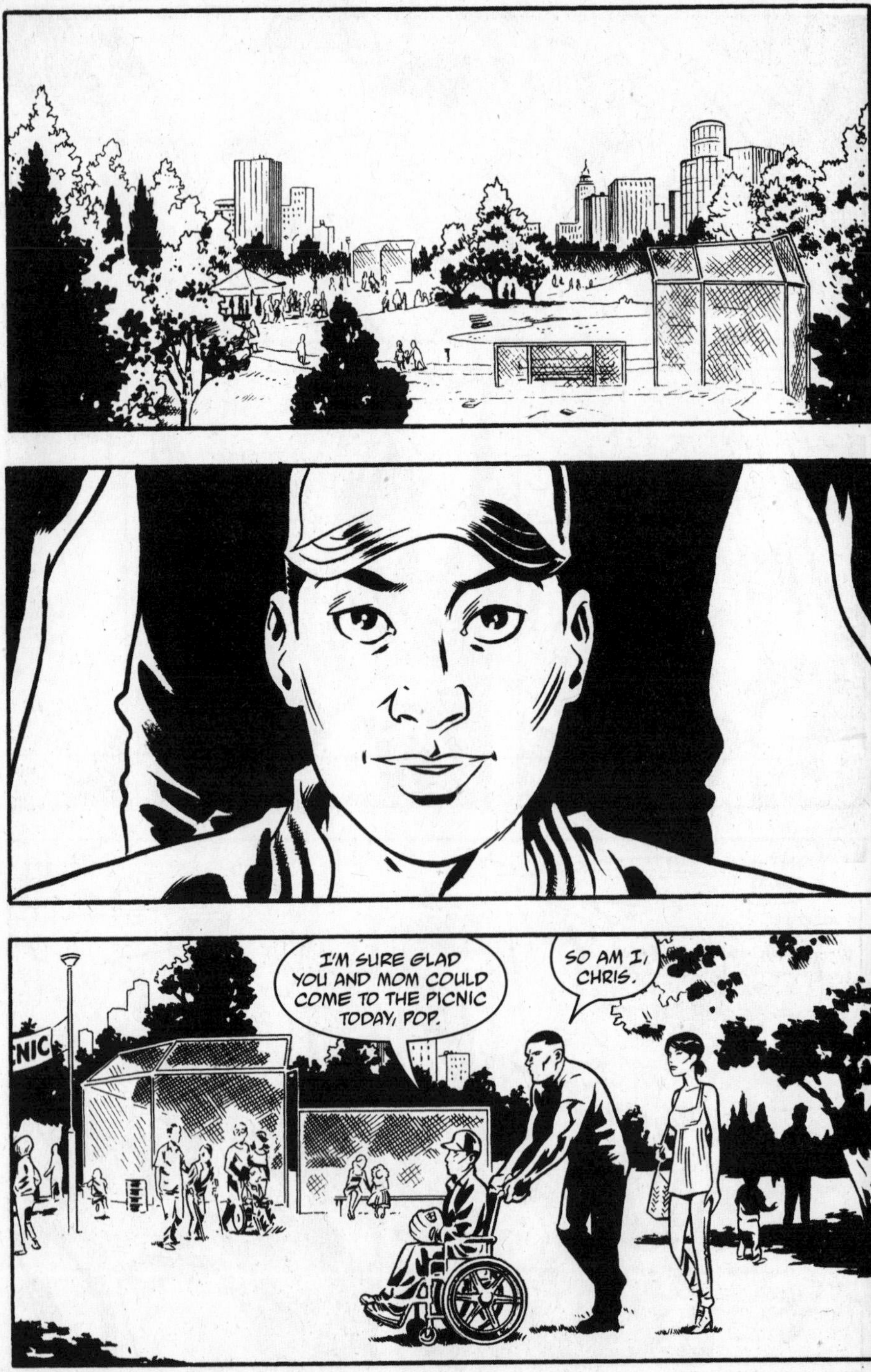
I'M SURE GLAD YOU AND MOM COULD COME TO THE PICNIC TODAY, POP.
SO AM I, CHRIS.
NIC

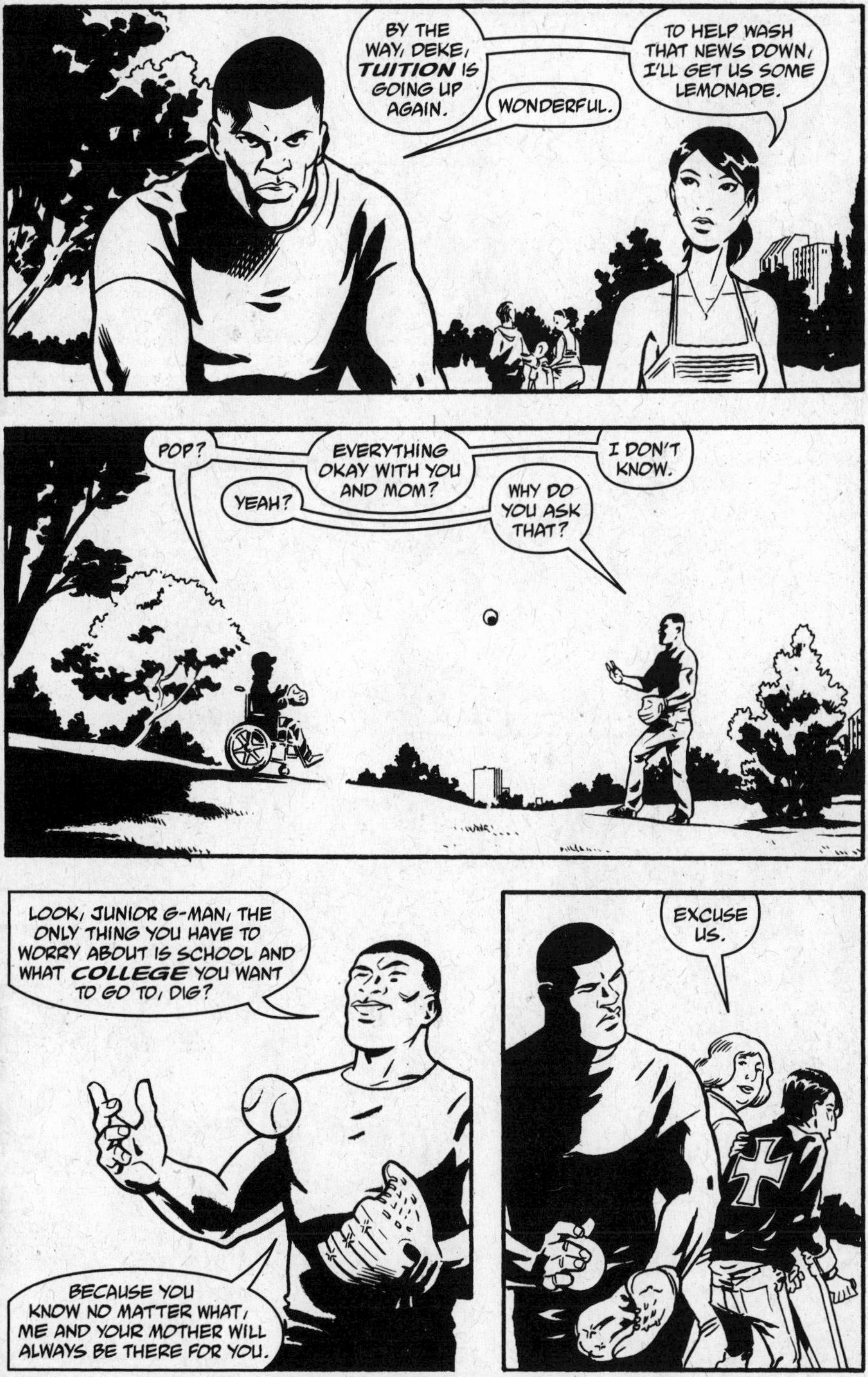
BY THE WAY, DEKE, TUITION IS GOING UP AGAIN.
WONDERFUL.
TO HELP WASH THAT NEWS DOWN, I'LL GET US SOME LEMONADE.
POP?
YEAH?
EVERYTHING OKAY WITH YOU AND MOM?
WHY DO YOU ASK THAT?
I DON'T KNOW.
LOOK, JUNIOR G-MAN, THE ONLY THING YOU HAVE TO WORRY ABOUT IS SCHOOL AND WHAT COLLEGE YOU WANT TO GO TO, DIG?
BECAUSE YOU KNOW NO MATTER WHAT, ME AND YOUR MOTHER WILL ALWAYS BE THERE FOR YOU.
EXCUSE US.

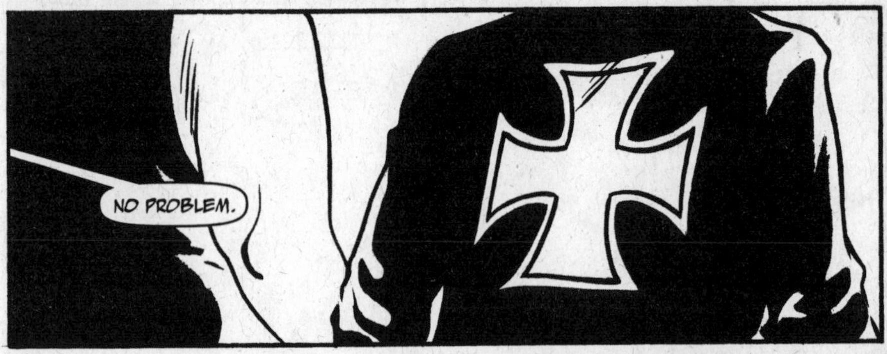
NO PROBLEM.

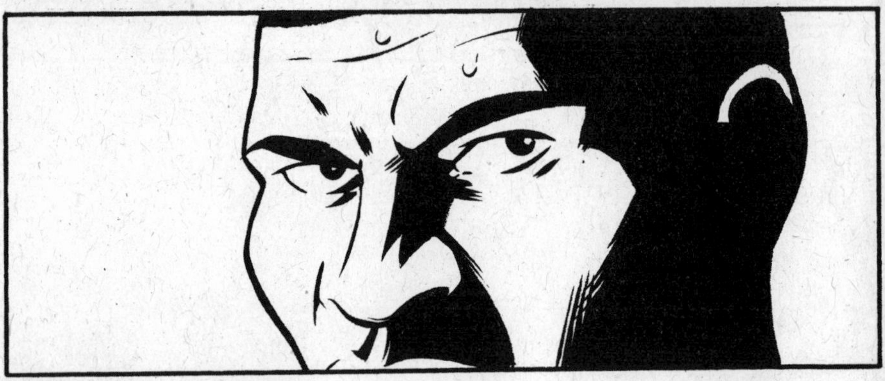

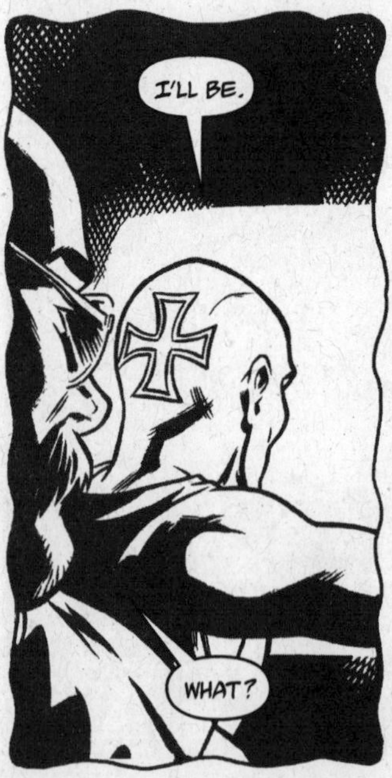
I'LL BE.
WHAT?

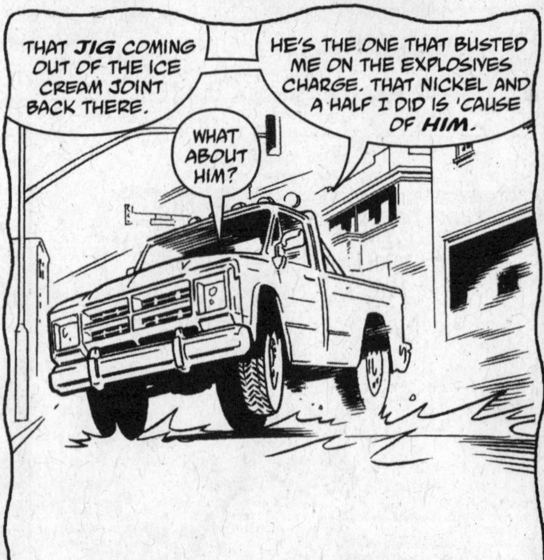
THAT JIG COMING OUT OF THE ICE CREAM JOINT BACK THERE.
HE'S THE ONE THAT BUSTED ME ON THE EXPLOSIVES CHARGE. THAT NICKEL AND A HALF I DID IS 'CAUSE OF HIM.
WHAT ABOUT HIM?

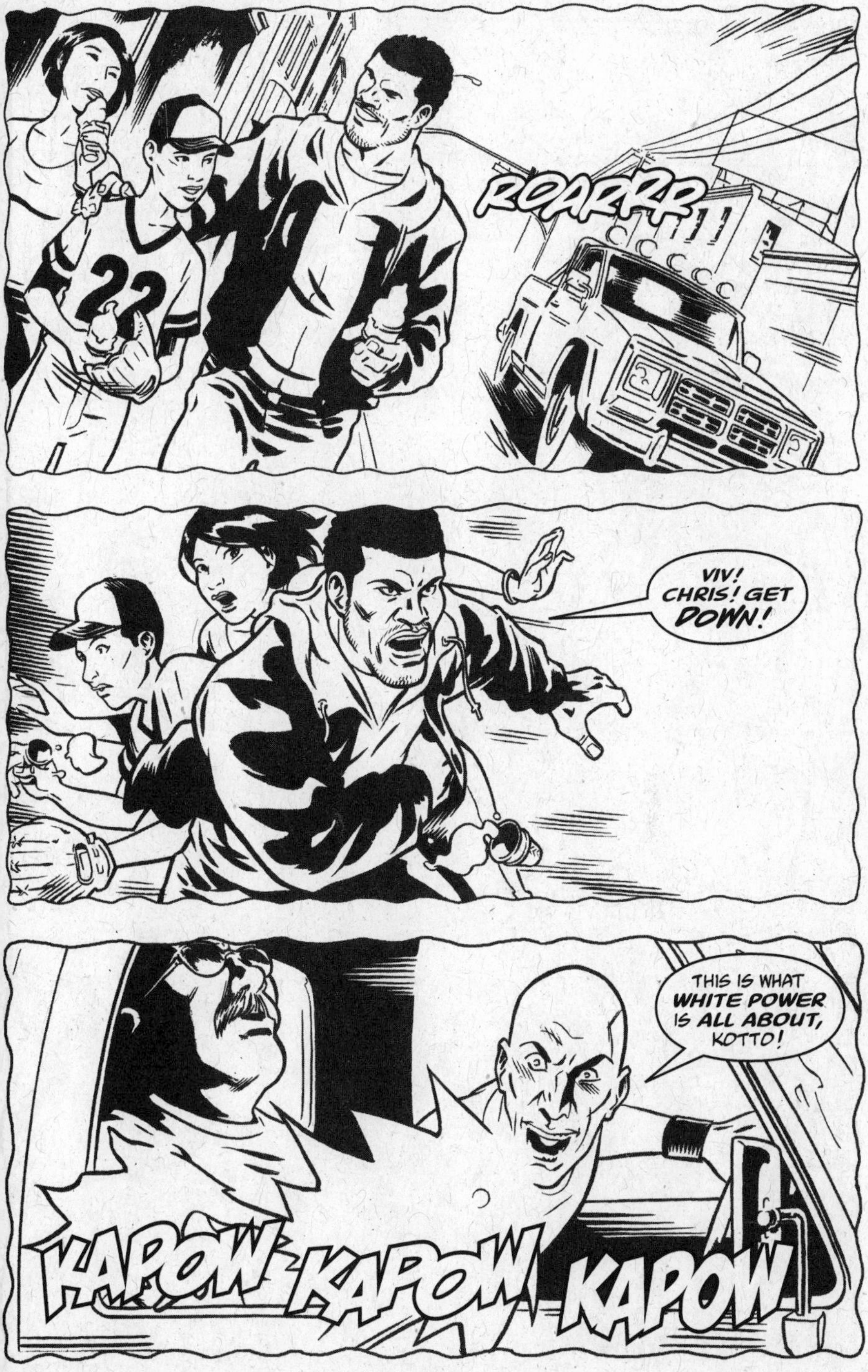
ROARRR
VIV! CHRIS! GET DOWN!
THIS IS WHAT WHITE POWER IS ALL ABOUT, KOTTO!
KAPOW KAPOW KAPOW

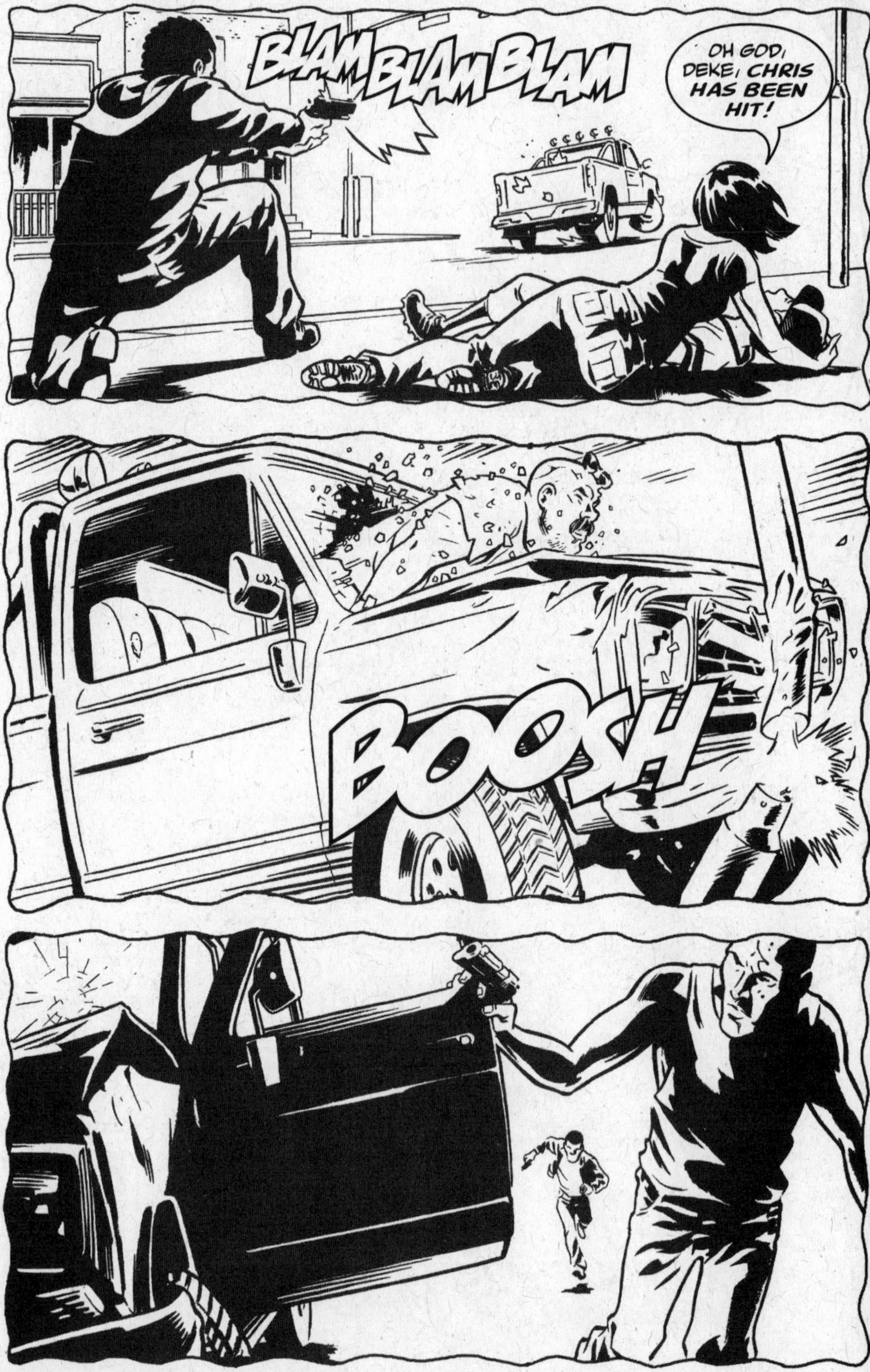
BLAM BLAM BLAM
OH GOD, DEKE, CHRIS HAS BEEN HIT!
BOOSH

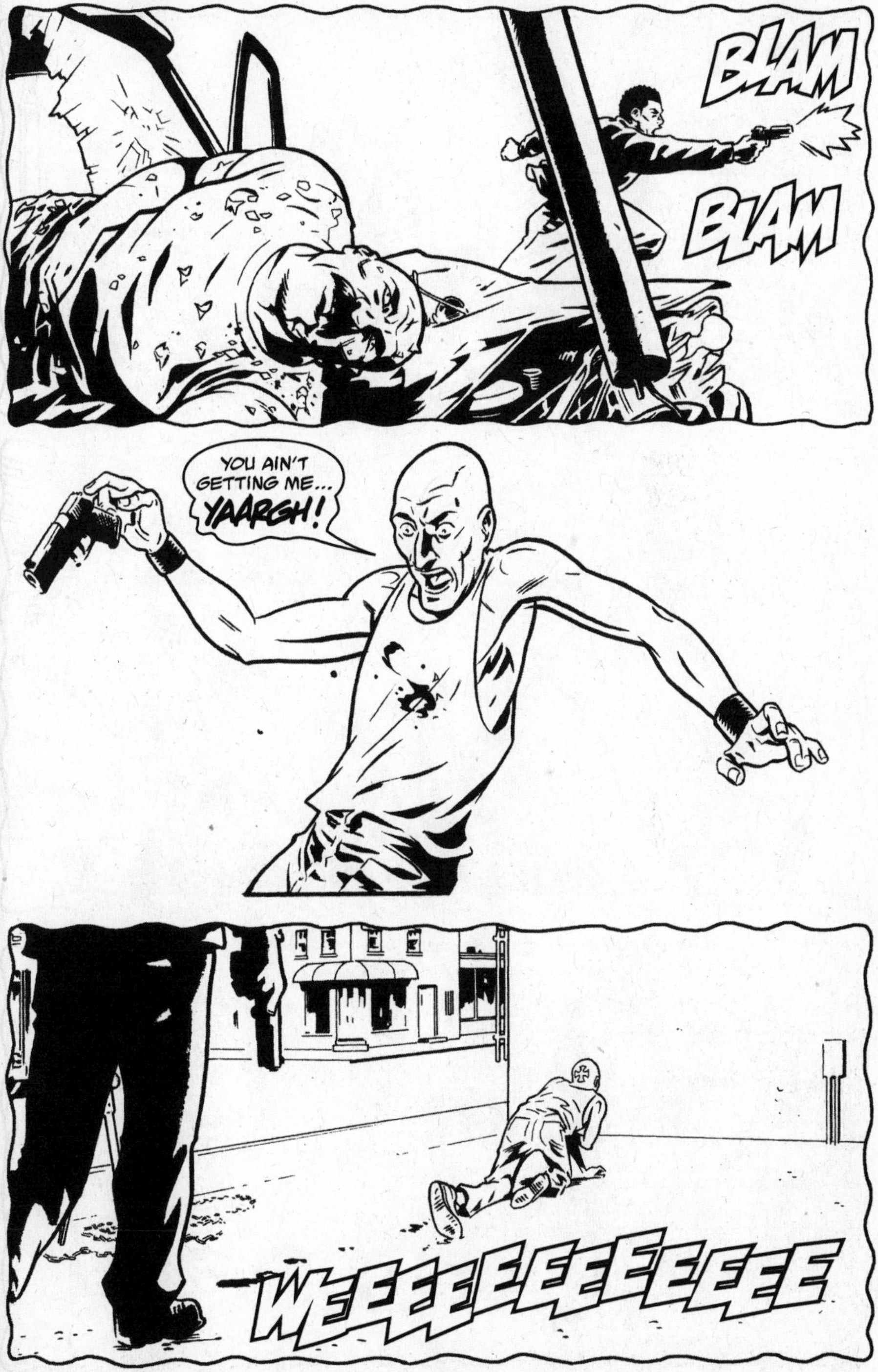

BLAM
BLAM
YOU AIN'T GETTING ME... YAARGH!
WEEEEEEEEEEEE

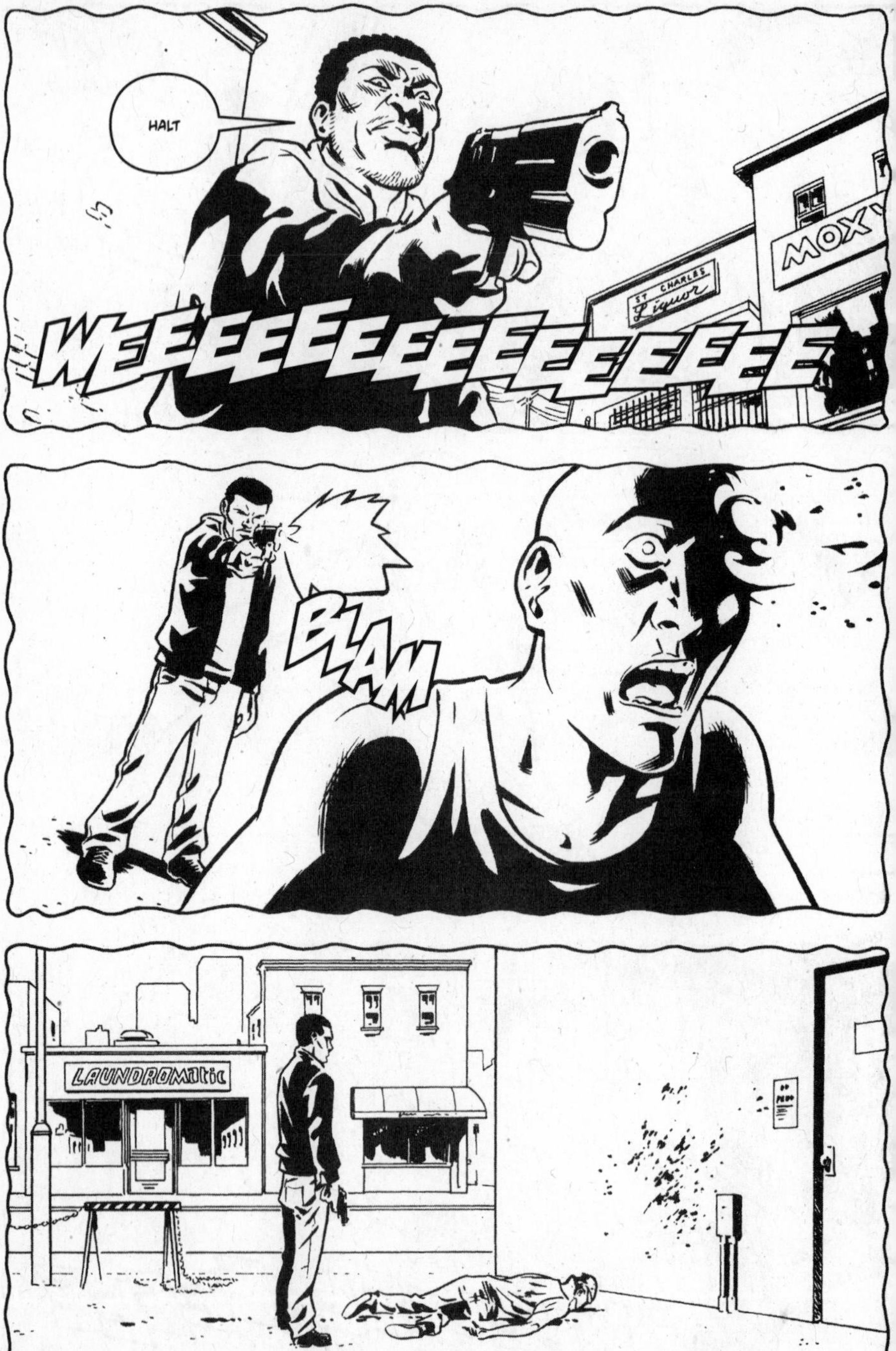
HALT
ST CHARLES Liquor
MOX
WEEEEEEEEEEEEEEE
BLAM
LAUNDROMATIC

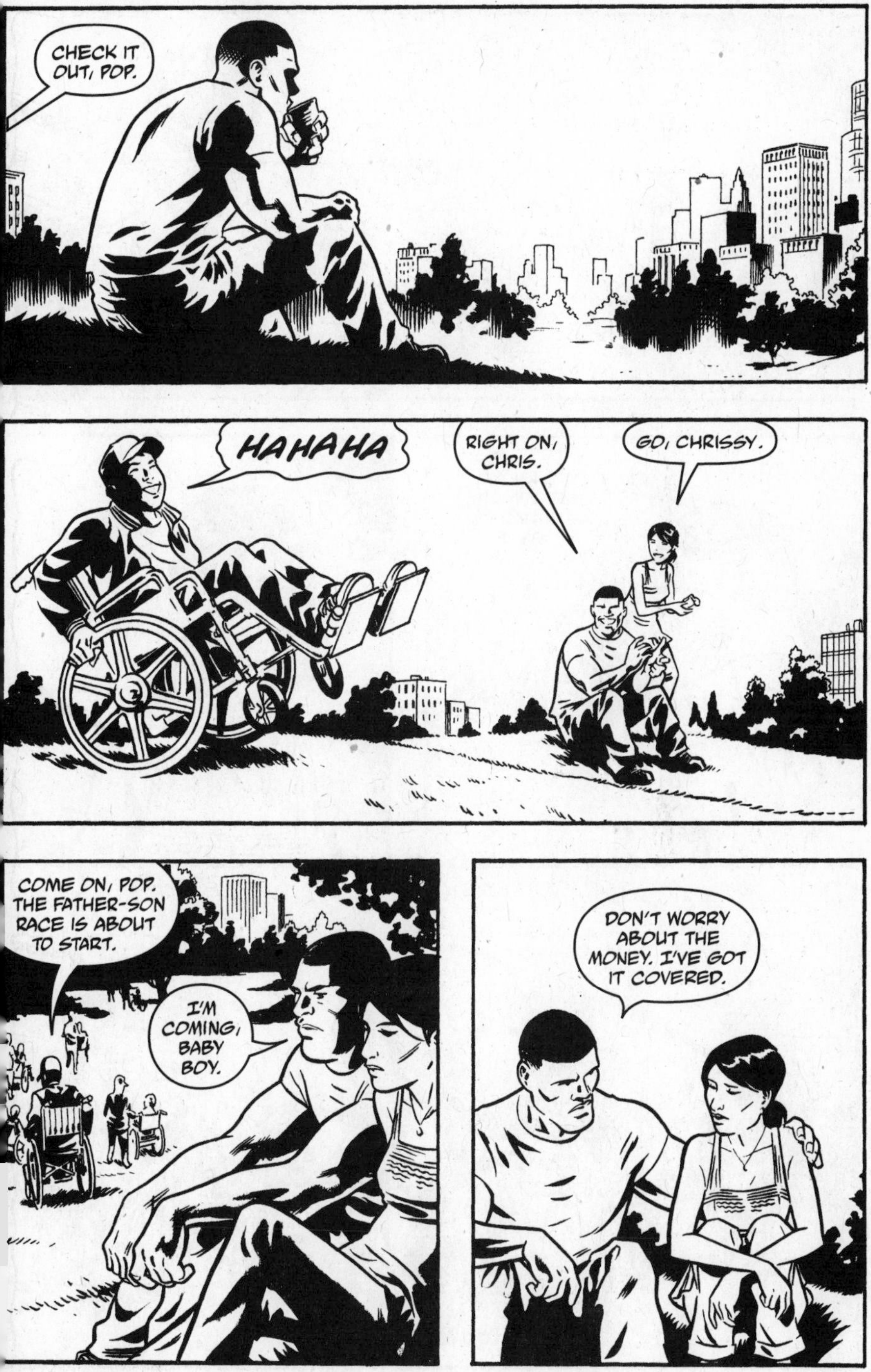
CHECK IT OUT, POP.
HAHAHA
RIGHT ON, CHRIS.
GO, CHRISSY.
COME ON, POP. THE FATHER-SON RACE IS ABOUT TO START.
I'M COMING, BABY BOY.
DON'T WORRY ABOUT THE MONEY. I'VE GOT IT COVERED.

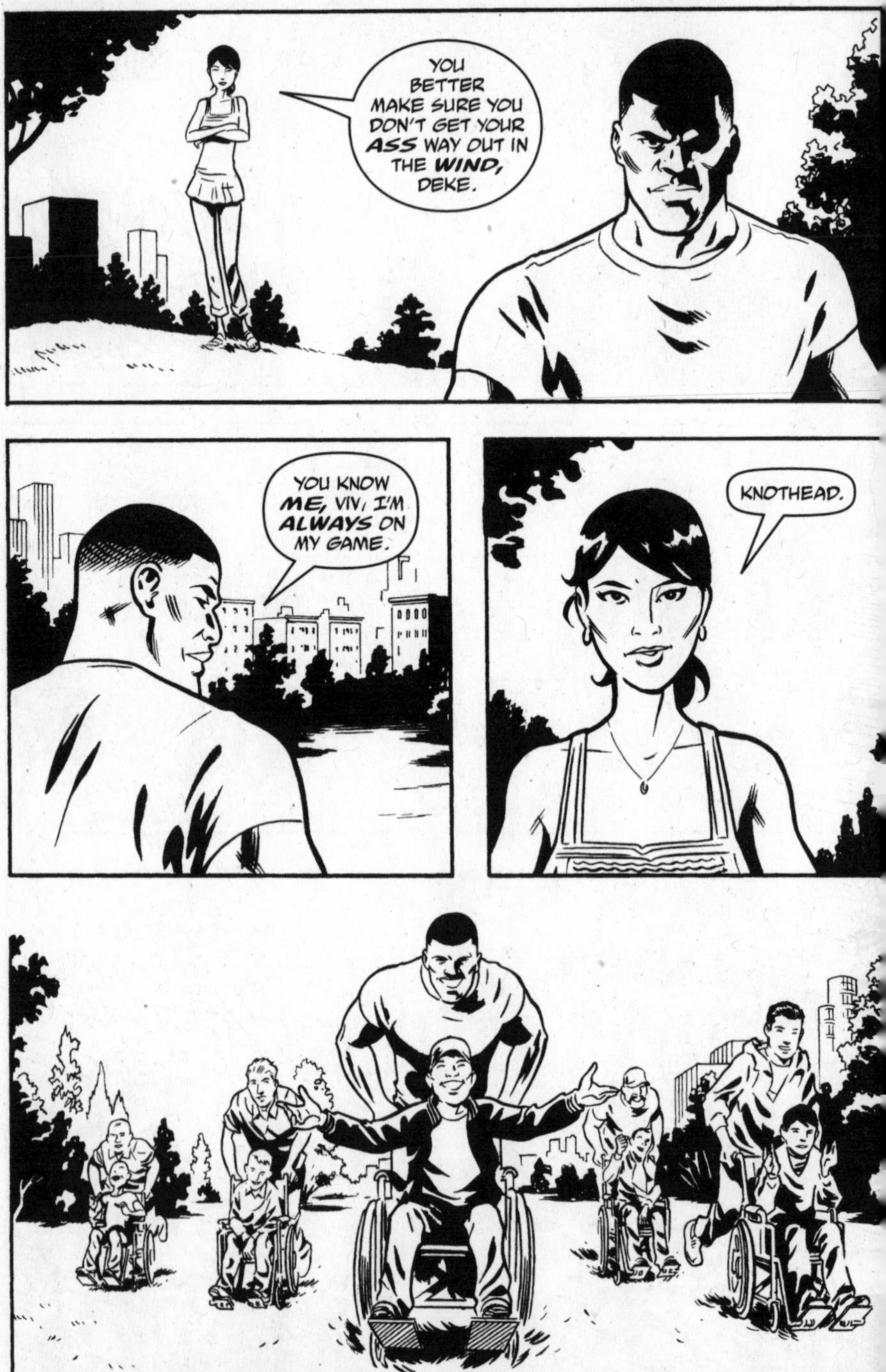
YOU BETTER MAKE SURE YOU DON'T GET YOUR **ASS** WAY OUT IN THE **WIND,** DEKE.
YOU KNOW **ME,** VIV, I'M **ALWAYS** ON MY GAME.
KNOTHEAD.

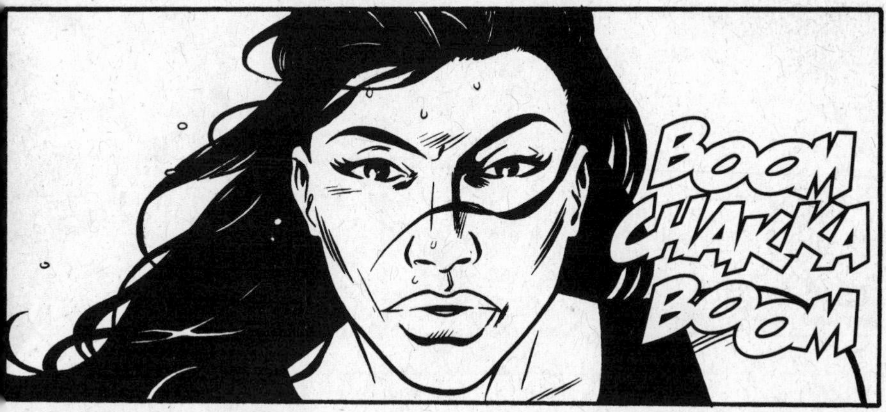
BOOM CHAKKA BOOM

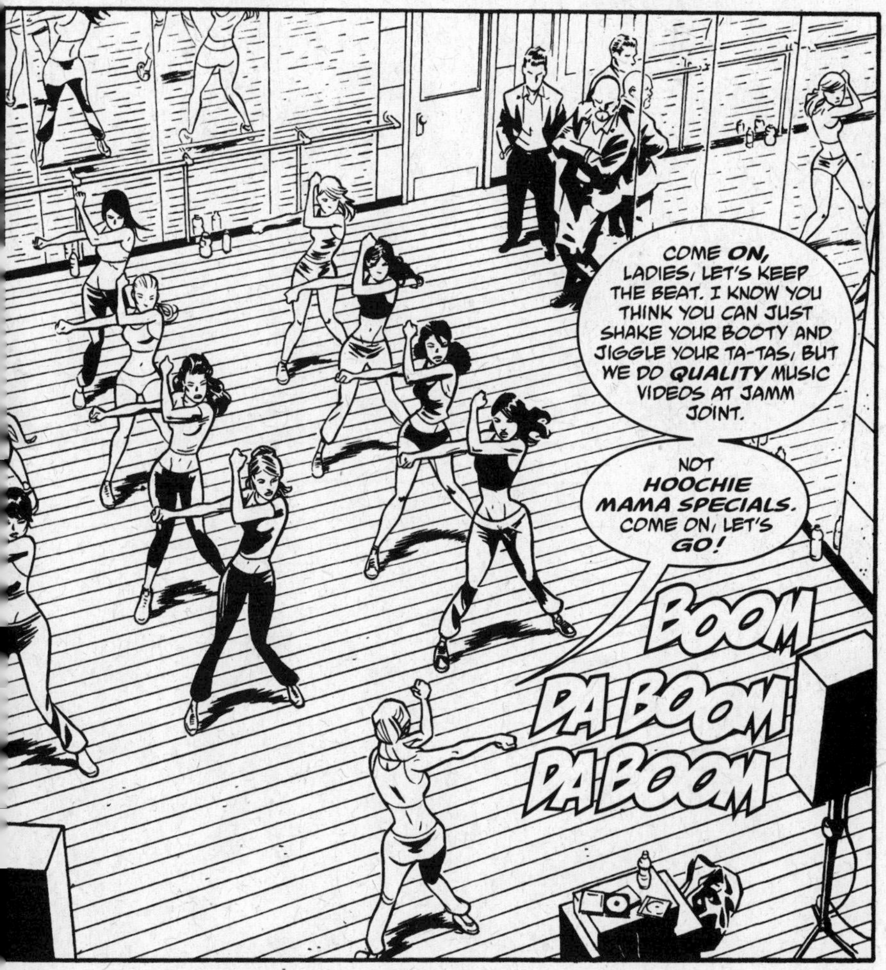
COME ON, LADIES, LET'S KEEP THE BEAT. I KNOW YOU THINK YOU CAN JUST SHAKE YOUR BOOTY AND JIGGLE YOUR TA-TAS, BUT WE DO QUALITY MUSIC VIDEOS AT JAMM JOINT.
NOT HOOCHIE MAMA SPECIALS. COME ON, LET'S GO!
BOOM
DA BOOM DA BOOM

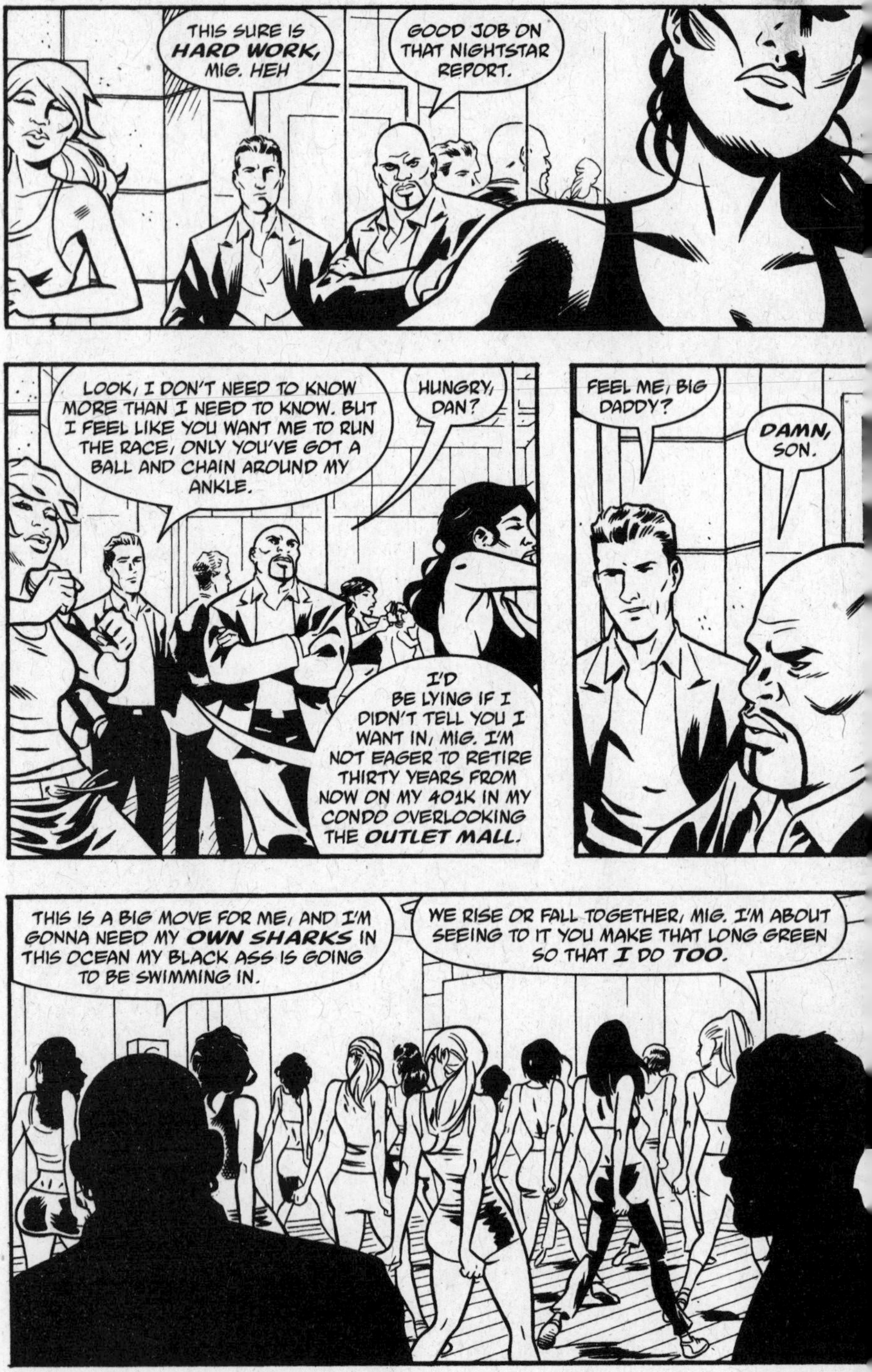

THIS SURE IS HARD WORK, MIG. HEH
GOOD JOB ON THAT NIGHTSTAR REPORT.
LOOK, I DON'T NEED TO KNOW MORE THAN I NEED TO KNOW. BUT I FEEL LIKE YOU WANT ME TO RUN THE RACE, ONLY YOU'VE GOT A BALL AND CHAIN AROUND MY ANKLE.
HUNGRY, DAN?
I'D BE LYING IF I DIDN'T TELL YOU I WANT IN, MIG. I'M NOT EAGER TO RETIRE THIRTY YEARS FROM NOW ON MY 401K IN MY CONDO OVERLOOKING THE OUTLET MALL.
FEEL ME, BIG DADDY?
DAMN, SON.
THIS IS A BIG MOVE FOR ME, AND I'M GONNA NEED MY OWN SHARKS IN THIS OCEAN MY BLACK ASS IS GOING TO BE SWIMMING IN.
WE RISE OR FALL TOGETHER, MIG. I'M ABOUT SEEING TO IT YOU MAKE THAT LONG GREEN SO THAT I DO TOO.

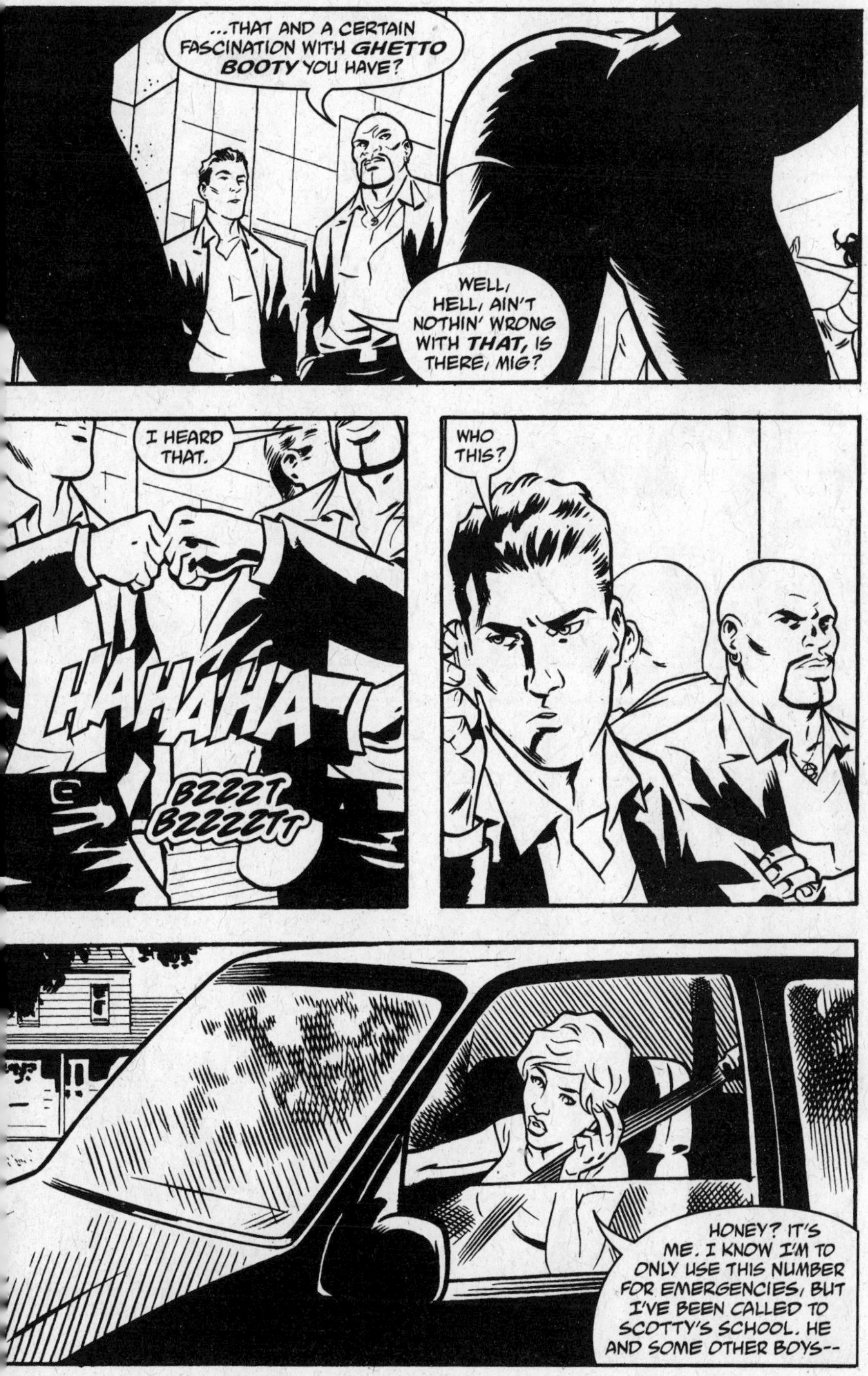
...THAT AND A CERTAIN FASCINATION WITH GHETTO BOOTY YOU HAVE?
WELL, HELL, AIN'T NOTHIN' WRONG WITH THAT, IS THERE, MIG?
I HEARD THAT.
HAHAHA
BZZZT BZZZZTT
WHO THIS?
HONEY? IT'S ME. I KNOW I'M TO ONLY USE THIS NUMBER FOR EMERGENCIES, BUT I'VE BEEN CALLED TO SCOTTY'S SCHOOL. HE AND SOME OTHER BOYS--

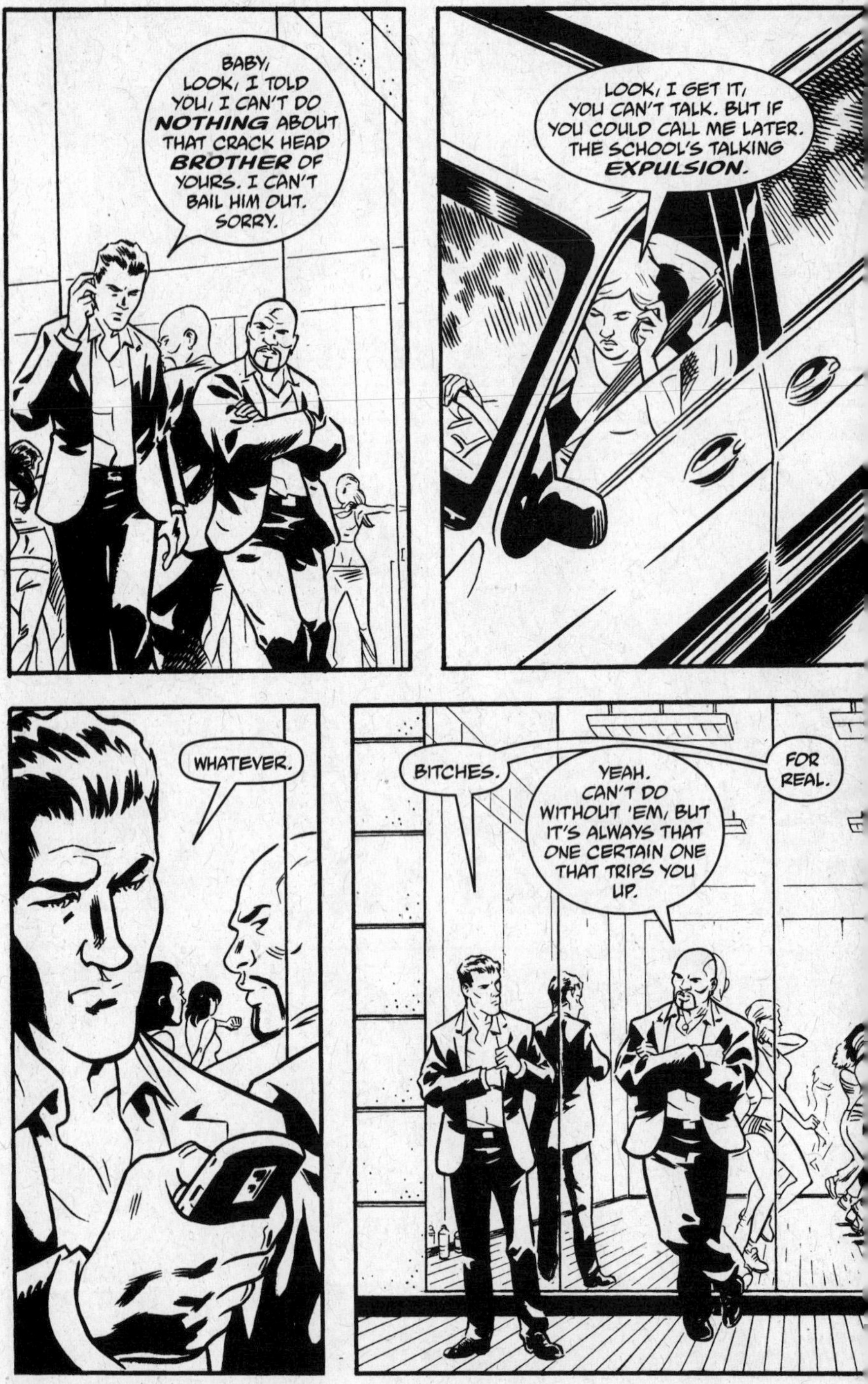

BABY, LOOK, I TOLD YOU, I CAN'T DO NOTHING ABOUT THAT CRACK HEAD BROTHER OF YOURS. I CAN'T BAIL HIM OUT. SORRY.
LOOK, I GET IT, YOU CAN'T TALK. BUT IF YOU COULD CALL ME LATER. THE SCHOOL'S TALKING EXPULSION.
WHATEVER.
BITCHES.
YEAH. CAN'T DO WITHOUT 'EM, BUT IT'S ALWAYS THAT ONE CERTAIN ONE THAT TRIPS YOU UP.
FOR REAL.

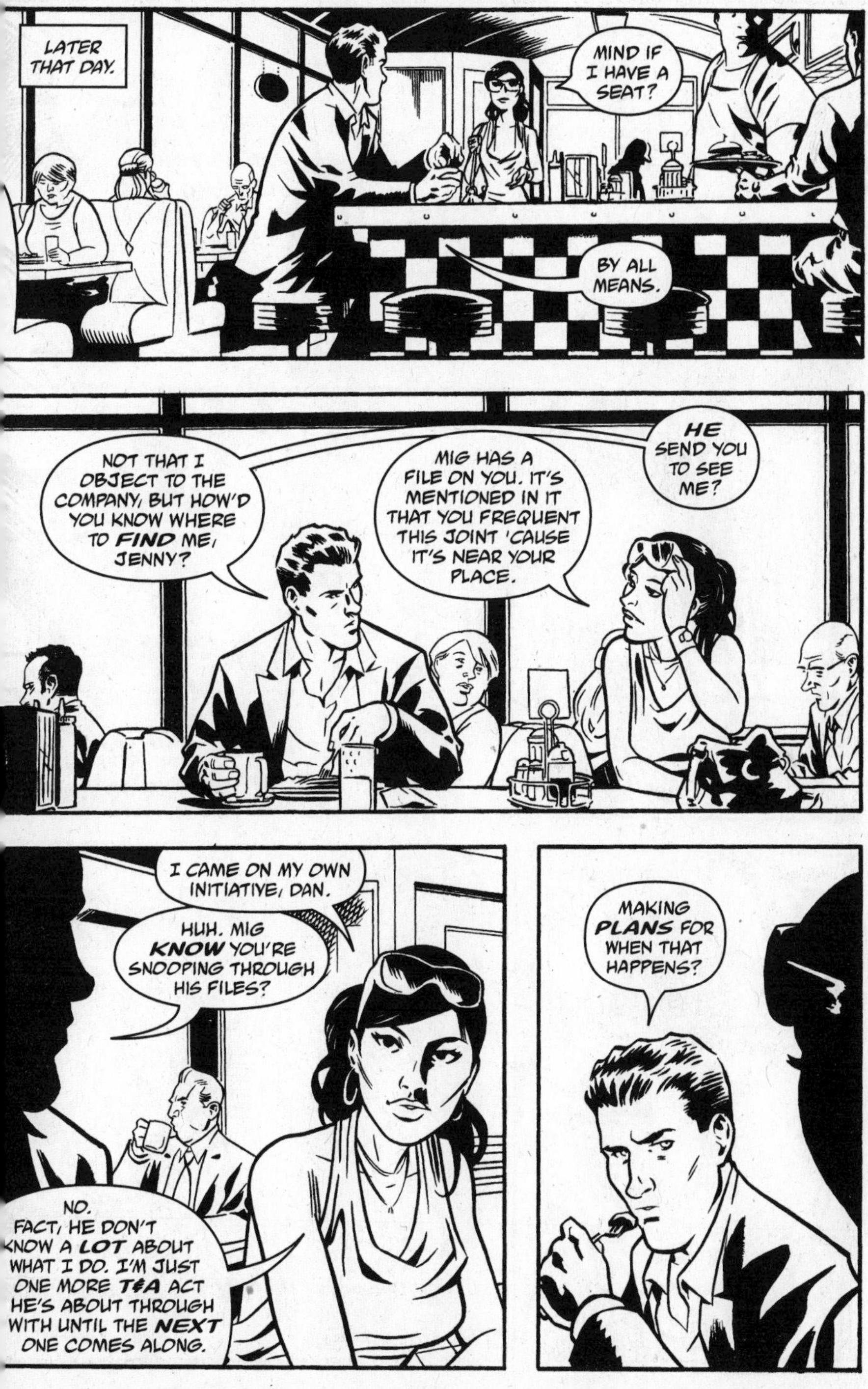
LATER THAT DAY.
MIND IF I HAVE A SEAT?
BY ALL MEANS.
NOT THAT I OBJECT TO THE COMPANY, BUT HOW'D YOU KNOW WHERE TO FIND ME, JENNY?
MIG HAS A FILE ON YOU. IT'S MENTIONED IN IT THAT YOU FREQUENT THIS JOINT 'CAUSE IT'S NEAR YOUR PLACE.
HE SEND YOU TO SEE ME?
I CAME ON MY OWN INITIATIVE, DAN.
HUH. MIG KNOW YOU'RE SNOOPING THROUGH HIS FILES?
NO. FACT, HE DON'T KNOW A LOT ABOUT WHAT I DO. I'M JUST ONE MORE T&A ACT HE'S ABOUT THROUGH WITH UNTIL THE NEXT ONE COMES ALONG.
MAKING PLANS FOR WHEN THAT HAPPENS?

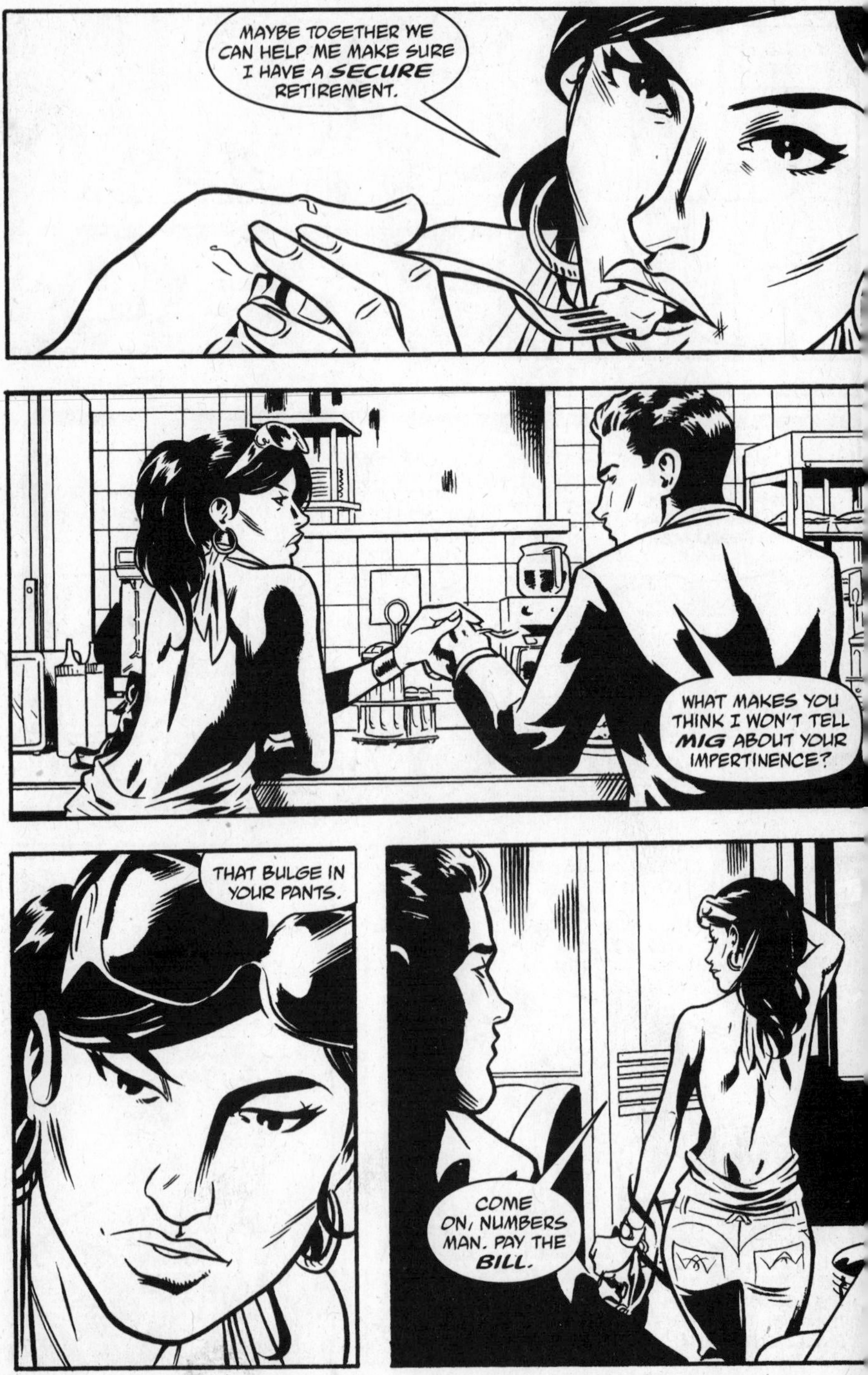
MAYBE TOGETHER WE CAN HELP ME MAKE SURE I HAVE A SECURE RETIREMENT.
WHAT MAKES YOU THINK I WON'T TELL MIG ABOUT YOUR IMPERTINENCE?
THAT BULGE IN YOUR PANTS.
COME ON, NUMBERS MAN. PAY THE BILL.

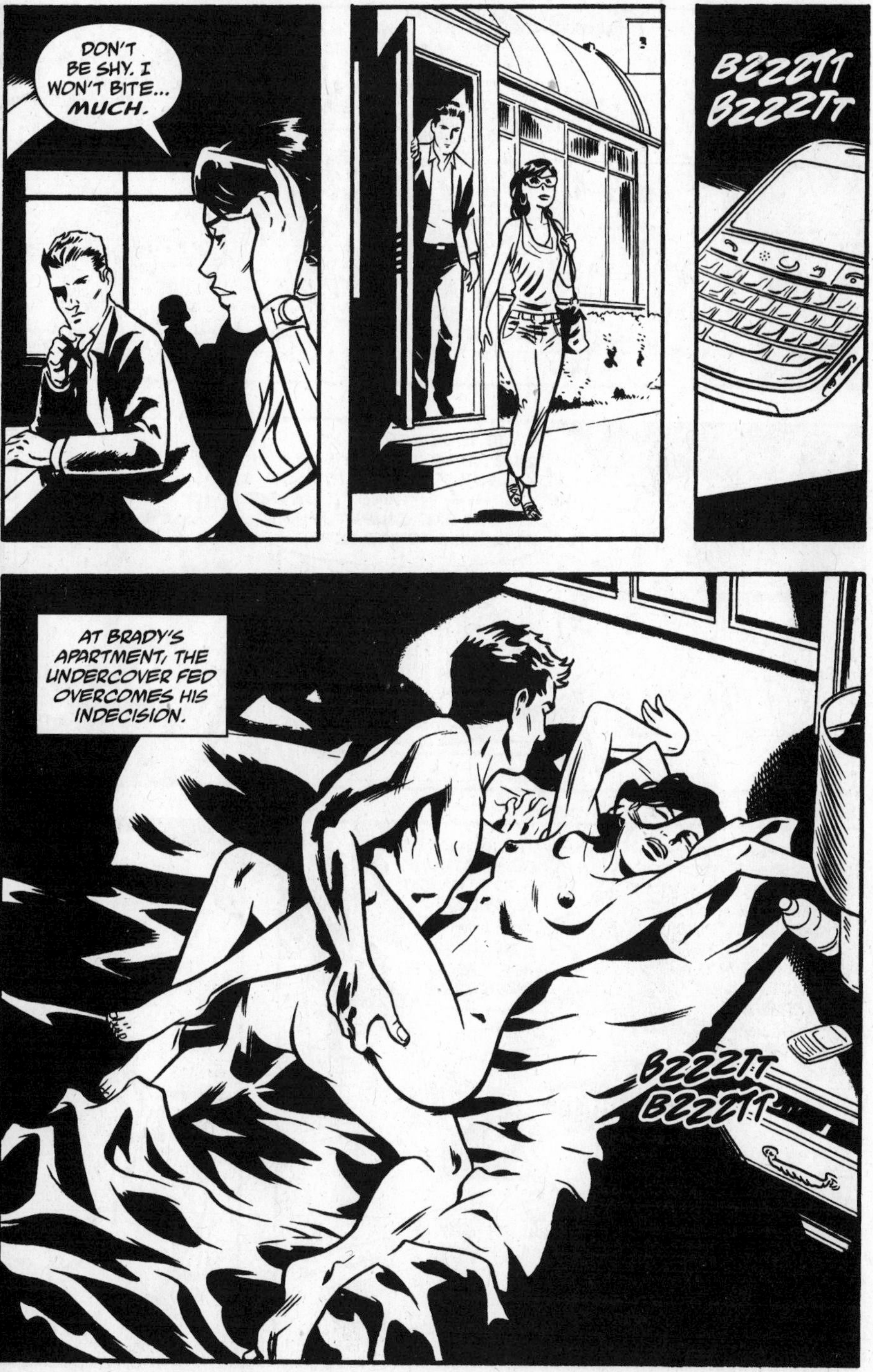
DON'T BE SHY. I WON'T BITE... MUCH.
BZZZTT
BZZZTT
AT BRADY'S APARTMENT, THE UNDERCOVER FED OVERCOMES HIS INDECISION.
BZZZTT
BZZZTT

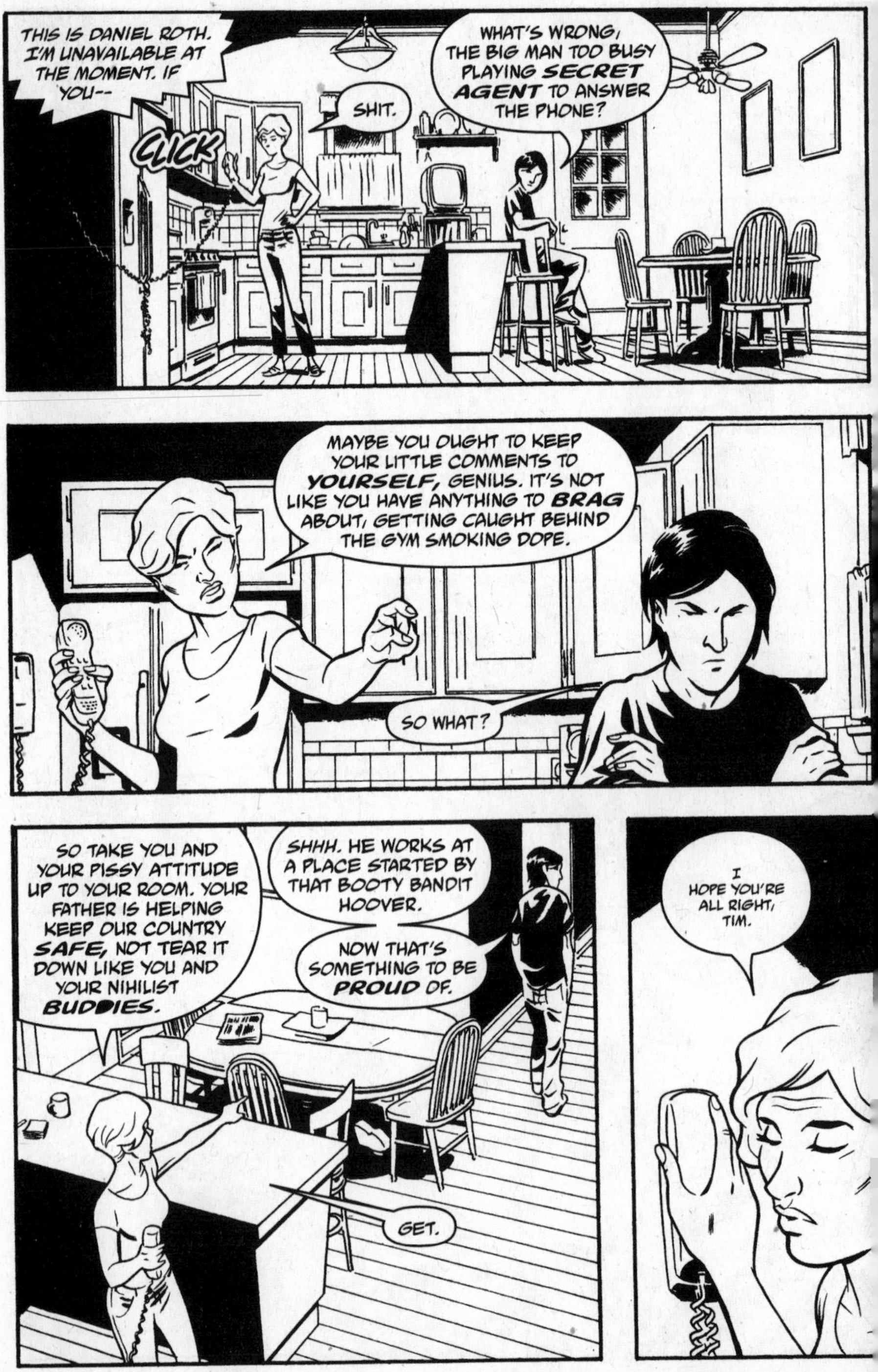
THIS IS DANIEL ROTH. I'M UNAVAILABLE AT THE MOMENT. IF YOU--
CLICK
SHIT.
WHAT'S WRONG, THE BIG MAN TOO BUSY PLAYING SECRET AGENT TO ANSWER THE PHONE?
MAYBE YOU OUGHT TO KEEP YOUR LITTLE COMMENTS TO YOURSELF, GENIUS. IT'S NOT LIKE YOU HAVE ANYTHING TO BRAG ABOUT, GETTING CAUGHT BEHIND THE GYM SMOKING DOPE.
SO WHAT?
SO TAKE YOU AND YOUR PISSY ATTITUDE UP TO YOUR ROOM. YOUR FATHER IS HELPING KEEP OUR COUNTRY SAFE, NOT TEAR IT DOWN LIKE YOU AND YOUR NIHILIST BUDDIES.
SHHH. HE WORKS AT A PLACE STARTED BY THAT BOOTY BANDIT HOOVER.
NOW THAT'S SOMETHING TO BE PROUD OF.
GET.
I HOPE YOU'RE ALL RIGHT, TIM.

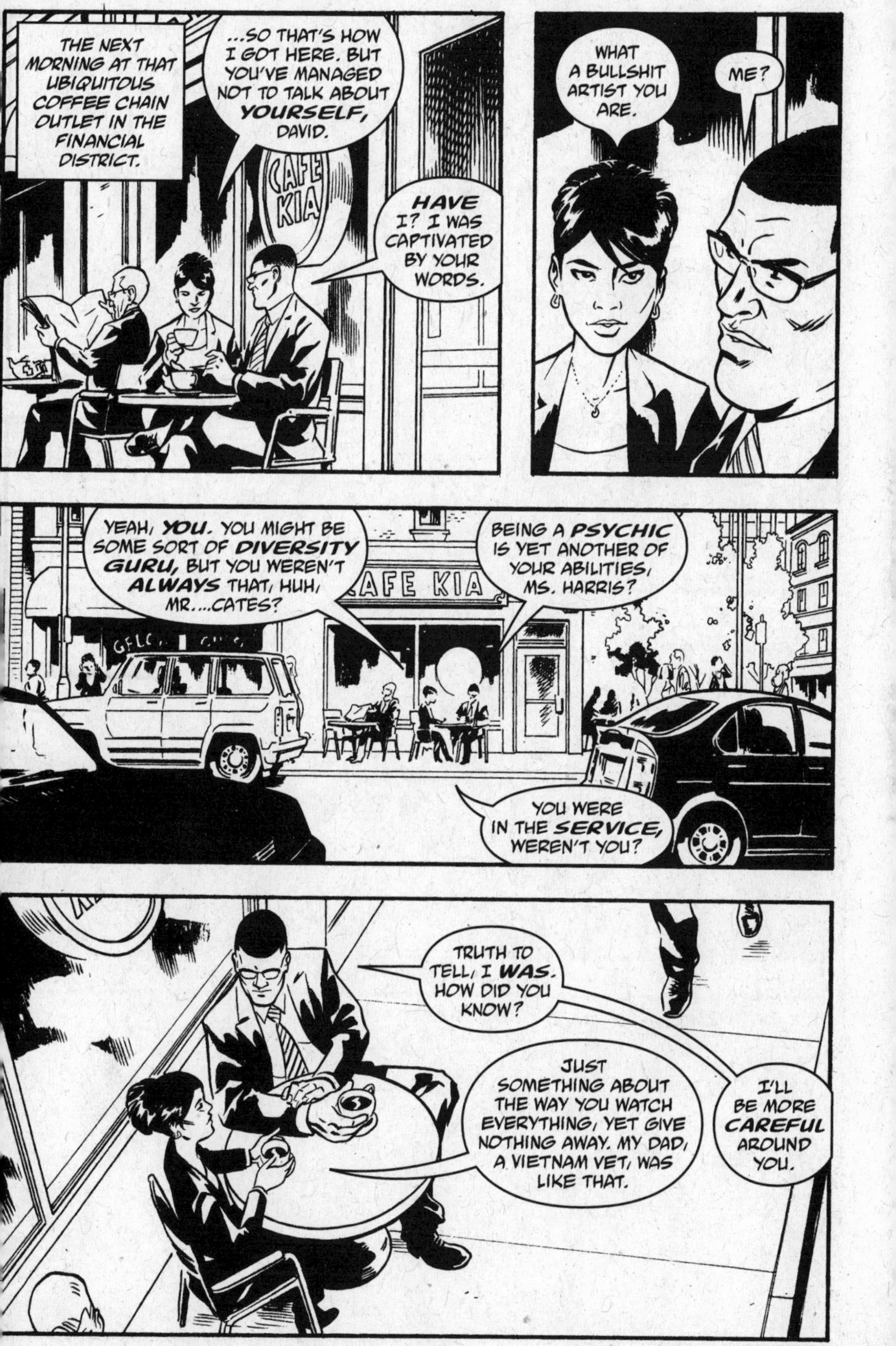
THE NEXT MORNING AT THAT UBIQUITOUS COFFEE CHAIN OUTLET IN THE FINANCIAL DISTRICT.
...SO THAT'S HOW I GOT HERE. BUT YOU'VE MANAGED NOT TO TALK ABOUT YOURSELF, DAVID.
CAFE KIA
HAVE I? I WAS CAPTIVATED BY YOUR WORDS.
WHAT A BULLSHIT ARTIST YOU ARE.
ME?
YEAH, YOU. YOU MIGHT BE SOME SORT OF DIVERSITY GURU, BUT YOU WEREN'T ALWAYS THAT, HUH, MR....CATES?
BEING A PSYCHIC IS YET ANOTHER OF YOUR ABILITIES, MS. HARRIS?
YOU WERE IN THE SERVICE, WEREN'T YOU?
TRUTH TO TELL, I WAS. HOW DID YOU KNOW?
JUST SOMETHING ABOUT THE WAY YOU WATCH EVERYTHING, YET GIVE NOTHING AWAY. MY DAD, A VIETNAM VET, WAS LIKE THAT.
I'LL BE MORE CAREFUL AROUND YOU.

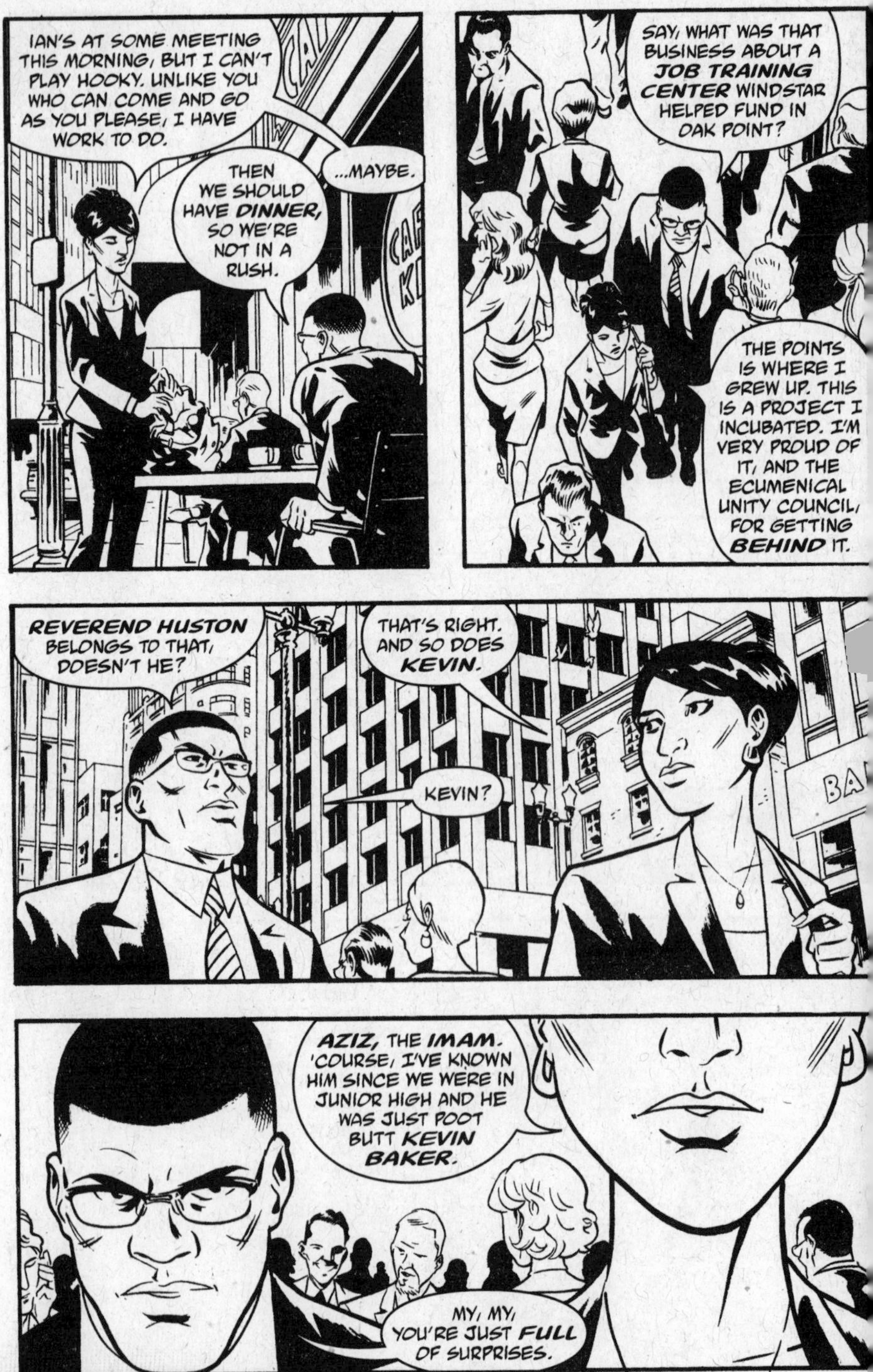
IAN'S AT SOME MEETING THIS MORNING, BUT I CAN'T PLAY HOOKY. UNLIKE YOU WHO CAN COME AND GO AS YOU PLEASE, I HAVE WORK TO DO.
THEN WE SHOULD HAVE DINNER, SO WE'RE NOT IN A RUSH.
...MAYBE.
SAY, WHAT WAS THAT BUSINESS ABOUT A JOB TRAINING CENTER WINDSTAR HELPED FUND IN OAK POINT?
THE POINTS IS WHERE I GREW UP. THIS IS A PROJECT I INCUBATED. I'M VERY PROUD OF IT, AND THE ECUMENICAL UNITY COUNCIL, FOR GETTING BEHIND IT.
REVEREND HUSTON BELONGS TO THAT, DOESN'T HE?
THAT'S RIGHT. AND SO DOES KEVIN.
KEVIN?
AZIZ, THE IMAM. 'COURSE, I'VE KNOWN HIM SINCE WE WERE IN JUNIOR HIGH AND HE WAS JUST POOT BUTT KEVIN BAKER.
MY, MY, YOU'RE JUST FULL OF SURPRISES.

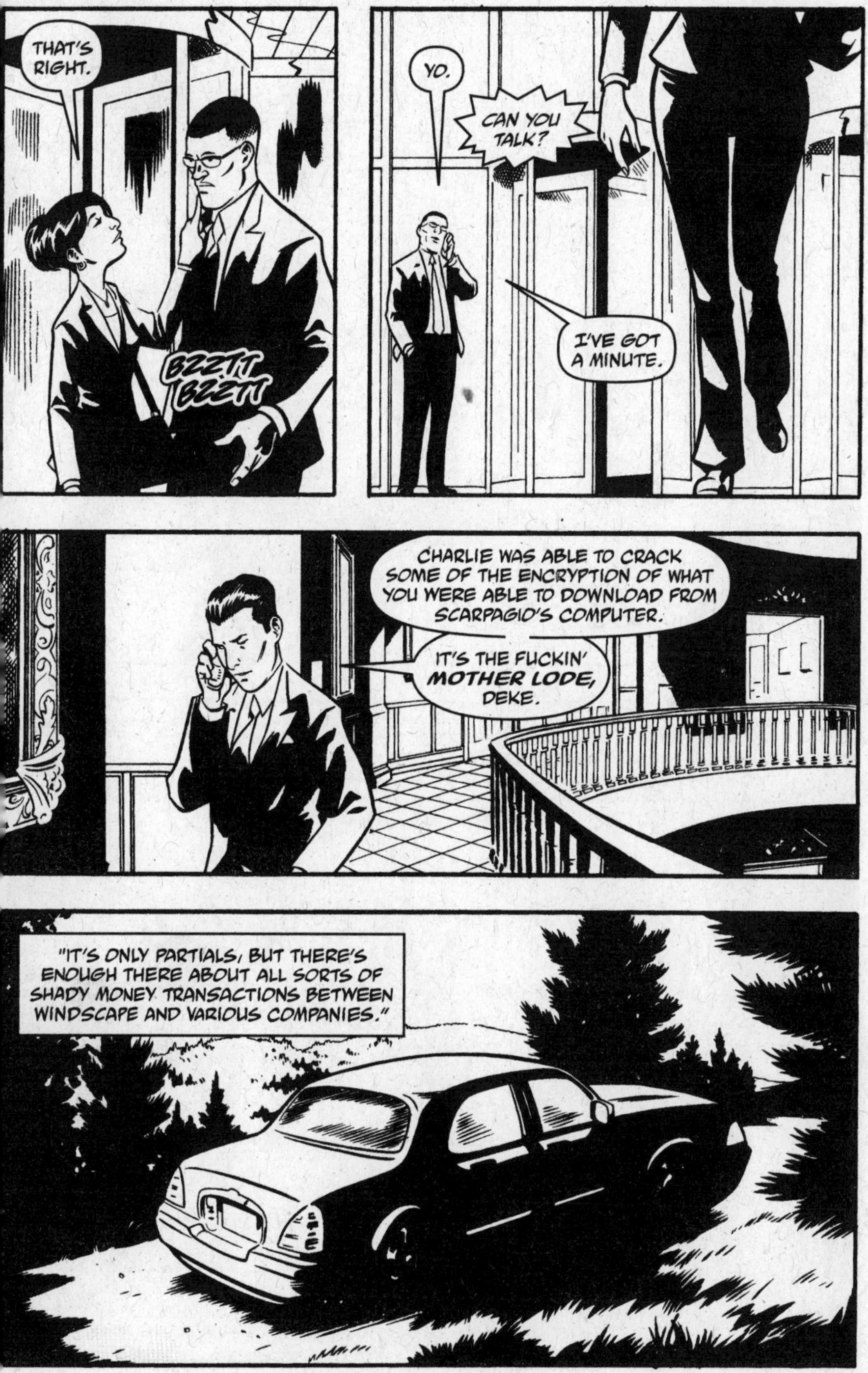
THAT'S RIGHT.
BZZTT BZZTT
YO.
CAN YOU TALK?
I'VE GOT A MINUTE.
CHARLIE WAS ABLE TO CRACK SOME OF THE ENCRYPTION OF WHAT YOU WERE ABLE TO DOWNLOAD FROM SCARPAGIO'S COMPUTER.
IT'S THE FUCKIN' MOTHER LODE, DEKE.
"IT'S ONLY PARTIALS, BUT THERE'S ENOUGH THERE ABOUT ALL SORTS OF SHADY MONEY TRANSACTIONS BETWEEN WINDSCAPE AND VARIOUS COMPANIES."

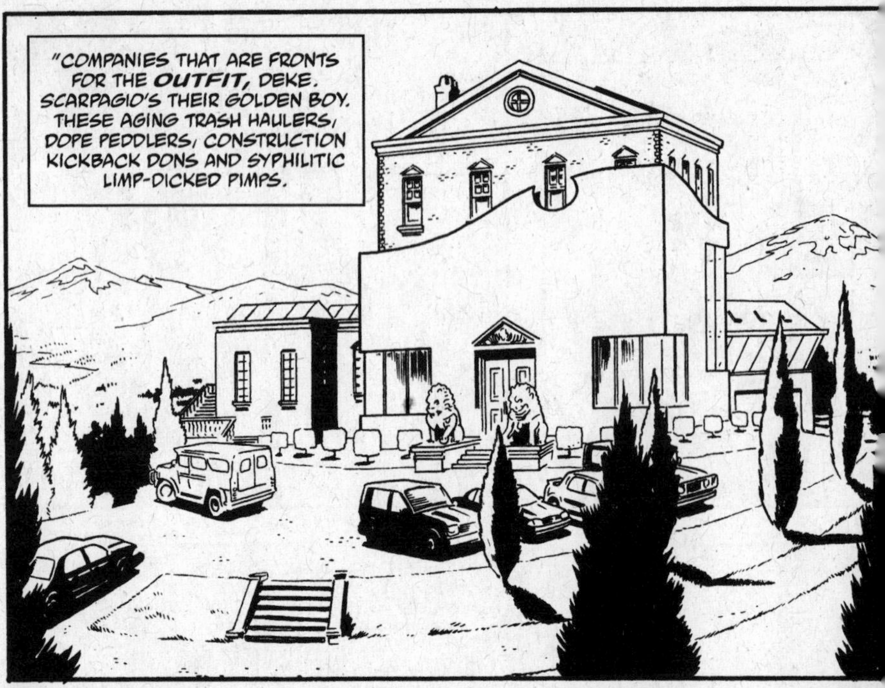
"COMPANIES THAT ARE FRONTS FOR THE OUTFIT, DEKE. SCARPAGIO'S THEIR GOLDEN BOY. THESE AGING TRASH HAULERS, DOPE PEDDLERS, CONSTRUCTION KICKBACK DONS AND SYPHILITIC LIMP-DICKED PIMPS.

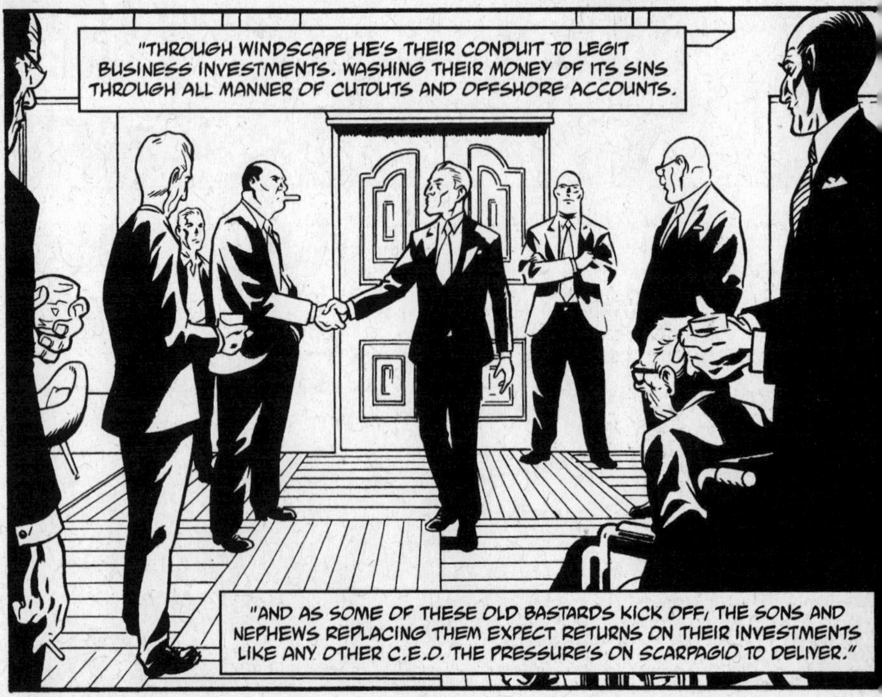
"THROUGH WINDSCAPE HE'S THEIR CONDUIT TO LEGIT BUSINESS INVESTMENTS. WASHING THEIR MONEY OF ITS SINS THROUGH ALL MANNER OF CUTOUTS AND OFFSHORE ACCOUNTS.
"AND AS SOME OF THESE OLD BASTARDS KICK OFF, THE SONS AND NEPHEWS REPLACING THEM EXPECT RETURNS ON THEIR INVESTMENTS LIKE ANY OTHER C.E.O. THE PRESSURE'S ON SCARPAGIO TO DELIVER."

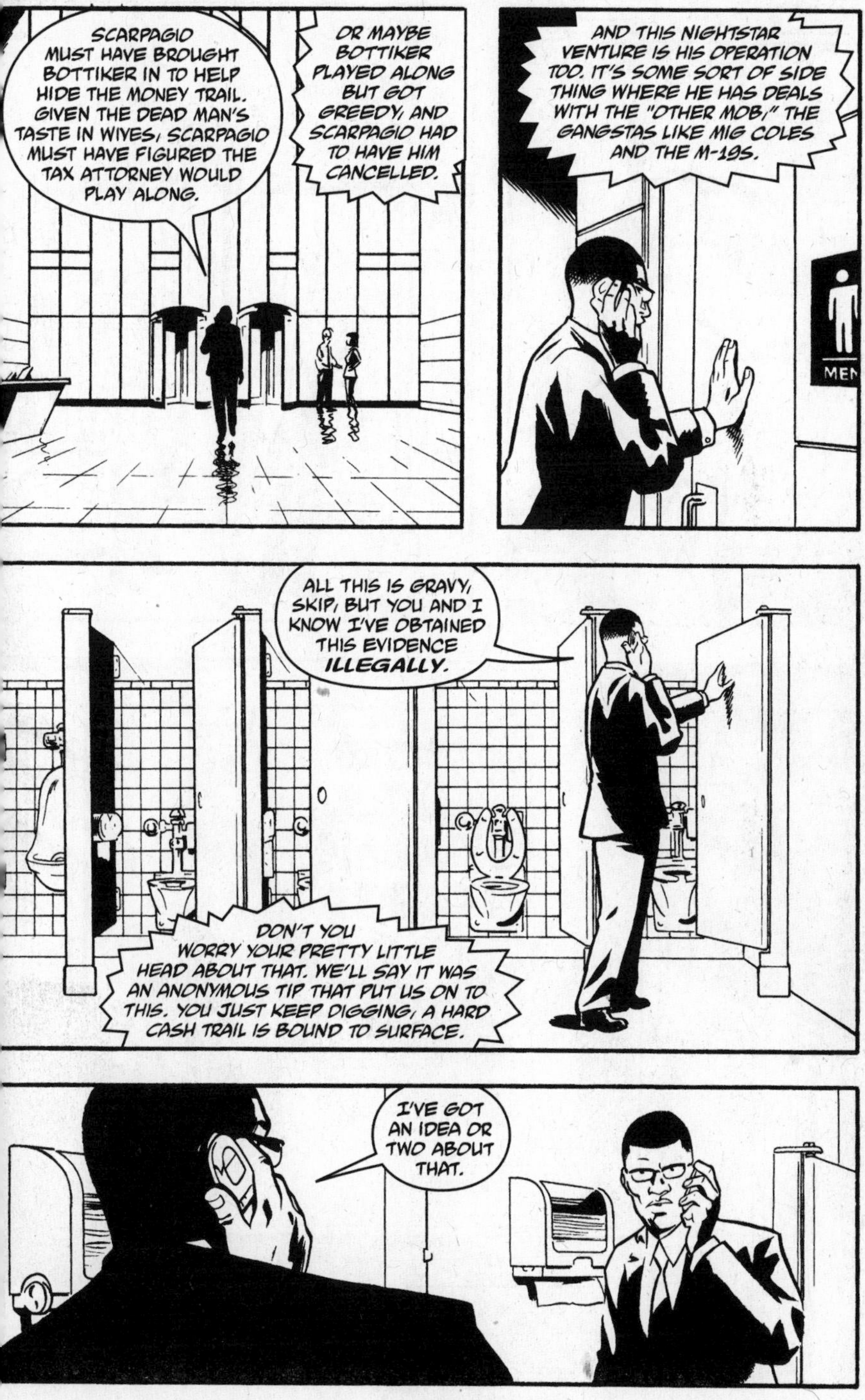
SCARPAGIO MUST HAVE BROUGHT BOTTIKER IN TO HELP HIDE THE MONEY TRAIL. GIVEN THE DEAD MAN'S TASTE IN WIVES, SCARPAGIO MUST HAVE FIGURED THE TAX ATTORNEY WOULD PLAY ALONG.
OR MAYBE BOTTIKER PLAYED ALONG BUT GOT GREEDY, AND SCARPAGIO HAD TO HAVE HIM CANCELLED.
AND THIS NIGHTSTAR VENTURE IS HIS OPERATION TOO. IT'S SOME SORT OF SIDE THING WHERE HE HAS DEALS WITH THE "OTHER MOB," THE GANGSTAS LIKE MIG COLES AND THE M-19S.
MEN
ALL THIS IS GRAVY, SKIP, BUT YOU AND I KNOW I'VE OBTAINED THIS EVIDENCE ***ILLEGALLY.***
DON'T YOU WORRY YOUR PRETTY LITTLE HEAD ABOUT THAT. WE'LL SAY IT WAS AN ANONYMOUS TIP THAT PUT US ON TO THIS. YOU JUST KEEP DIGGING, A HARD CASH TRAIL IS BOUND TO SURFACE.
I'VE GOT AN IDEA OR TWO ABOUT THAT.

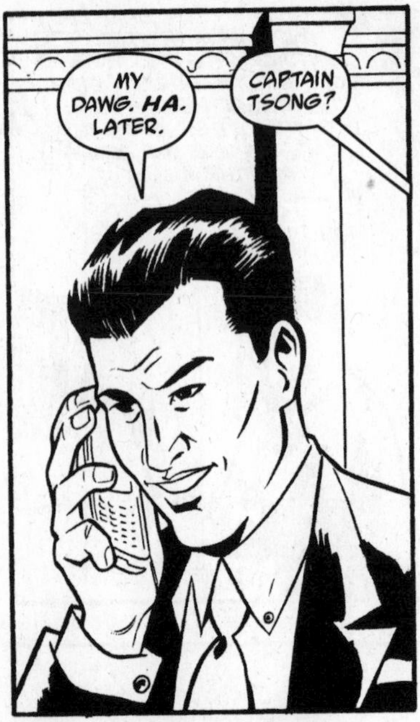
MY DAWG. HA. LATER.
CAPTAIN TSONG?

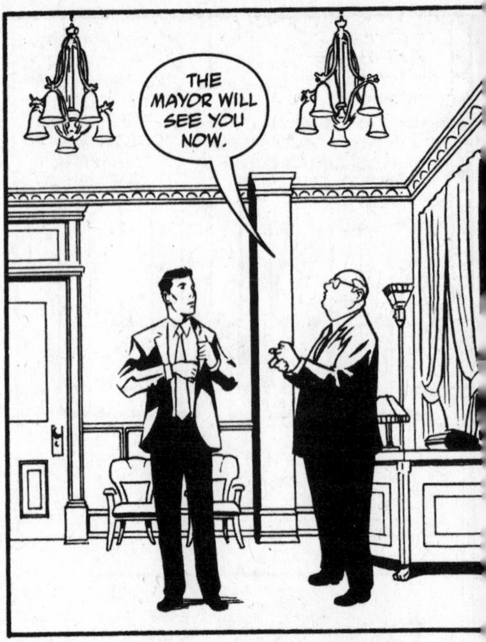
THE MAYOR WILL SEE YOU NOW.

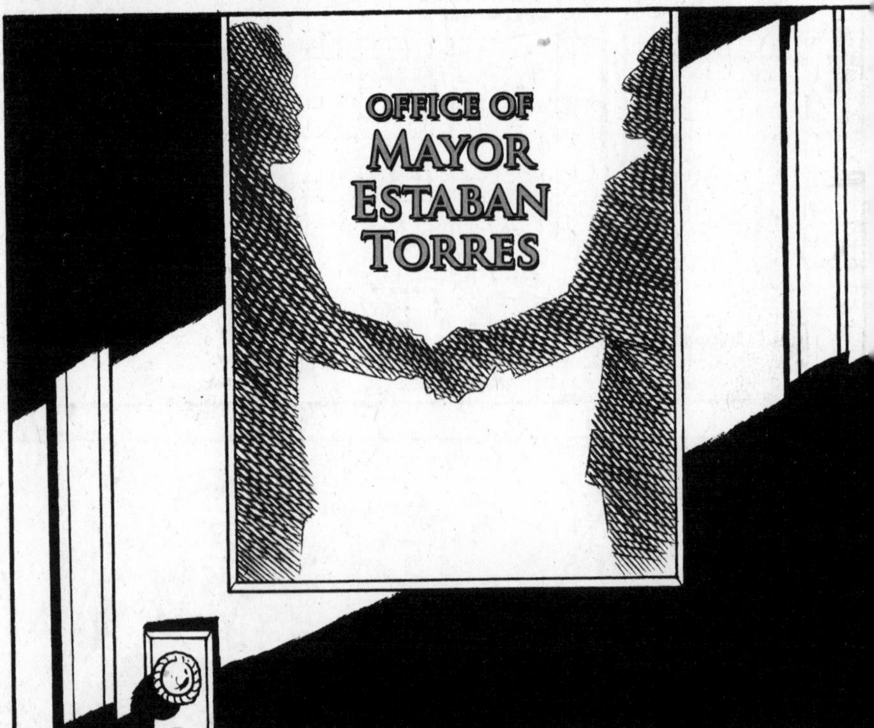
OFFICE OF
MAYOR
ESTABAN
TORRES

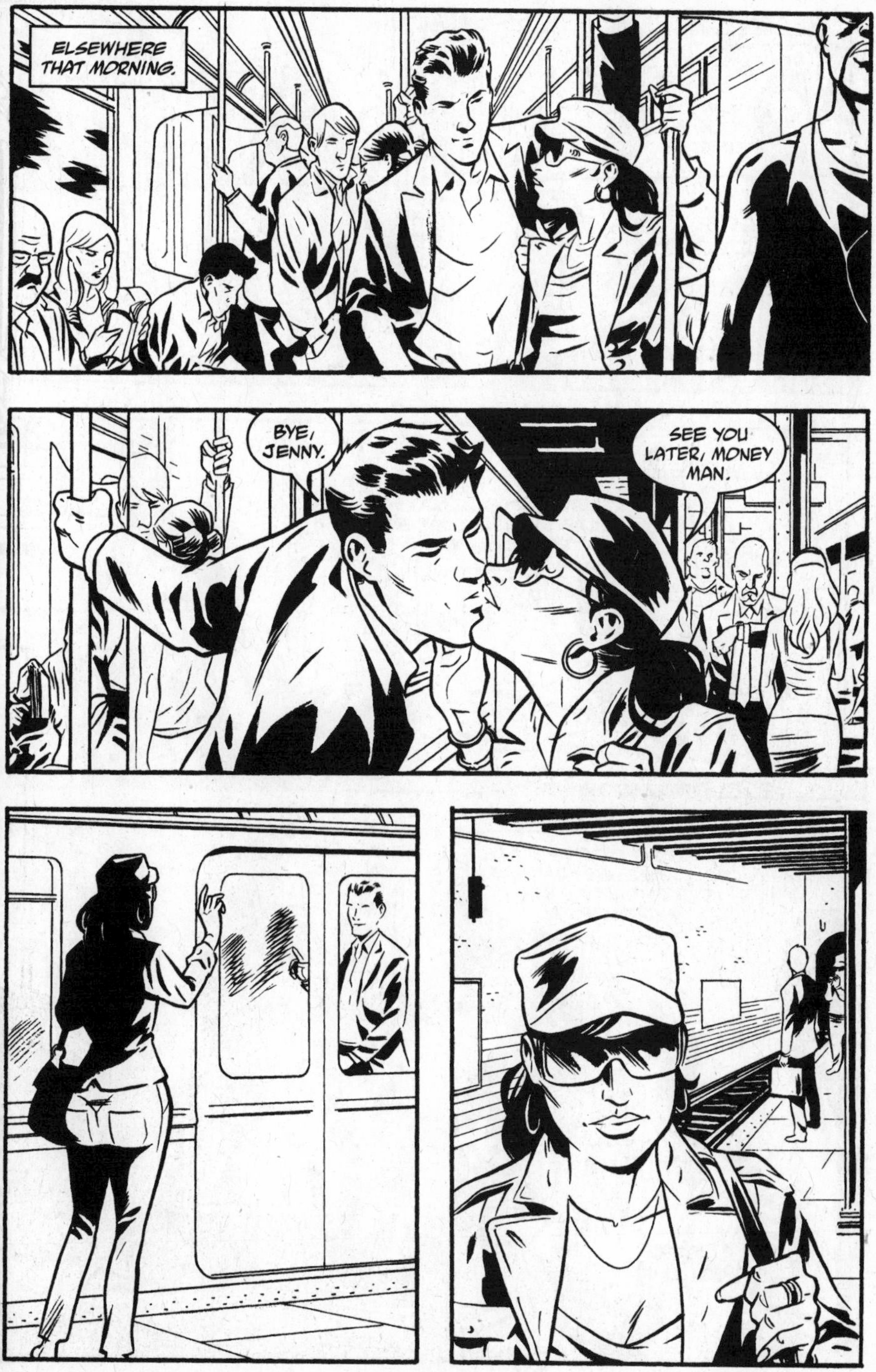
ELSEWHERE THAT MORNING.
BYE, JENNY.
SEE YOU LATER, MONEY MAN.

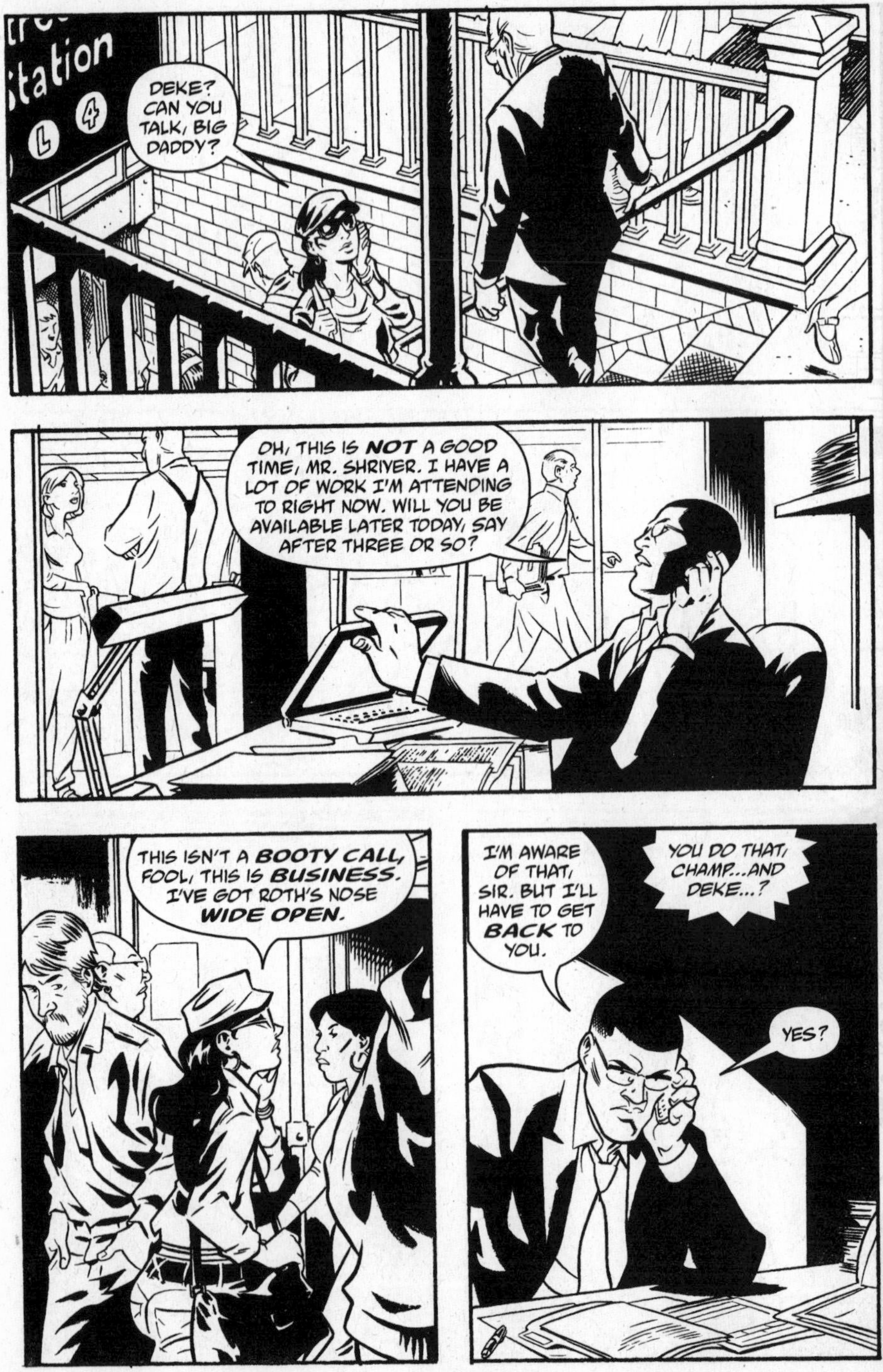

DEKE? CAN YOU TALK, BIG DADDY?
OH, THIS IS NOT A GOOD TIME, MR. SHRIVER. I HAVE A LOT OF WORK I'M ATTENDING TO RIGHT NOW. WILL YOU BE AVAILABLE LATER TODAY, SAY AFTER THREE OR SO?
THIS ISN'T A BOOTY CALL, FOOL, THIS IS BUSINESS. I'VE GOT ROTH'S NOSE WIDE OPEN.
I'M AWARE OF THAT, SIR. BUT I'LL HAVE TO GET BACK TO YOU.
YOU DO THAT, CHAMP...AND DEKE...?
YES?

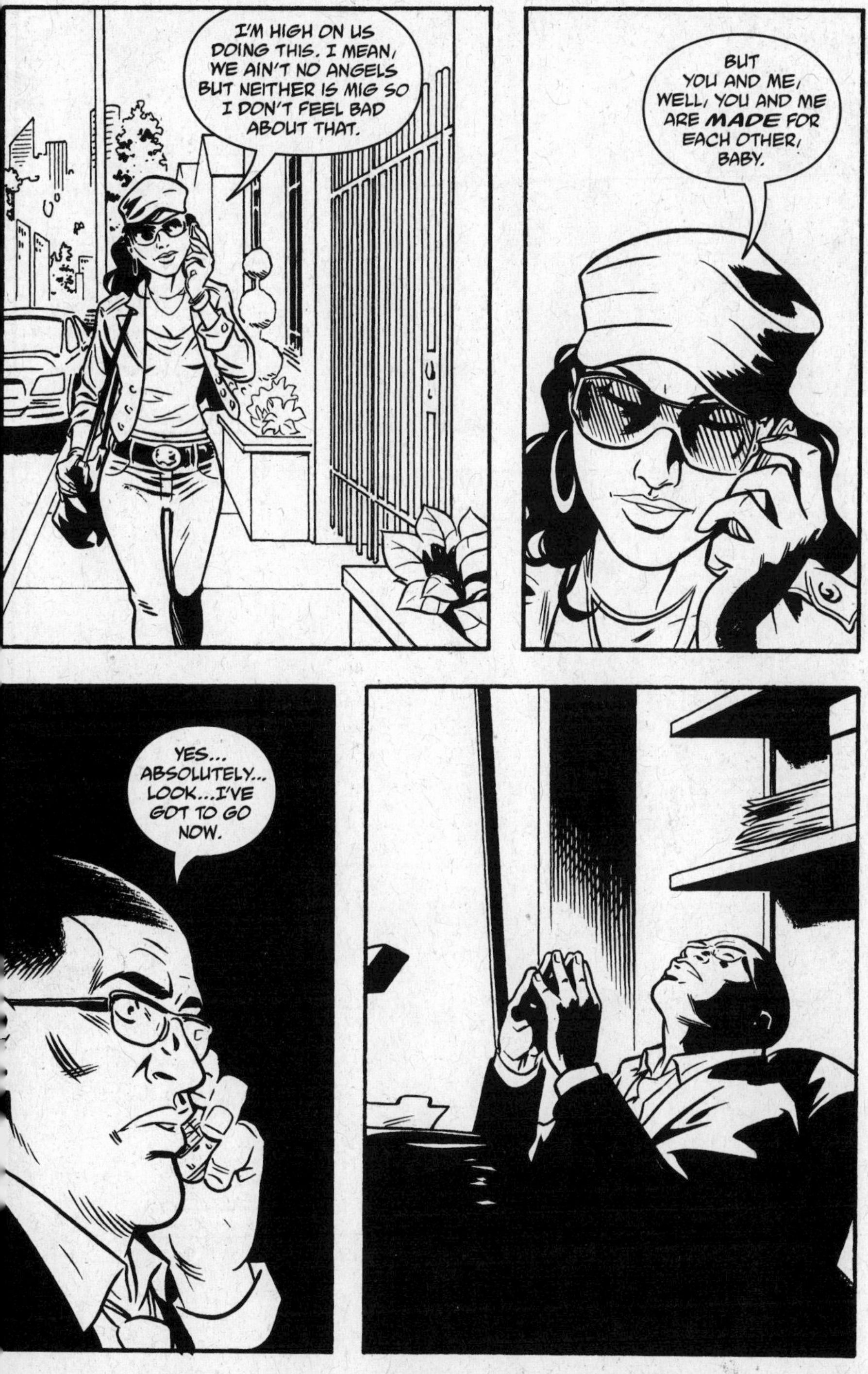
I'M HIGH ON US DOING THIS. I MEAN, WE AIN'T NO ANGELS BUT NEITHER IS MIG SO I DON'T FEEL BAD ABOUT THAT.
BUT YOU AND ME, WELL, YOU AND ME ARE **MADE** FOR EACH OTHER, BABY.
YES... ABSOLUTELY... LOOK...I'VE GOT TO GO NOW.

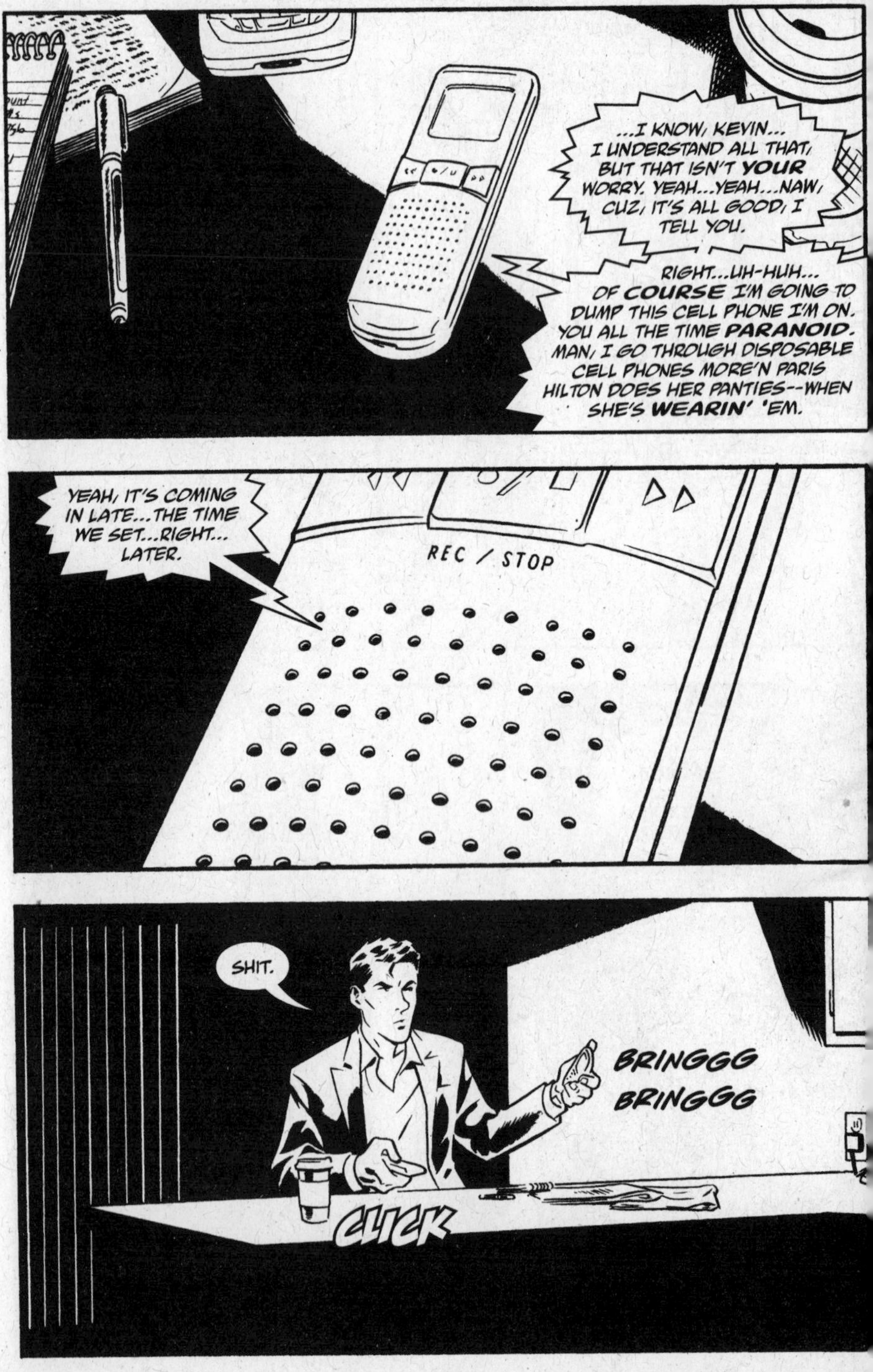
...I KNOW, KEVIN... I UNDERSTAND ALL THAT, BUT THAT ISN'T YOUR WORRY. YEAH...YEAH...NAW, CUZ, IT'S ALL GOOD, I TELL YOU.
RIGHT...UH-HUH... OF COURSE I'M GOING TO DUMP THIS CELL PHONE I'M ON. YOU ALL THE TIME PARANOID. MAN, I GO THROUGH DISPOSABLE CELL PHONES MORE'N PARIS HILTON DOES HER PANTIES--WHEN SHE'S WEARIN' 'EM.
YEAH, IT'S COMING IN LATE...THE TIME WE SET...RIGHT... LATER.
REC / STOP
SHIT.
BRINGGG
BRINGGG
CLICK

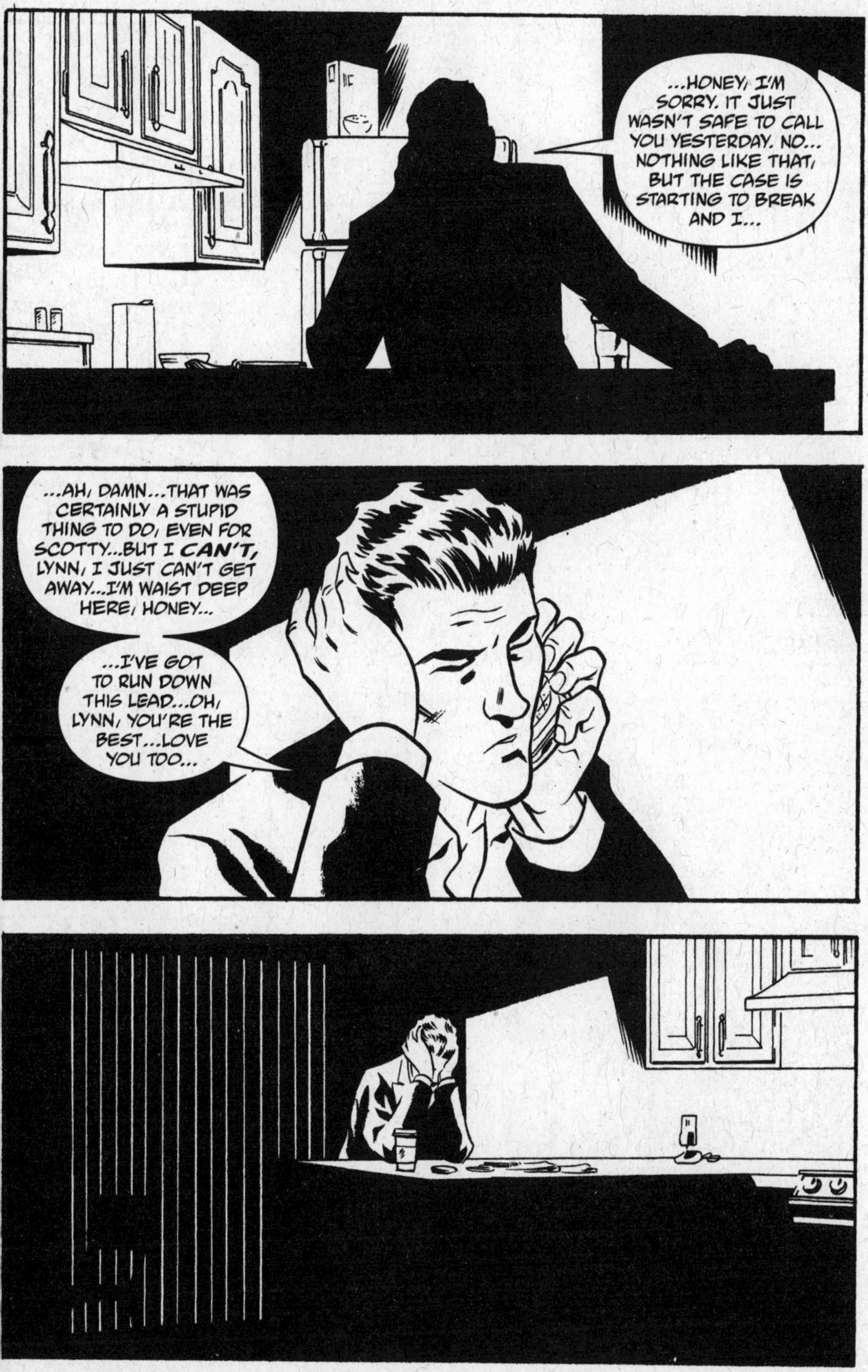
...HONEY, I'M SORRY. IT JUST WASN'T SAFE TO CALL YOU YESTERDAY. NO... NOTHING LIKE THAT, BUT THE CASE IS STARTING TO BREAK AND I...
...AH, DAMN...THAT WAS CERTAINLY A STUPID THING TO DO, EVEN FOR SCOTTY...BUT I CAN'T, LYNN, I JUST CAN'T GET AWAY...I'M WAIST DEEP HERE, HONEY...
...I'VE GOT TO RUN DOWN THIS LEAD...OH, LYNN, YOU'RE THE BEST...LOVE YOU TOO...

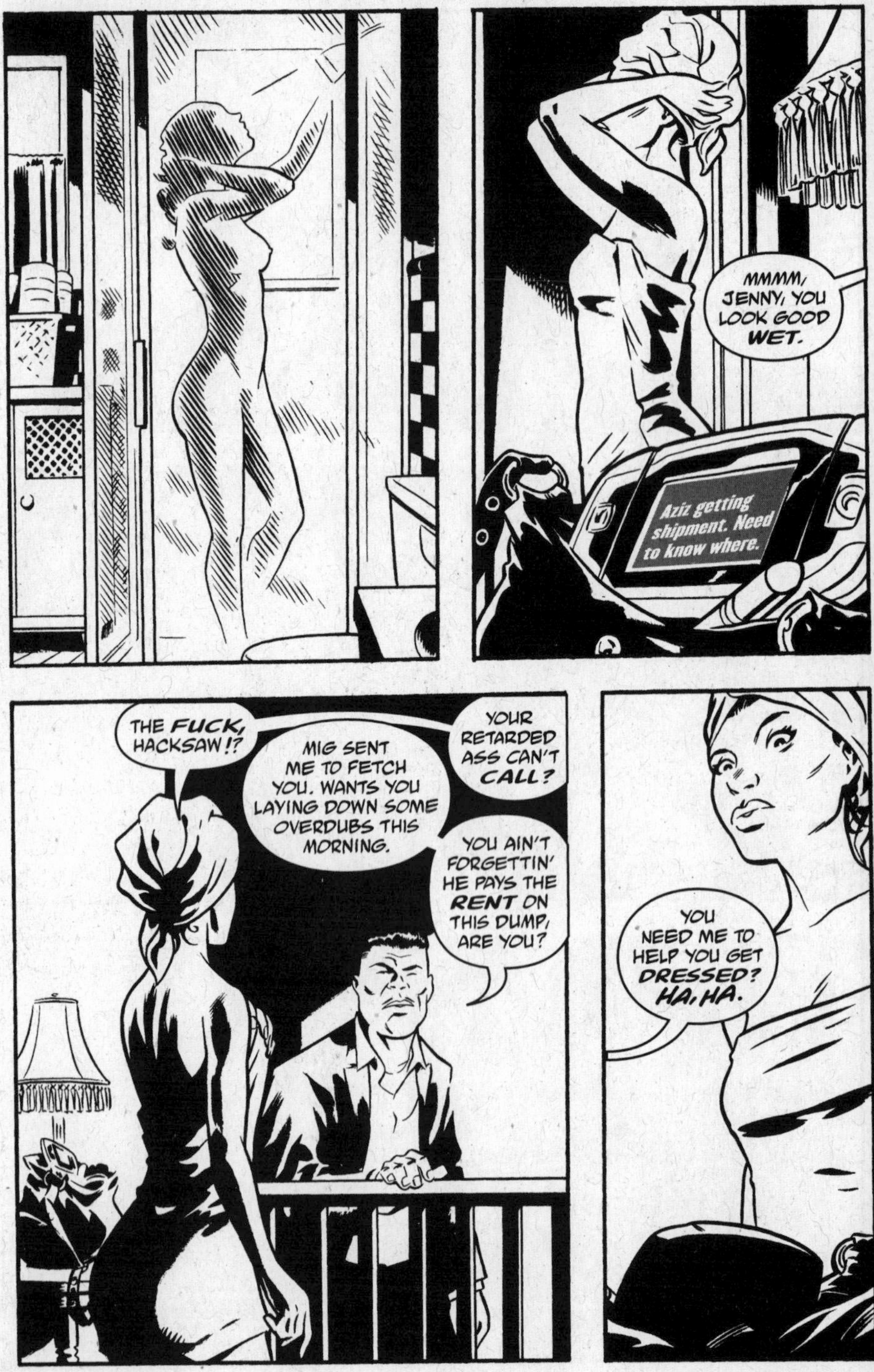
MMMM, JENNY, YOU LOOK GOOD WET.
Aziz getting shipment. Need to know where.
THE FUCK, HACKSAW!?
MIG SENT ME TO FETCH YOU. WANTS YOU LAYING DOWN SOME OVERDUBS THIS MORNING.
YOUR RETARDED ASS CAN'T CALL?
YOU AIN'T FORGETTIN' HE PAYS THE RENT ON THIS DUMP, ARE YOU?
YOU NEED ME TO HELP YOU GET DRESSED? HA, HA.

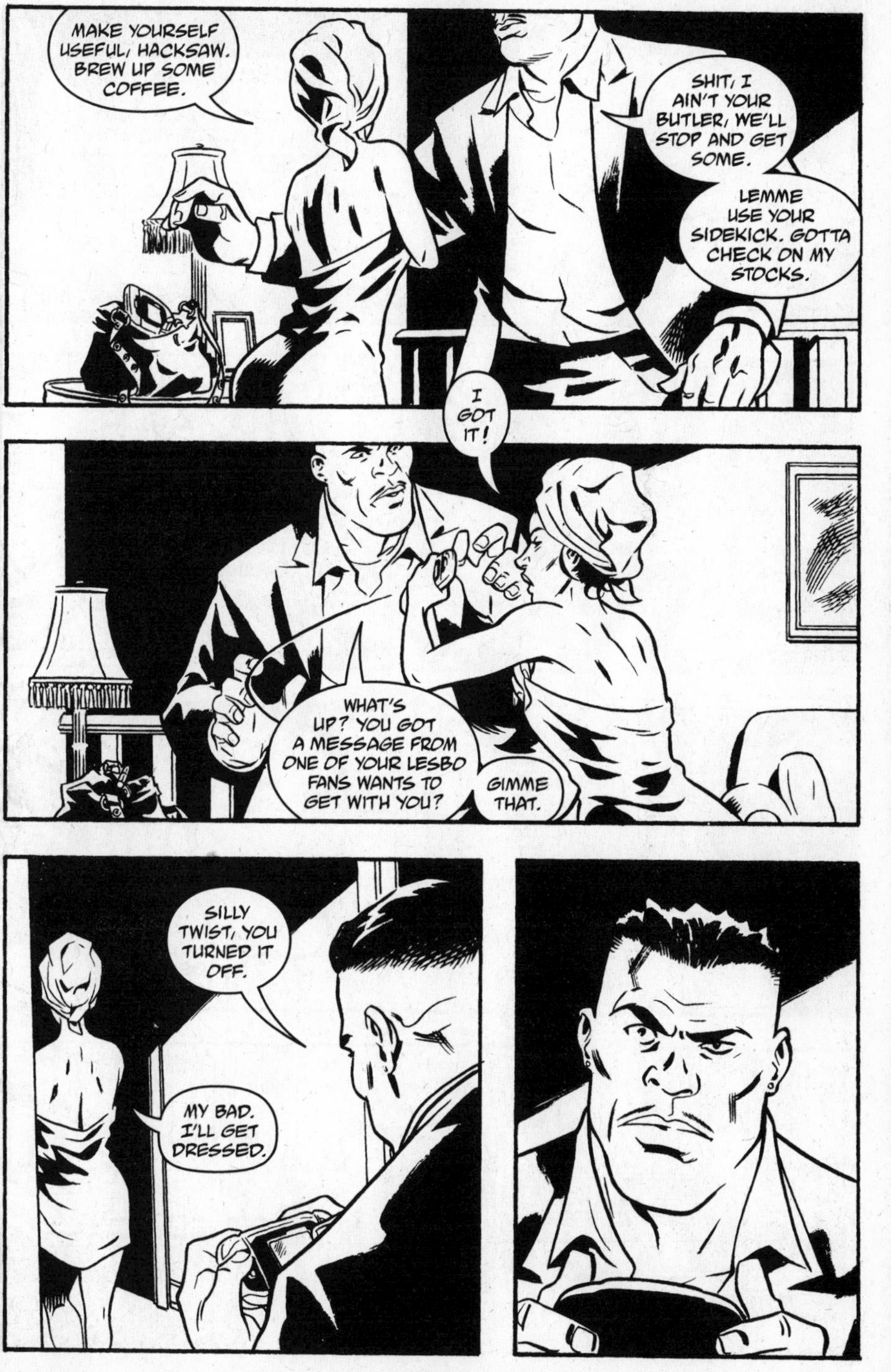
MAKE YOURSELF USEFUL, HACKSAW. BREW UP SOME COFFEE.
SHIT, I AIN'T YOUR BUTLER, WE'LL STOP AND GET SOME.
LEMME USE YOUR SIDEKICK. GOTTA CHECK ON MY STOCKS.
I GOT IT!
WHAT'S UP? YOU GOT A MESSAGE FROM ONE OF YOUR LESBO FANS WANTS TO GET WITH YOU?
GIMME THAT.
SILLY TWIST, YOU TURNED IT OFF.
MY BAD. I'LL GET DRESSED.

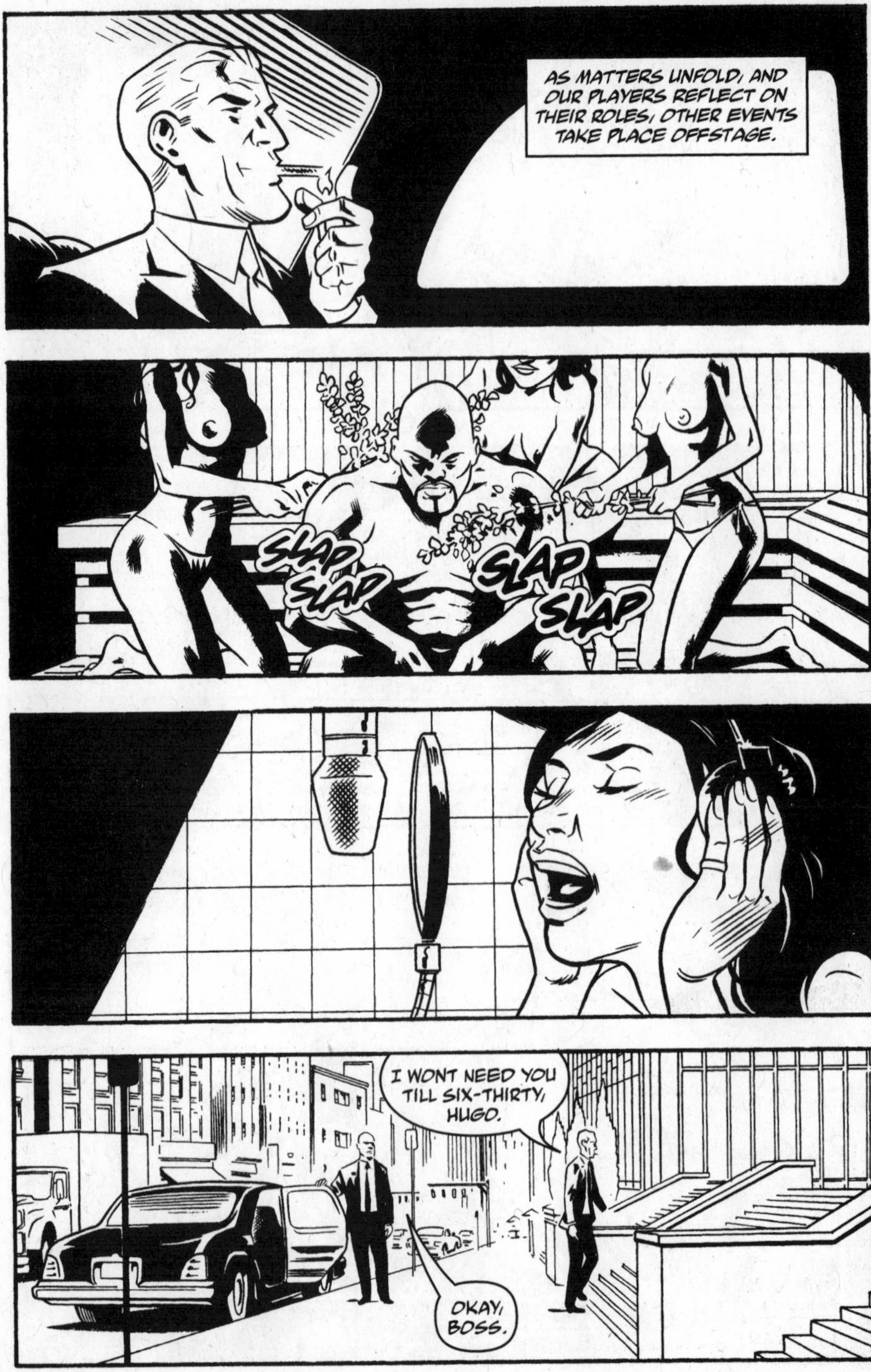
AS MATTERS UNFOLD, AND OUR PLAYERS REFLECT ON THEIR ROLES, OTHER EVENTS TAKE PLACE OFFSTAGE.
SLAP SLAP
SLAP SLAP
I WONT NEED YOU TILL SIX-THIRTY, HUGO.
OKAY, BOSS.

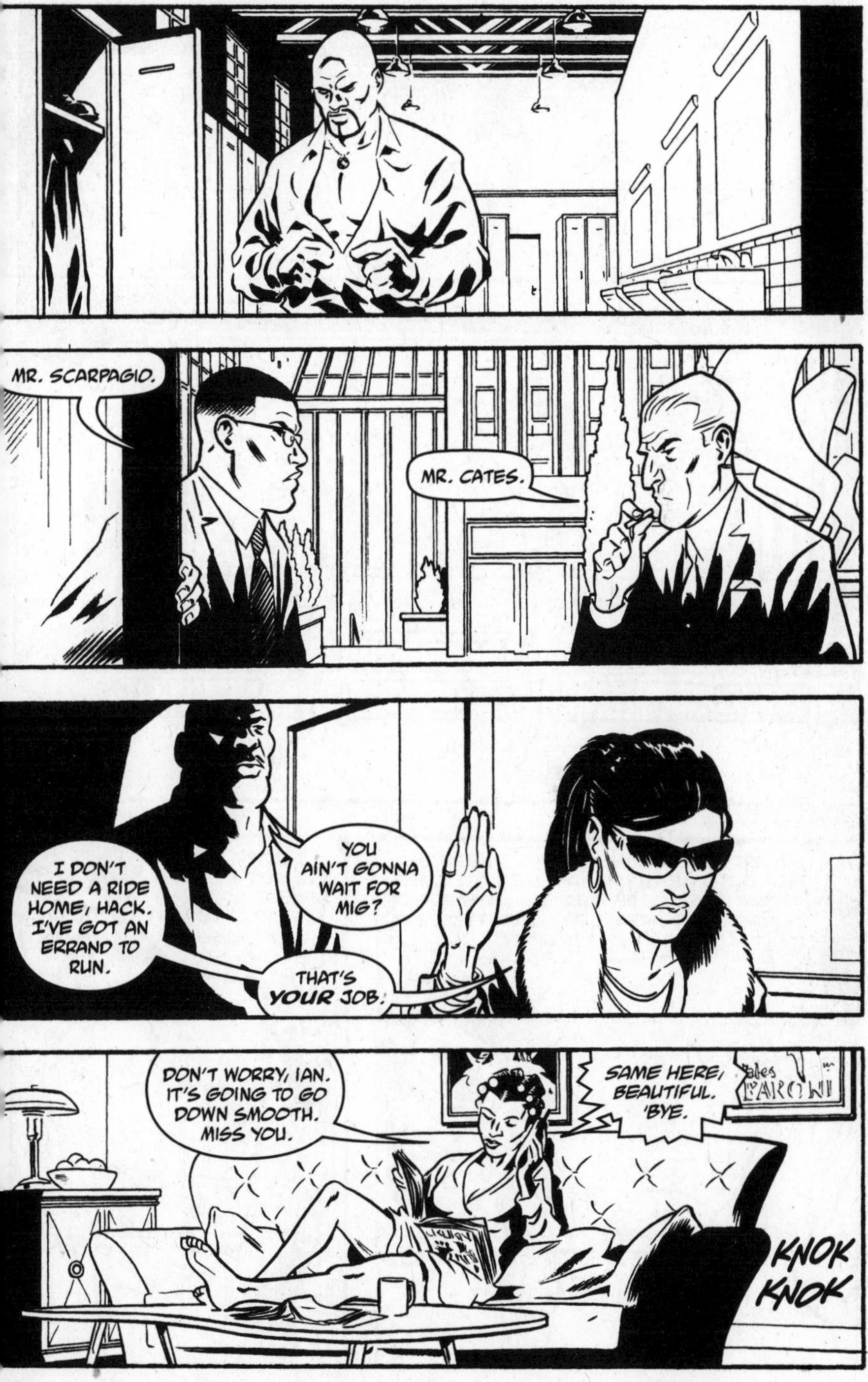
MR. SCARPAGIO.
MR. CATES.
I DON'T NEED A RIDE HOME, HACK. I'VE GOT AN ERRAND TO RUN.
YOU AIN'T GONNA WAIT FOR MIG?
THAT'S YOUR JOB.
DON'T WORRY, IAN. IT'S GOING TO GO DOWN SMOOTH. MISS YOU.
SAME HERE, BEAUTIFUL. 'BYE.
KNOK KNOK

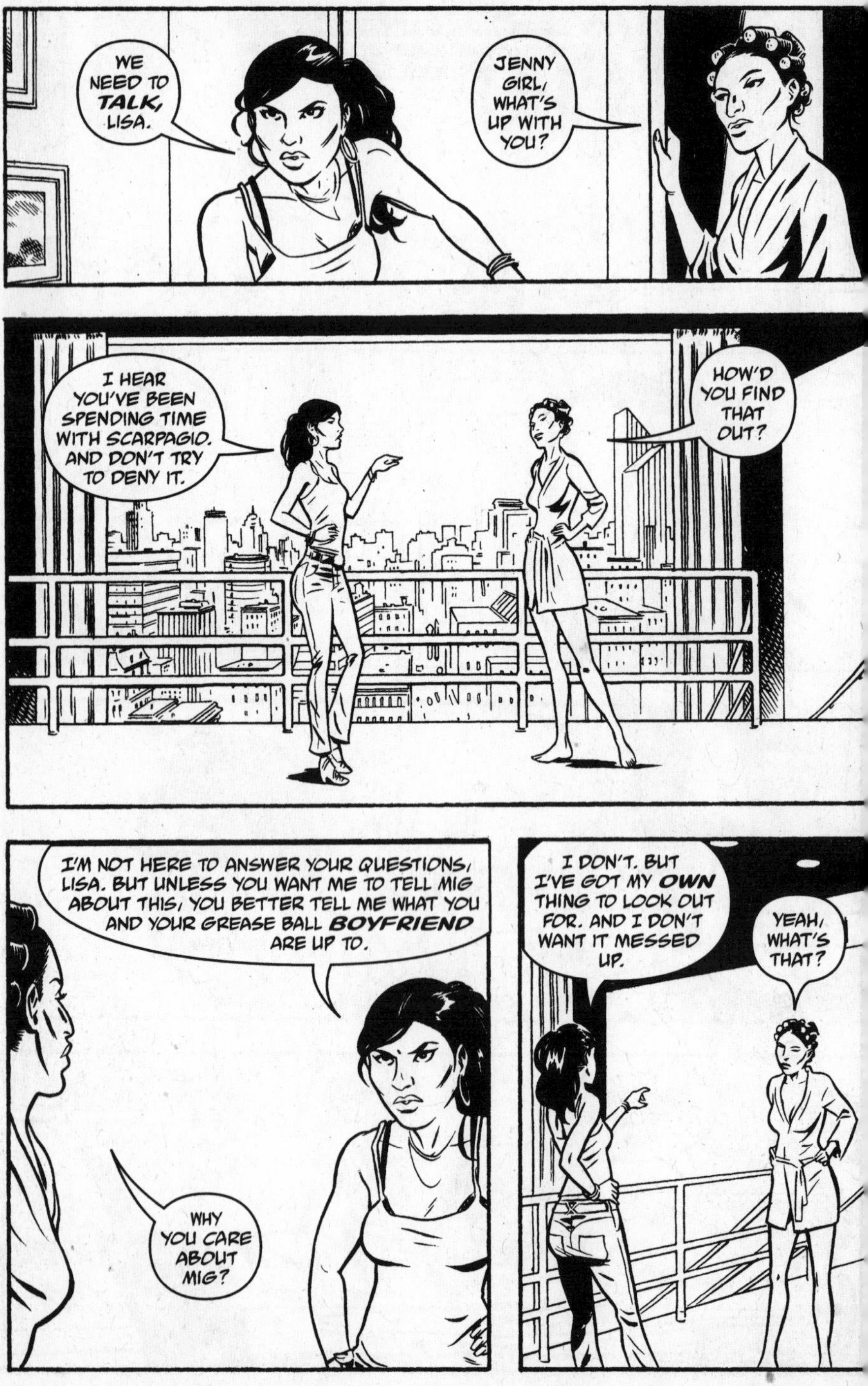
WE NEED TO TALK, LISA.
JENNY GIRL, WHAT'S UP WITH YOU?
I HEAR YOU'VE BEEN SPENDING TIME WITH SCARPAGIO. AND DON'T TRY TO DENY IT.
HOW'D YOU FIND THAT OUT?
I'M NOT HERE TO ANSWER YOUR QUESTIONS, LISA. BUT UNLESS YOU WANT ME TO TELL MIG ABOUT THIS, YOU BETTER TELL ME WHAT YOU AND YOUR GREASE BALL BOYFRIEND ARE UP TO.
WHY YOU CARE ABOUT MIG?
I DON'T. BUT I'VE GOT MY OWN THING TO LOOK OUT FOR. AND I DON'T WANT IT MESSED UP.
YEAH, WHAT'S THAT?

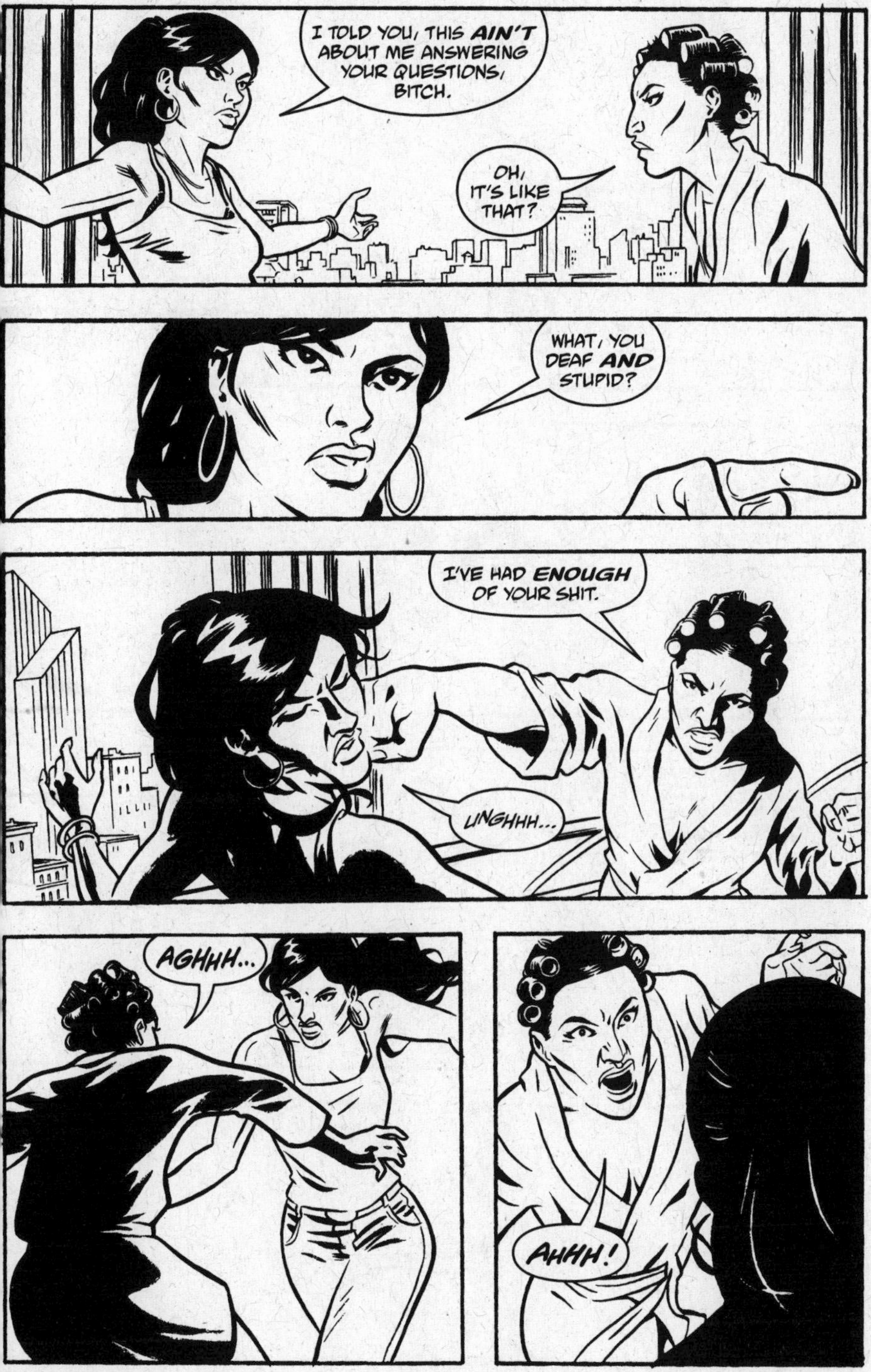
I TOLD YOU, THIS AIN'T ABOUT ME ANSWERING YOUR QUESTIONS, BITCH.
OH, IT'S LIKE THAT?
WHAT, YOU DEAF AND STUPID?
I'VE HAD ENOUGH OF YOUR SHIT.
UNGHHH...
AGHHH...
AHHH!

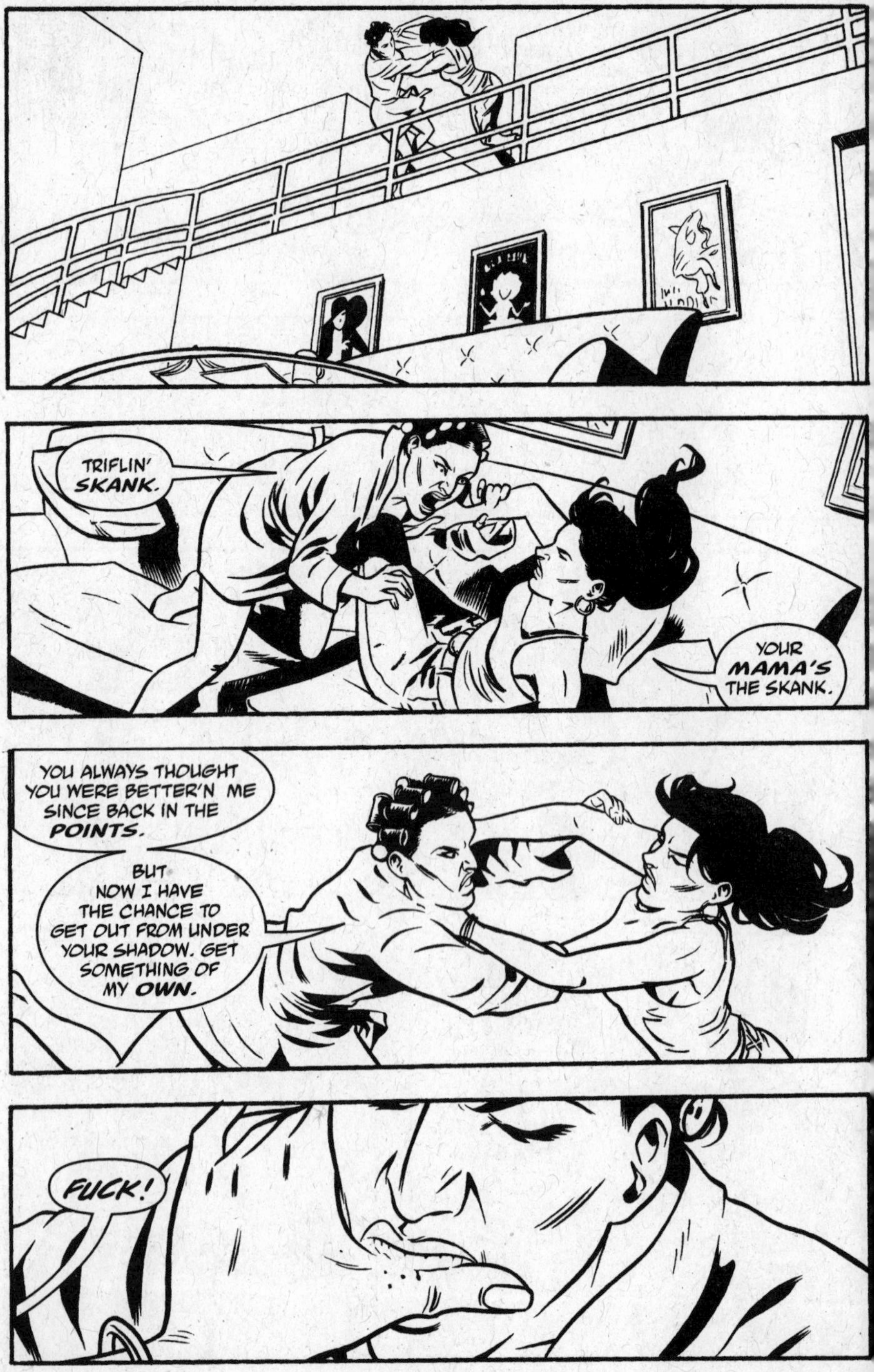
TRIFLIN' SKANK.
YOUR MAMA'S THE SKANK.
YOU ALWAYS THOUGHT YOU WERE BETTER'N ME SINCE BACK IN THE POINTS.
BUT NOW I HAVE THE CHANCE TO GET OUT FROM UNDER YOUR SHADOW. GET SOMETHING OF MY OWN.
FUCK!

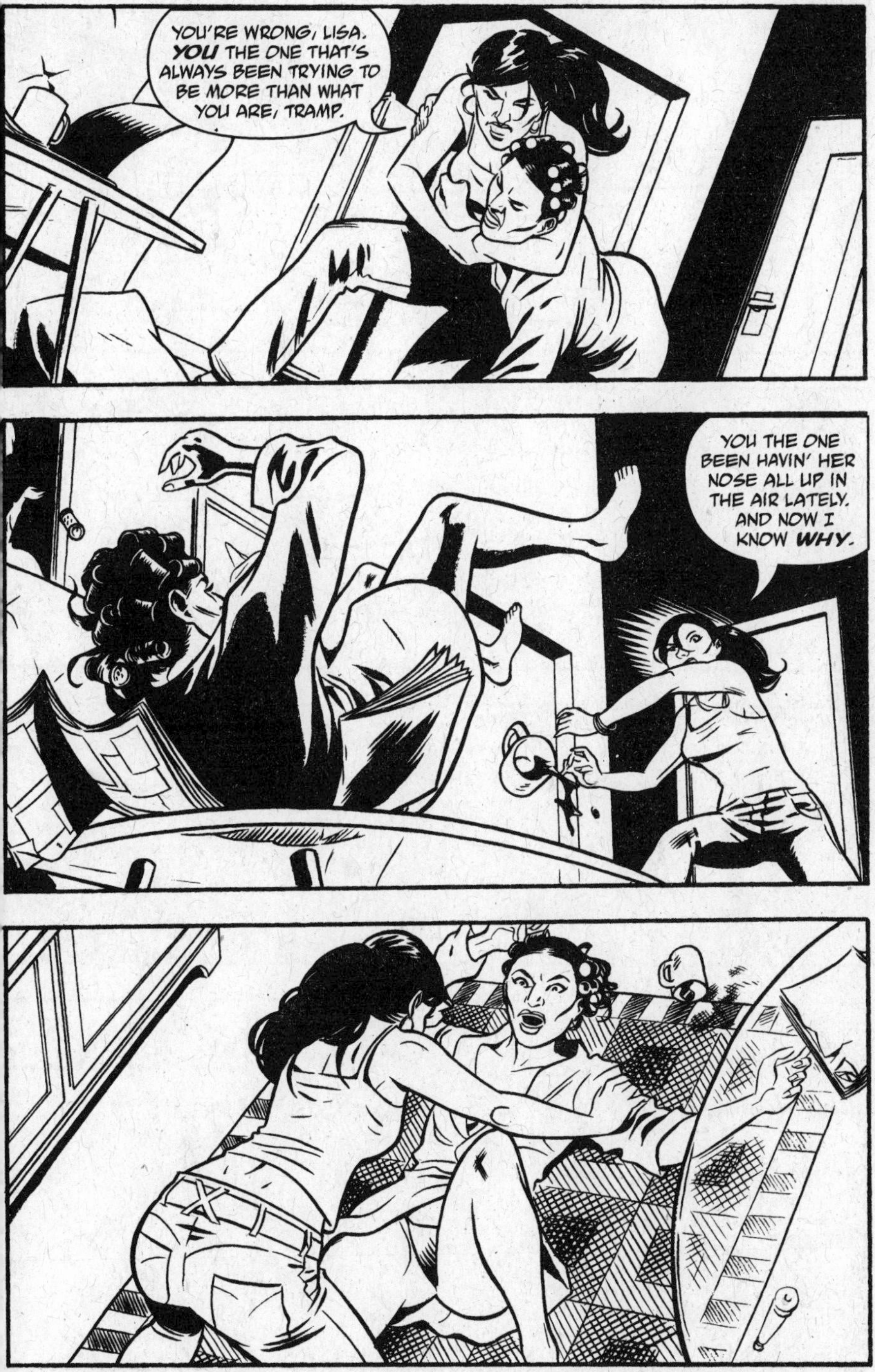
YOU'RE WRONG, LISA. YOU THE ONE THAT'S ALWAYS BEEN TRYING TO BE MORE THAN WHAT YOU ARE, TRAMP.
YOU THE ONE BEEN HAVIN' HER NOSE ALL UP IN THE AIR LATELY. AND NOW I KNOW WHY.

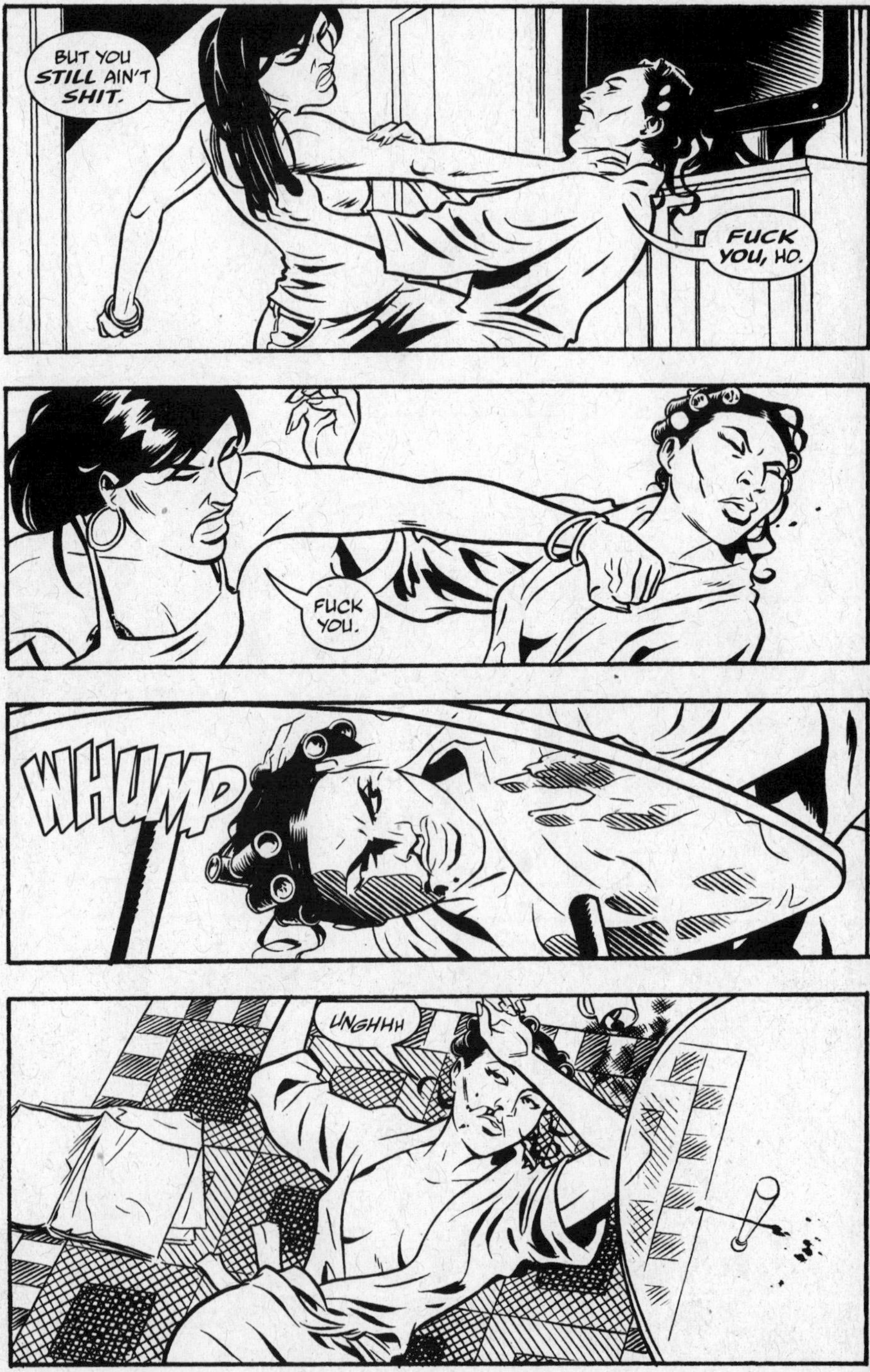
BUT YOU STILL AIN'T SHIT.
FUCK YOU, HO.
FUCK YOU.
WHUMP
UNGHHH

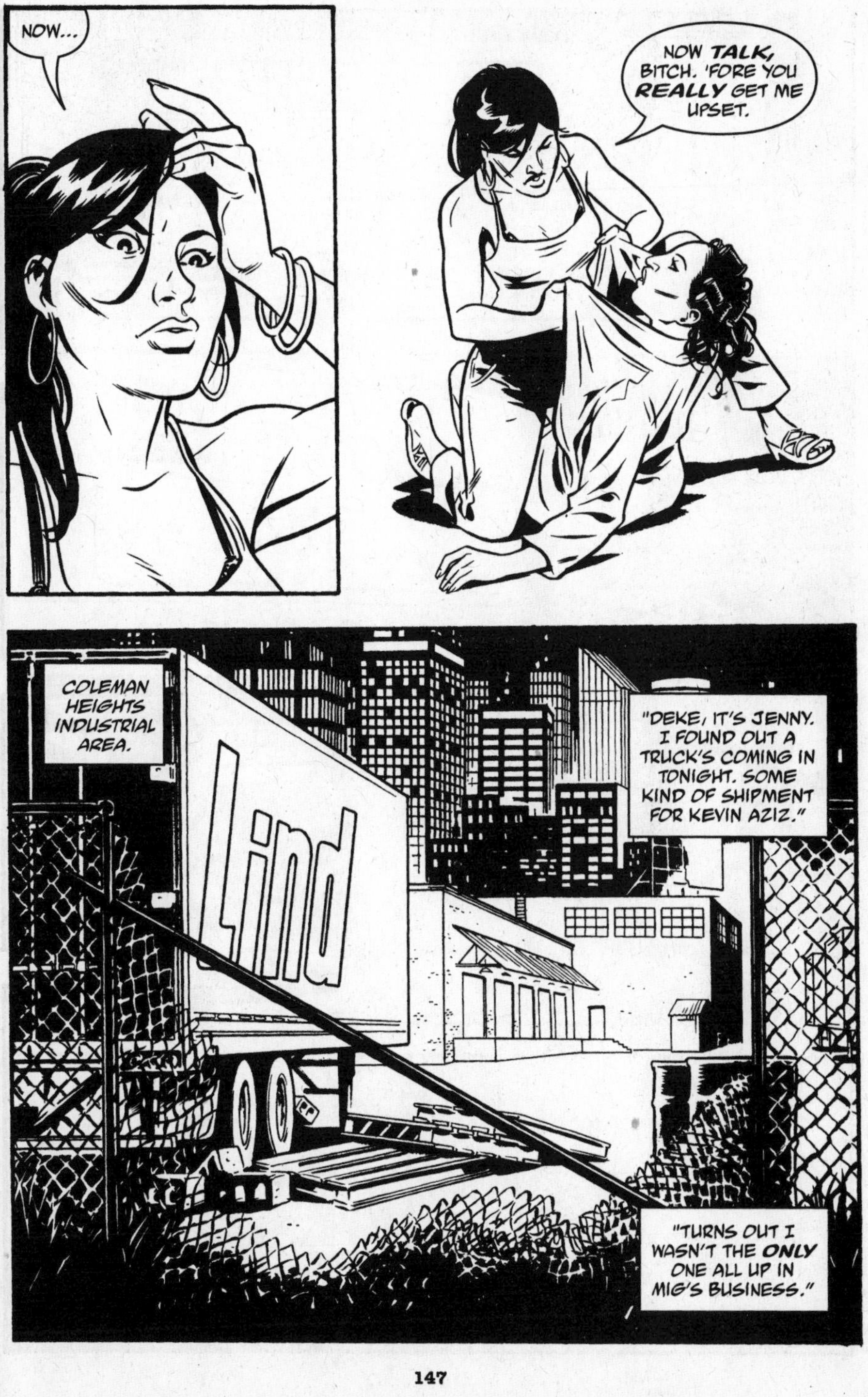
NOW...
NOW TALK, BITCH. 'FORE YOU REALLY GET ME UPSET.
COLEMAN HEIGHTS INDUSTRIAL AREA.
"DEKE, IT'S JENNY. I FOUND OUT A TRUCK'S COMING IN TONIGHT. SOME KIND OF SHIPMENT FOR KEVIN AZIZ."
Lind
"TURNS OUT I WASN'T THE ONLY ONE ALL UP IN MIG'S BUSINESS."

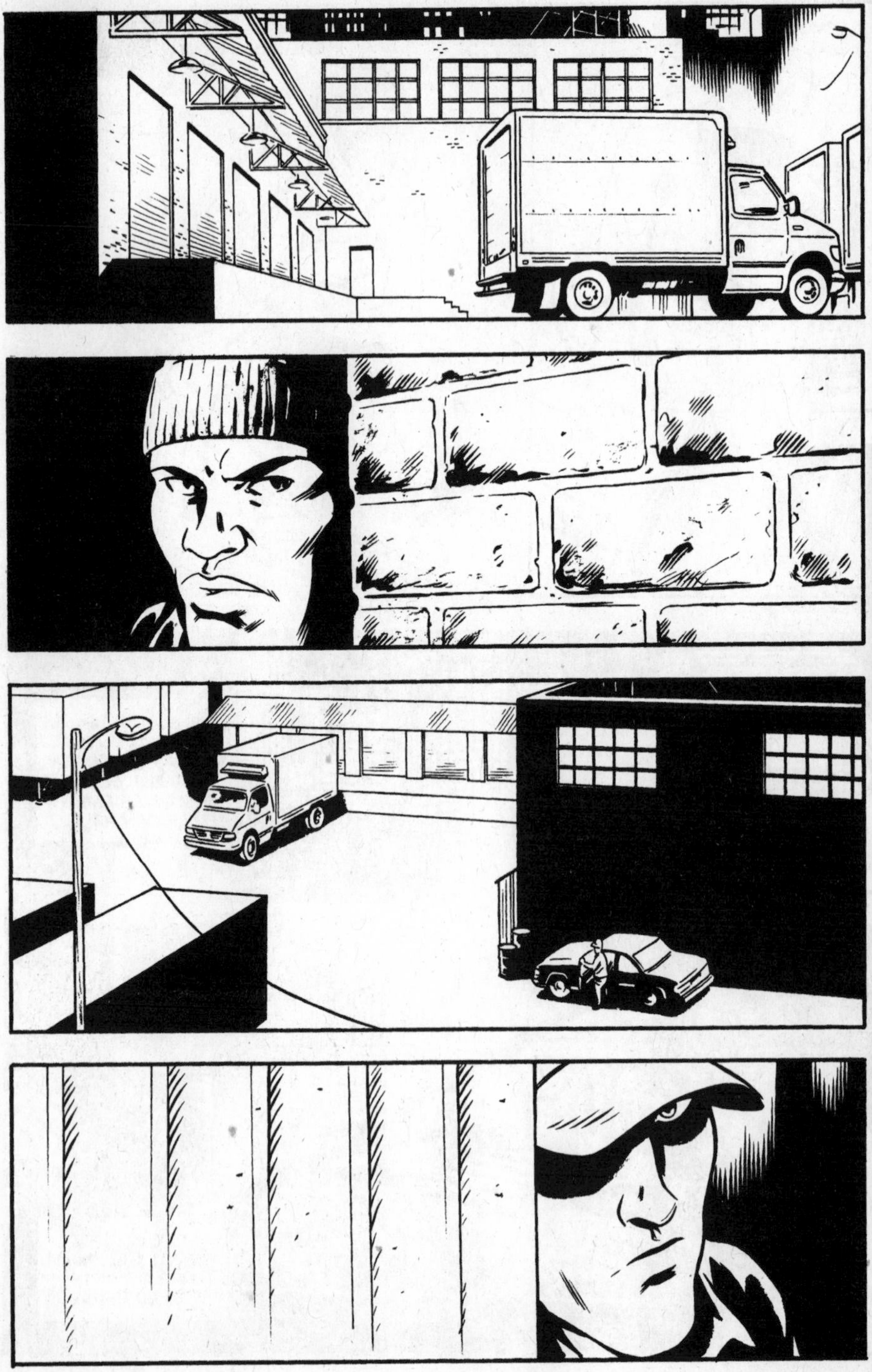

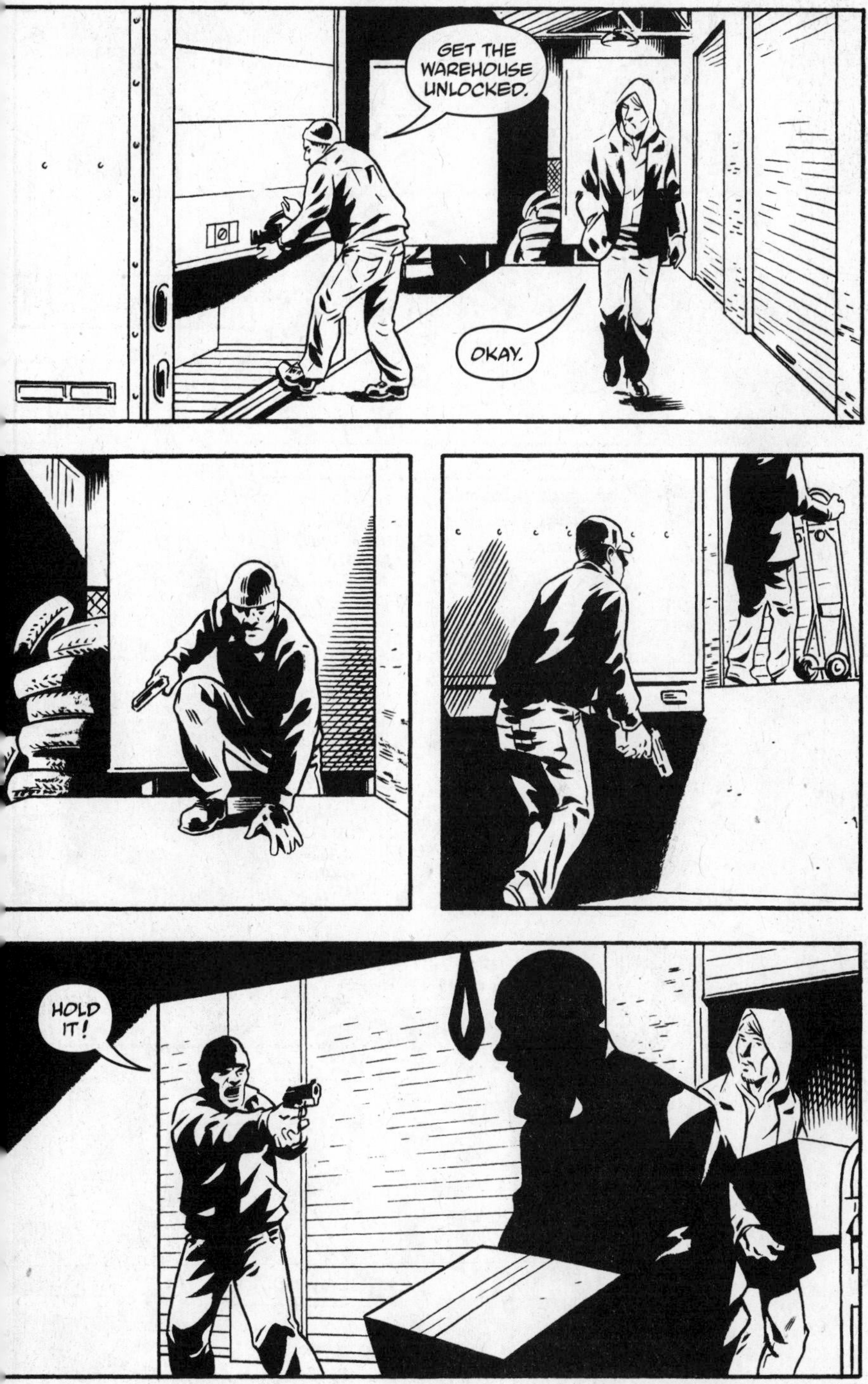
GET THE WAREHOUSE UNLOCKED.
OKAY.
HOLD IT!

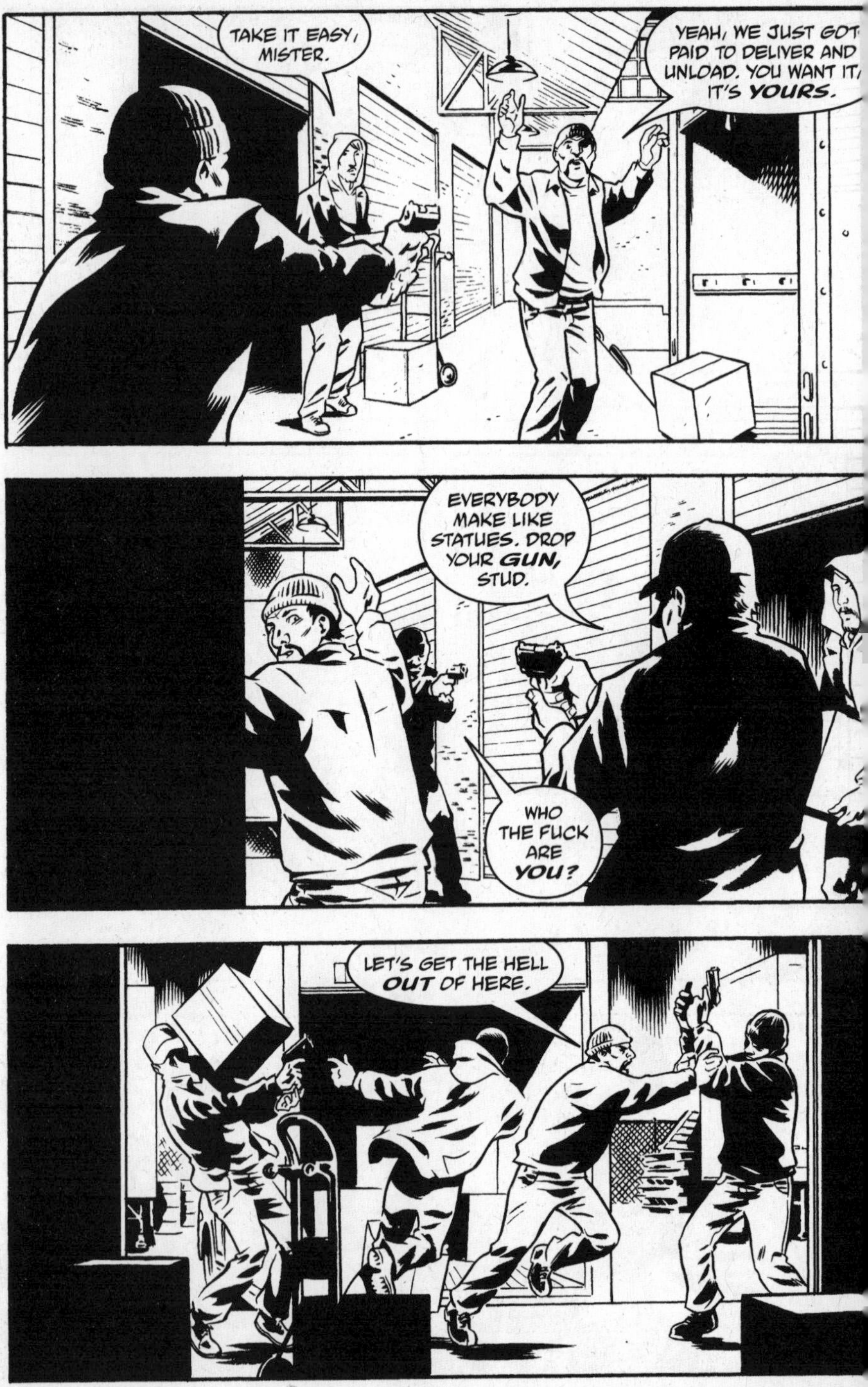
TAKE IT EASY, MISTER.
YEAH, WE JUST GOT PAID TO DELIVER AND UNLOAD. YOU WANT IT, IT'S YOURS.
EVERYBODY MAKE LIKE STATUES. DROP YOUR GUN, STUD.
WHO THE FUCK ARE YOU?
LET'S GET THE HELL OUT OF HERE.

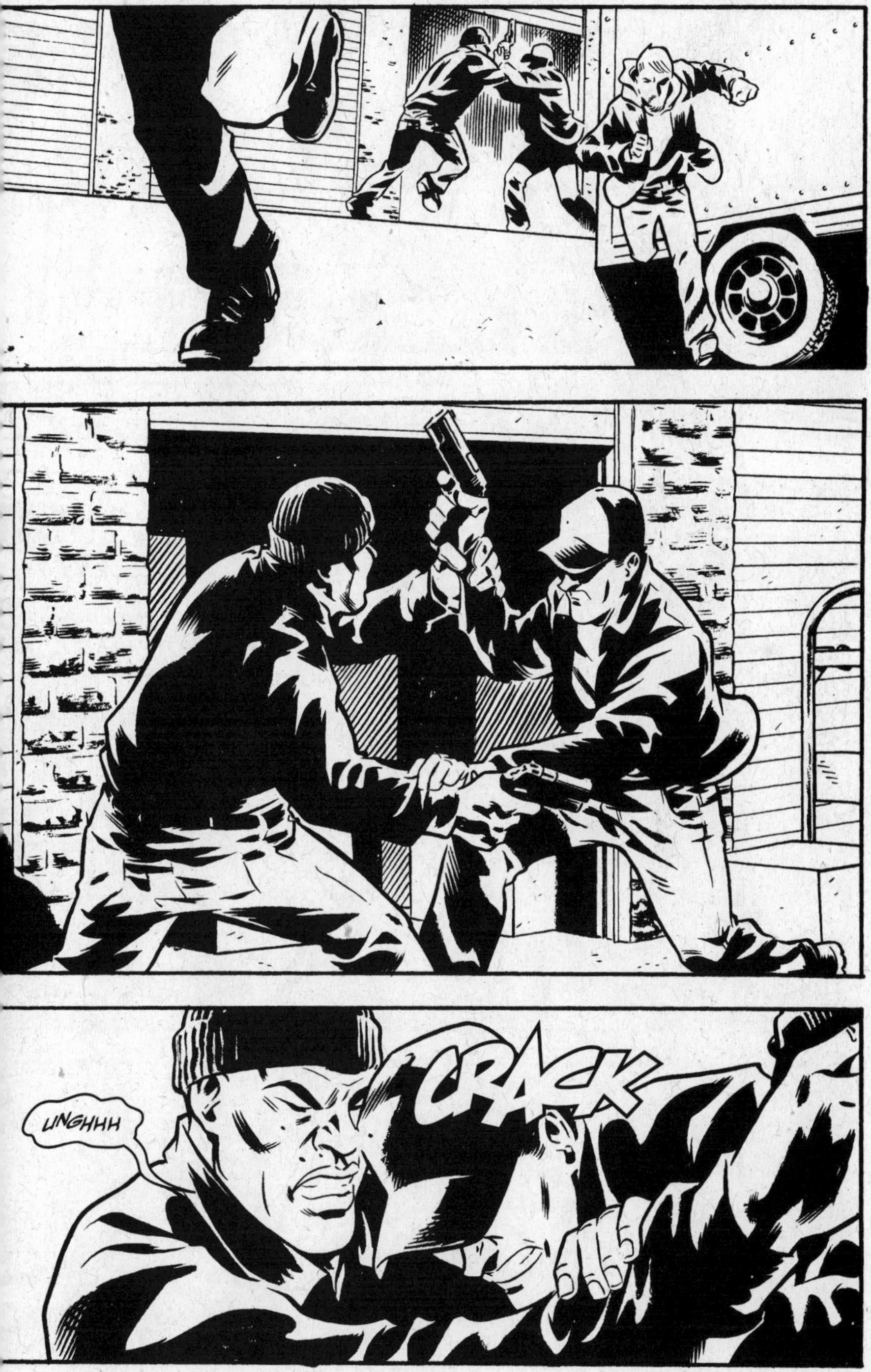
UNGHHH
CRACK

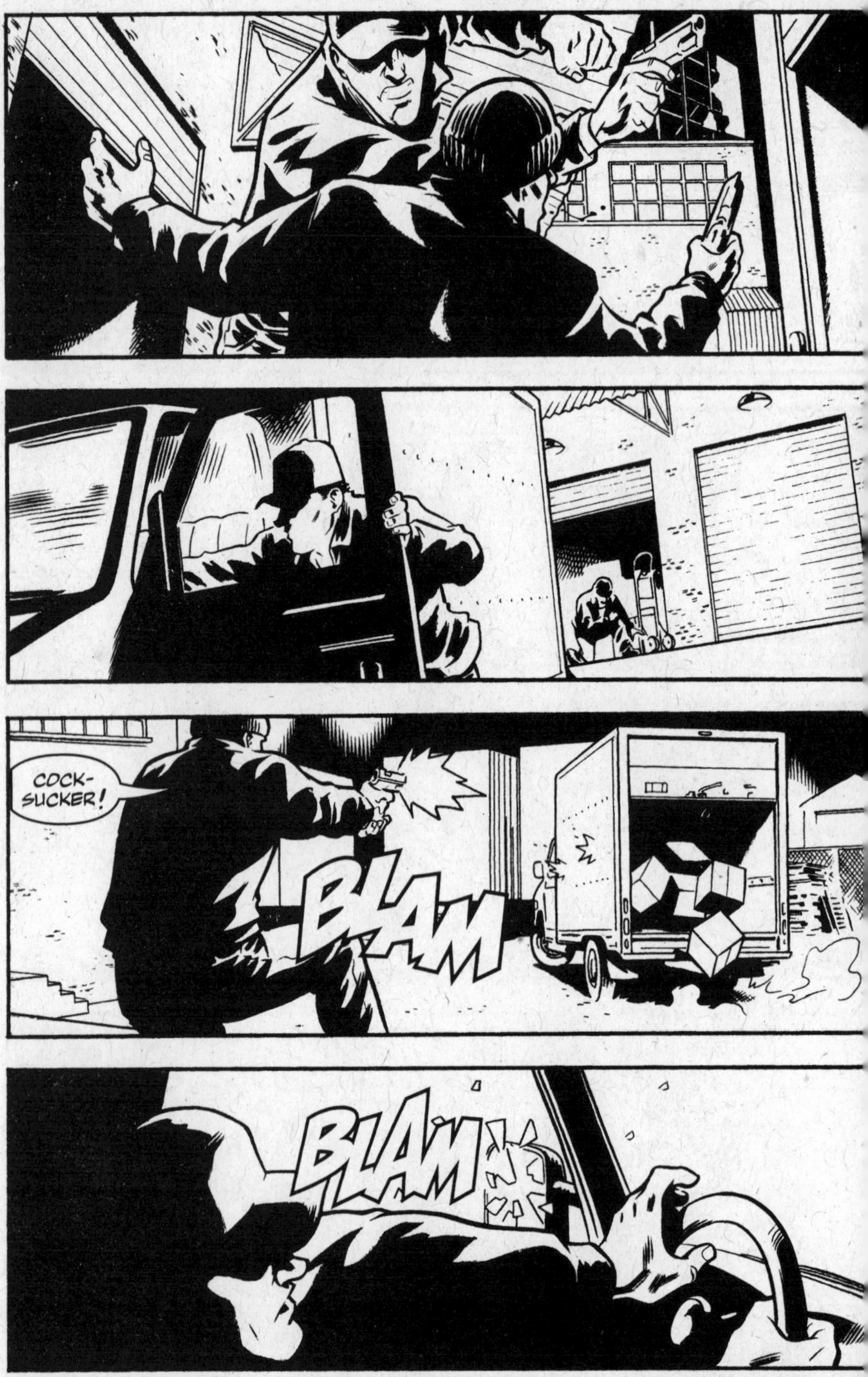
COCK-
SUCKER!
BLAM
BLAM

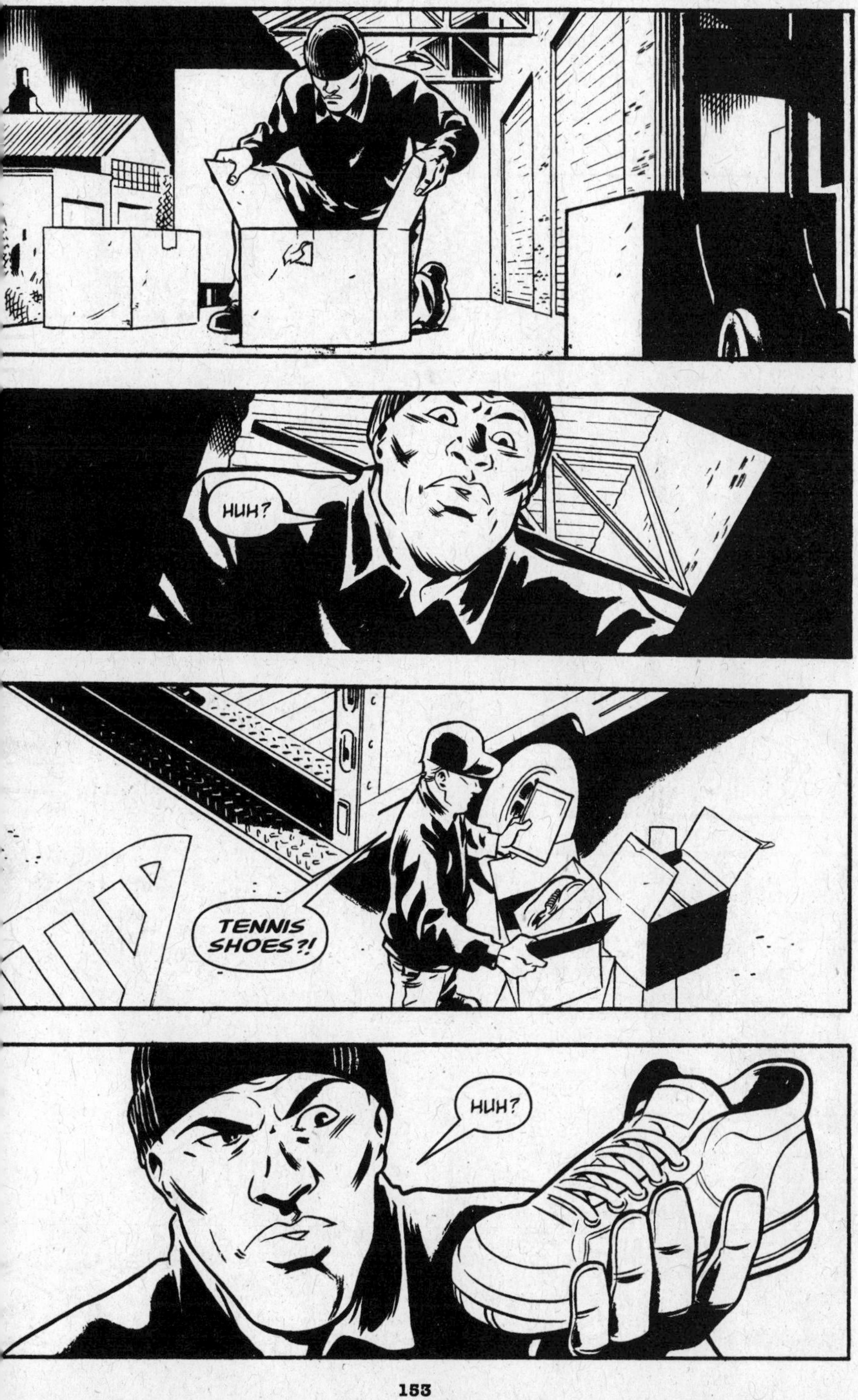
HUH?
TENNIS SHOES?!
HUH?

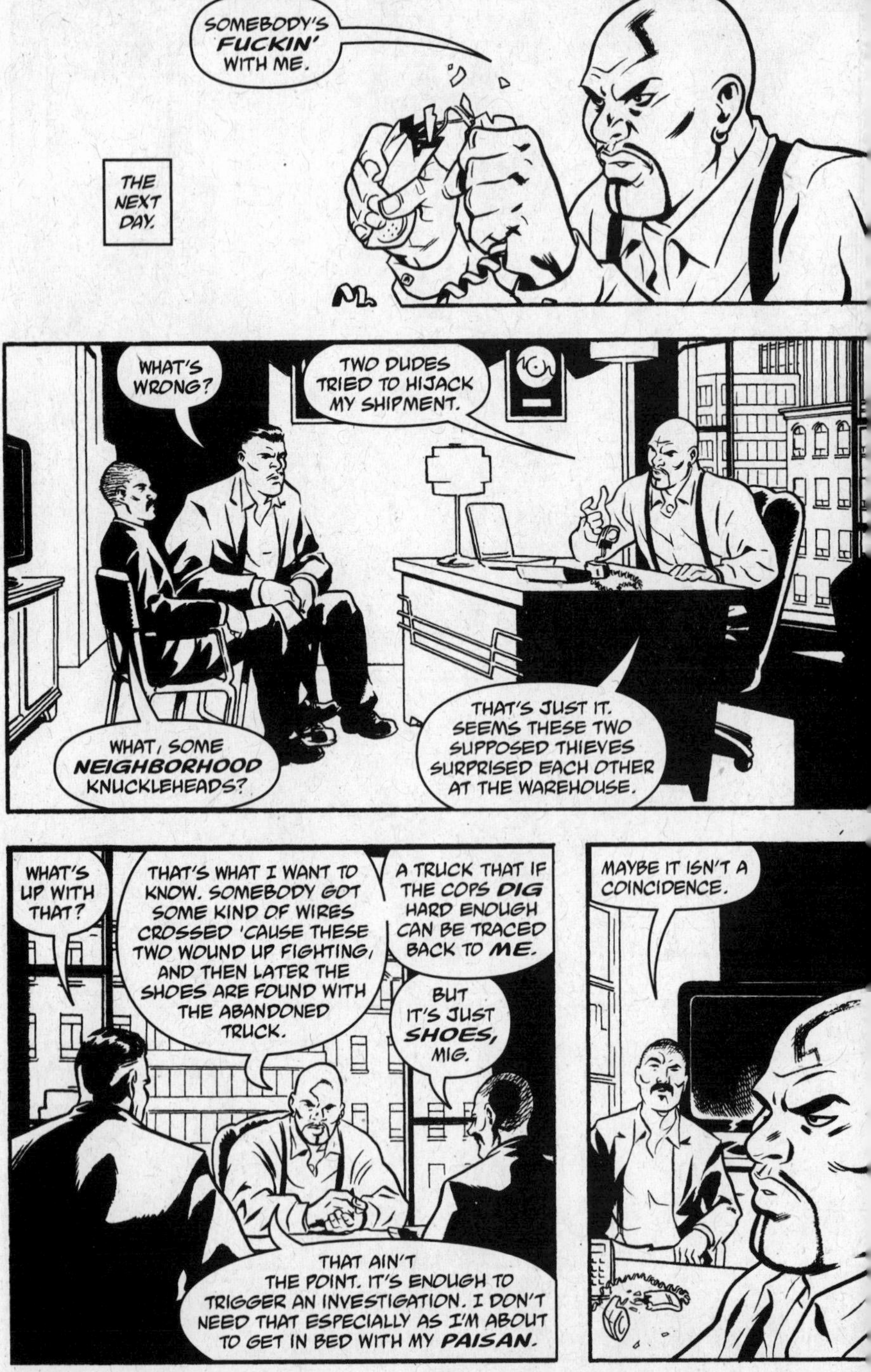

SOMEBODY'S FUCKIN' WITH ME.
THE NEXT DAY.
WHAT'S WRONG?
TWO DUDES TRIED TO HIJACK MY SHIPMENT.
WHAT, SOME NEIGHBORHOOD KNUCKLEHEADS?
THAT'S JUST IT. SEEMS THESE TWO SUPPOSED THIEVES SURPRISED EACH OTHER AT THE WAREHOUSE.
WHAT'S UP WITH THAT?
THAT'S WHAT I WANT TO KNOW. SOMEBODY GOT SOME KIND OF WIRES CROSSED 'CAUSE THESE TWO WOUND UP FIGHTING, AND THEN LATER THE SHOES ARE FOUND WITH THE ABANDONED TRUCK.
A TRUCK THAT IF THE COPS DIG HARD ENOUGH CAN BE TRACED BACK TO ME.
BUT IT'S JUST SHOES, MIG.
THAT AIN'T THE POINT. IT'S ENOUGH TO TRIGGER AN INVESTIGATION. I DON'T NEED THAT ESPECIALLY AS I'M ABOUT TO GET IN BED WITH MY PAISAN.
MAYBE IT ISN'T A COINCIDENCE.

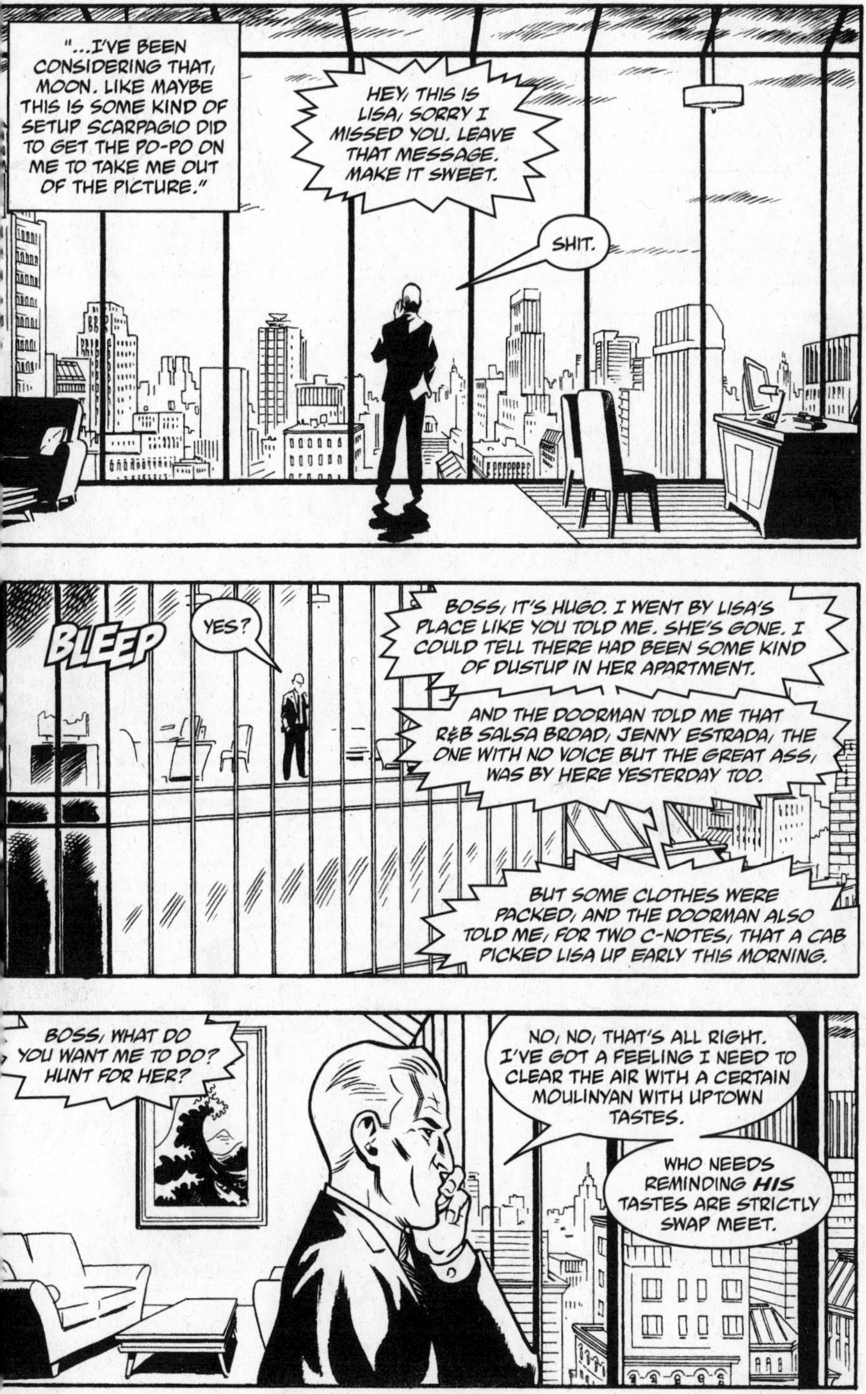
"...I'VE BEEN CONSIDERING THAT, MOON. LIKE MAYBE THIS IS SOME KIND OF SETUP SCARPAGIO DID TO GET THE PO-PO ON ME TO TAKE ME OUT OF THE PICTURE."
HEY, THIS IS LISA, SORRY I MISSED YOU. LEAVE THAT MESSAGE. MAKE IT SWEET.
SHIT.
BLEEP
YES?
BOSS, IT'S HUGO. I WENT BY LISA'S PLACE LIKE YOU TOLD ME. SHE'S GONE. I COULD TELL THERE HAD BEEN SOME KIND OF DUSTUP IN HER APARTMENT.
AND THE DOORMAN TOLD ME THAT R&B SALSA BROAD, JENNY ESTRADA, THE ONE WITH NO VOICE BUT THE GREAT ASS, WAS BY HERE YESTERDAY TOO.
BUT SOME CLOTHES WERE PACKED, AND THE DOORMAN ALSO TOLD ME, FOR TWO C-NOTES, THAT A CAB PICKED LISA UP EARLY THIS MORNING.
BOSS, WHAT DO YOU WANT ME TO DO? HUNT FOR HER?
NO, NO, THAT'S ALL RIGHT. I'VE GOT A FEELING I NEED TO CLEAR THE AIR WITH A CERTAIN MOULINYAN WITH UPTOWN TASTES.
WHO NEEDS REMINDING HIS TASTES ARE STRICTLY SWAP MEET.

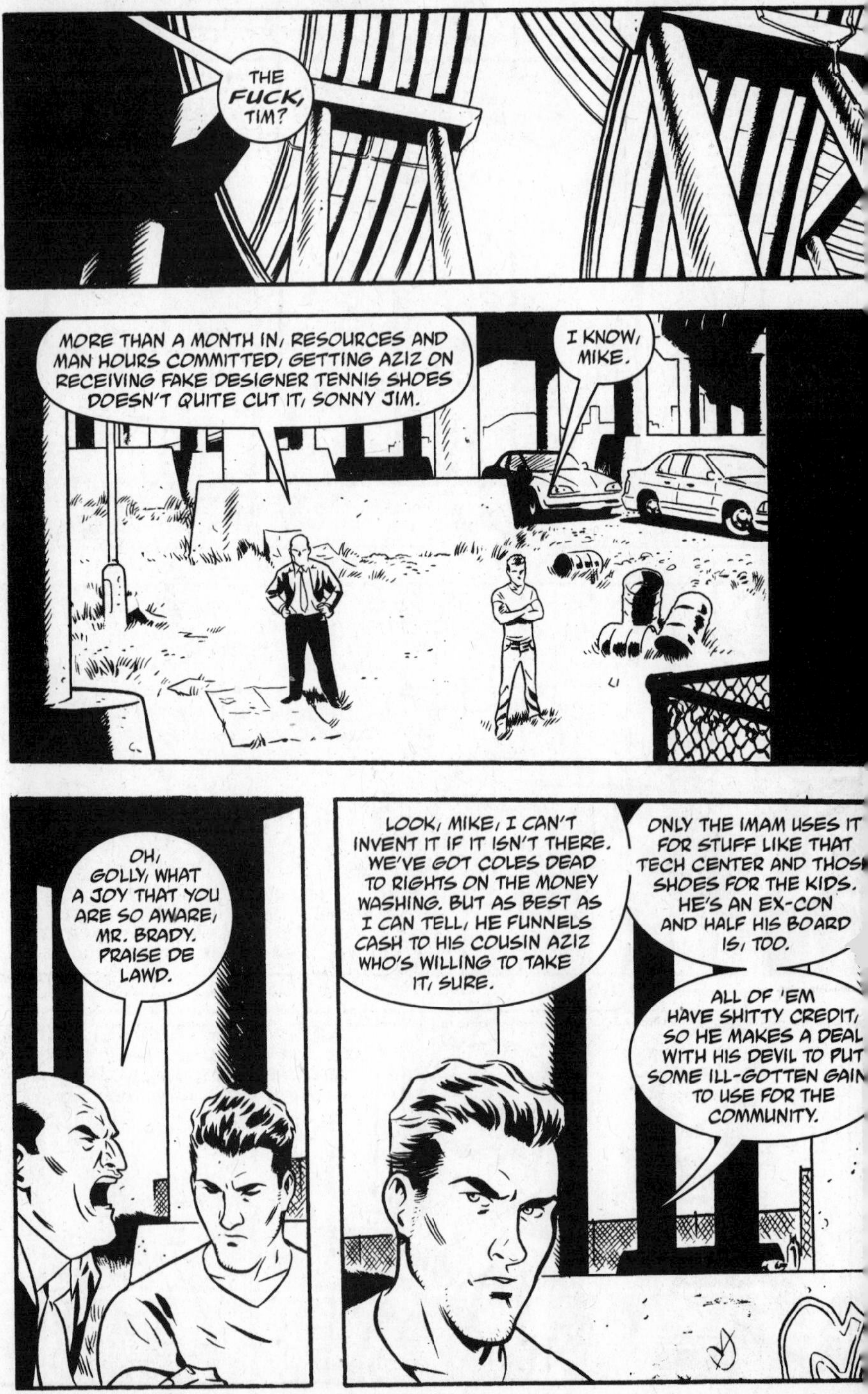
THE FUCK, TIM?
MORE THAN A MONTH IN, RESOURCES AND MAN HOURS COMMITTED, GETTING AZIZ ON RECEIVING FAKE DESIGNER TENNIS SHOES DOESN'T QUITE CUT IT, SONNY JIM.
I KNOW, MIKE.
OH, GOLLY, WHAT A JOY THAT YOU ARE SO AWARE, MR. BRADY. PRAISE DE LAWD.
LOOK, MIKE, I CAN'T INVENT IT IF IT ISN'T THERE. WE'VE GOT COLES DEAD TO RIGHTS ON THE MONEY WASHING. BUT AS BEST AS I CAN TELL, HE FUNNELS CASH TO HIS COUSIN AZIZ WHO'S WILLING TO TAKE IT, SURE.
ONLY THE IMAM USES IT FOR STUFF LIKE THAT TECH CENTER AND THOS SHOES FOR THE KIDS. HE'S AN EX-CON AND HALF HIS BOARD IS, TOO.
ALL OF 'EM HAVE SHITTY CREDIT, SO HE MAKES A DEAL WITH HIS DEVIL TO PUT SOME ILL-GOTTEN GAIN TO USE FOR THE COMMUNITY.

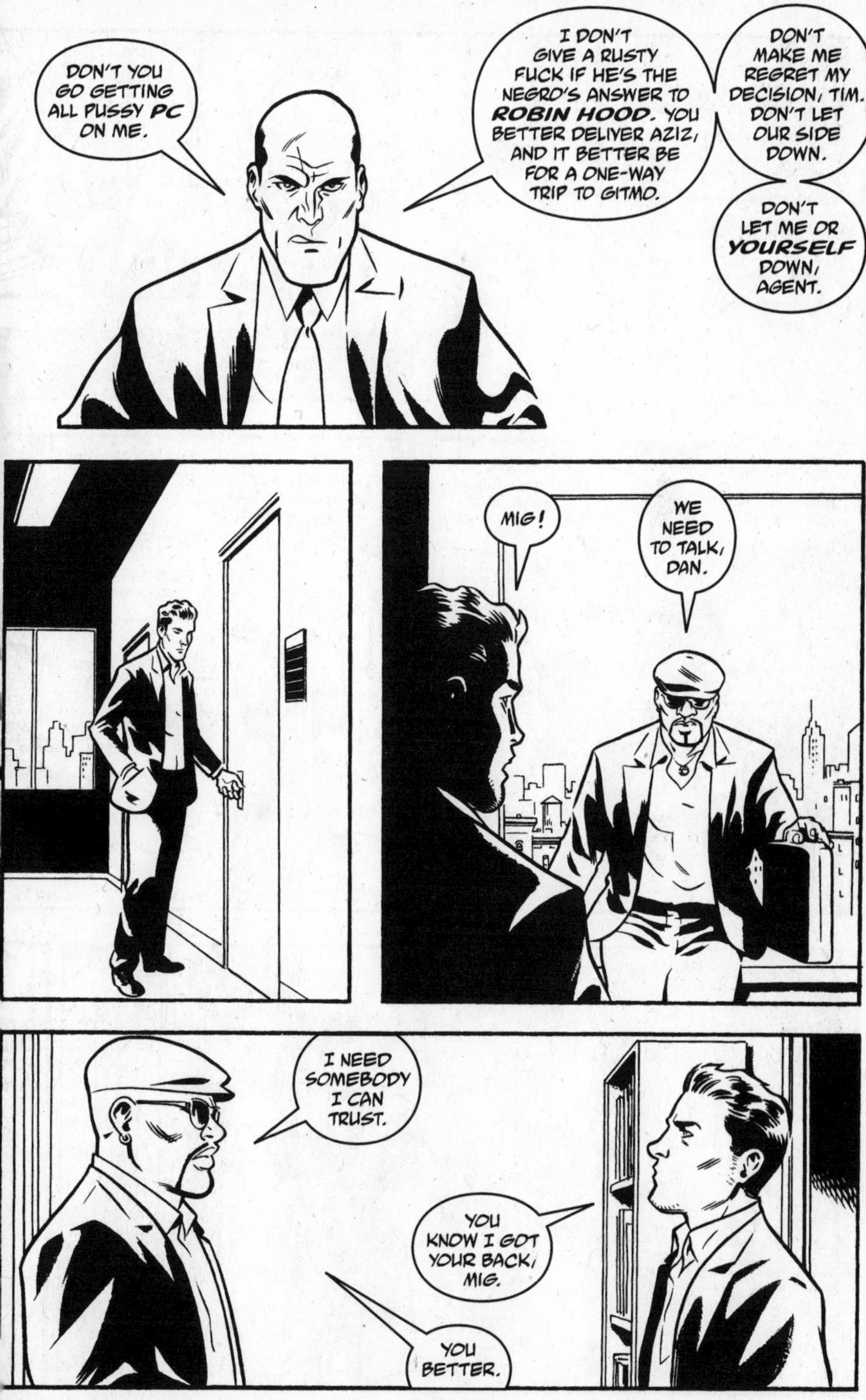
DON'T YOU GO GETTING ALL PUSSY PC ON ME.
I DON'T GIVE A RUSTY FUCK IF HE'S THE NEGRO'S ANSWER TO ROBIN HOOD. YOU BETTER DELIVER AZIZ, AND IT BETTER BE FOR A ONE-WAY TRIP TO GITMO.
DON'T MAKE ME REGRET MY DECISION, TIM. DON'T LET OUR SIDE DOWN.
DON'T LET ME OR YOURSELF DOWN, AGENT.
MIG!
WE NEED TO TALK, DAN.
I NEED SOMEBODY I CAN TRUST.
YOU KNOW I GOT YOUR BACK, MIG.
YOU BETTER.

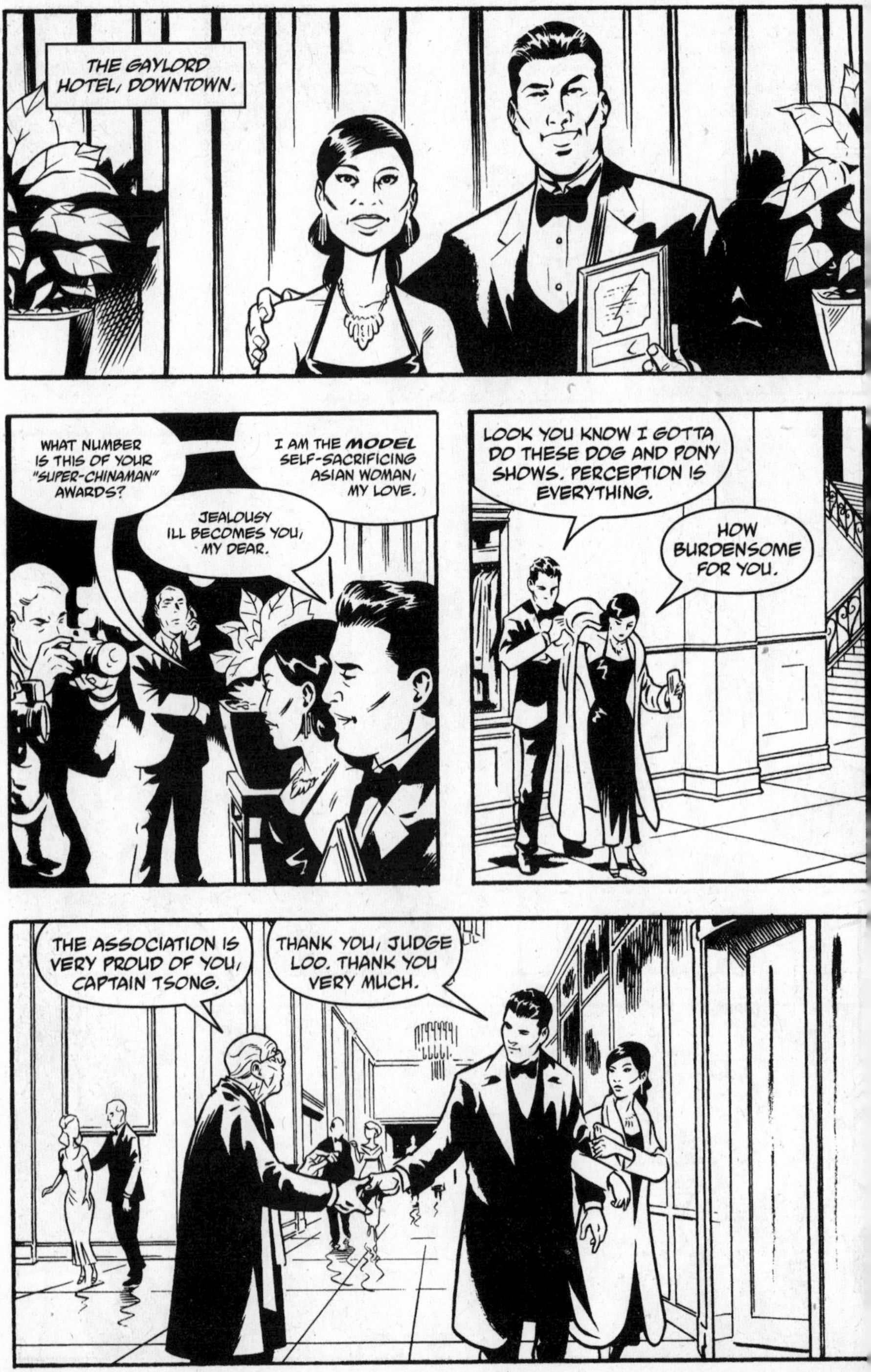
THE GAYLORD HOTEL, DOWNTOWN.
WHAT NUMBER IS THIS OF YOUR "SUPER-CHINAMAN" AWARDS?
I AM THE MODEL SELF-SACRIFICING ASIAN WOMAN, MY LOVE.
JEALOUSY ILL BECOMES YOU, MY DEAR.
LOOK YOU KNOW I GOTTA DO THESE DOG AND PONY SHOWS. PERCEPTION IS EVERYTHING.
HOW BURDENSOME FOR YOU.
THE ASSOCIATION IS VERY PROUD OF YOU, CAPTAIN TSONG.
THANK YOU, JUDGE LOO. THANK YOU VERY MUCH.

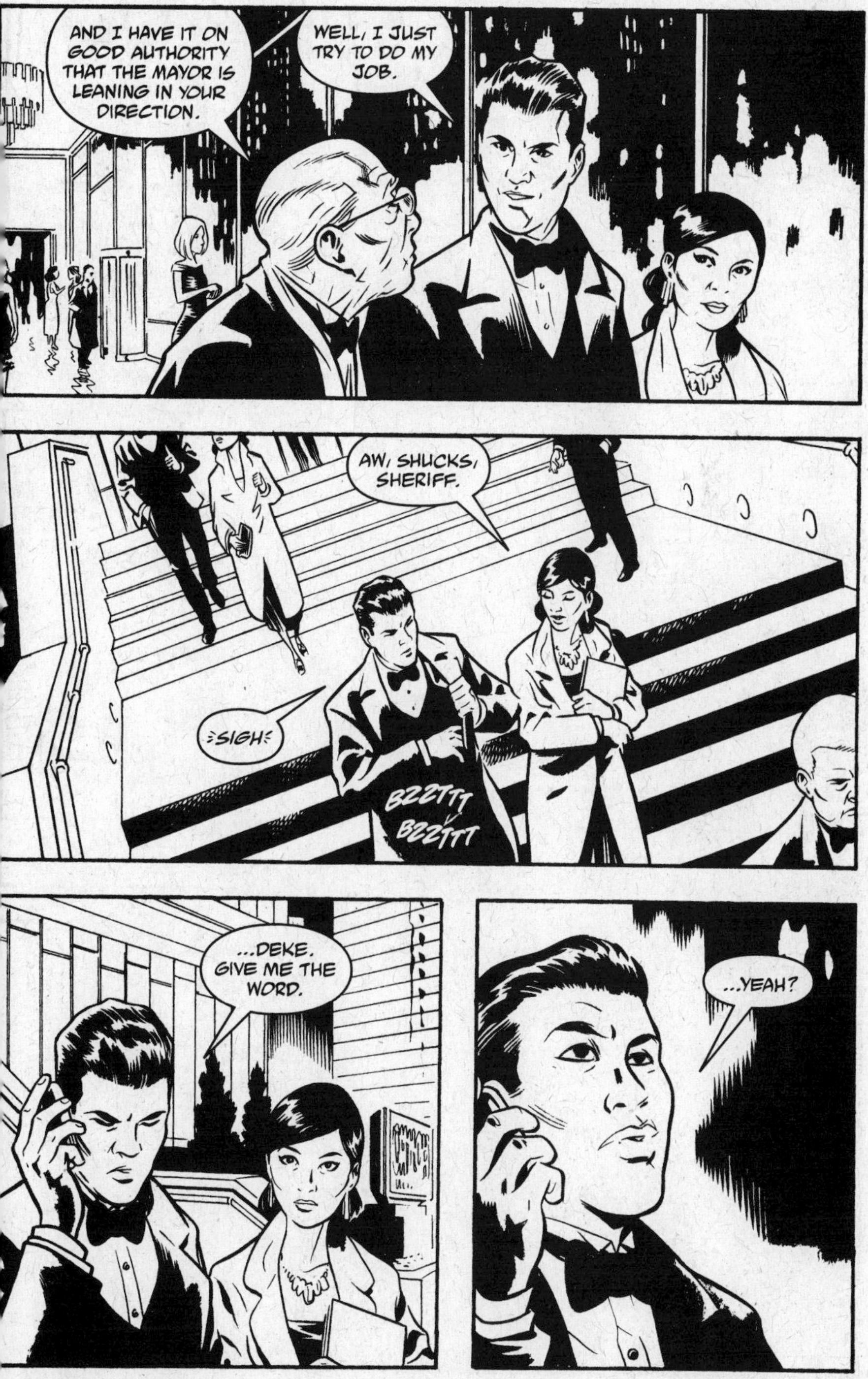
AND I HAVE IT ON GOOD AUTHORITY THAT THE MAYOR IS LEANING IN YOUR DIRECTION.
WELL, I JUST TRY TO DO MY JOB.
AW, SHUCKS, SHERIFF.
SIGH
BZZTTT
BZZTTT
...DEKE. GIVE ME THE WORD.
...YEAH?

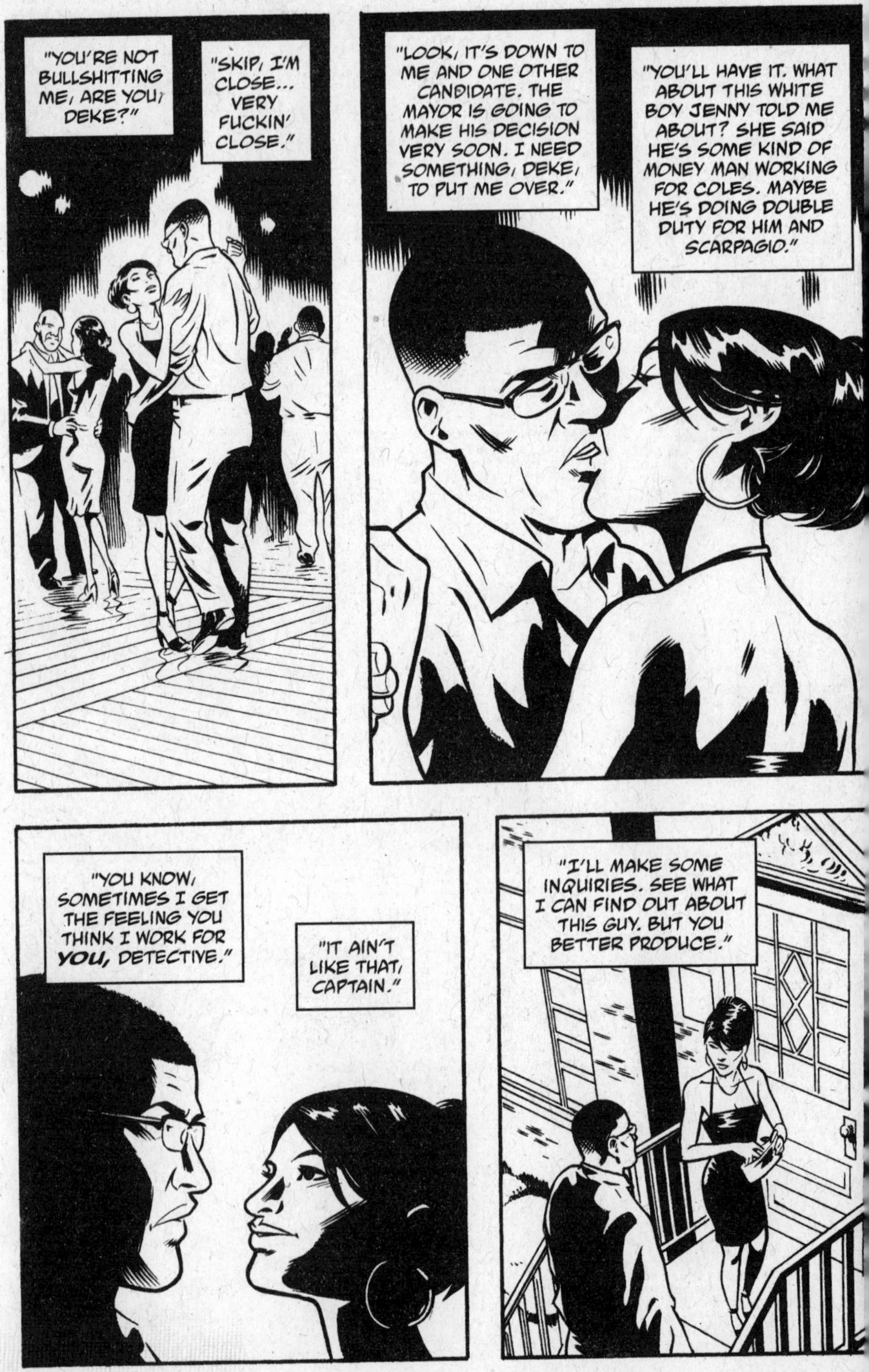

"YOU'RE NOT BULLSHITTING ME, ARE YOU, DEKE?"
"SKIP, I'M CLOSE... VERY FUCKIN' CLOSE."
"LOOK, IT'S DOWN TO ME AND ONE OTHER CANDIDATE. THE MAYOR IS GOING TO MAKE HIS DECISION VERY SOON. I NEED SOMETHING, DEKE, TO PUT ME OVER."
"YOU'LL HAVE IT. WHAT ABOUT THIS WHITE BOY JENNY TOLD ME ABOUT? SHE SAID HE'S SOME KIND OF MONEY MAN WORKING FOR COLES. MAYBE HE'S DOING DOUBLE DUTY FOR HIM AND SCARPAGIO."
"YOU KNOW, SOMETIMES I GET THE FEELING YOU THINK I WORK FOR *YOU,* DETECTIVE."
"IT AIN'T LIKE THAT, CAPTAIN."
"I'LL MAKE SOME INQUIRIES. SEE WHAT I CAN FIND OUT ABOUT THIS GUY. BUT YOU BETTER PRODUCE."

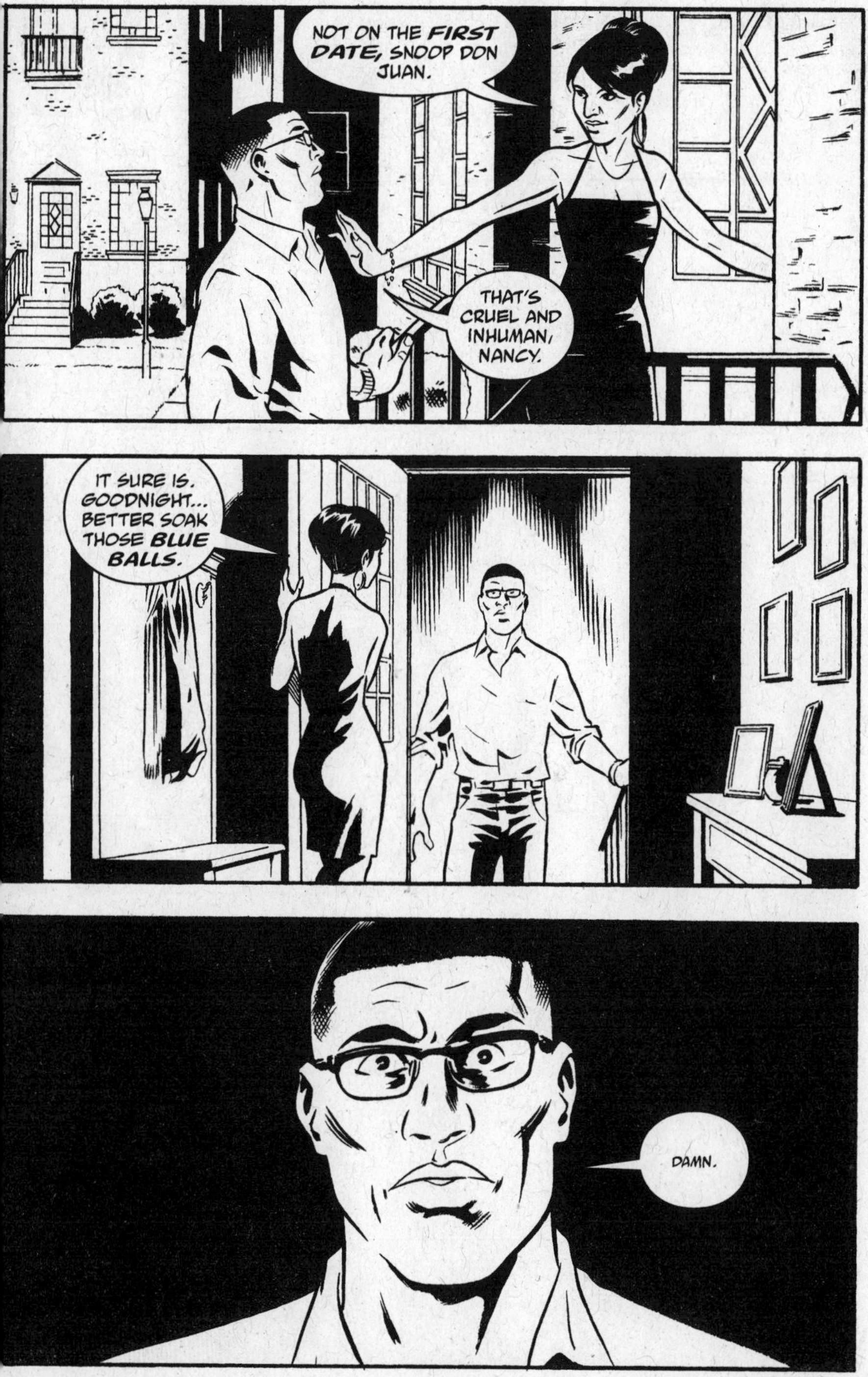
NOT ON THE FIRST DATE, SNOOP DON JUAN.
THAT'S CRUEL AND INHUMAN, NANCY.
IT SURE IS. GOODNIGHT... BETTER SOAK THOSE BLUE BALLS.
DAMN.

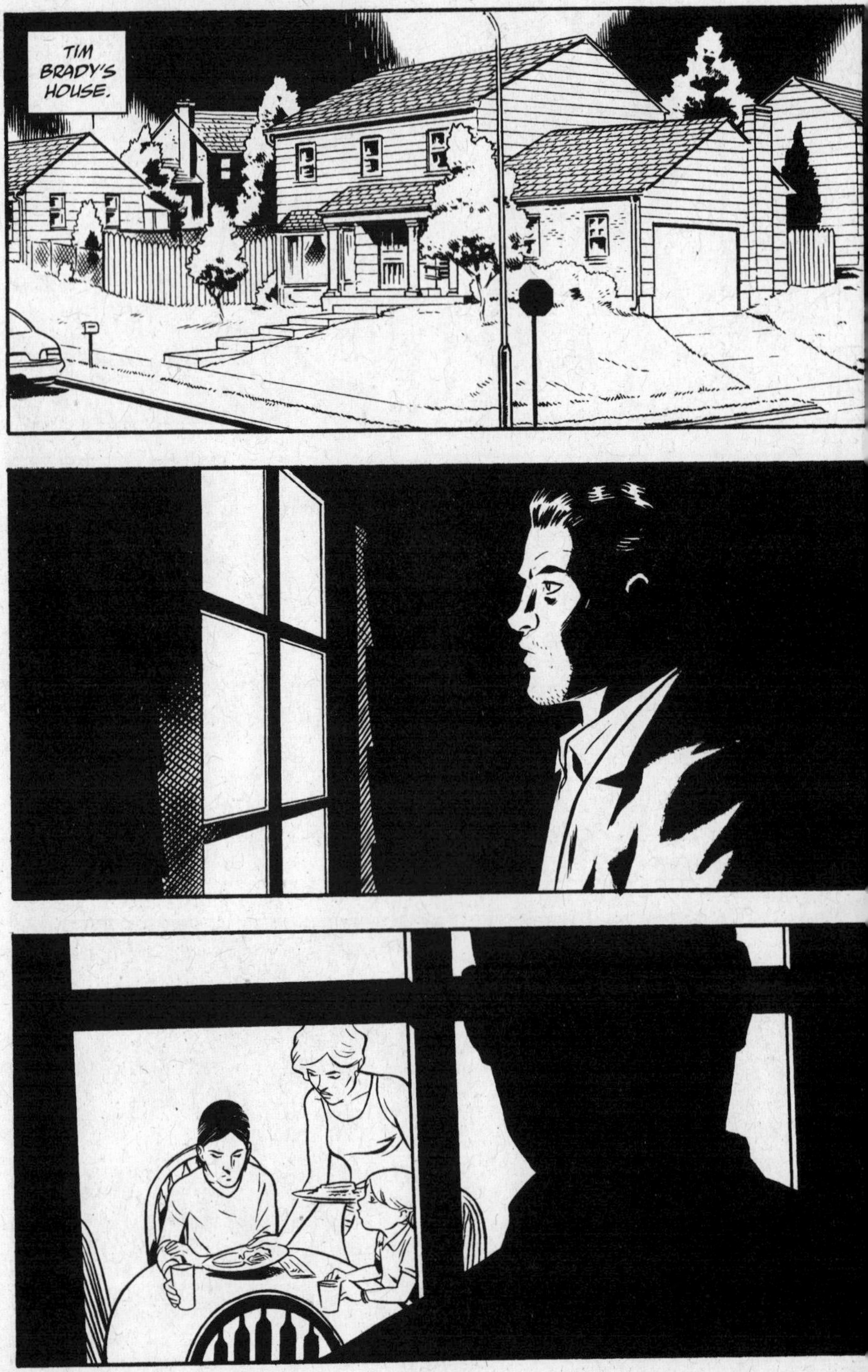
TIM BRADY'S HOUSE.

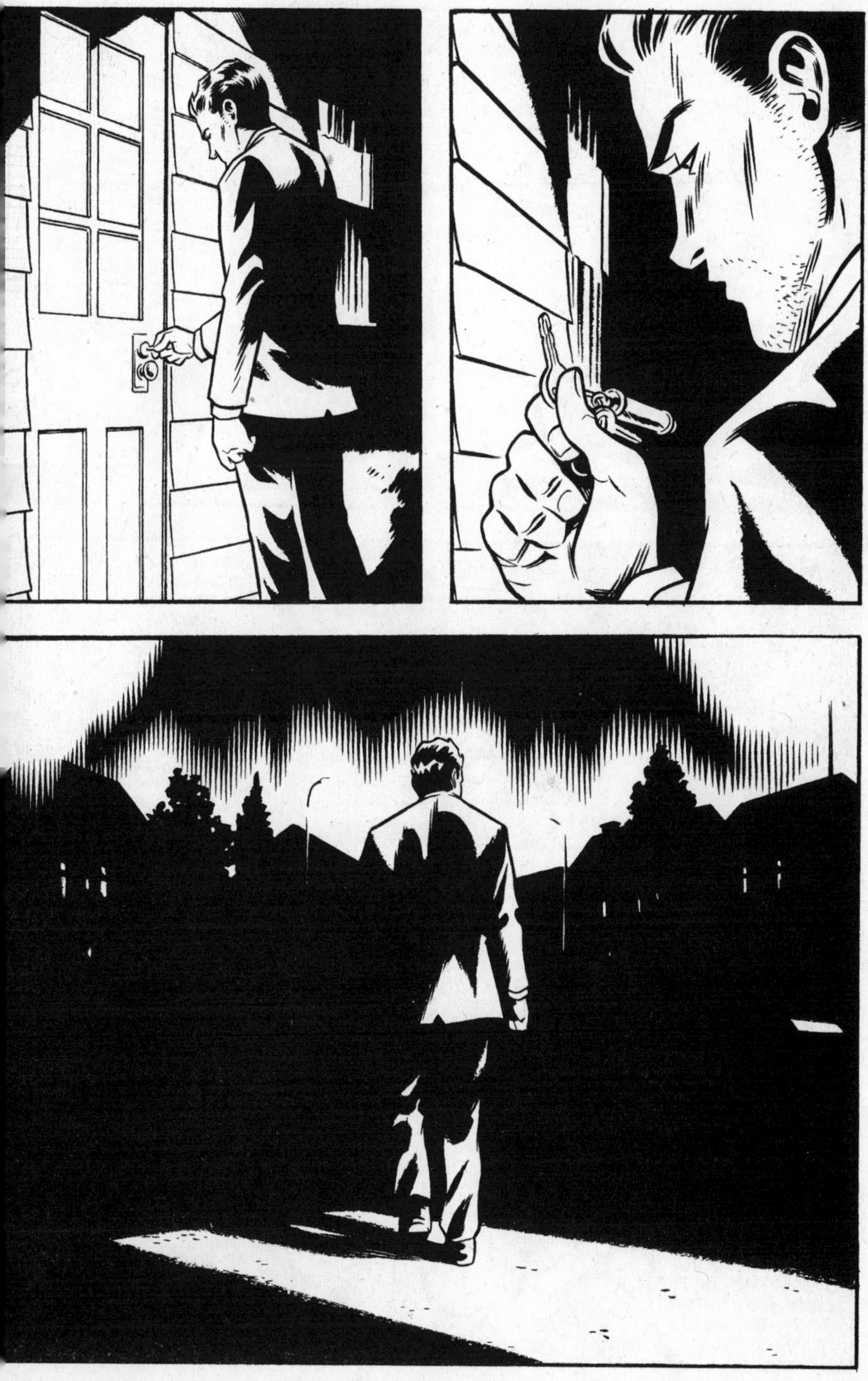

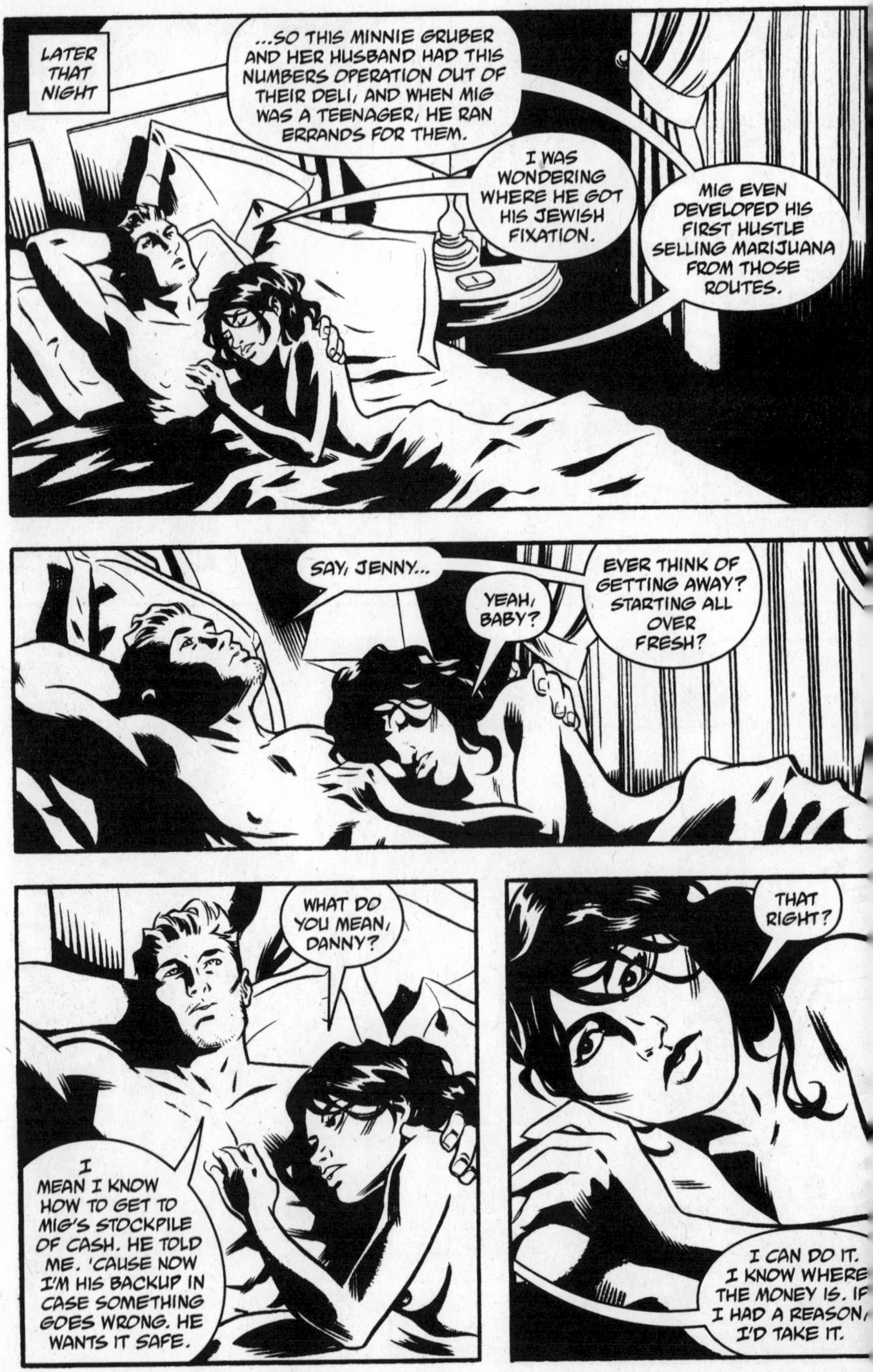
LATER THAT NIGHT
...SO THIS MINNIE GRUBER AND HER HUSBAND HAD THIS NUMBERS OPERATION OUT OF THEIR DELI, AND WHEN MIG WAS A TEENAGER, HE RAN ERRANDS FOR THEM.
I WAS WONDERING WHERE HE GOT HIS JEWISH FIXATION.
MIG EVEN DEVELOPED HIS FIRST HUSTLE SELLING MARIJUANA FROM THOSE ROUTES.
SAY, JENNY...
YEAH, BABY?
EVER THINK OF GETTING AWAY? STARTING ALL OVER FRESH?
WHAT DO YOU MEAN, DANNY?
I MEAN I KNOW HOW TO GET TO MIG'S STOCKPILE OF CASH. HE TOLD ME. 'CAUSE NOW I'M HIS BACKUP IN CASE SOMETHING GOES WRONG. HE WANTS IT SAFE.
THAT RIGHT?
I CAN DO IT. I KNOW WHERE THE MONEY IS. IF I HAD A REASON, I'D TAKE IT.

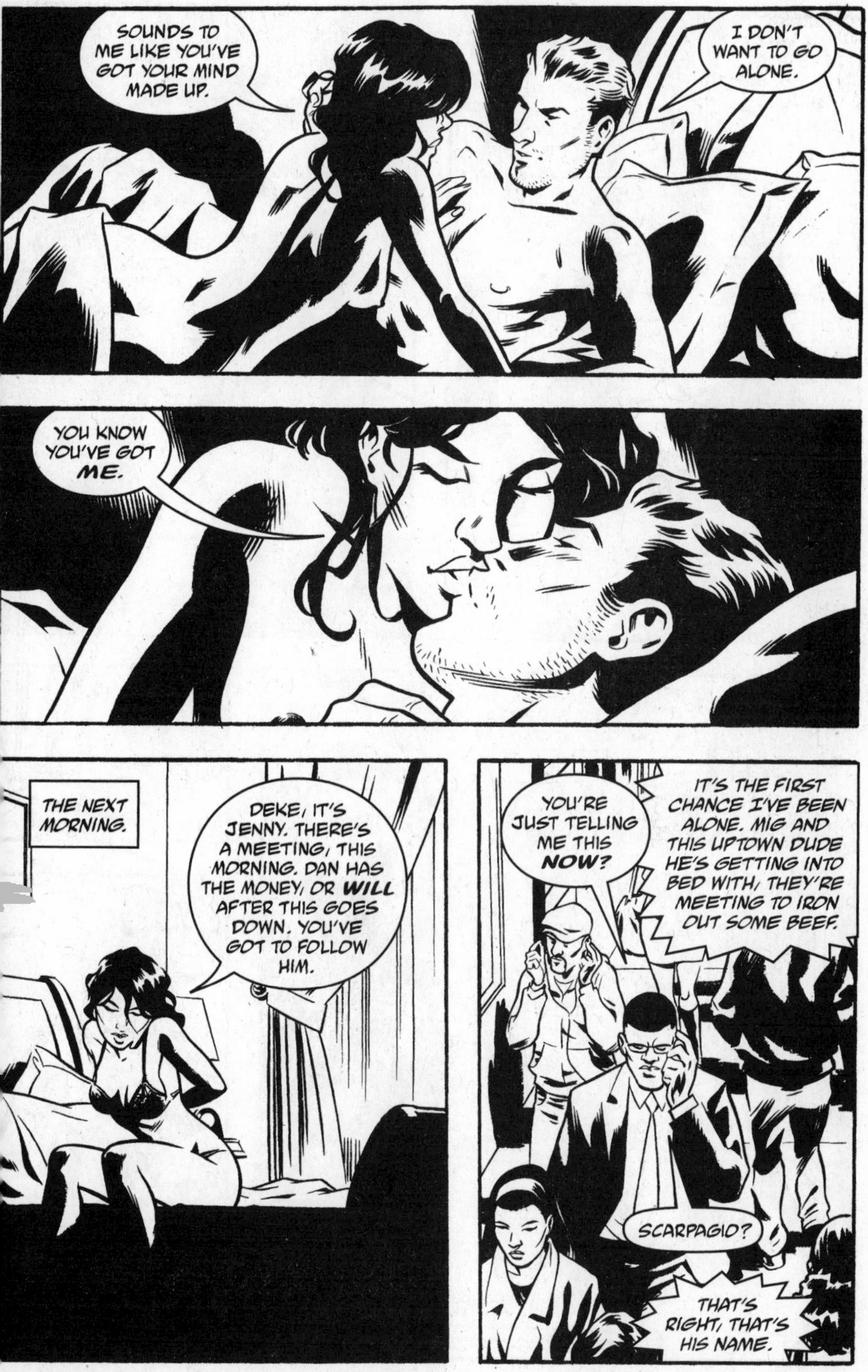
SOUNDS TO ME LIKE YOU'VE GOT YOUR MIND MADE UP.
I DON'T WANT TO GO ALONE.
YOU KNOW YOU'VE GOT ME.
THE NEXT MORNING.
DEKE, IT'S JENNY. THERE'S A MEETING, THIS MORNING. DAN HAS THE MONEY, OR WILL AFTER THIS GOES DOWN. YOU'VE GOT TO FOLLOW HIM.
YOU'RE JUST TELLING ME THIS NOW?
IT'S THE FIRST CHANCE I'VE BEEN ALONE. MIG AND THIS UPTOWN DUDE HE'S GETTING INTO BED WITH, THEY'RE MEETING TO IRON OUT SOME BEEF.
SCARPAGIO?
THAT'S RIGHT, THAT'S HIS NAME.

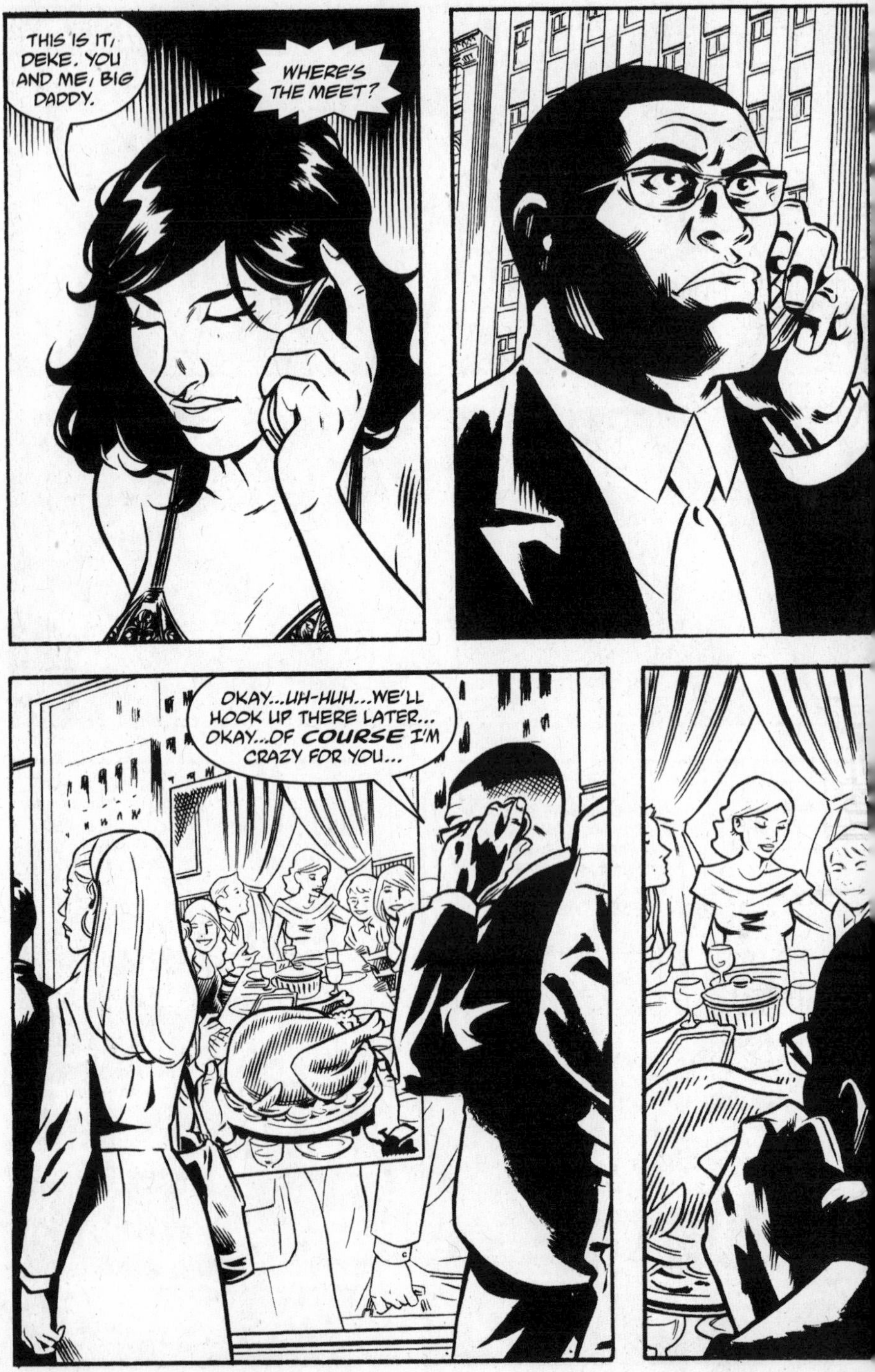
THIS IS IT, DEKE. YOU AND ME, BIG DADDY.
WHERE'S THE MEET?
OKAY...UH-HUH...WE'LL HOOK UP THERE LATER... OKAY...OF COURSE I'M CRAZY FOR YOU...

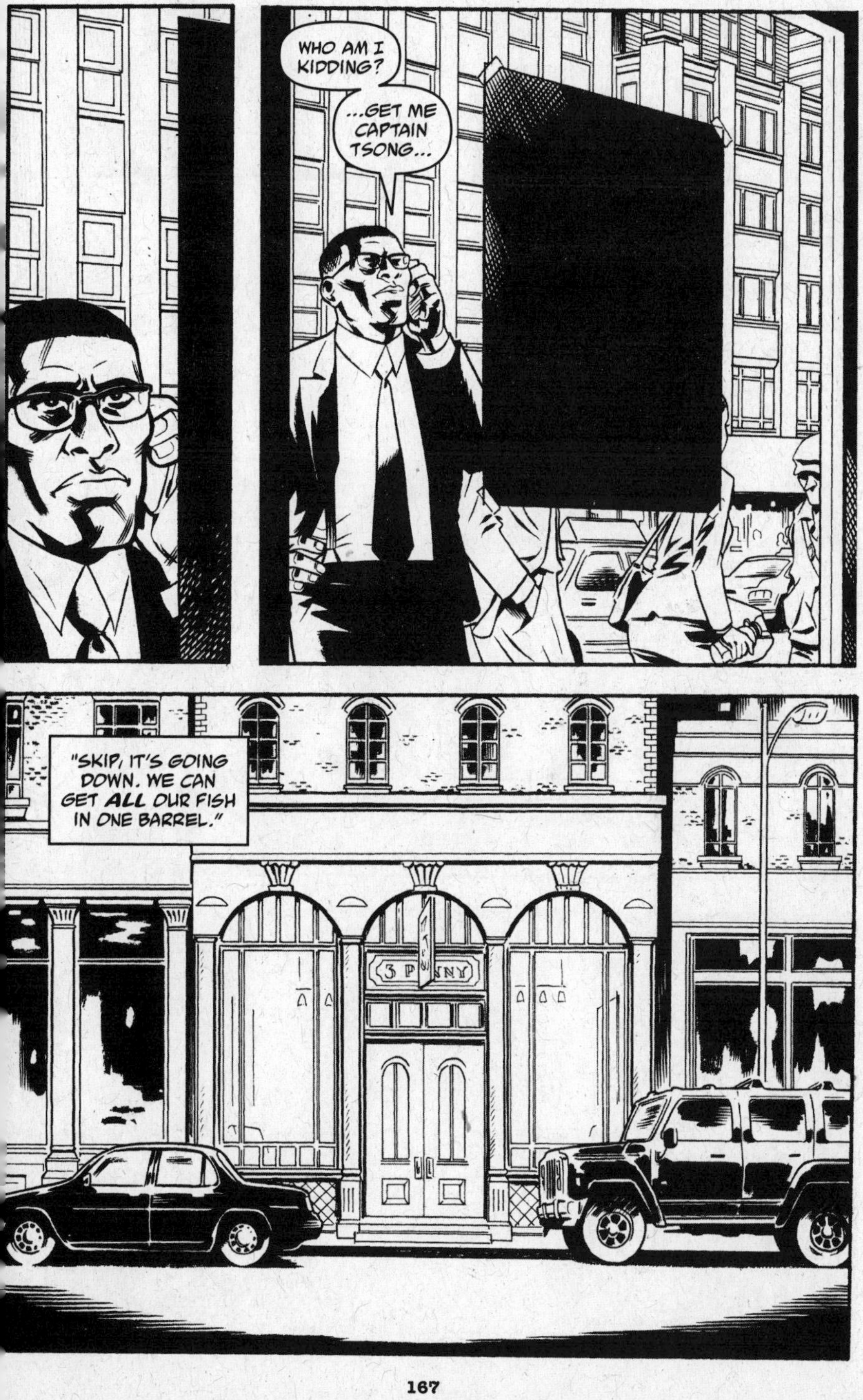
WHO AM I KIDDING?
...GET ME CAPTAIN TSONG...
"SKIP, IT'S GOING DOWN. WE CAN GET **ALL** OUR FISH IN ONE BARREL."

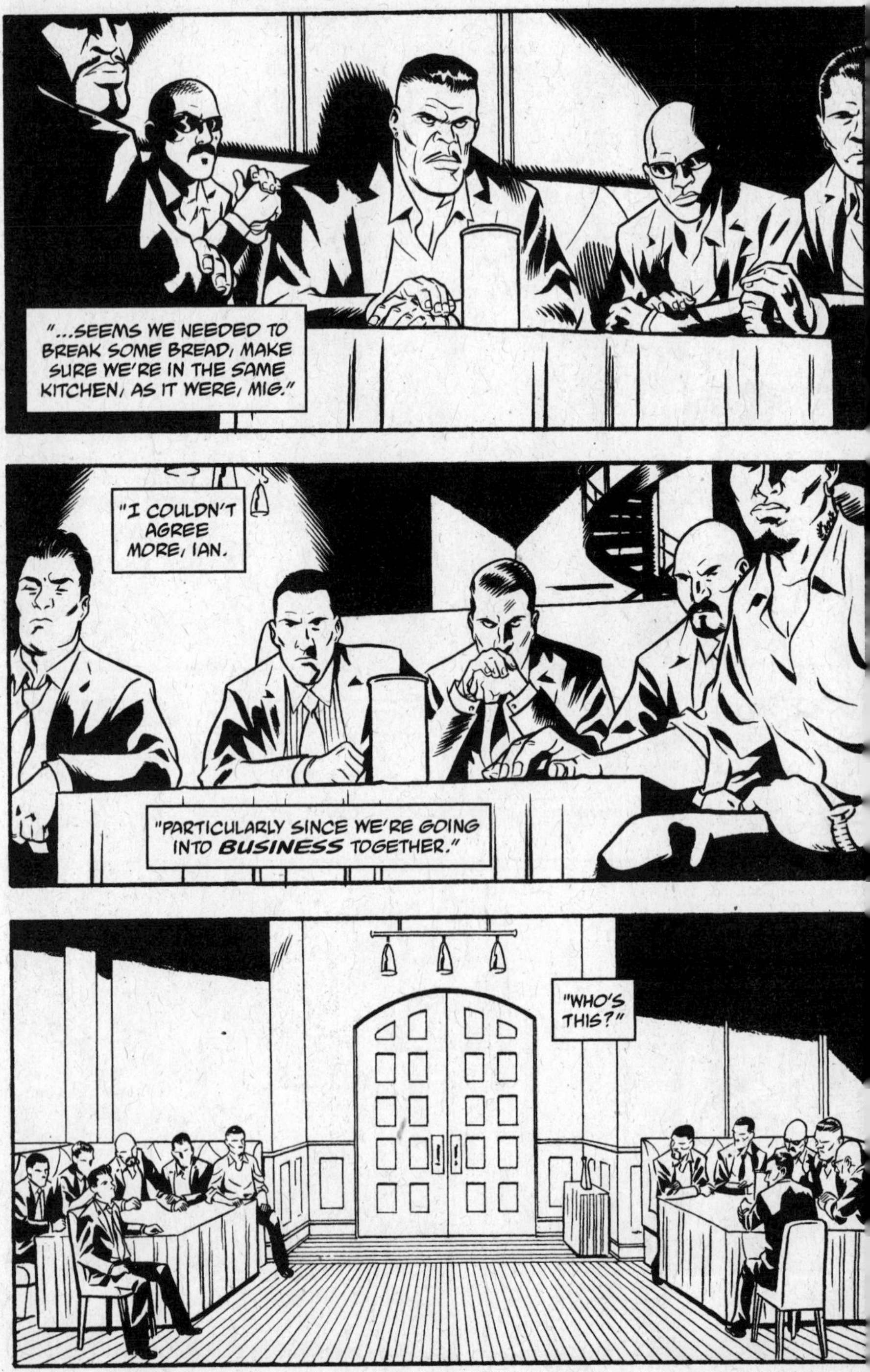
"...SEEMS WE NEEDED TO BREAK SOME BREAD, MAKE SURE WE'RE IN THE SAME KITCHEN, AS IT WERE, MIG."
"I COULDN'T AGREE MORE, IAN.
"PARTICULARLY SINCE WE'RE GOING INTO BUSINESS TOGETHER."
"WHO'S THIS?"

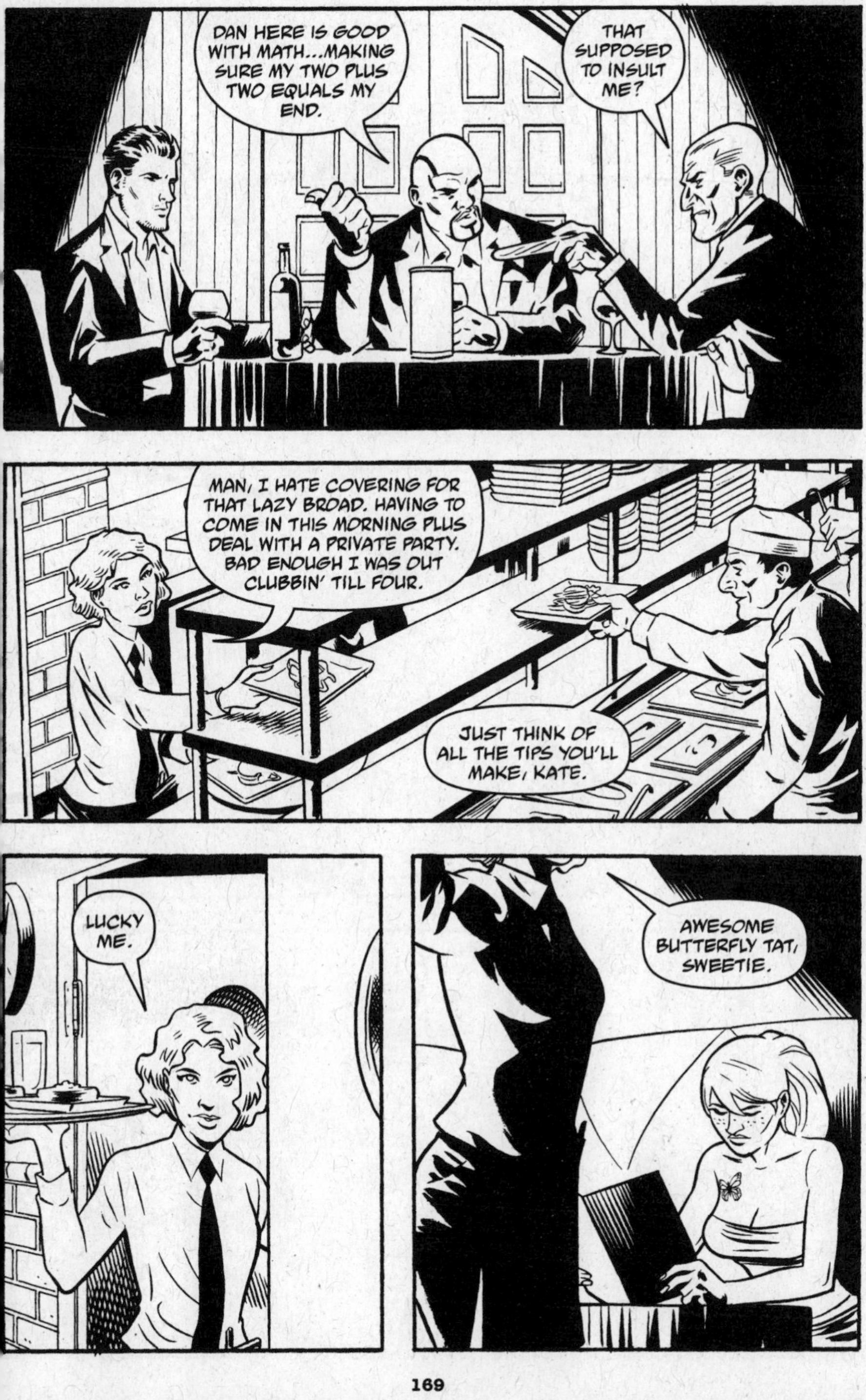
DAN HERE IS GOOD WITH MATH...MAKING SURE MY TWO PLUS TWO EQUALS MY END.
THAT SUPPOSED TO INSULT ME?
MAN, I HATE COVERING FOR THAT LAZY BROAD. HAVING TO COME IN THIS MORNING PLUS DEAL WITH A PRIVATE PARTY. BAD ENOUGH I WAS OUT CLUBBIN' TILL FOUR.
JUST THINK OF ALL THE TIPS YOU'LL MAKE, KATE.
LUCKY ME.
AWESOME BUTTERFLY TAT, SWEETIE.

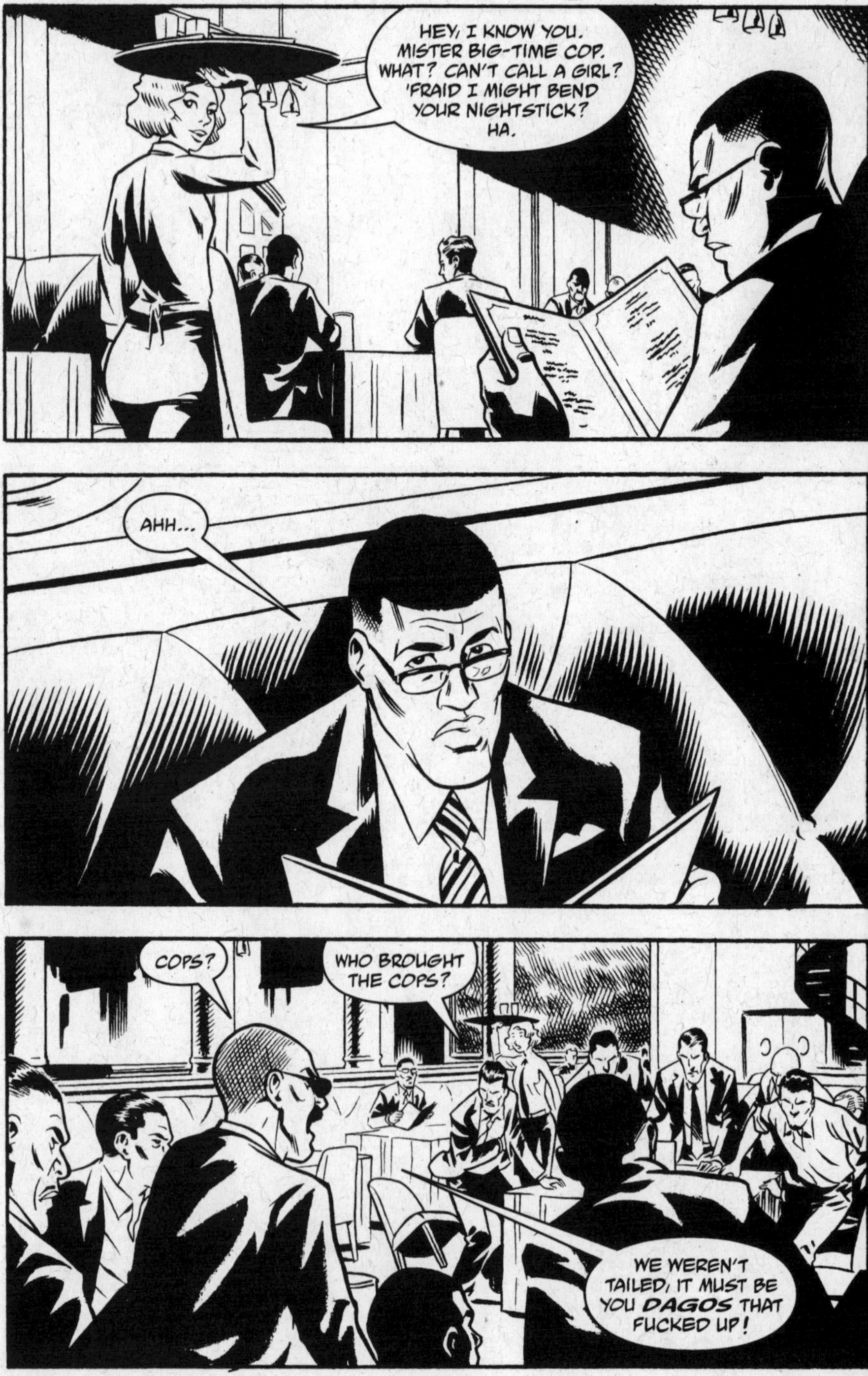
HEY, I KNOW YOU. MISTER BIG-TIME COP. WHAT? CAN'T CALL A GIRL? 'FRAID I MIGHT BEND YOUR NIGHTSTICK? HA.
AHH...
COPS?
WHO BROUGHT THE COPS?
WE WEREN'T TAILED, IT MUST BE YOU DAGOS THAT FUCKED UP!

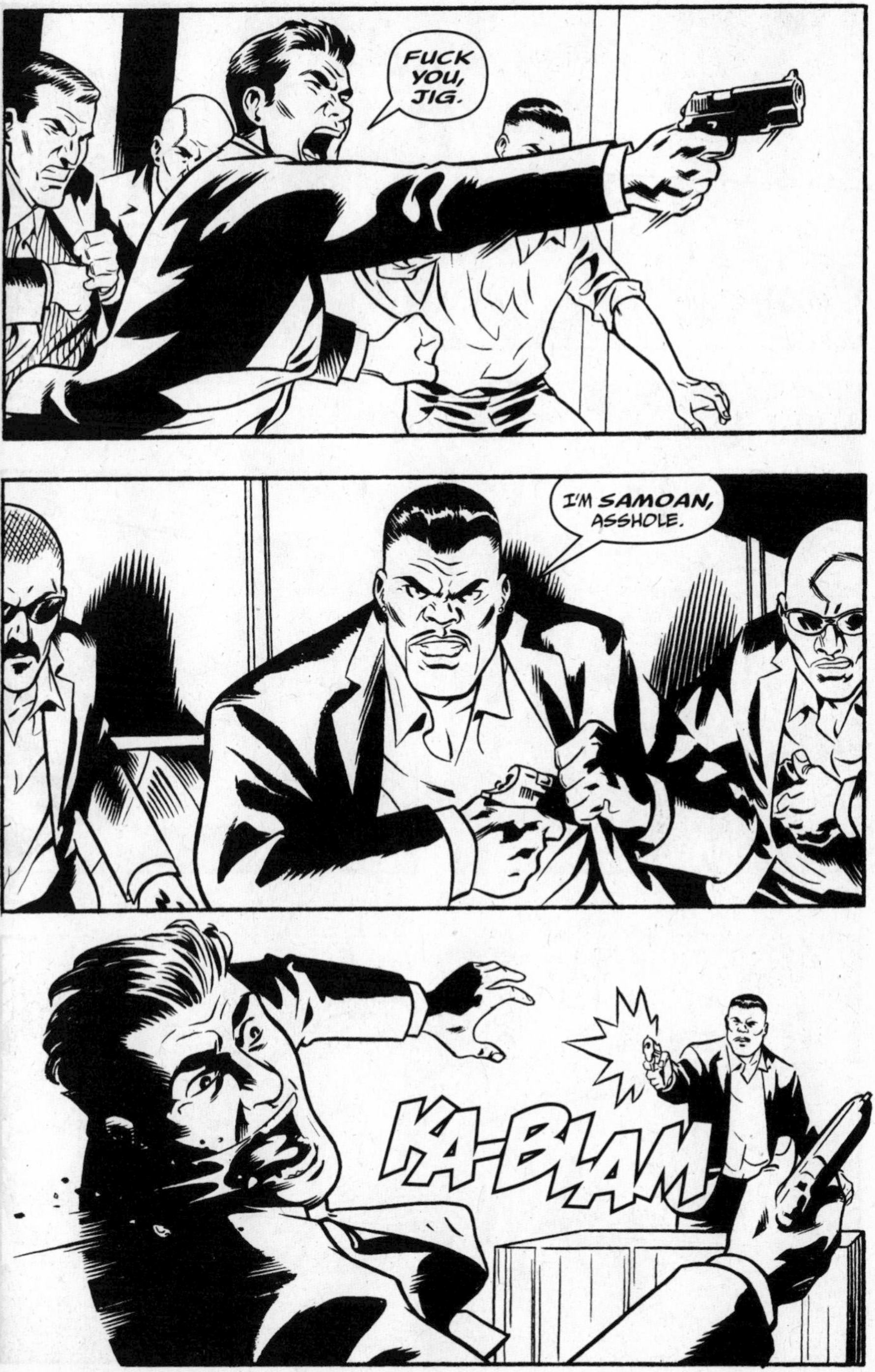
FUCK YOU, JIG.
I'M SAMOAN, ASSHOLE.
KA-BLAM

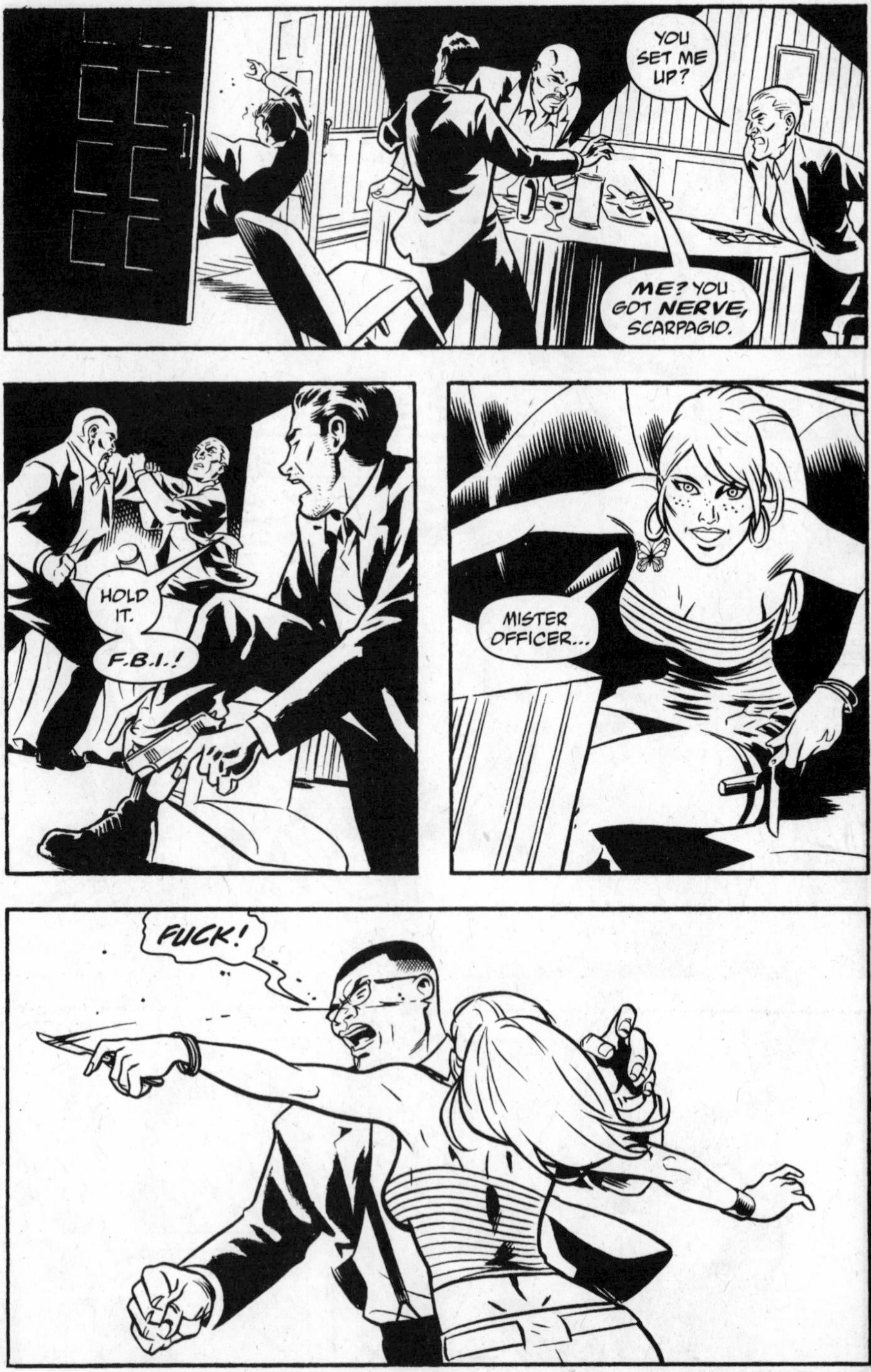
YOU SET ME UP?
ME? YOU GOT NERVE, SCARPAGIO.
HOLD IT.
F.B.I.!
MISTER OFFICER...
FUCK!

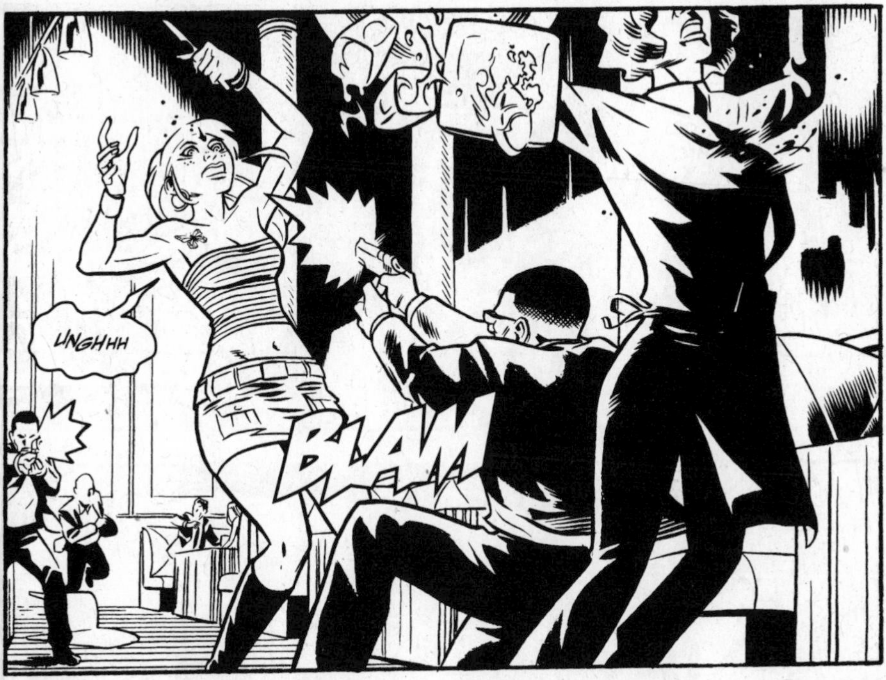
UNGHHH
BLAM

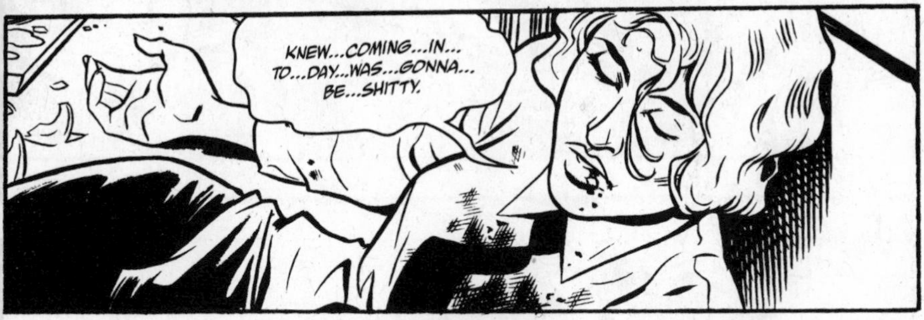
KNEW...COMING...IN... TO...DAY...WAS...GONNA... BE...SHITTY.

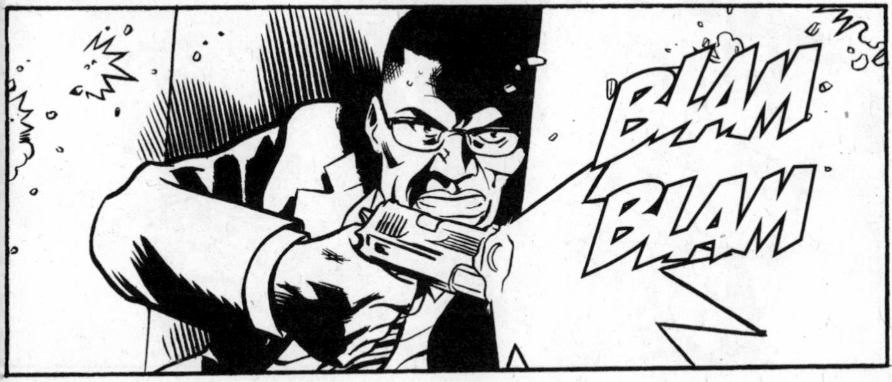
BLAM
BLAM

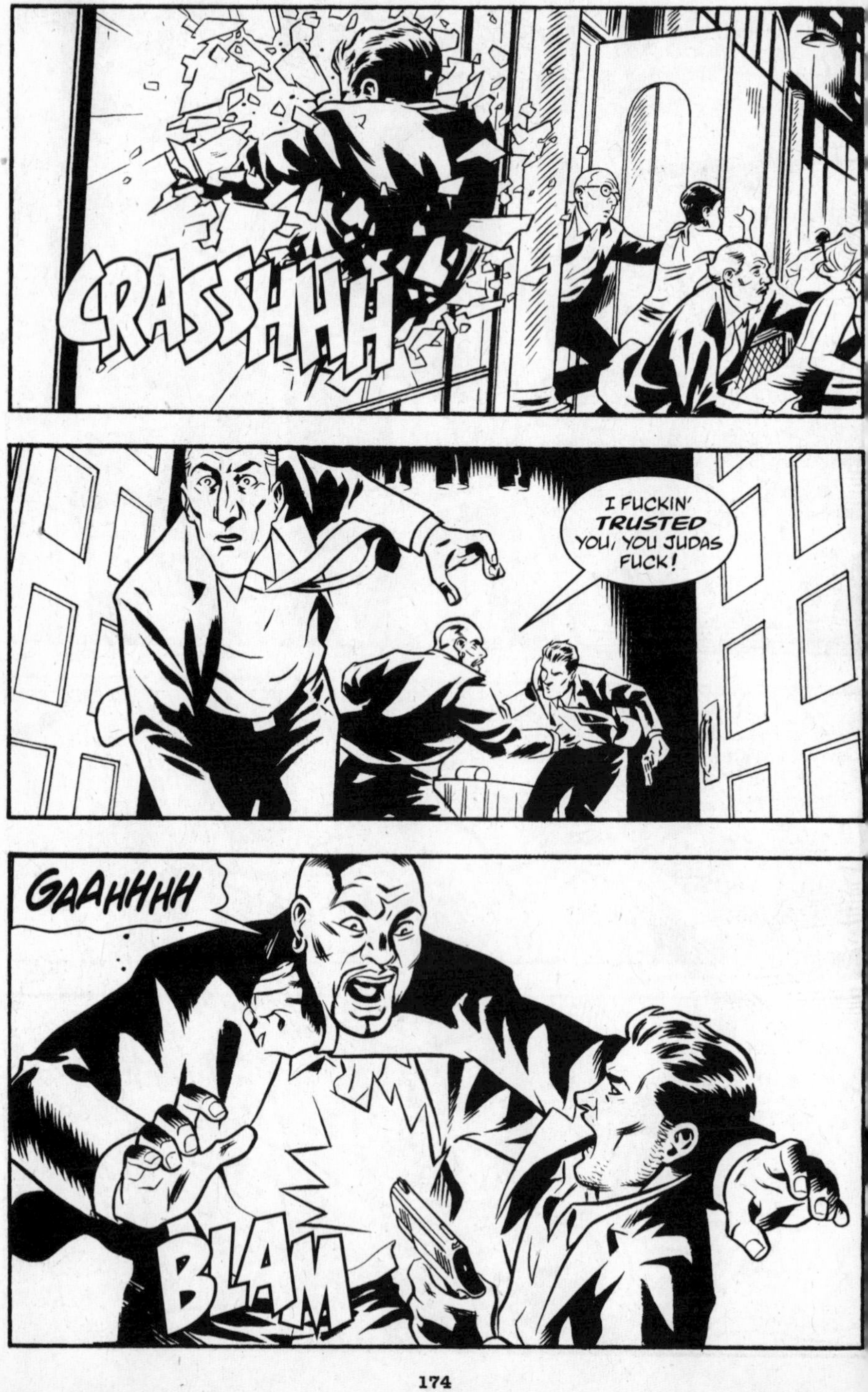
CRASSHHH
I FUCKIN' TRUSTED YOU, YOU JUDAS FUCK!
GAAHHHH
BLAM

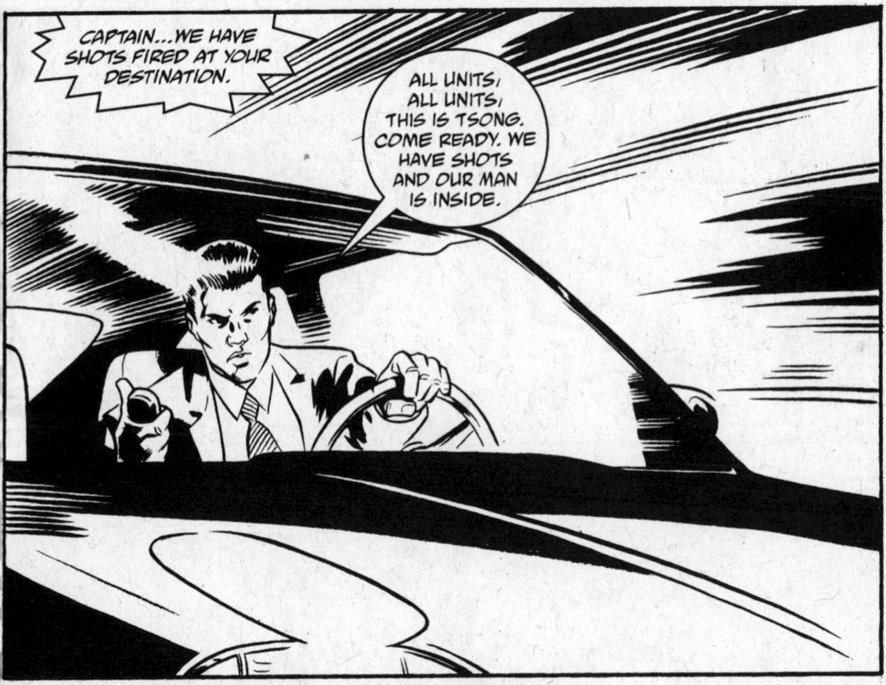
CAPTAIN...WE HAVE SHOTS FIRED AT YOUR DESTINATION.
ALL UNITS, ALL UNITS, THIS IS TSONG. COME READY. WE HAVE SHOTS AND OUR MAN IS INSIDE.

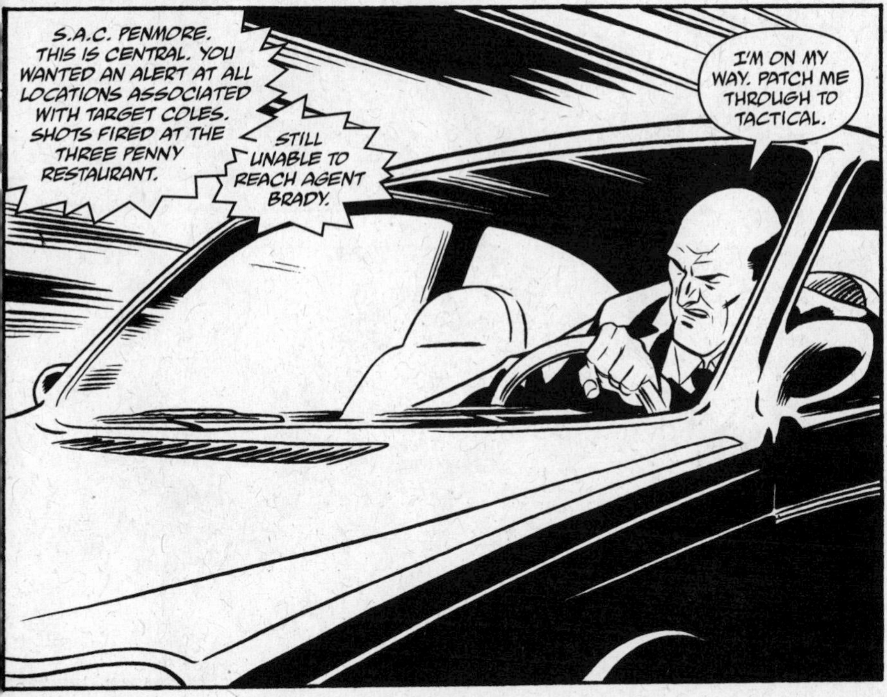
S.A.C. PENMORE. THIS IS CENTRAL. YOU WANTED AN ALERT AT ALL LOCATIONS ASSOCIATED WITH TARGET COLES. SHOTS FIRED AT THE THREE PENNY RESTAURANT.
STILL UNABLE TO REACH AGENT BRADY.
I'M ON MY WAY. PATCH ME THROUGH TO TACTICAL.

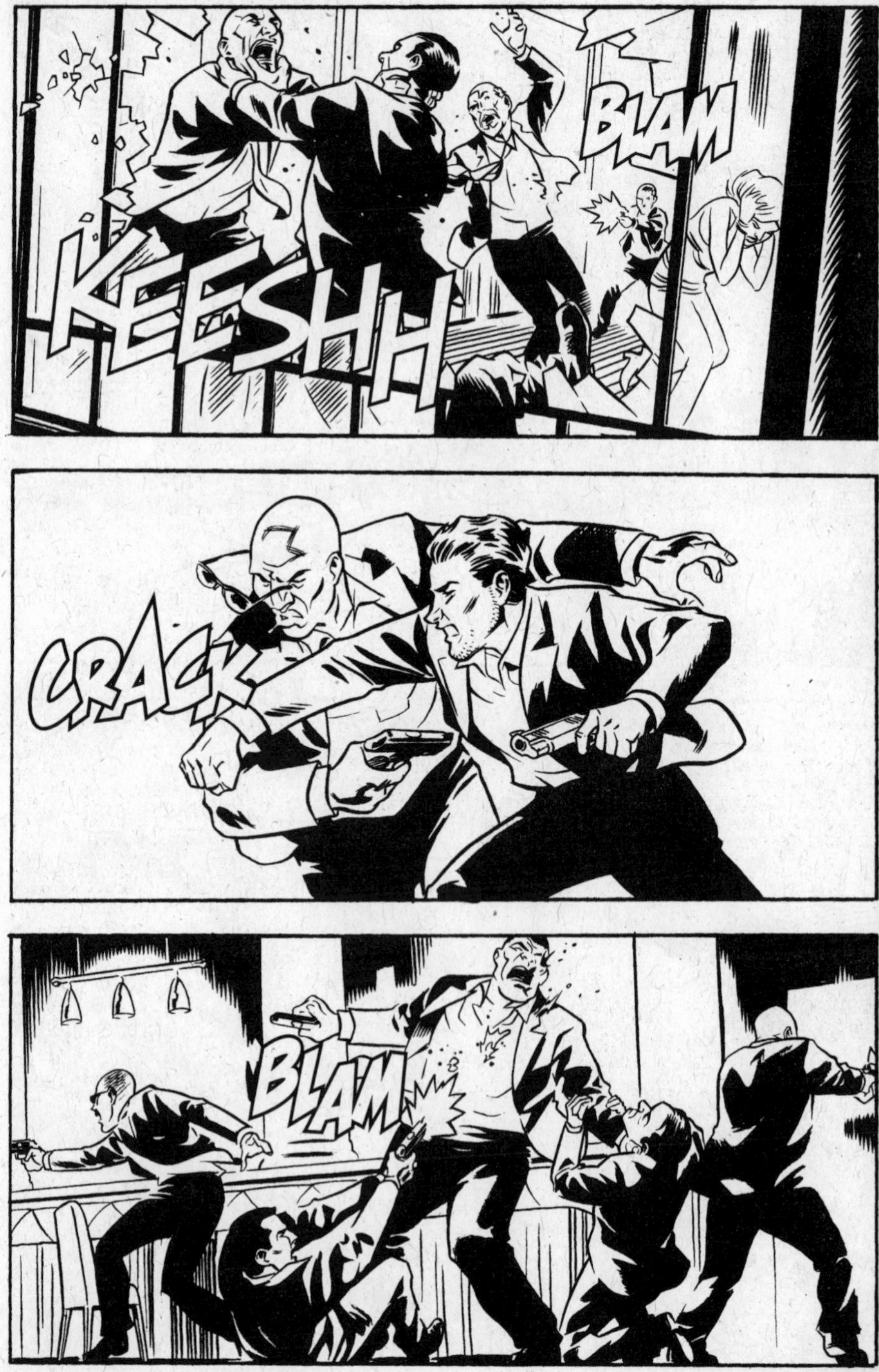
BLAM
KEESHH
CRACK
BLAM

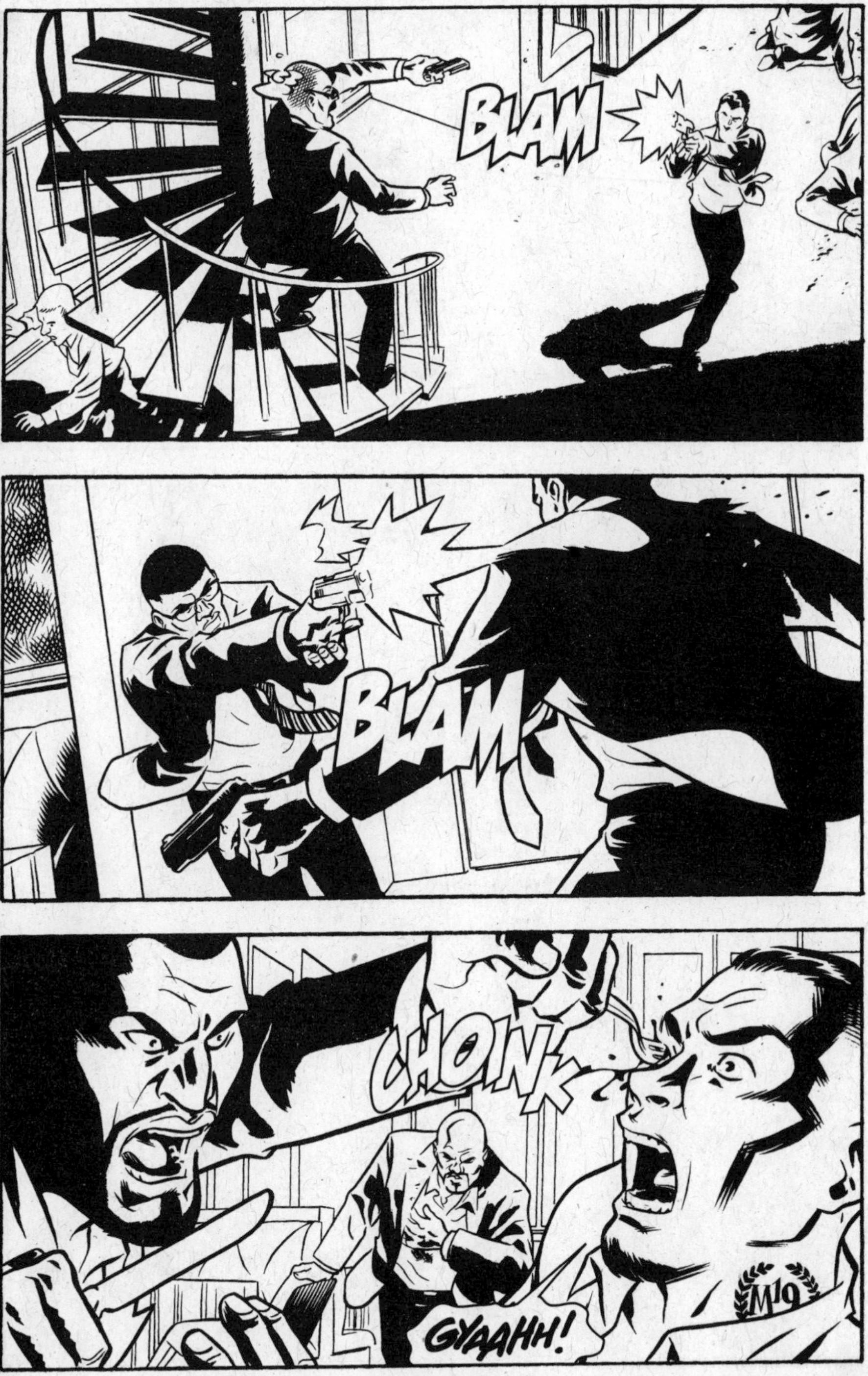
BLAM
BLAM
CHOINK
GYAAHH!

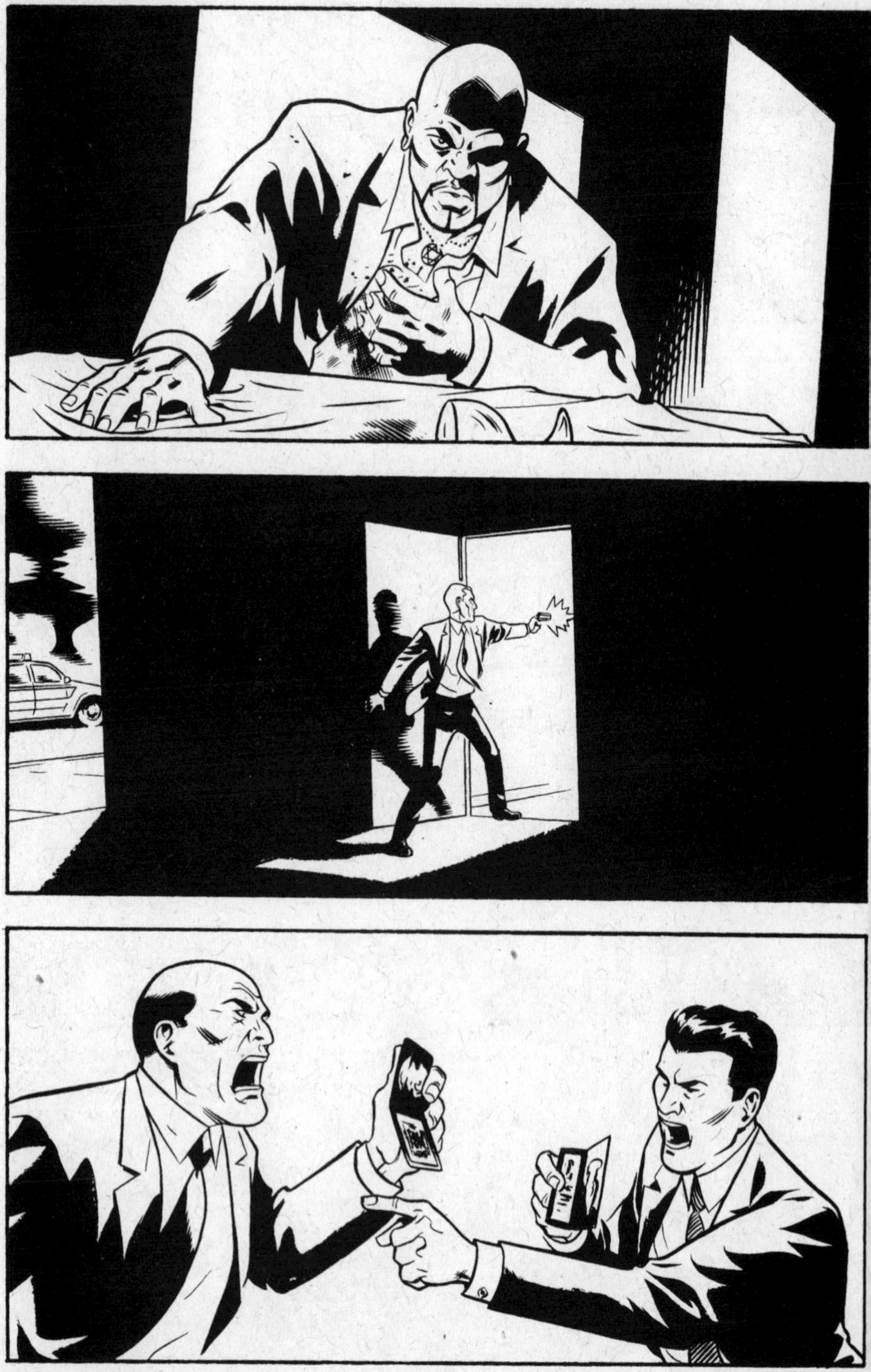

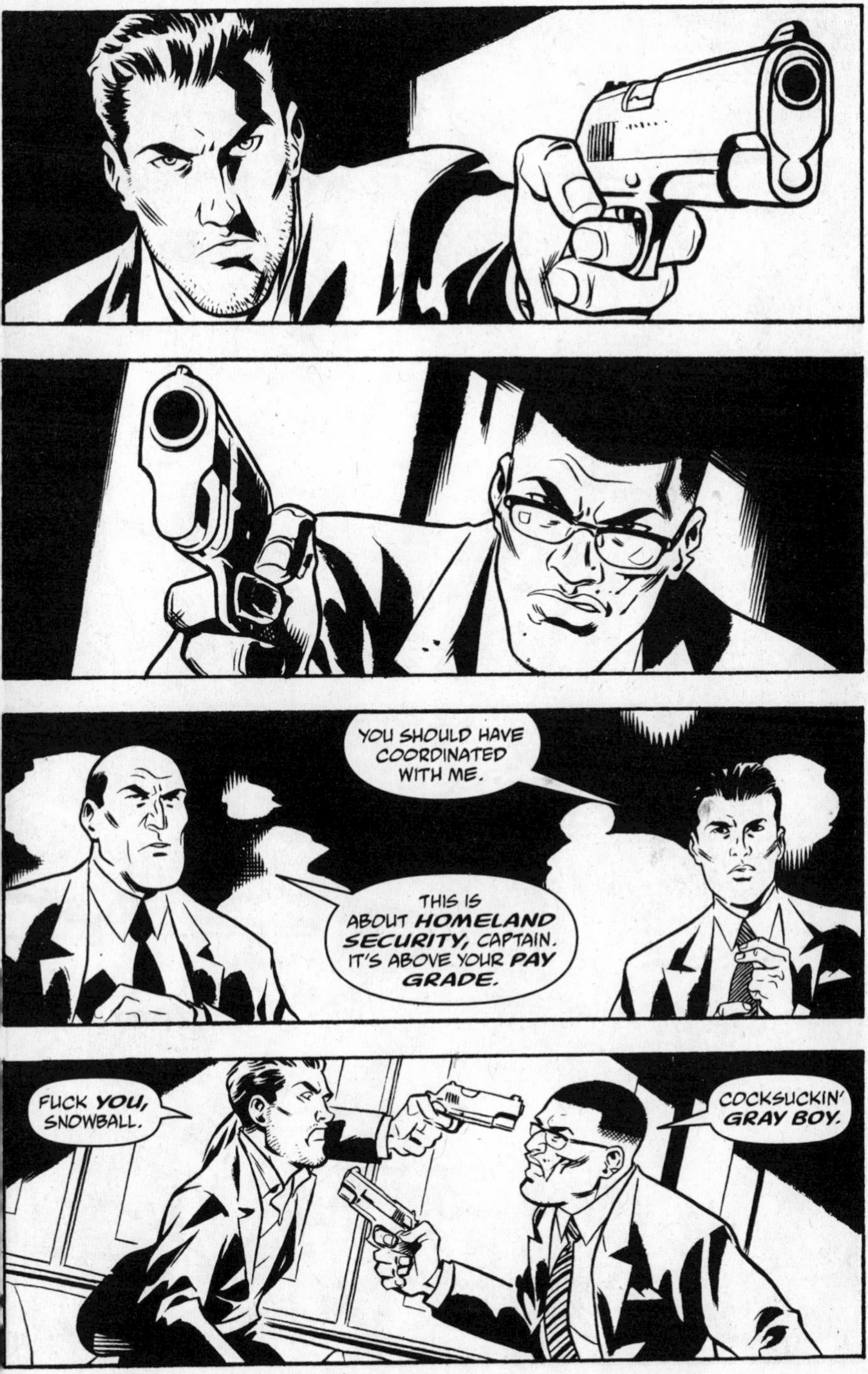
YOU SHOULD HAVE COORDINATED WITH ME.
THIS IS ABOUT *HOMELAND SECURITY,* CAPTAIN. IT'S ABOVE YOUR *PAY GRADE.*
FUCK *YOU,* SNOWBALL.
COCKSUCKIN' *GRAY BOY.*

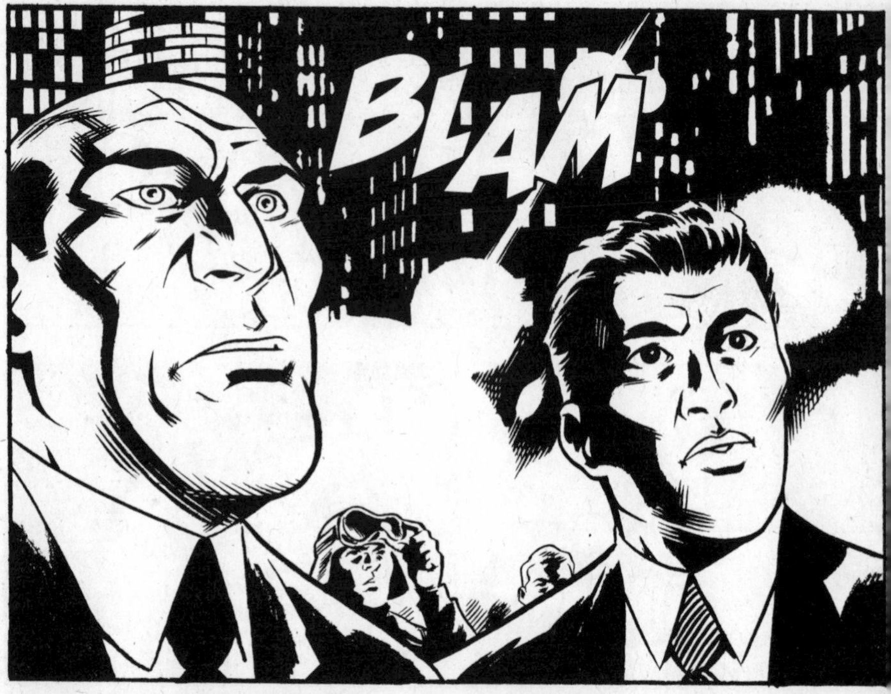
BLAM

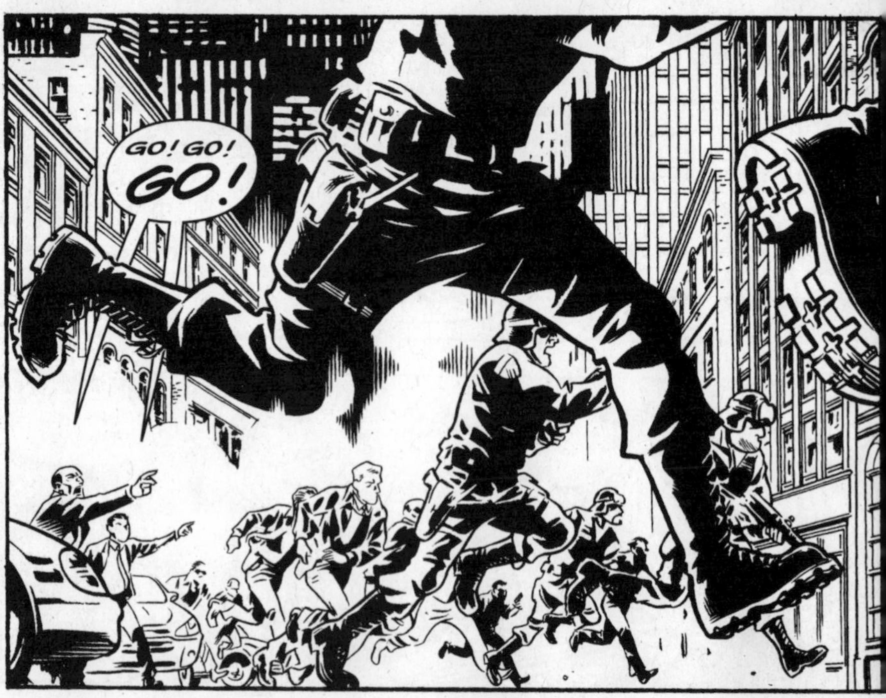
GO! GO! GO!

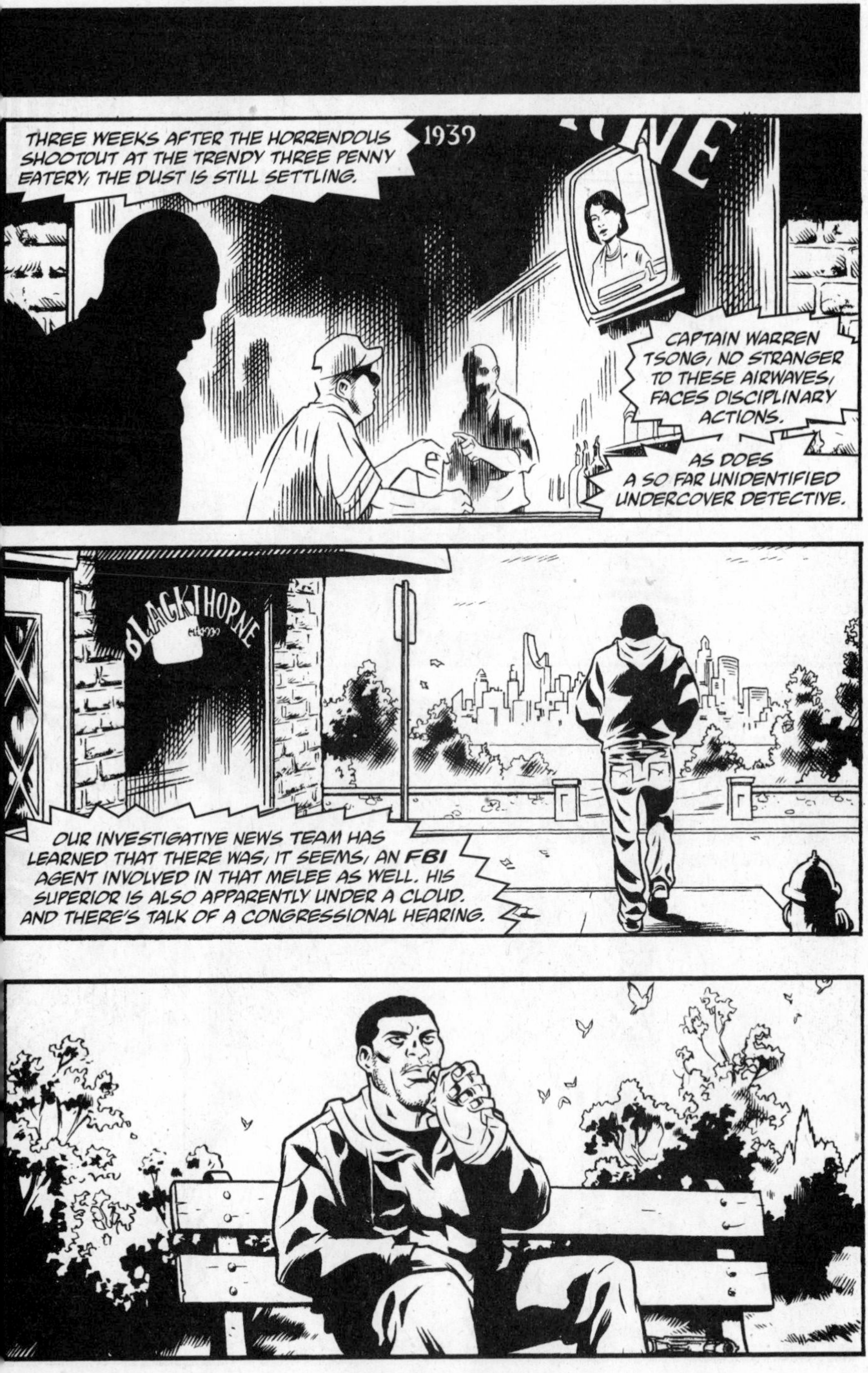
THREE WEEKS AFTER THE HORRENDOUS SHOOTOUT AT THE TRENDY THREE PENNY EATERY, THE DUST IS STILL SETTLING.
1939
CAPTAIN WARREN TSONG, NO STRANGER TO THESE AIRWAVES, FACES DISCIPLINARY ACTIONS.
AS DOES A SO FAR UNIDENTIFIED UNDERCOVER DETECTIVE.
BLACKTHORNE
OUR INVESTIGATIVE NEWS TEAM HAS LEARNED THAT THERE WAS, IT SEEMS, AN FBI AGENT INVOLVED IN THAT MELEE AS WELL. HIS SUPERIOR IS ALSO APPARENTLY UNDER A CLOUD. AND THERE'S TALK OF A CONGRESSIONAL HEARING.

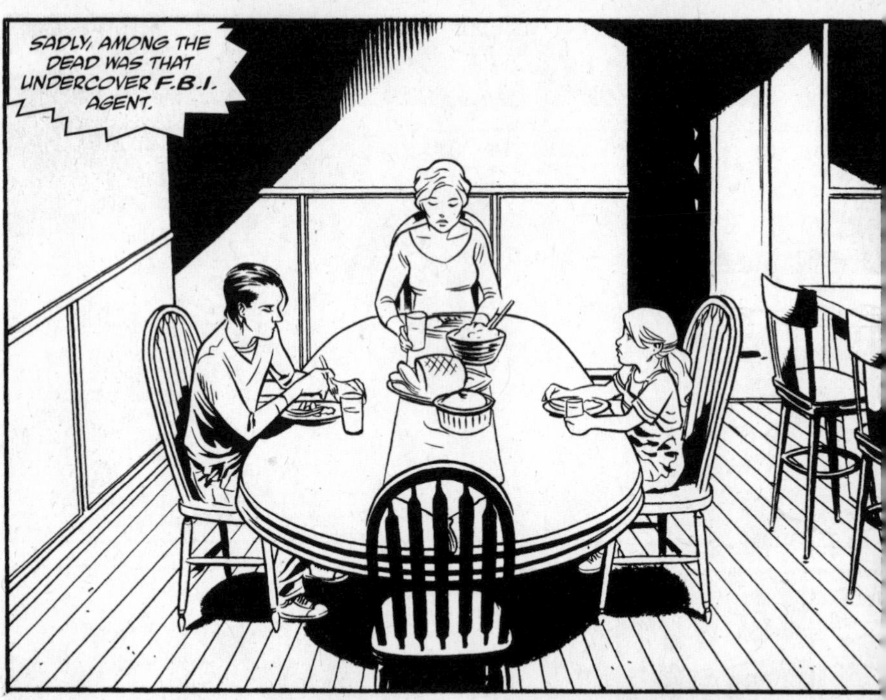
SADLY, AMONG THE DEAD WAS THAT UNDERCOVER F.B.I. AGENT.

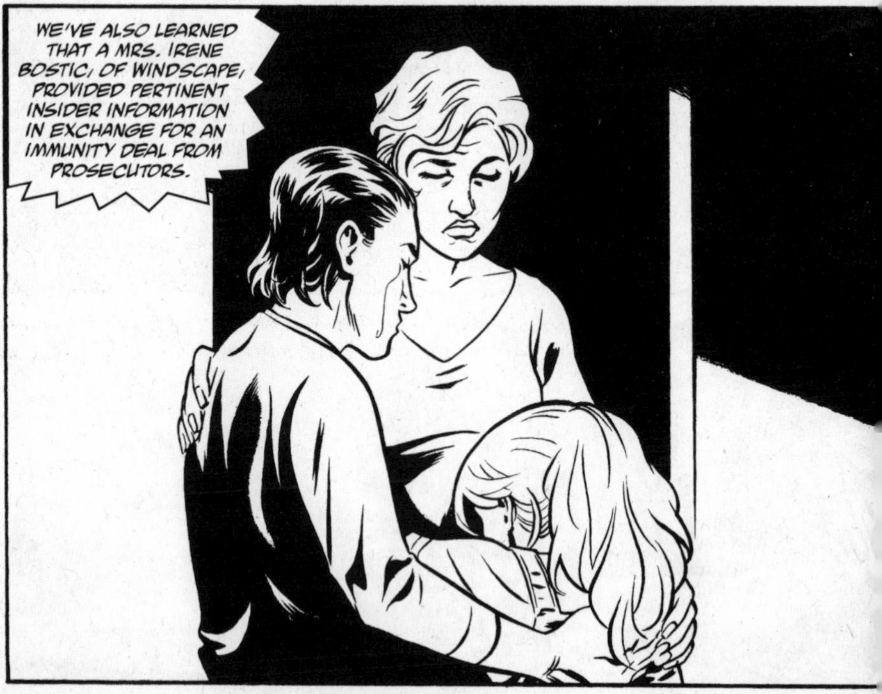
WE'VE ALSO LEARNED THAT A MRS. IRENE BOSTIC, OF WINDSCAPE, PROVIDED PERTINENT INSIDER INFORMATION IN EXCHANGE FOR AN IMMUNITY DEAL FROM PROSECUTORS.

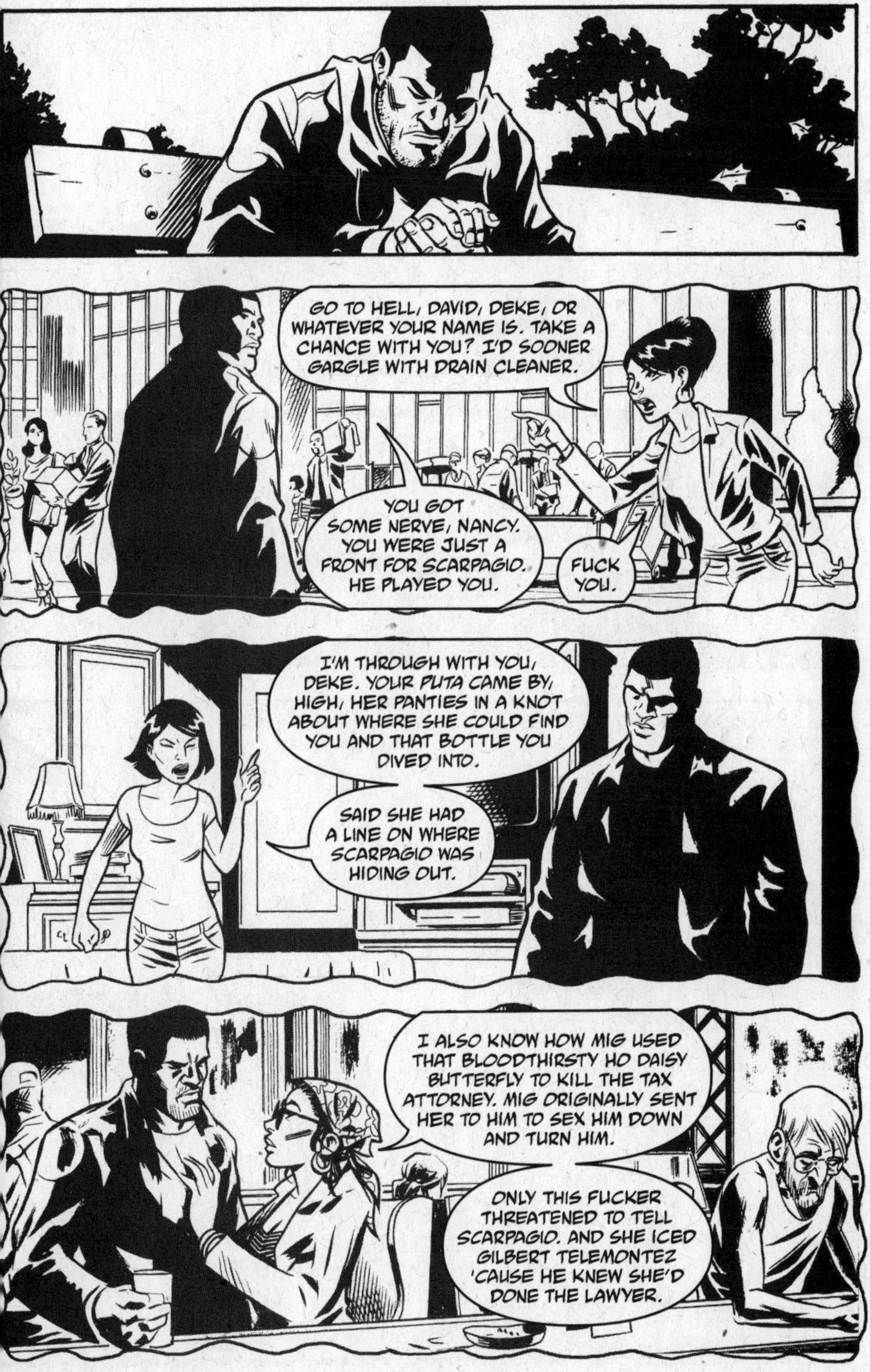
GO TO HELL, DAVID, DEKE, OR WHATEVER YOUR NAME IS. TAKE A CHANCE WITH YOU? I'D SOONER GARGLE WITH DRAIN CLEANER.
YOU GOT SOME NERVE, NANCY. YOU WERE JUST A FRONT FOR SCARPAGIO. HE PLAYED YOU.
FUCK YOU.
I'M THROUGH WITH YOU, DEKE. YOUR PUTA CAME BY, HIGH, HER PANTIES IN A KNOT ABOUT WHERE SHE COULD FIND YOU AND THAT BOTTLE YOU DIVED INTO.
SAID SHE HAD A LINE ON WHERE SCARPAGIO WAS HIDING OUT.
I ALSO KNOW HOW MIG USED THAT BLOODTHIRSTY HO DAISY BUTTERFLY TO KILL THE TAX ATTORNEY. MIG ORIGINALLY SENT HER TO HIM TO SEX HIM DOWN AND TURN HIM.
ONLY THIS FUCKER THREATENED TO TELL SCARPAGIO. AND SHE ICED GILBERT TELEMONTEZ 'CAUSE HE KNEW SHE'D DONE THE LAWYER.

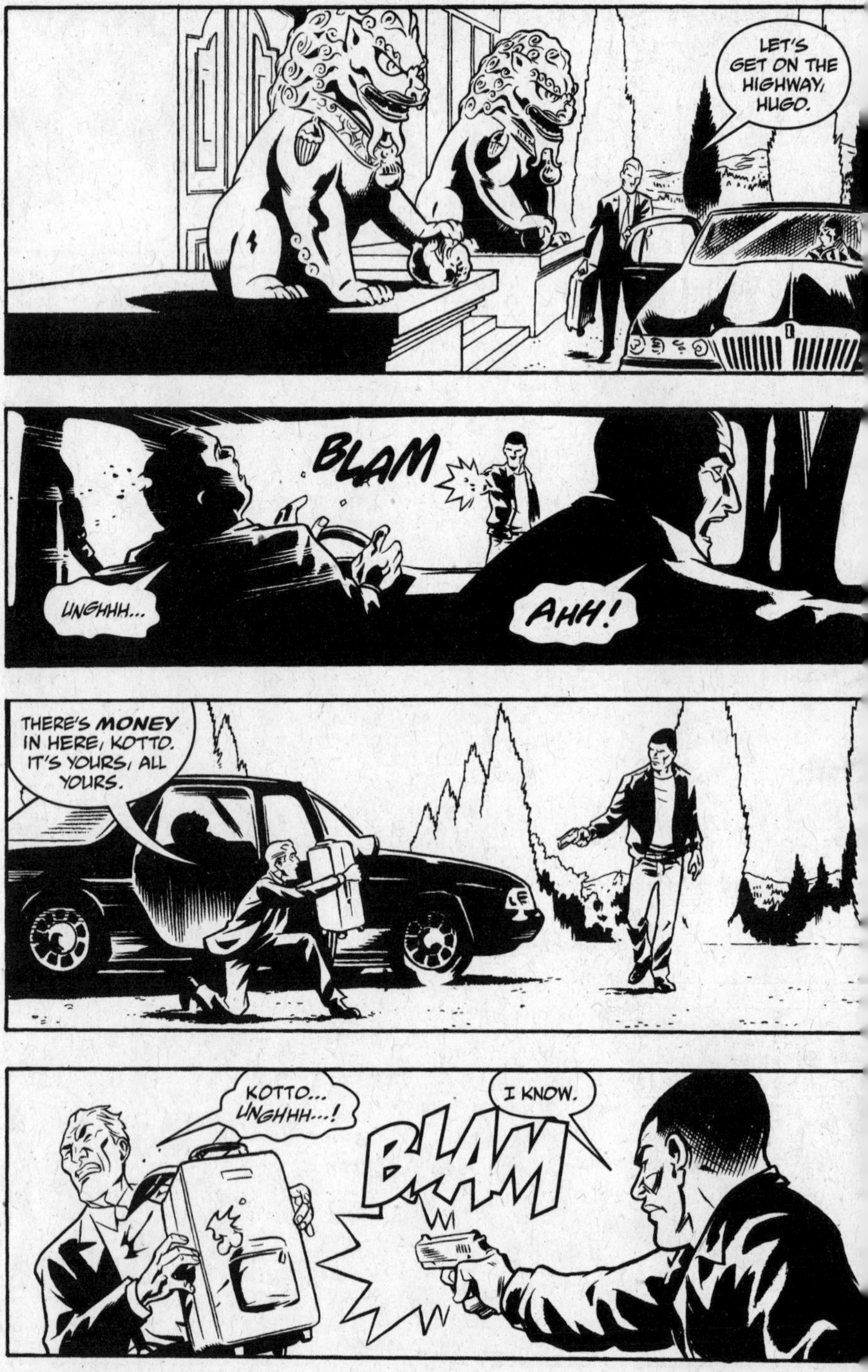
LET'S GET ON THE HIGHWAY, HUGO.
BLAM
UNGHHH...
AHH!
THERE'S MONEY IN HERE, KOTTO. IT'S YOURS, ALL YOURS.
KOTTO... UNGHHH...!
I KNOW.
BLAM

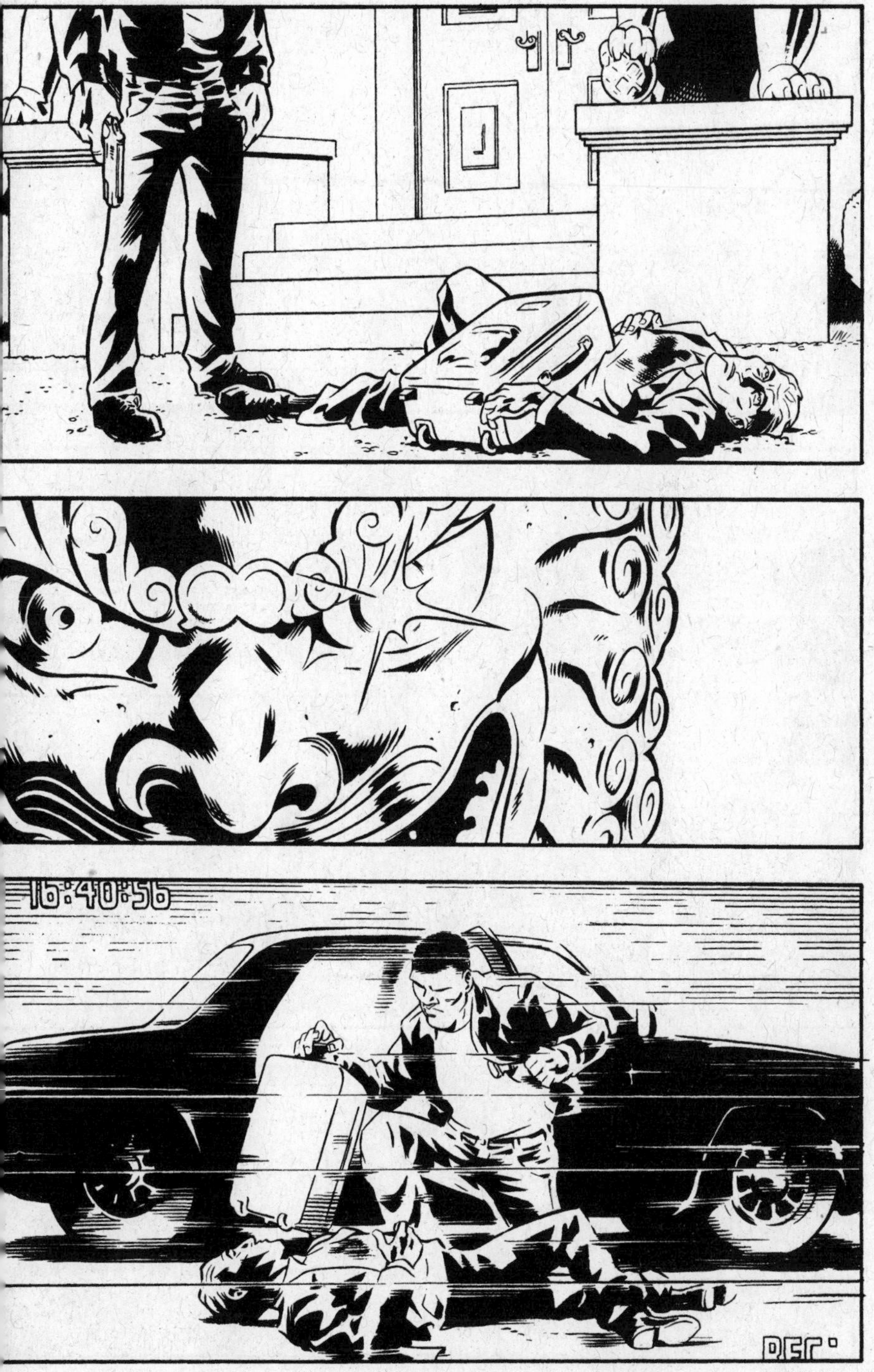
16:40:56
REC

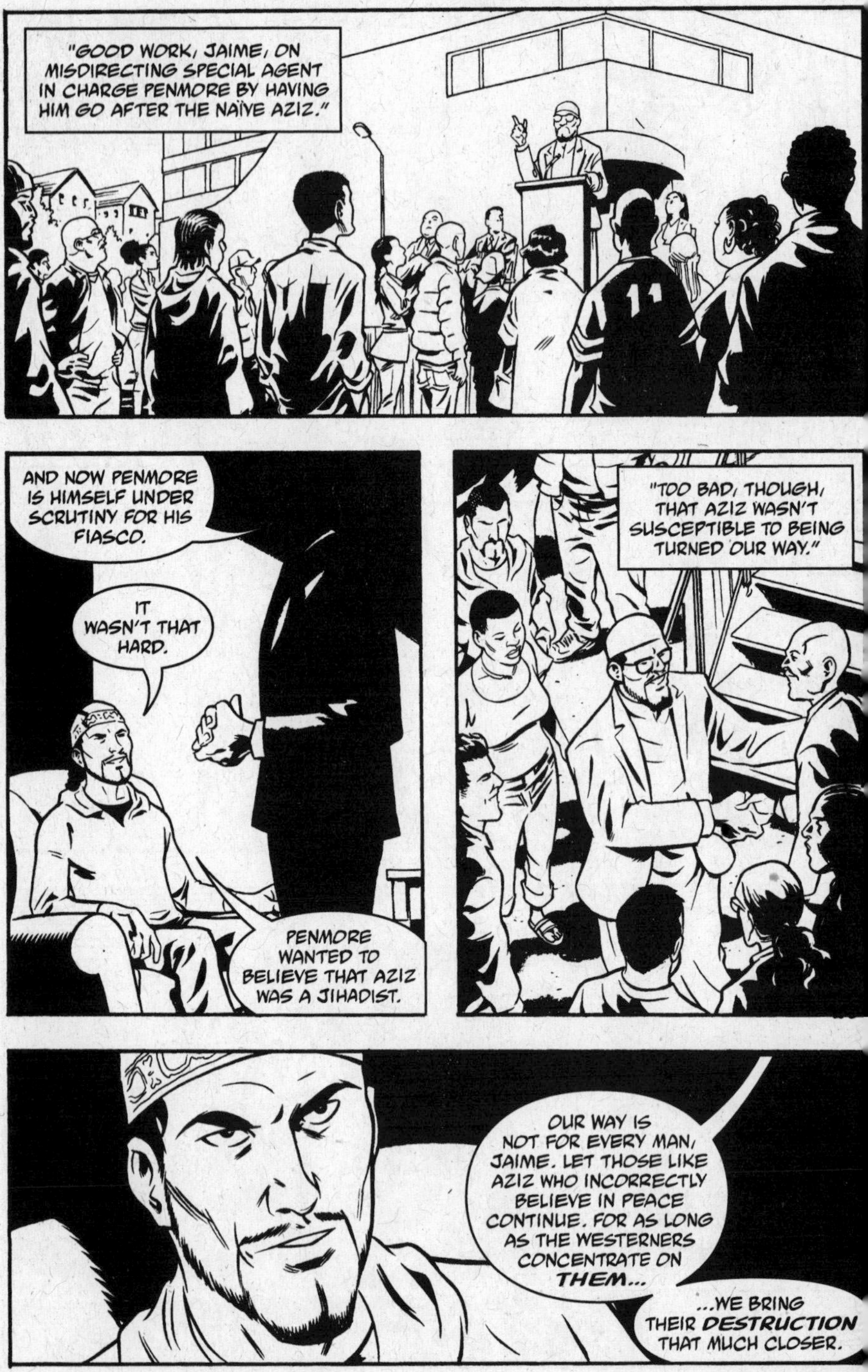
"GOOD WORK, JAIME, ON MISDIRECTING SPECIAL AGENT IN CHARGE PENMORE BY HAVING HIM GO AFTER THE NAÏVE AZIZ."
AND NOW PENMORE IS HIMSELF UNDER SCRUTINY FOR HIS FIASCO.
IT WASN'T THAT HARD.
PENMORE WANTED TO BELIEVE THAT AZIZ WAS A JIHADIST.
"TOO BAD, THOUGH, THAT AZIZ WASN'T SUSCEPTIBLE TO BEING TURNED OUR WAY."
OUR WAY IS NOT FOR EVERY MAN, JAIME. LET THOSE LIKE AZIZ WHO INCORRECTLY BELIEVE IN PEACE CONTINUE. FOR AS LONG AS THE WESTERNERS CONCENTRATE ON *THEM*...
...WE BRING THEIR *DESTRUCTION* THAT MUCH CLOSER.

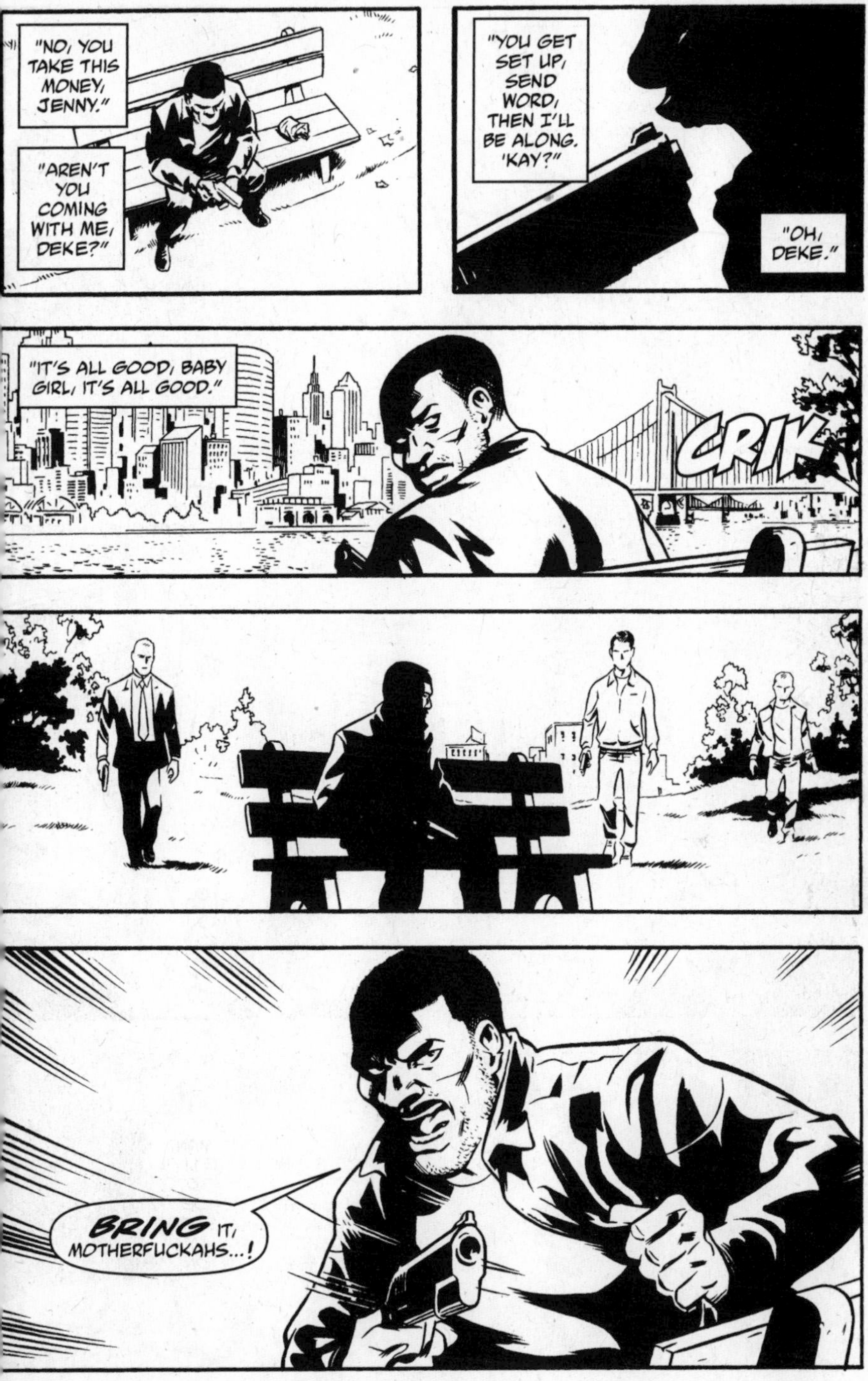
"NO, YOU TAKE THIS MONEY, JENNY."
"AREN'T YOU COMING WITH ME, DEKE?"
"YOU GET SET UP, SEND WORD, THEN I'LL BE ALONG. 'KAY?"
"OH, DEKE."
"IT'S ALL GOOD, BABY GIRL, IT'S ALL GOOD."
CRIK
BRING IT, MOTHERFUCKAHS...!

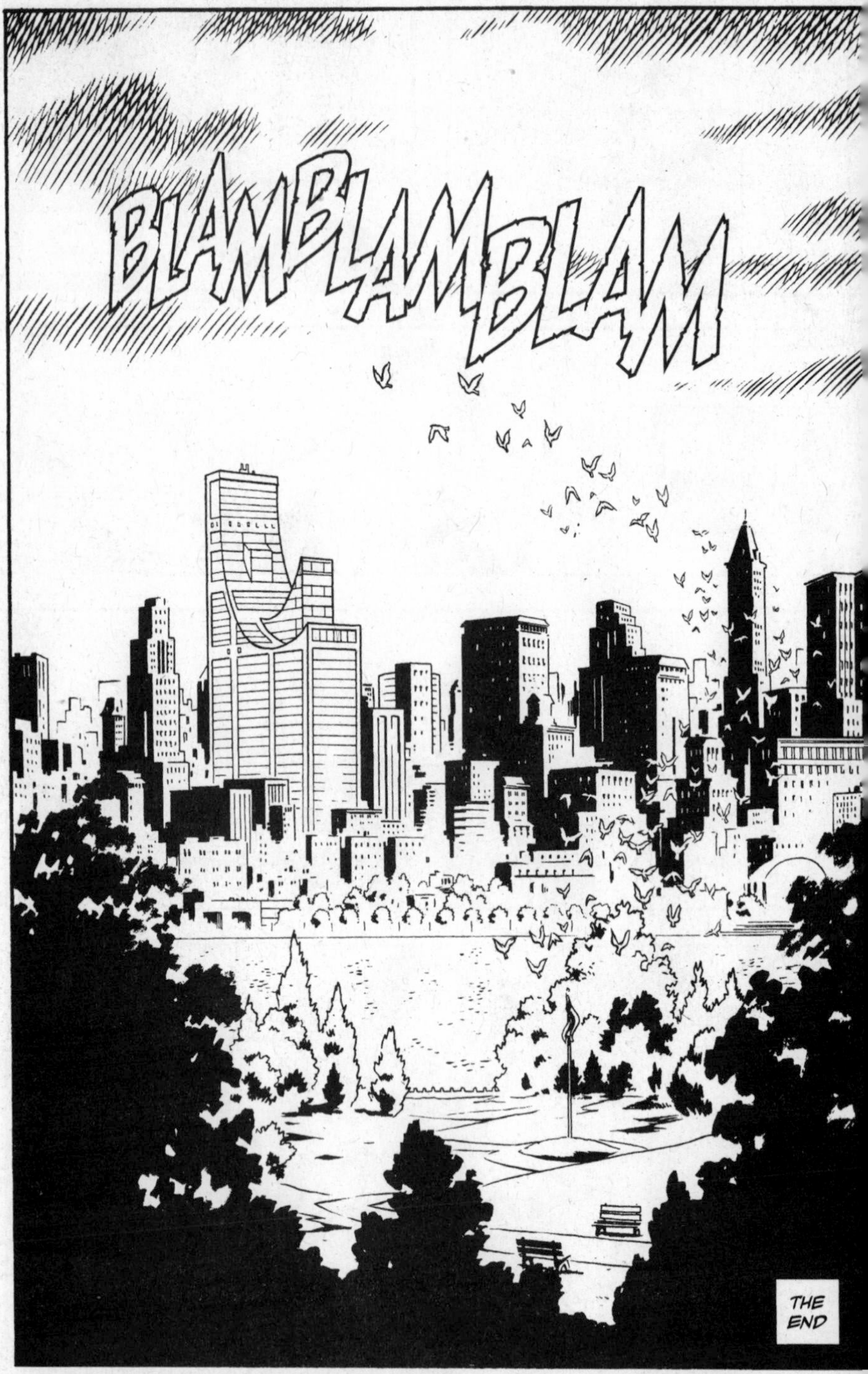
BLAMBLAMBLAM
THE END

DON'T MISS THESE OTHER VERTIGO CRIME BOOKS

NOCHE ROJA
SIMON OLIVER
JASON LATOUR
VERTIGO CRIME

NOCHE ROJA

Written by **Simon Oliver**
Art by **Jason Latour**

At the border, life is cheap. But death costs nothing at all.

"Deftly merges noir with a torn-from-the-headlines story. Noir is timeless, and this book proves it!"
– **Christos Gage** (AREA 10)

RAT CATCHER

Written by **Andy Diggle**
(THE LOSERS)
Art by **Victor Ibañez**

A washed-up FBI agent on a desperate hunt for a notorious mob hit-man finds out the hard way that he's the assassin's latest target!

"Compelling graphic storytelling, full of twists, turns and vivid characters."
– **Dave Gibbons** (WATCHMEN)

ANDY DIGGLE
ART BY VICTOR IBAÑEZ
RAT CATCHER
VERTIGO CRIME

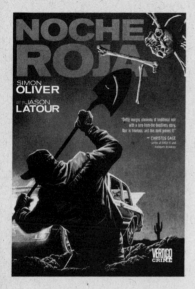

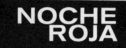

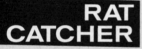

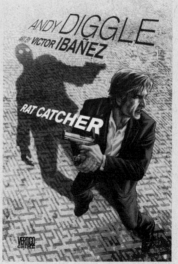

MORE FROM VERTIGO CRIME

AVAILABLE NOW

JASON
STARR
THE CHILL

THE CHILL

Written by **JASON STARR**
(Best-selling author of *Panic Attack* and *The Follower*)

Art by **MICK BERTILORENZI**

A modern thriller steeped in Celtic mythology — a broken-down cop tracks a seductive killer who possesses the supernatural power known as "the chill." Can he stop her before her next victim dies horribly... but with a smile on his face?

PETER
MILLIGAN
JAMES
ROMBERGER
THE BRONX KILL
VERTIGO CRIME

THE BRONX KILL

Written by **PETER MILLIGAN**
(GREEK STREET)

Art by **JAMES ROMBERGER**

A struggling writer is investigating his Irish cop roots for his next novel. When he returns home from a research trip, his wife is missing and finding her will lead him to a dark secret buried deep in his family's past.

AREA 10
CHRISTOS N.
GAGE
CHRIS
SAMNEE

AREA 10

Written by **CHRISTOS N. GAGE**
(*Law & Order: SVU*)

Art by **CHRIS SAMNEE**

When a detective — tracking a serial killer who decapitates his victims — receives a bizarre head injury himself, he suspects a connection between his own fate and the killer's fascination with Trepanation — the ancient art of skull drilling.

VERTIGO CRIME

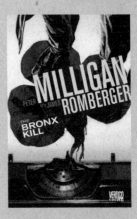